SIX ROUNDTABLE DISCUSSIONS
OF CORPORATE FINANCE
WITH JOEL STERN

Six Roundtable Discussions of Corporate Finance with Joel Stern _____

EDITED BY DONALD H. CHEW, JR.

Q

QUORUM BOOKS
New York • Westport, Connecticut • London

Library of Congress Cataloging-in-Publication Data

Six roundtable discussions of corporate finance with
  Joel Stern.

  Includes index.
  1. Corporations—Finance.   I. Stern, Joel.
II. Chew, Donald H.
HG4026.5.S59   1986   658.1'5   86–12382
ISBN 0–89930–162–2 (lib. bdg. : alk. paper)

Library of Congress Catalog Card Number: 86–12382
ISBN: 0–89930–162–2

First published in 1986 by Quorum Books

Greenwood Press, Inc.
88 Post Road West, Westport, Connecticut 06881

Printed in the United States of America

∞

The paper used in this book complies with the
Permanent Paper Standard issued by the National
Information Standards Organization (Z39.48–1984).

10 9 8 7 6 5 4 3 2 1

Copyright Acknowledgment

Portions of Chapter II, "Do Dividends Matter?: A Discussion of
Corporate Dividend Policy," were previously published in *Chase Financial
Quarterly*, vol. 1, no. 2 (Winter 1982), Copyright 1982, The
Chase Manhattan Bank, N.A. All rights reserved.

Contents

Participants

JEFF BECK heads the Mergers & Acquisitions Department at OPPEN-HEIMER & COMPANY, and is also a member of OPPENHEIMER'S Executive Committee.

STEPHEN BOOKE is President of BOOKE & COMPANY, a corporate public relations firm in New York.

GARRETT BLOWERS is Vice President, Investor Relations for CBS.

LOUIS BRINDISI is Senior Vice President of BOOZ ALLEN & HAMILTON, Inc., and a member of the Firm's Board of Directors. Lou is the managing officer of BOOZ ALLEN's Executive Compensation Strategy Practice.

JOHN CHILDS is a Vice President at KIDDER PEABODY, and is widely known in the field of corporate finance as an advisor and lecturer.

PETER DODD holds a dual appointment as Associate Professor of Finance at the UNIVERSITY OF CHICAGO's Graduate School of Business and the UNIVERSITY OF NEW SOUTH WALES in Australia.

CARL FERENBACH is a Managing Director of THOMAS H. LEE CO., a firm specializing in the arrangement of leveraged buy-outs. Carl was formerly head of MERRILL LYNCH's Mergers & Acquisitions Department.

DANIEL FISCHEL is Associate Professor of Law at the UNIVERSITY OF CHICAGO LAW SCHOOL.

STEVEN FRIEDMAN, who has been a Partner of GOLDMAN SACHS & COMPANY since 1973, heads both Goldman's Mergers & Acquisitions and its Private Financing Departments. He is also a member of its Management Committee.

FABIANNE GERSHON is Vice President and Director of Corporate Communications for MORGAN STANLEY.

CHESTER GOUGIS is a Group Vice President of DUFF AND PHELPS.

PATRICK HESS is Associate Professor of Finance at the UNIVERSITY OF MINNESOTA.

GAILEN HITE is Associate Professor of Finance at SOUTHERN METHODIST UNIVERSITY, and has published a number of studies on divestitures, liquidations, and spin-offs.

MICHAEL JENSEN holds a dual appointment as both LaClare Professor of Finance and Business Administration (and Director of the Managerial Economics Research Center) at the UNIVERSITY OF ROCHESTER, and as Professor of Business Administration at the HARVARD BUSINESS SCHOOL.

ALAN JOHNSON is a principal consultant at SIBSON & CO., a compensation consulting firm in Princeton, New Jersey. Alan was formerly part of Hewitt Associates' compensation consulting practice.

DAVID KRAUS recently formed his own consulting firm, DAVID KRAUS & CO., which, in conjunction with Arthur Andersen, advises corporate clients on executive compensation.

ANDREW KALOTAY is a Vice President of SALOMON BROTHERS in its Bond Portfolio Analysis group.

WILLIAM KEALY is Partner and Director of Research for GOLDMAN SACHS & COMPANY, with whom he has been associated for the past 15 years.

DAVID LARCKER is Professor of Accounting at NORTHWESTERN UNIVERSITY's J. L. Kellogg Graduate School of Management.

ROBERT LITZENBERGER is COG Miller Distinguished Professor of Finance, STANFORD UNIVERSITY.

JOSIAH LOW III is Managing Director of MERRILL LYNCH's Corporate Finance Department, and presently runs its "emerging growth" group.

DENNIS MCCONNELL is Assistant Professor of Finance at the UNIVERSITY OF MAINE at Orono.

JUDSON REIS has been a Managing Director of MORGAN STANLEY since 1976, and is a member of its Mergers and Acquisitions Department.

DAVID SCHULTE recently formed his own merchant banking firm, CHILMARK PARTNERS, based in Chicago. He was formerly a Senior Vice President at SALOMON BROTHERS, where he created the Corporate Reorganization Group.

JAMES SCOTT is Chairman of the Finance Department at COLUMBIA UNIVERSITY's Graduate School of Business.

G. WILLIAM SCHWERT is Professor of Finance at the UNIVERSITY OF ROCHESTER's Graduate School of Management, and also serves as an Editor of the *Journal of Financial Economics*.

MICHAEL SEELY is President of INVESTOR ACCESS CORP., a financial communications firm in New York.

MICHAEL SHERMAN is Senior Vice President and Chairman of Investment Policy at SHEARSON LEHMAN/AMERICAN EXPRESS.

CLIFFORD SMITH is Associate Professor of Finance at the UNIVERSITY OF ROCHESTER and an Editor of the *Journal of Financial Economics*.

BENNETT STEWART is a Senior Partner of STERN STEWART & CO.

ROBERT TAGGART is Professor of Finance at BOSTON UNIVERSITY and Editor of *Financial Management*.

MARK UBELHART is HEWITT ASSOCIATES' national practice leader in the field of Corporate Finance/Compensation.

BRIAN WALSH is Assistant Treasurer of GENERAL FOODS CORPORATION.

ASHLEY WEARE is a Senior Vice President at BANKERS TRUST, where he is in charge of investor and financial relations.

WILLIAM WHITE is HAY MANAGEMENT CONSULTANTS' national practice director for executive compensation.

JOSEPH T. WILLETT works on MERRILL LYNCH's Treasury staff.

HARRY WINN is Treasurer of AMERICAN HOSPITAL SUPPLY.

Preface

Since 1969, when he presented his first two-day corporate finance seminar to the senior management of Pepsico, Joel Stern has been waging a continuous campaign against "accounting-driven" financial management. Under the banner of "earnings per share don't count," he has stimulated (and often provoked) executives from over 800 public corporations by arguing that public firms should be run largely as if they were private. His unvarying message has been that, because capital markets are "efficient," the public corporation best serves its stockholders by maximizing neither reported earnings nor earnings growth, but after-tax "free cash flow." The sophisticated investors that dominate the markets (the "lead steers," in Stern's parlance) are accustomed to distinguishing between accounting illusion and economic reality in setting stock prices; and they can be counted on to reward such "value-maximizing" behavior by management.

To many of the businessmen who have heard him preach the gospel of "market efficiency" over the past fifteen years, Stern must have sounded like a strange prophet crying out in the wilderness. But his advice to corporate executives has had behind it the weight of the greater body of academic research in finance conducted over the last three decades. Beginning principally with the work of Franco Modigliani and Merton Miller back in the late fifties, there has been a major revolution in the theory of corporate finance at our leading business schools. Now firmly grounded in principles of economic logic, and aided by sophisticated statistical methods and powerful computers, the study of finance has made steady progress toward achieving the predictive power of a positive science. Supported by an impressive body of empirical research, finance scholars have been challenging much of the accounting-oriented intuition that continues to pass for the collective wisdom of Wall Street.

In this sense, then, Stern has been far from alone in his advocacy of the theory of "modern finance." Indeed, his efforts are backed by what amounts to a remarkable consensus about market efficiency (at least in its so-called "semi-strong" form) that prevails today in the academic finance community. To say this, of course, is not to minimize important remaining disagreements among financial economists about aspects of the theory. The Capital Asset Pricing Model, for example, has not done as good a job in explaining actual corporate returns as its formulators had hoped; and a challenger, known as Arbitrage Pricing Theory, is now on the rise. As another example, the widely accepted DCF valuation framework, which has been under attack in the past few years, is now being supplemented by the use of options pricing theory to evaluate strategic business options. But, as Michael Jensen has commented on a number of occasions, the relentless testing of the proposition of market efficiency from the late sixties onward has made it "without doubt the best-documented hypothesis in the social sciences."

A LITTLE MORE BACKGROUND

In the fall of 1981, under the aegis of the Chase Manhattan Bank, Joel and I (with the help of Joe Willett) founded a publication called the *Chase Financial Quarterly* in order to supplement our corporate finance advisory work for the bank. Its purpose, more broadly, was to help bridge what we saw as a "gulf" between modern finance theory and much corporate practice by translating current research into practical recommendations for corporate policy. Four issues later, in November 1982, we and other members of our Chase Financial Policy division left the bank to form Stern Stewart & Co., a private corporate finance advisory firm. We also renewed our publishing efforts by starting the *Midland Corporate Finance Journal (MCFJ)*. The purpose of the *MCFJ*, like that of its predecessor, was to bring to the attention of senior management the practical import of theoretical developments in finance for a wide range of corporate decisions: capital budgeting, dividend policy, capital structure planning, international performance measurement, acquisition and divestiture pricing, corporate risk management, and executive compensation.

Now beginning its fourth year of publication, the *MCFJ* has achieved a distinction we think unique among financial publications: while making a strong appeal to practicing corporate executives, it has also established a reputation among financial academics as the most creditable corporate finance publication written for the layman. For this reason, besides attracting a growing corporate following, the *MCFJ* is beginning to be used extensively in graduate business schools, especially in Executive Development Programs. The articles are now being assigned in the classrooms at such prestigious institutions as the University of Chicago (where Merton Miller, incidentally, has been using an entire issue of the *MCFJ* as the main text of a course he teaches in corporate policy), MIT's Sloan School, Wharton, Dartmouth's Tuck School, Stanford, Berkeley, UCLA, the University of Virginia, the University of Rochester, and the Harvard Business School.

"SIX ROUNDTABLE DISCUSSIONS OF CORPORATE FINANCE"

Perhaps the most successful feature of the *MCFJ*—both in the sense of reaching a large corporate audience and in directing academics' attention to some of the major concerns of the practicing business community—has been our series of "Roundtable Discussions." In bringing together senior corporate executives, investment bankers, and prominent academics, the six discussions reprinted in this book present a high-spirited (at times heated) exchange of ideas and experience between financial theorists and practitioners that should be of strong interest to both groups. Each, as we think these discussions bear out, has much to learn from the other.

Our aim in selecting the topics was to make the discussions both timely, on the one hand, and as perennially useful as possible, on the other, by engaging subjects which all corporate financial officers must address at some point in the planning cycle. We settled on the following six (and they are presented in the following order): (1) Financial Communication; (2) Dividend Policy; (3) Mergers and Acquisitions; (4) Corporate Restructuring; (5) Capital Structure; and (6) Management Compensation. We also include after each of the six discussions a position paper on that subject by a member of Stern Stewart & Co. (for which shameless propagandizing we ask the indulgence of our readers).

Our thinking in so ordering the topics is this: The scientific revolution in finance is at bottom a change in the theory of valuation. And, to the extent management views its function as the maximization of stockholder value, all financial decisions are grounded in some theory of capital market pricing. How management decides to use the corporate assets at its disposal, how it chooses to fund its investment opportunities, and what it chooses to tell investors, all depend fundamentally on its understanding of how the stock market works.

Accordingly, we begin the book with those discussions which reveal most clearly the theory of corporate valuation which underlies (implicitly, if not explicitly) the policy prescriptions by members of the practicing business community. What becomes palpably obvious in the first three discussions (on financial communication, dividend policy, and M & A) is that, however much the tenets of modern finance have demolished all rivals in the academy, the theory of "efficient markets" and its corollary of valuation by discounted cash flow are far from universally accepted in the practicing business community. Given this very fundamental difference in the two groups' views of the capital market pricing process, it is not so difficult to understand the sharp differences that often arise between the policy recommendations proffered by businessman and by academic.

And, as the latter three discussions suggest, the implications of market efficiency for corporate investment and financing decisions do not appear to be well understood outside the academic finance community. (Or, if they are understood, they are certainly resisted.) The persistent claim by practitioners of corporate finance—especially those investment bankers who pride themselves on their intimate familiarity with markets—is that the theory needs to be greatly modified to make it square with the "facts" of the "real world." Investment bankers, to be sure, often have a strong vested interest in taking a view of the world that is sharply at odds with that of "modern finance." But even when this subjectivity of self-interest is discounted, there nevertheless seems much that is persuasive in their defense of their own time-honored practices. At the same time, however, it also seems clear that investment bankers, as well as much of the practicing business community, need to examine more critically some of their own most cherished convictions about the "irrationality" of market behavior. We suspect that Truth in this matter, though inclining sharply toward the more disinterested group of academics, lies somewhere in between the provinces of theorist and practitioner, the Academy and Wall Street.

Having acknowledged possible limitations of the theory in its present form, we think it is important to point out that the continuing effort of financial researchers is to make the theory ever more realistic, to accommodate ever more complexities, while still providing a useful way of generalizing. We believe that the academic finance profession is making real and rapid progress in this attempt. (In fact, as I have been told repeatedly by observers both interested and disinterested, corporate finance is undoubtedly the "growth industry" in the business school curriculum of the future.) We also feel, however, that more and better dialogue between the two groups can help the theory evolve more surely toward greater realism, relaxing some of the more troubling assumptions along the way, and thus overcoming much of the resistance from the business community that is evident in the pages that follow.

I would like to close by expressing both Joel's and my gratitude to all those representatives of both the business and academic worlds who were kind enough to take time out of their busy schedules to participate in these discussions. ("Interrogations," as some of the panelists have suggested, is probably a better word to describe Joel's version of the Socratic method.) I think you will agree that, collectively, they have done an admirable job in giving expression to a fascinating variety of experience and perspective.

Donald H. Chew, Jr.
Partner, Director of Publications
Stern Stewart & Co.

November 8, 1985
New York City

SIX ROUNDTABLE DISCUSSIONS
OF CORPORATE FINANCE
WITH JOEL STERN

Introduction:
Mis-Accounting for Value

The principal issues financial executives must address on a continuing basis are those of resource allocation and funding. It is principally through the careful evaluation of investment opportunities and the selection of appropriate financing instruments that financial management may hope to increase the value of its shareholders' investment. This is the essence of corporate finance.

But lest you think this is too simple, the basic principles of corporate finance hold out a great number of prescriptions for policy, and lend themselves to an impressive range of practical applications, that go well beyond the mechanics of capital budgeting and capital structure planning. Once management has a thorough grounding in the conceptual foundations of finance (which means, most important, a good understanding of how capital markets set corporate stock prices), it can use that foundation as the basis for establishing value-creating approaches in a number of apparently unrelated areas. For example, management's understanding of the market pricing process should certainly guide its strategy for financial communication both within the company—especially in communicating the financial goals of the company to operating management—and with the investment community at large. Somewhat less obviously, a better understanding of investors' behavior should also lead to improvements in a company's performance measurement and capital budgeting criteria, its pricing of acquisitions and divestitures, its long-range financial planning (including dividend policy, my favorite topic in all of corporate finance) and, last but certainly not least, its management incentive plan.

THE CONCEPTUAL FOUNDATIONS: MARKET EFFICIENCY AND DISCOUNTED CASH FLOW _____

My experience in discussions with representatives of more than 800 public companies over the past fifteen years has only served to deepen my conviction that the majority of our corporate directors and senior executives remain blissfully ignorant of, if not actively hostile toward, the central tenets of "modern" finance. Contrary to the results of almost all of the significant research over the past twenty-five years, most corporate managers I've encountered continue to subscribe to what I call the "accounting model" of the firm. This view holds that stock prices are determined primarily by reported earnings. In its most simplistic form, it maintains that investors respond uncritically to financial statements, mechanically capitalizing published EPS figures at standard, industry-wide multiples. Corporate executives subscribing to the accounting model view the goal of financial management as the maximization of reported earnings per share.

The rival view, which I call the "economic model," holds that the market value of corporate stock (like the value of a bond or any other investment) is the present value of a company's future expected after-tax free cash flow, discounted at rates which reflect investors' required returns for bearing risk. According to this view, accounting earnings may offer a reasonably good measure of corporate performance, but only insofar as they reflect real *cash* profitability. When earnings seriously misrepresent operating cash flows, accounting statements distort performance and provide an unreliable guide to value.

Now, you may say to me, "Stern, this is all well and good. But who cares what model of the firm we have in our heads as long as our business continues to generate the operating profits?" My answer is that performance measurement is a critical function of corporate senior management. Appropriate measures are necessary to allocate capital among competing operating divisions of companies, to choose among investment projects, to evaluate acquisition plans, and to devise incentive-based compensation programs. And, unfortunately, the critical task of performance measurement is often grossly distorted by accounting measures. Accounting measures sometimes sound appealing, but often they miss the fundamental economic determinants of value. And it is the economic valuation process that should drive performance measurement.

In what remains of this introduction, I want to provide a critique of two of the most popular accounting measures—earnings and earnings per share. But before I show you how blind adherence to the accounting model leads managers to make the wrong decisions, let me say a few more words about the proper standard of measurement, the "economic model." This will allow us to see more clearly the shortcomings of accounting measures of performance.

The Economic Model of the Firm

Economic value, as distinguished from accounting attempts to measure value, is determined in the marketplace. The value of publicly held corporations is assessed every trading day by the stock market. Privately held companies, although without traded shares, are held to the same standards of value when they are bought and sold. The fundamental determinants of value that drive stock prices are the same for private as well as public companies; and such determinants should accordingly provide the main criteria of any corporate performance measurement process.

You might then say to me (as have many), "Stern, how can you ignore accounting statements when every security analyst's report I've ever read attempts to forecast EPS and EPS growth?" My answer depends critically on the distinction between "average investors"—those for whom most security analyst reports are intended—and the "marginal investors," those wealthy institutions and individuals that dominate the market pricing process.

My first aim as a financial advisor is always to make management appreciate the critical role of what I call "the lead steers" in the marketplace for corporate securities. These dominant investors see to it that companies' shares are priced properly. By this, I mean that the lead steers focus on economic value—the cash-generating ability of the firm and the risks associated with it—rather than on accounting values that can be altered through bookkeeping entries that have no effect on cash.

To my way of thinking, all corporate managers are basically in the same business: the competition for investors' savings. A company's stockholders are rewarded only when cash invested in the business yields a greater return (properly measured) than lead steers can duplicate elsewhere while bearing equal risk. Economic value is created by investments that provide (or are expected by the market to provide) a risk-adjusted return greater than that investors can earn on their own. The greater the number and amounts of such investment, the higher the value of the firm. But when rates of return on corporate investment fall below this standard, each additional dollar of investment actually causes the market value of the company to *fall*—even though EPS may continue to grow at a steady rate.

Note that the creation of economic value need not be related to winning the competition for business; that is, improving market share may be irrelevant, if not actually reducing the value of the enterprise. Division managers often commit excessive amounts of capital to achieve only modest improvements in sales. Such a strategy destroys market values.

The chief financial officer and chief planning officer also must focus on winning the competition for *capital*. This is achieved by finding investments that earn attractive rates of return after adjusting for risk.

In essence, then, the "economic" model of the firm emphasizes cash and risk. Also important to consider is how the financing of the firm affects its risk. Funding of the company's assets can be raised in a number of different ways. But each method—whether debt, equity, or some innovative mixture—requires investors, the providers of capital, to assess the risk of the venture and its probable return. The attractiveness of the prospective return is compared against that available from alternative investments of similar risk. Risk assessment relative to expected return, in short, is a key function of the capital allocation and valuation process.

EARNINGS AND EARNINGS PER SHARE (EPS) ───────────

Now let's turn to the problems of the accounting model. Such traditional accounting measures as earnings and earnings per share can severely distort the true economic picture. The flaws in these measures come from their failure both to measure cash flows and to reflect the effects of risk. First, they encourage managers to boost earnings with non-cash accounting entries that do not add value. Second, they confuse finance with business and therefore do not measure risk properly.

Failure to Represent Cash Flow

When the corporate goal is to increase reported earnings or EPS, decisions can be made that harm the economic value of a firm. Such decisions will result in a lower stock price in spite of the increase in reported EPS. There are two classic examples of the failure of accounting earnings and EPS to represent cash flows and, thus, to measure value. They are the inventory costing method (LIFO versus FIFO) decision and the amortization of goodwill in acquisitions.

LIFO inventory accounting results in lower earnings relative to FIFO when inflation is increasing the market value of inventory items. Lower earnings, however, mean lower taxes, and that means a savings of cash. If one compares two companies with exactly the same operating profits before taxes, the LIFO company will report lower earnings than the FIFO company. But the LIFO company will have more cash in the bank at the end of the day because the lower earnings result in lower taxes paid. Which company is worth more? The answer, of course, is the one with more cash in the bank. In fact, a number of studies have demonstrated that investors respond favorably to changes from FIFO to LIFO inventory accounting, regardless of the fall in accounting earnings and EPS. (For a concise summary of these studies, see "Tax-Cutting Inventory Management," by Gary Biddle and Kipp Martin, in the Summer 1985 issue of our *Midland Corporate Finance Journal*.)

Equally misleading is the accounting treatment of goodwill in acquisitions. Many companies refuse to undertake acquisitions if pooling of interest accounting cannot be employed. But amortization of goodwill represents neither a cash cost nor a tax shield and, consequently, has no effect on economic value. Again, the evidence indicates that what matters most to investors is the total amount paid relative to the cash-flow benefits that are realized. The subsequent accounting recognition of the acquisition is not relevant if it does not affect cash or taxes. Managers who are concerned about goodwill write-offs will be biased against strategically sensible acquisitions, and thus may fail to make the appropriate decisions to enhance economic value.

Mixing Finance with Business

Reported earnings and EPS reflect the outcome of financing as well as operating decisions. In the economic model of the firm, value is created by the operating cash flows generated principally by the company's investment plans. Then, after the investment strategy is formulated, financing decisions are made which provide the capital for the operating units and which optimize tax considerations and financial risk. Mixing the operating decisions with the financing decision can be misleading because of a failure to consider the effects of increased financial risk on the economic value of the firm.

For example, any company can use debt to increase earnings and EPS as long as the after-tax rate of return on investment exceeds the after-tax cost of borrowing money. When yields on high-grade corporate bonds are, say, 12 percent, the after-tax borrowing cost may be as little as 6 percent. Corporate investments, including acquisitions, that yield more than 6 percent will increase earnings if financed with debt. Unfortunately, this is hardly an acceptable standard of profitability. Why? Because it fails to consider risk.

Equity investors do not ignore the additional financial risk they bear when a company increases its leverage. Increased leverage, with its higher required fixed-interest payments, will increase the variability of earnings over a business cycle. The increase in financial risk will lower the price-to-earnings (P/E) multiple that investors will assign to the company's stock price. The original P/E multiple (pre-leveraging) will be maintained only if the profits from the new investments cover the full cost of debt and equity financings— because financing with debt today means that equity financing will have to take place in the future to maintain a prudent capital structure.

Increased leverage can involve tax savings and can be the most appropriate vehicle for financing new investments. The key to adding economic value, however, is not earning a return that simply matches the after-tax cost of debt. Instead, returns must be judged against a cost of capital that appropriately accounts for the increased riskiness of the company. Earnings and EPS fall disastrously short in this regard. They assume that the P/E multiple will remain constant, and it most certainly will not.

Another Look at Risk

Accounting measures are also flawed in their treatment of expenditures for product development and market-building, such as R&D and advertising. Accounting rules often require that these outlays be expensed in the year they are incurred because their future returns are uncertain. Businessmen, however, know that these outlays create value and should be capitalized.

It is true that these expenditures are among the most risky that a company makes, and in many instances the outlays do not pay off. In the aggregate, though, these outlays lay the foundation for the future value of corporations. Investors do not expect every expenditure to pay off, but they do expect that there will be enough winners creating sufficient value to cover the costs of the losers.

To compute the return on their investment, investors relate the cash benefits realized in future years to their initial cash outlays. To be consistent in measuring performance, management should adopt the same "full cost" measurement procedure employed by investors. For performance measurement purposes, R&D and market-building expenses should be capitalized, not expensed as accounting rules prescribe.

Using earnings or EPS as a corporate yardstick encourages management to shy away from the risks associated with new investment. Management's decisions are focused on the near-term costs of value-creating expenditures without proper consideration of the longer-term benefits these expenditures may bring. Thus, the time horizon for payback narrows considerably, putting managers at a disadvantage to more patient competitors. To remedy this problem, performance measurement must ignore certain accounting conventions and ignore reported EPS. Performance measurement (and management compensation as well) must be structured to value fairly the long-term benefits of value-creating investments; they should not simply focus managers' attention on the near-term costs.

EPS and Acquisitions

Another extremely serious shortcoming of EPS arises when evaluating acquisitions consummated through an exchange of shares. EPS will *always* increase following a merger with a company bearing a lower P/E ratio; it will *always* decrease after a merger with a higher P/E ratio company. Is it therefore logical to conclude that the acquisition of companies with lower P/E ratios will always benefit investors, whereas the acquisition of higher P/E ratio companies will always be harmful? Stated differently, can an acquisition be judged "good" or "bad" without knowing whether there are any operating synergies to be realized or if the premium paid is excessive? Common sense would say the answer is "no." But why is this the case?

The reason lies in the fact that P/E ratios change in the wake of acquisitions to reflect either an improvement or a deterioration in the overall quality of earnings. The dilution in EPS following the acquisition of a higher multiple company can be offset by an increase in the P/E multiple, so that the stock price need not be adversely affected. The multiple rises because higher quality earnings are added to lower quality earnings. Add high octane gas to low octane gas, and the rating will increase. The same is true for earnings.

The opposite happens with the acquisition of a lower multiple company. It is true that EPS will increase, but it is possible that the dilution in the multiple will more than offset it, leading to a lower stock price. Investors care about both the quality and the quantity of earnings in setting stock prices. EPS represents only one-half of the story.

In conclusion, EPS is misleading as a basis for judging the merits of an acquisition with an exchange of shares. Companies that currently sell at high P/E ratios can make acquisitions that harm shareholders while at the same time increasing EPS. By diluting their P/E ratio, such companies mortgage their future in order to show higher per share earnings today. Equally questionable is the reluctance of the management of companies selling at modest P/E ratios to acquire attractive candidates just because of potential earnings dilution.

Cash, Risk, and EPS

The measurement of corporate performance should always focus on the determinants of economic value, not on purely accounting measures. Economic value is determined by the interplay of cash returns relative to the risks taken. Accounting conventions often involve non-cash (and non-tax) entries. Accounting measures also rarely measure changes in risk. Thus, such favorite accounting standards of measurement as earnings or EPS can be severely flawed and lead to value-damaging rather than value-enhancing decisions.

In many ways the Mom and Pop grocery store understood these concepts all along. What matters is how much cash is in the till at the end of the day relative to the risk taken in the business. A return to the basics of cash and risk can improve substantially the management decision-making process at all firms, no matter their size. The key is adopting performance measurement criteria that reflect these principles instead of "managing" earnings and EPS through the manipulation of accounting techniques.

NOW, ABOUT THIS BOOK... ─────────────────

One of our most important objectives in producing this volume on corporate finance has been to take a step beyond the principles of finance— beyond its conceptual underpinnings, if you will—and toward an examination of how the theory of "modern finance" stands up in the "real world." What are its strengths and what are its limitations for corporate practitioners? To this end we have brought together a group of distinguished academics and practitioners to discuss the why and how of six critical issues in corporate financial management: (1) financial communication, (2) dividend policy, (3) capital structure planning, (4) mergers and acquisitions, (5) corporate restructuring, and (6) management incentive compensation.

Since my colleague, Don Chew, has ably summarized the issues raised by the individual discussions (in his accompanying introductions to each), I will simply close by repeating my own suggestions to management on some of these subjects. Such policy recommendations, the reader will recognize, are those that come directly out of the "economic model" of the firm:

- In communicating with investors, speak to the lead steers. Forget the standard discussions of past performance. Emphasize instead the factors that drive stock prices; offer a concrete, realistic picture of the company's future. This means explaining how much capital is to be invested in various businesses, how the firm is to be financed and, perhaps most important, what performance objectives are motivating management to perform. Lead steers need to know how management evaluates its own operating profitability, and on what basis it rewards its people.

- In setting a target capital structure, aim for a debt ratio which makes the fullest use of the tax advantage of leverage while still retaining financing flexibility. Set a dividend policy that does not subordinate the company's investment opportunities to a high annual fixed cost commitment. (What is the sense in paying out funds with one hand only to have to recapture the cash by issuing new debt or equity?) Measure the true cost of convertibles (believe me, it is far higher than the coupon yield your investment banker would have you think it is); convertibles offer investors a valuable option on the firm's equity, one that can be costly to the company's stockholders. Give some thought to straight preferred stock. Like debt, prefs sell fairly on a yield-to-maturity basis; and they thus provide an effective equity financing vehicle for undervalued companies.

- In pricing acquisitions, avoid overpaying. If the entry price is too high, the buying company can never earn an adequate rate of return on its investment—and its stock price will suffer, most likely on the day the deal is announced. Successful acquisitions are what I like to call "win-win" situations; that is, both the buying and the selling companies' stockholders hold shares of greater value when the deal is completed.

- In setting required rates of return, measure hurdle rates by type of business, so that managers of divisions with differing risks understand what lead steers expect of them. A failure by corporate management to develop (and achieve) sensible divisional performance standards must, in my opinion, be responsible for much of the restructuring activity (especially the divestitures and LBOs) we have been seeing in the past few years.

- In the case of international operations, set goals from the perspective of well-diversified investors who focus only on risks they cannot eliminate by international diversification. And try to see through the distorting effects—as lead steers do—

of temporary exchange rate movements on translated earnings. Most of these changes are likely to reverse themselves with time, especially those caused by short-sighted government policies.

- In structuring compensation plans, make operating managers partners in the firm's success by linking bonus payments directly to what we call "economic value added." (Using EPS, or growth in EPS, as the principal criterion is liable to be a big mistake!) Make liberal use of stock options where appropriate. Also, especially in the case of highly cyclical industries, try to *reward good management, not good luck*. Instead of compensating the business cycle, as most compensation plans do, design a plan which partly insulates operating managers from broad economic and industry effects beyond their control. This will allow the company to reward good performance (and keep good managers) during bad times, and to avoid paying out unearned largesse when times are good. The key is rewarding truly discretionary management performance.

In short, management should use carefully constructed techniques of financial analysis to interpret signals from the lead steers, and to communicate *with* them. Such signals can be used profitably by management to improve its allocation and financing of corporate resources. The key words, again, are "cash" and "risk"; forget those bookkeeping entries that have no bearing on economic value—the lead steers have been ignoring them for years.

Joel M. Stern
Managing Partner
Stern Stewart & Co.

November 8, 1985
New York City

I

Reaching the "Lead Steers"
A DISCUSSION OF CORPORATE FINANCIAL COMMUNICATION

INTRODUCTION

The critical role of a theory of value in determining corporate policy is no more clearly shown than in the following "Discussion of Financial Communication." Featuring a distinguished group of investor relations executives, corporate public relations consultants, and financial advisors, the discussion addresses three principal questions: Are there dominant price-setting investors in the market? and if so, who are they? What are the most important factors that such investors consider in setting stock prices? And, finally, how does one communicate with those investors most effectively? The answers to the first two questions seem, in large part, to condition the response to the third.

The discussion begins by taking up the timely issue of the role of large institutional investors in pricing stocks. There seemed to be considerable disagreement among the panelists as to whether the institutions were indeed the "dominant," or even most the sophisticated, investors (especially since so many of them seem to underperform broad market averages). Nevertheless, the investor relations professionals concurred in the belief that a strong institutional following was valuable. Michael Seely, for example, reported that his own studies showed that institutional ownership tended to (1) improve liquidity, (2) reduce the volatility of stock prices, and (3) reduce the likelihood of takeover. Given the relatively new development in which institutions have begun to back stockholder dissidents, however, the last advantage may prove to have been ephemeral at best.

The discussion also lays the groundwork for future discussions by revealing considerable differences about the degree of financial sophistication displayed by the market; and such differences lead in turn to some pronounced differences in approach to investor relations. The more conventional approaches to investor relations proposed by some practitioners emphasize the need to "sell" corporate stocks to investors through massive public relations campaigns. The primary effect of such public relations campaigns, however—at least according to Seely—appears to be an increase in the volume of trading, but *not* in stock price.

This observation, which proved quite controversial to some of the other investor relations (IR) professionals in the group, leads to the revelation of a very fundamental conflict between academic and practitioner in their views of market pricing. The implicit premise behind the corporate PR campaign is that the demand curve for securities is downward sloping, and that the function of an investor relations program is to increase the *supply* of investors interested in the stock. A broader base of investors, it is argued, should not only increase stock prices, but also keep the stock from falling drastically during a temporary downturn in earnings, or some other piece of bad news.

Advocates of market efficiency, by contrast, argue that a better approximation of the demand curve for stocks is a horizontal line. This means that stock prices are determined not by the number of potential stockholders, but by the information (and the quality of that information) about the underlying value of the company possessed by the most influential investors. As Bennett Stewart and David M. Glassman comment in the article which follows the discussion, "*The fallacy of the supply-and-demand description of the market is the assumption that money must enter or leave the market to send prices up or down.* In reality...shares can change price without changing hands and...can change hands without changing price."

The modern theory thus implies that the large masses of "average" investors to which PR campaigns are traditionally pitched may be largely irrelevant in the pricing process. If so, the investor relations effort would be better spent in attempting to identify and impress the so-called "marginal" investors—those influential "arbitrageurs" with lots of money and somewhat privileged access to information who expect to make even more money by stepping in to "correct" under- or overvalued situations. If the latter is indeed a better description of the market pricing process, and the primary objective of the corporate IR program is to support the company's stock price, then many of the standard public relations functions like "road shows" and the production of glossy annual reports may be an inordinate waste of corporate dollars and effort.

The discussion finally turns to questions like the following: What sort of information do the most sophisticated investors use in pricing securities? For example, are statements about a company's long-range investment program likely to influence investors' assessments of the values of companies today? What is being communicated through such management actions as dividend changes, changes in capital structure, and stock repurchases? And why is the market responding so favorably to announcements of corporate restructuring transactions like spin-offs and divestitures? What sort of information is being released by these changes?

The presumption throughout most of this latter part of the discussion is that management's actions speak louder than its words. But the future role of the investor relations function, at least as Seely articulates it, is to develop a more direct means for senior management to communicate its policies and prospects to the investment community—more direct than, say, the relatively oblique (and costly) methods of raising the dividend and buying back shares at large premiums over market. Such a suggestion, of course, arouses the skepticism of many of the investor relations professionals present. But, as Ashley Weare of Bankers Trust comments, "Though I'm not sure your proposals are realistic, I would love to see you kick the tires and show us all a new way."

DHC

REACHING THE "LEAD STEERS":
A DISCUSSION OF CORPORATE FINANCIAL
COMMUNICATION
December 14, 1983

JOEL STERN, MODERATOR: I would like to welcome you all to this roundtable discussion. Our topic, as you know, is the role of investor relations or, more generally, of financial communication in the corporation. I suspect that, on occasion, we will wander pretty far afield from investor relations per se. But let me just post some guidelines by saying that we want the discussion to explore three major issues: First, are there dominant, price-setting investors in the market? and if so, who are they? Second, what are the crucial variables or factors investors consider in setting stock prices? And, finally, how does one communicate with those investors most effectively? In the course of exploring these broad issues, we want to focus on specific aspects of these issues such as:

1. Are prices set predominantly by institutions, or is the individual investor still a force to be reckoned with in investor relations campaigns? What are the advantages and disadvantages of having a large institutional following?

2. Are most companies fairly priced? If so, what are the mechanisms that make the market so efficient? How important are stock analysts in this process? What are the channels by which information travels?

3. What information is used by stock analysts and institutions in pricing stocks? For example, are short-term financial statements the crucial determinant of stock prices? How effective is the market in seeing through accounting illusion? Is the market capable of taking the longer view? Are statements about a company's long-range investment program likely to influence investors' assessments of the values of companies today?

4. If the market is reasonably efficient, why would there be a discrepancy between a company's intrinsic or fair value and its current market value? Are there a

great many undervalued companies in need of improved financial communication to raise stock prices?

5. How do companies communicate? and are there changes taking place in communications strategies? What are the dominant schools of thought among investor relations experts? How does "corporate image" translate into stock prices? Does more publicity mean a more successful IR program?

6. What are the most successful instances of financial communication you can recall? and why were they successful? What are the crucial variables management should attempt to focus upon in reaching the market? How important are presentations to security analysts, and how should presentations be structured?

7. Are there other, perhaps more forceful, means of communicating to investors? What is being communicated through such management actions as dividend changes, changes in capital structure (new debt or equity issues), stock splits, and stock repurchases? Furthermore, why is the market responding so favorably to announcements of corporate restructuring transactions like spin-offs, divestitures, leveraged buy-outs? What sort of information is being released by these changes?

With this as an overview, I would like to introduce our distinguished group of participants, who bring to the table a variety of viewpoints, experience, and achievement. As we move around the table to my left, we have:

GARRETT BLOWERS is Vice President, Investor Relations for CBS, Inc.;

STEPHEN BOOKE is President of Booke & Company, a corporate public relations firm in New York;

JOHN CHILDS is a Vice President at Kidder Peabody and is widely known in the field of corporate finance as an advisor and lecturer;

FABIANNE GERSHON is Vice President and Director of Corporate Communications for Morgan Stanley;

DENNIS MCCONNELL is Assistant Professor of Finance at the University of Maine at Orono;

MICHAEL SEELY is President of Investor Access Corp., a financial communications firm in New York; and

ASHLEY WEARE is a Senior Vice President at Bankers Trust, where he serves as an advisor on financial policy, and is in charge of investor and financial relations.

THE "LEAD STEERS"

JOEL: I'd like now to turn initially, if I could, to Fabianne Gershon of Morgan Stanley. Fabianne, based on your experience and discussions with public companies and companies that intend to go public, and based also on your dealings with institutions and the larger individual investors, what do you think about this notion of dominant, price-setting investors? Do you think there are people like that? And if there are people like that, could you identify one or two of them?

FABIANNE GERSHON: I have talked to portfolio managers, investment analysts, institutional salesmen, and M & A specialists, and they all seem to feel that the situation varies very much from company to company. There are certain institutional "buy-side" people who have a lot of cash, research, and intelligence at their disposal. And they undoubtedly are trendsetters for a limited number of stocks.

JOEL: You are suggesting, then, that the dominant investors are either institutions or individuals who have large sums of money?

FABIANNE: I am talking now only about institutional investors. But I agree that the institutional investor is not the only investor in the market for every company. Institutions generally follow a fairly small percentage of all public companies. The individual investor is still very much in high-yield stocks, especially utilities or high-growth emerging companies. You find that individuals' interests run the gamut much more that than the institutions' interests do.

STEVE BOOKE: Joel, I think your "lead steer" terminology is certainly accurate. As a general rule, it is the institutions—the pension funds, the insurance companies, the banks—that are definitely the lead steers. Without identifying them individually, institutional investors are undoubtedly the dominant price-setters. And they in turn are heavily influenced by the top flight, the "all-American" analysts advising them.

JOEL: But isn't it the institutions themselves which make the final decisions to invest or sell? It is not the analyst who is actually making the choice to buy or sell, but rather the portfolio manager who controls the large sums of money.

STEVE: True. But the analyst has tremendous influence with the institution, with the portfolio manager. The fund managers will frequently go with the analyst's judgment, just as opportunists, even when they have questions about his projections and forecasts. If they have confidence in that analyst, they will go with him. So the analyst comes to represent the firm as well.

JOEL: Well, Steve, let me explain that I have a bit of a problem with the assurance with which you identify institutions as the price-setting investors. Academics like Michael Jensen of the University of Rochester and Eugene Fama at Chicago performed research in the mid-sixties which examined stock market data that ran from 1926 through the late fifties, maybe even into the early sixties. And their data showed that markets behaved in a financially sophisticated manner over that period of time. Now that was long before the advent and growth of institutions in the market. In fact, the institutional element of the market began to grow very rapidly in the fifties. But prior to the 1950s it was a very small fraction of the market as a whole. Yet they found that markets were highly sophisticated.

STEVE: Are you saying that they found that the stock market was totally efficient?

JOEL: They found that the markets behaved in what they would call an "efficient" manner. That is, risks and rewards were very highly correlated. Put another way, the market was a fair game, investors got what they paid for as long as they had reasonably diversified portfolios. They also found that stock prices followed a "random walk." This meant that you couldn't reliably make money by riding trends in market prices. So, even back then, charting or technical analysis, which attempts to identify and exploit market "trends," would not have provided a reliable means of outperforming the market.

Those types of studies were based on market movements that preceded the period of the 1960s. And because the institutions only came into their own in the mid and late 1950s in a very big way, my question is: If institutional investors dominate market prices today, and the sophistication of the market can be attributed largely to their investment in research, their teams of analysts, etc., then what enabled the markets prior to institutions to price securities? Or is it possible that the institutions are not as dominant a force in pricing as is commonly believed?

ASHLEY WEARE: Joel, I would make the proposition that there has been a very substantial and ongoing change in the security markets. If this academic research were brought up to date to reflect developments in the late seventies and early eighties, it would show an ever-increasing domination of our markets by institutions. We know that institutional trading now accounts for 75 percent of the volume on the Big Board. And I was recently informed that the volume of institutional business on the American Exchange has increased in the last three years from 5 percent to 20 percent of total trading. So we have a lot of continuing data to show that the cash flow that institutions have is in fact setting the prices.

But, while I believe that institutions are very influential, I would also challenge Steve's statement about the power of the "sell-side" analyst. I have some data which I think gives the lie to that myth. As a large investment organization, the Trust Department at Bankers Trust gets inputs on 900 companies every month from thirty broker/dealers. We want to know their opinion on those companies' investment attractiveness. We want to know what they are actually telling their clients in terms of the rank order of their investment attractiveness.

As it turns out, this investment ranking often has little correspondence with current stock valuations. For example, a bank like Morgan is *not* highly recommended by sell-side analysts at this time. Yet it has the highest P/E of all the major banks. What I am experiencing in this case—and I believe it is a representative one—is a very interesting "disconnect" between sell-side recommendations and buy-side actions. That is, "sell-side" analysts do not seem to have the complete power over the buy-side fund managers that people often attribute to them. The sell side may propose what they think the buyers should be using in their portfolios. But these portfolio men live with their own myths, they live with their own perceptions of what value is. So I have considerable doubt in my mind about how direct that linkage is. It is not a simple, direct "push-pull."

MICHAEL SEELY: Could I add a couple of points to that? This is more in the nature of cleansing the soul, getting it off my chest.

JOEL: Mike, we want you to have a religious experience.

MIKE: To give you one thought, the firm of Lynch, Jones and Ryan gathers published earnings estimates from about seventy firms on the sell side and twenty buy-side firms. They say they have observed a strong positive correlation (I haven't examined the data myself and can't confirm the validity of their tests) between stock price performance and the number of earnings estimates on that stock. For a typical Big Board company, the greater the number of estimates on a stock, the better its price performance. Each additional estimate, from the first analyst up to, say, the twelfth, seems to correlate with a statistically observable, positive stock price effect. But only up to a certain point—only, say, up to the twelfth analyst. In short, the thirteenth guy on IBM doesn't bring anything to the picnic.

JOEL: What you are saying, then, is that it's good to have a certain number of analysts following your stock. But once you reach a certain minimum, you get . . .

MIKE: Diminishing returns in terms of insight, or in terms of contribution to market efficiency—however you want to put it. Diminishing marginal value.

JOEL: Well, then, does this contradict the idea that there are certain key analysts who, when they say "go," we go, and when they say "stop," we stop?

MIKE: Joel, you know as well as I do that if somebody does a good piece of research, two more are going to be written that are derived from the first piece; there can be a "snowballing" effect.

And that brings me to my second footnote, and that is the myth of the "all-star" analyst. It is a concept which, frankly, I think is terribly over-blown. The salaries of analysts get set on the basis of whether somebody winds up on *Institutional Investor*'s cover every year. If I were running a research department, the last thing I would want would be to have my entire research department on *Institutional Investor*'s all-star team. And my logic is very simple. The polling that *II* uses is entirely on the basis of what the buy side thinks. As a result, there is a tremendous bias in the sampling toward analysts who interface with clients rather than with companies. But if I am paying the guy to study companies and develop superior analytical insights (which, incidentally, I think *are* possible even in the context of an efficient market, I don't find the concepts mutually exclusive), I want him to be evaluated by the people who work on the basis of his recommendations. Not "do the customers like him?," but "did we outperform?"

STEVE: Yes, I agree with you about the all-star analysts. But we are not talking about fairness, we are talking about perceptions.

MIKE: Well, if the lead steer investor is indeed a sell-side analyst, I suspect he is not the guy who every year appears on the cover of *Institutional Investor*. But, to carry this point to the portfolio manager himself, and to apply this concept of the lead steer to a specific company situation, I would argue that there clearly are "lead steer" investors...

JOEL: How do you know that?

MIKE: Let me give you an example. Take the case of a Coleco. Coleco was a hot stock. It screamed on the basis of what the Adam computer was going to do. And, for nothing, you got this new doll—the Cabbage Patch kids. Now I suspect that there was a very small group of *very* "lead steer" investors—the kind who eschew any kind of publicity or notoriety—and they decided that this was bullshit. They then went out and shorted Coleco. And they shorted Coleco big.

STEVE: Who put the stock up though, Michael? Who put it up in the first place?

MIKE: Institutions. But I think you will also find in the case of Coleco, Steve, that there was a tremendous amount of retail volume in that stock on the upside. So then what? Our lead steers probably got together and said, "Gee, that stock is not fairly valued because my spy in the factory in upstate New York tells me that they can't make the thing." In this way, lead steer investors function as a kind of self-correcting mechanism. Here, they set up a hugh short—which they probably still haven't covered. The Bob Wilsons of the world—these are the guys out there that are lead steer investors.

JOEL: Are you saying, then, that the institutions have a tendency to underperform the market because the lead steers take advantage of them on a consistent basis?

MIKE: I would hesitate to say "on a consistent basis."

JOEL: Then the example that you are giving us is merely for its entertainment value? Can we draw any significance from this, in terms of how we might help the chief financial and chief executive officers of companies see markets functioning? You see, I am interested in whether there is any basis for us saying that there are lead steer investors. At the beginning of this discussion, I started by asking the question: If there are lead steers who might they be? And some people said, "It is the institutions, that's for sure." And I say, "Well, that may be true today, but the markets seem to have been fairly sophisticated, when evaluated by current measures of sophistication, during periods that preceded the growth of institutions. How did that happen?" So that leads me to question at least the degree to which institutions dominate pricing in the markets.

I recently heard a prominent economist from Salomon Brothers state that there were some 2,200 players in the game that account for about 88 percent of the volume on the New York Stock Exchange. Now this tells us that institutional investors clearly account for large percentages of the daily trading volume. But microeconomic theory suggests that prices are not determined primarily by the size of trade and by the largest traders. But

rather prices are set by the so-called "marginal" investors, by those investors—be they analysts, individual investors, institutions, whomever—who
come in to correct an under- or overvalued situation on the basis (generally)
of proprietary information. To the extent this theory holds, the institutions
may not be as influential as everyone seems to believe. They do not appear
to have functioned as the lead steer in your Coleco example. It may well
be true that institutions do not consistently do better than the average
investor—because they just don't have access to the lead steer. Because the
lead steers may require specific "boutique-type" returns for themselves in
order to play as lead steers.

MIKE: Let's just say your lead steer investors are the "smartest guys in
the room." They can be anyone at any given time on any given stock. But
they are *not* named "Aunt Jane."

ASH: Well, let me give you some absolutely fascinating evidence for the
proposition that stocks are sold, not bought. There is a foreign-based company of world-class dimension that I know about. They had 4 million shares
in ADRs in the fourth quarter of '82. Five quarters later, it had 45 to 50
million shares in its ADRs.

How did this happen? Who bought these shares and why? Well, what
happened was that a handful of sell-side analysts—three or four at the
most—decided that they were going to really take a swat at this. One of
these analysts was in a retail-oriented firm with a large sales force. Another
was with a much more institution-oriented firm. The marketing of the stock
was extraordinarily successful. In fact, the stock doubled. It went from X
to 2X. It is now at 1.5X. The large American ownership was bid away from
foreign owners.

When you try to find out from the institutional analysts who bought the
ADRs, they will tell you that the people who bought it were primarily their
own customers. But, if you go to the 13F report, you find that only about
a third of the ownership is institutional. What I found on closer inspection—
and I think this is fascinating—is that the lead retail firm recommending
the stock has 25,000 customers in it. It was a very profitable stock for the
firm in 1983. It's an interesting case because nobody knew where the sales
really were. The people talking to institutions thought it was an institutional
stock because they have institutional customers. The retail guys thought it
was a retail stock because they sold it to their retail system.

JOEL: I guess we are asking the question: Does it make any difference
whether a company has or seeks its ownership among institutions or
individuals?

ASH: I think this story supports the notion that a company itself has
little influence over its ownership, and that it probably doesn't matter.

JOEL: Well, one reason I ask this question is that how you answer it
may very much affect the marketing of corporate securities. As just one
example, when companies are going public for the first time, they are almost

invariably advised by their investment banker that the first step is to stage a "road show." That is, three or four of the key officers of the firm must travel around to the major financial centers in the United States—to Los Angeles, Chicago, New York and maybe Houston or Dallas—and perhaps even to Western Europe, and they must promote the company's future to brokers, analysts, etc.

When I hear investment bankers affirm the absolute necessity of "road shows," my first impulse is to say, "What is this? Is this anything like the old Ed Sullivan program? Do we get jugglers? What do we do here?" And if I'm feeling courageous that day, I will raise my hand and ask, "Why are we doing all of this if there are lead steer investors? Why not simply assemble that little group (whoever they might be) and have the chairman and these three other people in the company speak to them, be interviewed by them, satisfy their expectations regarding the future course of this company, and be done with it? Why are we going through this whole two-and-a-half week song and dance?"

MIKE: Many public offerings for smaller companies pervert their natural investor base. The underwriters push the stock out [to institutions] and over the next two years it comes back to the headquarters—to those who know the company.

STEVE: Well the answer, Joel, at least partially, to that question is that this is a consumer company, a consumer retail type company. Presumably the investment banker will already have talked to the lead steers. He will have the principals of the company talking to them already. And he will have sold one or two of them on the company. And if he is not successful in his initial selling effort, then he might still use the road show on the premise that he is going to snag some people along the way.

JOEL: Let's assume, though, that there were five or six so-called lead steer investors in the industry. And he knew who they were. Let's say they were investment bankers, and he invited them to come to the company headquarters and the top people in the company made their pitch and the lead steers were satisfied. Then why are we going through the rest of it?

GARRY BLOWERS: Well, Joel, the lead steers are not the same all the time, and that's what you seem to be assuming. You claim that before the advent of the analysts and the institutional dominance of trading in the market, the market nonetheless seemed to be efficient over time. Well, I think that, at any given point in time, there is functioning an information network of some kind. But I would also suggest that the nature or dynamics of the information network have changed radically since the sixties.

JOEL: Why? And how do you know?

GARRY: The key change has been from an "old-boy" network to a much larger and more complex information grid.

STEVE: Well, for one thing, computer speed today has made a dramatic change in the whole approach to market analysis.

JOEL: But if information travels more quickly today, and the evaluation and translation of information into share prices is even quicker today than it used to be, then...

GARRY: It makes it even tougher to make money in the market.

JOEL: But this begs the question: Why, if the market is so efficient at processing information, do we need corporate investor relations programs at all?

GARRY: Well, the truth of the matter is that the market is efficient *only* over extended periods of time. Unless there are some remaining inefficiencies at some points in time, no one is ever going to make any more money than the market on average. And there will be no incentive for anybody to seek out information. In fact, the growth of index funds today reflects this belief that it is very difficult to outperform the market.

Nevertheless, I would still insist the market can be under- and overvalued in short time frames, and even over a longer time period...

JOEL: It's easy to say that, of course, with the benefit of hindsight. But it's much harder to take advantage of such under- or overvaluations using only what you know on any given day. However, I'm basically in agreement with you about this.

THE ROLE OF INVESTOR RELATIONS

JOEL: I have a little analogy to describe how investors operate in capital markets, one that I often use with our clients. It has to do with the behavior of bees. Not "the birds and the bees," which is much more interesting, but just the bees. Why do bees pollinate flowers? Do you think bees know that they are pollinating flowers? Not a chance. They are just out to have a good time. A flower is like the local pub. The bees go there, they go "slurp" and go on to the next one. And the process by which they go from one pub to the next happens to be the process by which flowers get pollinated.

Now, it is my contention that investment analysts function essentially the same way in markets. That is, if an analyst felt that by seeking information he or she could spot under- and overvalued shares, act on it, and pocket a significant piece of change, then the process by which she or he would be accessing the information and translating it into new share prices would also be the process by which information was rapidly disseminated throughout the market. And thus the market is made efficient.

The question I have for you is this: If that process has changed (and let's assume for the sake of argument it has, so that it may be faster today or whatever), then why do we need people in the area of investor relations to convey information to the market? The reason I say this is that people who have been involved in investor relations seem to be announcing principally *historical* information. They are not talking about forecasts for the next three to five years. They are not talking about how management intends to finance the business.

FABIANNE: You are talking about only a very small part of the investor relations program.

GARRY: I disagree with you, Joel. I spend much more time talking about the future than I do about the past.

JOEL: Specifically about the future?

GARRY: Regularly about the future. We tell investors why we do what we are doing, what we think we are going to get out of it, why we think the industry is going where it is going, and how we are playing. But because we are dealing with the future, we are dealing with unknowns. When you talk to any group of analysts, some of them for their own set of reasons are going to respond positively to the same story that others may see in a more negative way. You are going to have a difference of opinion. That is what makes opportunities in the market and that allows money to be made in trading.

Now, what investor relations people do is to package and market information. As a practical matter somebody has got to take care of the business of simple data assembly and data publication. And I suppose you could write the investor relations people off and say that it is largely almost a secretarial function: just type it up and ship it out. But in fact when you are dealing with the issues of the company's future, there is a need for someone to articulate what it is that senior management is endeavoring to do. The CEO does not have the time to sit down with twenty different sell-side analysts and 120 buy-side analysts who may want some regular information from a company.

JOEL: I would like to suggest two reasons why—or two sets of conditions in which—investor relations *might not* serve a useful or valuable function. And, Steve or Garry, I would like either of you, if you don't mind, to offer your rejoinder. The first one is that investor relations people, at least in my experience, have provided information principally of an historical nature. Most chief executive officers I've met do not like to forecast anything if they can avoid it. They don't forecast sales, they don't forecast earnings, they don't forecast capital appropriations, they don't forecast dividend payments, they don't forecast anything. They sometimes will announce how much they plan to spend on new plants and equipment in the next twelve months, but that's about it. Even that they are somewhat reluctant to talk about. So they are focusing principally on historical information. And I feel fairly confident that if all you are going to do is merely announce what happened yesterday and talk about it in some detail, you are not going to add much of anything to the valuation process.

The other problem I have with standard investor relations is that if in fact companies have effective IR people, it would still not pay for lead steers to spend time with them, even if they were going to announce information about the future. Because if they announce information to the entire world at the same time, then it will be almost impossible for any one investment analyst to outfox the other foxes, so to speak. It will be impossible for him to outperform somebody else since they are all accessing the same relative information at about the same time. Therefore, the investment analyst who is really outstanding must spend most of his time not with the company and people like you, but with the suppliers, with customers, and competitors. They might also look to the academic community, to outstanding scientific researchers who might give them a lead as to what the pathbreaking developments are going to be like, and which firms are likely to benefit from those developments.

STEVE: Why do you think that good investor relations people—whether they are in-house or outside—do not use the same people that you are talking about and package *them* and make *them* available? Because we do exactly that.

JOEL: Well, that is an excellent suggestion. But let me just elaborate a bit on my own experience. I am a director of a company in the photography industry. And the head of research for that company is a brilliant optics physicist. I also have a friend who has the reputation of being among the best, if not the very best, optics security analyst on the street. I asked him once, "What do you do when you want to find out how Kodak or Polaroid are doing?" "Oh," he said, "you never visit the company. You won't learn beans visiting the company because they are providing you only with information they are willing to give everybody else. And if they do that I don't have any proprietary information. Therefore I spend my time visiting with suppliers to the firms. They tell me in effect how well the company is likely to do. Because if Optical Coating Laboratories is not coating the lenses of the Polaroid camera, you know pretty much that the near term sales and market acceptance of the Polaroid camera have not been good. I also visit the optics physicist whom you and I both know, and he provides me with a certain insight about the relative quality of the products from a Polaroid versus a Nikon versus a Canon lens."

ASH: Joel, I want to take issue with you on some of your assumptions because I think that your model of investor relations activity at this time is not valid. I agree with you that the only useful time that is being spent in the so-called "investor relations interface" is forward-looking. But that's where most of the time in investor relations *is* being spent. And, believe me, those practitioners and the people advising those practitioners are working hard. I am sure Steve and Mike and their clients are really trying to paint pictures of that future world, of how companies intend to generate future revenue and returns.

JOEL: Well, that's the right approach because the market value of the company *today* is based on what is going to happen in the future.

ASH: Absolutely. And while some historical figures are necessary perhaps to satisfy a small base of investors and analysts, this is not the part of investor relations that adds value to the corporation. So, as one who has had a good deal to do with financial communication, I don't accept your statement that IR activity is oriented toward the past.

The second faulty premise you make revolves around the equal intake of information. Just because you get up and put something on the Dow Jones or blow your trumpet, that doesn't mean that the message gets across to all participants equally, and at all times. Your theory seems to suggest that it does. The real world has time constraints. The world that I live in, and the world that I believe we all live in, is overburdened with information. Stocks, like insurance policies, are sold based on this information stream. That multinational company I described earlier is a good example of the importance of the marketing effort. That dramatic change in ownership was the result of *selling* to people. It did not come about because people were waiting at their tickers or waiting to open their mail to read about it. It was sold to people.

So that is what this IR interface is attempting to do, whether it is with the sell-side analyst or the institutional person. The chief executive of this European company came to New York a couple of times during that five-quarter period, made presentations, and meandered around, probably under the guidance of people like Steve and Mike. And they were out there *selling* that stock. That experience brought home to me the fact that something really happens out there—something I was rather skeptical about before. Something like that can happen because you make a claim on people's time. People do not have time, because the world that we live in has more information than we can use or absorb. So what this activity is doing is asking people to stop for a minute and pay some attention to me. That can have tremendous value.

GARRY: Can I just throw in one quick thing on this "lead steer" business? I think it is naive to assume that the lead steers are all the same. The truth of the matter is that the lead steers change. And sometimes in fact the interface between the investor relations side and the investment side leads to that change.

JOEL: Even if the lead steers change, are you capable of identifying who the lead steers are? So that the chief executive officer of your company can spend time with the lead steer and stop wasting his time on all the other steers around?

GARRY: My answer to that, number one, is yes, I can. And number two, part of my job is to make sure that my CEO does not waste his time. I take care of a lot of people that my CEO should never bother with. At the same time, however, there is also some public relations value to providing all people who require information some ability to communicate with the company.

JOEL: That is an interesting point. Because if the job of investor relations is one of taking care of the claims of all kinds of investors, that is important. I am not saying that it is not. However, I want to focus this discussion on the pricing process in the market, and whether that process is dominated by so-called lead steers, or whether all the other investors collectively have an important role in establishing the prices of securities.

ARE MARKETS UNIFORMLY EFFICIENT?

JOEL: I'd like to turn here to Dennis McConnell, whom we haven't heard from. Dennis, you are a scholar who focuses attention on issues in corporate finance like valuation and capital structure, and you have also looked into some of these questions concerning financial communication. I am sure this is not the first time you are hearing many of these observations we have been making today. But it may be one of the few times that you have heard it from so many of the professionals in the field. Do you find the comments we are making to be outrageous in view of the research that you have done? What does the research have to tell us here?

DENNIS MCCONNELL: Let me start by backtracking just a little bit. To this point we have discussed the possible existence of "lead steers" and the role of the investor relations function in identifying and communicating with those price-setting investors. Academics, to date, do not have any special expertise in either of these areas. Nor am I aware of any research papers that focus on these issues. The kind of data which might be useful in resolving these issues is very difficult for us, as outsiders, to obtain.

One of the issues we have looked at, however, is what we call "differential efficiency." We have talked a lot about lead steers and suggested that they are affiliated, to a large extent, with institutional investors. But it is my impression that institutional investors have major holdings in only about 300 companies in a universe of some 10,000 publicly traded companies. Several studies have examined the relative efficiency of different securities markets. Frank Reilly of Illinois, for example, has divided the market into two or three tiers and found that the market becomes less efficient as you move into companies with smaller capitalization. That is, investors seem to earn abnormally large risk-adjusted returns when holding small-cap stocks. This has become known as the "small firm effect" in the finance literature.

Thus, when we talk about the function of the investor relations officer, it strikes me that there are probably some major differences in how you would go about it if you are working with a top-tier or a bottom-tier firm. It seems fair to say that the observations made so far may apply only to a fairly small number of stocks. We may, in some important ways, be ignoring the other 9,700 publicly trading companies that are confronted by entirely different circumstances.

JOEL: Why do you think there would be different tiers if there were tremendous incentives to make money at all times across all segments of the market? Why would it be significantly easier to buy low and sell high in one tier than in another?

DENNIS: Well, some of the work that has been done—again I hark back to Frank Reilly—has categorized firms in terms of capitalization, liquidity possibilities for institutions and so on. His studies suggest that there may be 300 firms that all institutional investors can take a position in, stocks which offer the liquidity to get in and out of without moving prices around. Of a total universe of 10,000 firms, you can then identify maybe another 400 in which all but the top 30 or 40 institutions could get in and get out of without degrading market prices. And this would leave something like 9,300 firms that most major institutions would not touch, either because of capitalization or size or liquidity requirements.

JOEL: You are implying, then, that the proper valuations can come only from institutions?

DENNIS: No. What I am suggesting is that the smoothly efficient markets that we always talk about probably are not those in which the majority of stocks trade. If, as the empirical evidence suggests, various markets exhibit differing degrees of efficiency, there may be some money to be made on the so-called "neglected stocks."

JOEL: But that seems to fly in the face of common sense. If you could consistently, reliably make money trading those shares, why wouldn't other traders come in until the prices of the shares would become fairly valued?

DENNIS: Nobody seems to know the answer to that question at this point, but the evidence suggests that the traders have not moved into these markets in sufficient numbers to remove the opportunities in such markets for excess returns. This failure to respond has permitted investors in such markets to earn what has been termed an "information deficiency premium."

MIKE: I don't know the answer to your question either, Joel. But consider a point that Mike Milken of Drexel likes to make about the "Nifty 50" and junk bonds. Between 1972 and 1982, the fifty institutionally favored stocks underperformed the S & P by 48 percent. In the case of junk bonds, the facts show they've produced a 3 to 5 percent yield advantage over Treasuries, risk-adjusted, for decades. What this implies is a structural flaw in how fiduciaries run money and how sponsors run fiduciaries. It's "okay" to lose money in IBM and credit ratings are still revered—even though, as Mike likes to observe, Bowmar went from four times book to Chapter 11 in six months and Martin Marietta went from a "AA" to "B" in two weeks!

JOEL: My own experience suggests that regional investment bankers and brokers seem to spend a lot of their time looking for the under- and overvalued shares in their own neck of the woods. When I go to Minneapolis and meet with a firm like, say, Dain Bosworth, they will tell me how they found Medtronic before anyone else did. And I believe that. I think that is where the Dain Bosworths make their money. And they will continue to do so until the Medtronics get large enough to interest the Goldman Sachses of the world. The Dain Bosworths serve as the investment bankers for these small local firms, and they provide the kind of information to investors in general that should provide a fair value for such companies.

GARRY: That is absolutely right. An investor relations person in a small company may indeed be more important. He has to look at the world in a completely different way than I do at CBS—simply because the visibility factor that I deal with today has a wholly different set of ramifications. I sometimes spend less time communicating new information to institutions than I do correcting "misinformation" that derives from the almost excessive media attention given to my industry and company. But if you are the investor relations person at a small company, you shouldn't have an institutional focus, you shouldn't have a national focus. Instead you should have a regional brokerage firm and regional investor focus. You should concentrate initially on potential investors in a more narrow universe until you can achieve some level of visibility and begin to have some means of expanding your appeal.

JOEL: Well, when a moderately sized company goes public for the first time, would you be willing to tell the senior officers of the company that they should *not* make an attempt to place their stock in the hands of institutional investors, but to go for small investors instead?

GARRY: I think the answer really depends on how large the company is, and on how long it has been a public company. You would also want to consider where this company fits in its industry, how the industry is followed, how big a player it is, and therefore what the appeal of that firm's equity is likely to be relative to whatever competition there is.

STEVE: Certainly the retail broker, the regional or wirehouse broker who is bringing out an issue, wants the institutions to participate, even if he has the capacity to put away the deal himself without going outside his system. Because he knows the institutions set a tone. They also give him a more stable after-market for a period of time. So, a regional broker clearly wants the institutions.

MORE ON MARKET EFFICIENCY

JOEL: Well, the academic research on valuation seems to imply that what matters in the markets is not the size of a firm necessarily, nor where it is located—although there are some of the effects that Dennis mentioned. But what matters primarily is the quality of the information that the market has. If new information comes into the market, such that the expectations of so-called lead steer investors are changed—and let's assume this information was disclosed after the market closed—at the opening the following day the market price would adjust and open at its fair value without a single trade having been made. In other words, demand and supply would meet at a new price because all players in the game who mattered would now have a new estimate of the fair value of the company.

STEVE: I would like to respond to that by pointing to an article on the front page of this morning's *New York Times*. It was announced today that Japan has come up with super-computers that will go one hundred times faster than IBM's or Control Data's. Now certainly your lead steers in technology have been watching this development, especially since the development has taken place largely under the architecture of the two U.S. firms I mentioned. Bill Norris of Control Data has long been screaming at the top of his lungs about the fact that Japan is doing precisely what was announced in the *New York Times*. In fact, Japan has been doing it for years. Now, based on our discussion of the stock market, what do you think has happened to IBM's stock this morning?

JOEL: I guess today if I were a lead steer and I was taken by surprise by this announcement, I would call the Garry Blowers' equivalent at IBM as fast as I could get him on the phone and ask, "What is the response of Mr. Opel and the management committee of IBM?"

STEVE: They did that. And they said, "Our policy is not to comment."

JOEL: I see. Then I think I would at least buy a put option on IBM to cover myself.

MIKE: No, you wouldn't.

JOEL: To cover myself, yes.

MIKE: Oh, to hedge your investment?

JOEL: Yes, that is correct.

MIKE: It is probably too late.

JOEL: It may be too late. It is interesting that Michael Seely says it might be too late because as soon as the information is available in the market, IBM's new share price will reflect this information.

STEVE: Yes, but it should have reflected it before.

GARRY: If your analyst doesn't have you on top of this question, then you have got a problem with whoever is following the computer business.

JOEL: But then the question I would return with to you, Garry, is this: Why do I need Garry Blowers if I have outstanding analysts following my stock? If lead steer investors regularly get their information from sources not readily available to the market—not from investor relations people, but rather from suppliers, researchers, and so forth—then what is the proper role of the investor relations person in that kind of a marketplace?

You see, you might all to say to me, "I don't believe there are lead steers out there." In which case, my response to you would be, "It is possible you are right. But it is also possible that if there are lead steers, the reason you don't know about them is that they don't waste their time with you. Because the kind of information you are going to provide them with is at best redundant." If I were an investment analyst and I needed to learn the information before the *New York Times* reported it, you can be sure I would not waste my time talking to the investor relations guy. I am going to talk to the suppliers and the customers and the competitors to learn what I need to know to price the shares properly.

GARRY: Were there any analysts quoted in that *New York Times* story?

STEVE: Yes.

GARRY: What did they say?

STEVE: Basically they said that this represented a "serious problem."

DENNIS: Academics would say that the job of management and the investor relations staff in a situation like that is to avoid surprises. However, I would be embarrassed if I walked out of this room and found IBM's stock had fallen substantially. I can't believe everything is working right if that's happened. Everybody trades IBM like crazy every day.

MIKE: IBM is the most liquid stock in the United States.

GARRY: I agree with all of that. I also think that it is possible that even though IBM did not make a direct comment to the *New York Times*, they may have communicated some of management's attitude and level of concern to their major stockholders over the last few months prior to this announcement. I don't think there is a question of materiality involved here.

ASH: I would like to comment because I have watched the IBM situation. Not the technical side, but their communications. The people who do investor relations work for IBM, I have a hunch, sometimes may feel frustrated. The top management has a long history of apparent aloofness. If you look at their annual report, they give fewer numbers than practically any major company in this country. Yet IBM is the most widely held stock. Management basically feels that, based on sustained, superior performance, the long-term value of IBM will essentially establish itself, will take care of itself, without an elaborate investor relations program.

JOEL: So, you may be saying, then, that the lead steers who follow IBM don't spend their time with IBM, but with other sources of information. Therefore, the lead steers probably aren't now racing up to IBM for interpretation of the news. Because essentially they have been Pavlovianly trained not to get the information from IBM, but to seek out more proprietary sources.

MARKET EFFICIENCY AND THE "ROAD SHOW" REVISITED

JOHN CHILDS: Joel, I would like to offer a few comments. In the first place, while I think this has been an interesting conversation, I don't think it is getting anywhere as far as the role of investor relations is concerned. My second comment is this: The professors say the market is efficient. But I think all this means is that the demand for securities equals the supply. As far as I am concerned, the market is extremely irrational. I lecture our trainee brokers and I spend a lot of time explaining that the market is a very irrational market. It is rational only over the very long run. It gets way, way out of line. The Dow sold at 920 or something like that in 1972. It should then have sold around 600. When the Dow goes from the high 1200s down to what it is today, you can't tell me that that is rational. Do things really turn that quickly?

JOEL: Well, if you want to explore the reason why the stock market may have fallen over 130 points in the last six weeks, remember that during that period of time the rate of growth in the money supply has contracted very, very sharply. This has led more and more people to forecast a precipitous downturn in the rate of economic growth in the next quarter or two, as well as an increase in interest rates. Only a month ago, however, the prospects for the economy seemed very different to many because the central bank had not yet acted to tighten things as much as they had.

STEVE: I subscribe to John's theory. Let me offer you another instance of market irrationality. On Wednesday, February 8, 1984, a *New York Times* headline read, "Not Much Time Left to Resolve Deficits Volcker Tells House." Then, two days later, on February 10, "Volcker Discerns Hope on Deficits—Says that Financial Markets Overreacted to Remarks."

JOEL: Well, there is great uncertainty about what central bank policy is, and about what it is likely to be. And because Fed policy seems to be critical in terms of the outlook for economic activity, the information Volcker provides can be of tremendous importance to any analysts, lead steers or otherwise.

STEVE: Yes, but the information that Volcker imparted has been available. It has been available to lead steers, to good analysts.

JOEL: I would say no. The information about the size of the deficits has clearly been available. Information about what the Federal Reserve was likely to *do* about the size of those deficits has *not* been readily available. The Fed tries as best it can to keep highly secret the minutes of the open market committee meetings. It is very difficult to discern what their future policies are going to be. In fact I know of studies of the Fed's behavior which have found very little correspondence between Fed statements of intent and their actual policies. So for Volcker to be making a statement that would clearly specify what their future policies might be could be terribly important.

JOHN: Investors are irrational. They overreact. In boom periods when everybody is optimistic, they act like the guys who are going down to Atlantic City on the bus to beat the gambling houses. And when things turn pessimistic they act like the guys coming back. And this isn't rational.

But let me get back to the issue of the "road show" you raised earlier—because I don't think you have any understanding how they work. In fact, I suggest you go on some of the road shows and see how important it is. And I think Morgan Stanley would say the same thing. If you have a stock that is going to be sold to two or three institutions, you don't need a road show. But who sells stocks? If you have a new issue of 5 million shares and, let's say, 4 million went to the institutions, then you have a million shares to sell. The people who are going to sell those remaining shares are brokers or dealers. If you don't have a road show, they are going to be paying attention to some other security, and the offering is going to be a total flop. So it is an absolute essential to have a road show unless you have a stock that is well-known by everybody or unless it goes completely to the institutions.

JOEL: John, what is the content of the presentation at one of these "road shows"? Unless management intends to talk about its future investment and financing plans in some detail, I don't see how it can be of much value.

JOHN: Joel, you don't know how the road show works or how brokers work. They want to be able to say, "I just talked to the president of the company, and he said so and so." It is done on a pretty superficial basis. That is the essence of a road show. But if you don't do it and get your brokers keyed up, they are going to sell some other security.

Another question, Joel: Do you recommend that companies give out forecasts of earnings?

JOEL: Forecasts of earnings? I would say forecasts, yes. But it doesn't have to be earnings. Earnings come out of the accounting model of the firm. And I am not a strong advocate of the accounting model. But if you said a forecast of the cash-generating ability of the company, I would say yes.

JOHN: I have one other important disagreement with you, Joel. You seem to be arguing that there is no job for the investor relations person if forecasts are not given out. I don't think that is true at all. Take the case of an acquisition pricing. Your acquisition pricing is going to be based on a forecast. But if you are going to do a good job with an acquisition pricing, I would assume that you would spend maybe two or three weeks learning about the company in order to make the forecast.

Now you take a company like CBS. It is a pretty complicated company. Very exotic business. And maybe a few analysts understand exactly how it works. But there is a major educational problem, and this job of educating investors about the company is one of the important aspects of investor relations.

JOEL: Well, John, let's assume you are talking about an analyst who happens to be about forty or forty-five years of age, and who has spent the last fifteen to twenty years covering an industry. He is a specialist. This analyst will not require this kind of education, right?

Well, the reason I raise this question is that many chief executive officers have told me they are very unimpressed with the quality of analysts who call on them. Leon Levy at Oppenheimer & Company once said, "There is a reason for that, Joel. The reason is that the analysts who are new at the game try to use the company they are covering to educate them about the business. The really experienced analysts, meanwhile, are elsewhere talking to suppliers and customers and competitors and so on." So it's no wonder so many senior officers of companies think the market can't be efficient. Because the best analysts are largely invisible to—or conveniently forgotten by—these same senior managers who are telling me about how unsophisticated the market seems.

THE ROLE OF FINANCIAL COMMUNICATION IN AN EFFICIENT MARKET

MIKE: We have been talking around the issue of market efficiency. And I think the general consensus is that the markets are reasonably sophisticated in setting stock prices. They process information rapidly and reach appraisals of value that are not flawless, but generally fair, given the remaining uncertainty about the future. Now, the issue I would like to approach is this: Is there a role for the investor relations person in reasonably efficient markets? And, if so, what is it? And what effect does a good one have?

For the record, there was a study done by an academic (and the method or structure could withstand any kind of scrutiny). He studied the price performance relative to the general market of the clients of five major financial public relations firms. And he found no correlation. That is, the retention of a big PR firm appeared to have no detectable effect on the company's stock price.

At my own firm we have been working on another study for the past three years to discern more exactly the effect of good financial communications, not only on share price but on the quality of market-making and a whole host of other things. It is a complicated undertaking, but I will describe it very briefly. We started with the Financial Analysts Federation's evaluation of the quality of corporate reporting for four years. Corporate annual reports, the responsiveness of the corporate contact, the quality of interim reporting, consistency of accounting policies, and so forth. The FAF evaluation reveals the disparity in the quality of reporting by different companies and industry groups. We took eight industry groups over four years. Within eight homogeneous industry groups, we took the best communicators, the worst communicators, and we took average communicators.

We found that effective communication does *not* appear to lead to higher stock prices. The more interesting conclusion, however, is that companies that communicate well enjoy better liquidity. And this is liquidity defined in the conventional sense: the ability to buy or sell large quantities of the stock without a discount from the prior trade. Now, this finding does not necessarily minimize the role of an inside or outside investor relations manager. It simply says that if you communicate well, there is more and better information out there. And all investors, probably especially dominant price-setters, are more willing to trade because nobody has a superior insight.

JOHN: I don't think price should be the test of effective investor relations.

In fact, there are times when a good investor relations program should bring the price down.

MIKE: There certainly are overvalued securities, John, but in those cases, I'm not sure that Steve's clients or mine would pay us to herald the intrinsic value of the company until they get all their financing off.

JOHN: Don't you think that is something you should convince your client of—that the price is not the end result? Some investor relations people talk mainly in terms of price to their clients.

MIKE: We will talk about it in this sense: it is very possible I think, whether anecdotally or more formally, to develop an estimate of what a company is worth. Not what it is selling at, but what it is worth.

STEVE: But who makes that estimate?

MIKE: You can, I can.

JOEL: How do you do it?

MIKE: That is a long story.

JOEL: I mean, what are the key variables that you would focus on? Would you focus on future results as opposed to past results of the company?

MIKE: Ultimately, I think valuation comes down to a company's rate of return on invested capital relative to its cost of capital. And its *prospective* rate of return on capital is infinitely more important than historical returns. There is, however, a lot of persistency in rates of return. So that historical returns may provide some indication of future returns.

JOEL: Yes. In other words, you are saying that historical information may provide lead steer investors with better estimates of future returns than there might be in the absence of that information.

MIKE: Also, we focus on cash flows, try not to rely on the accounting model of the firm.

JOEL: So then you are talking about knocking out the accounting model, forecasting the cash-generating ability of companies into the future.

MIKE: Yes, and the ability to reinvest that cash in investments offering high rates of return—rates of return required by investors for bearing the risks inherent in those lines of business. Which brings me to an important aspect, I think, of this IR job—one that we haven't talked about. Management should understand the fair value of their firm, how that value is created and enhanced (or diminished). If there is a large discrepancy between the intrinsic or fair value of the company and its stock price, then management may be communicating poorly. And it is here that the investor relations executive can play a major role—by inducing or dramatizing management's commitment to cohering intrinsic and market values.

To illustrate this point, take the case of Dillingham. Dillingham had enormous "stored" values, but was earning low rates of return, negative capital spreads. They were earning considerably less than their cost of capital.

JOEL: They were earning low rates as measured by the *accounting* model.

MIKE: They were low rates of return any way you want to measure them.

JOEL: But the land values...

MIKE: They had stopped appreciating.

JOEL: That may be true, but historically the rates of return were quite high because the value of their holdings in that Ala Moana Shopping Center went up tremendously.

MIKE: Yes, but that was over a period of many years, and the appreciation had largely ceased.

JOEL: Yes, but the annual rate of return was still high if you include that appreciation.

MIKE: No, the play was over, but the "stored value" was high. So, the issue for Dillingham became this: Are we willing to harvest the stored value that had accumulated over the years—even if it means dismembering the company? And the aspect of the IR job that we haven't talked about, but which I think is essential, is not an issue of communication per se. Rather it is a matter of listening to the market, and interpreting what the market is saying for a management like Dillingham's which faces the toughest kind of decisions a management ever has to face.

JOEL: Is that the major role that you see for investor relations?

MIKE: It is an important role.

JOEL: You read from the existing share price certain implied...

MIKE: You read the entrails. You give the stock a voice and you let it speak through you to the management.

THE VALUE OF AN INSTITUTIONAL FOLLOWING (WITH A DIGRESSION ON DIVIDENDS)

MIKE: We started out talking about the lead steers. The conventional wisdom on the part of chief executives is that there are lead steers, and that they are the institutional investors and their agents. The consensus is that having a large institutional following is a bad thing. Nine out of ten chief executives believe that institutions create volatility, diminish liquidity, and increase vulnerability to takeover. Our studies, however, have shown that these chief executives are wrong on all counts. Increased institutional ownership is accompanied by improved liquidity, diminished volatility, and a reduced vulnerability to a hostile bid.

JOEL: So therefore you would recommend that companies that can access institutional ownership should do so?

MIKE: Absolutely.

ASH: Absolutely. It is the only game in town.

JOEL: Let me tell you a story that will perhaps surprise you. One of our clients in the Midwest is a very well-known pharmaceutical company. Their chief executive officer came from the political arena to take over the executive office of the company.

And he said to me, "I have a problem in that I don't know anything about finance and I don't know anything about accounting. Yet I would like to make some decisions about our dividend policy and our capital structure policy in general."

I said, "Well, then you have an advantage. If you don't know anything about finance and accounting, you won't have any of the preconceived biases that so many other chief executive officers come to these questions with. What I think you should do is merely to use your common sense. Run your public company as if it were private, and you'll make the right decisions for your public shareholders."

So then he said to me, "Well, what would you do, then, about our dividend policy?"

I said, "Well, let me ask you a question. What do you see as the expected rates of return on the new investment in the business?"

"Very high," he said. "In fact, we are going to get rid of a lot of the junk we now have. And if the remaining businesses don't earn their required returns, if our people can't get it up to an acceptable level within a reasonable amount of time, then we are getting out of those businesses."

I said, "Well, what are you going to do about your dividend?"

He said, "It wouldn't make any sense to increase our dividend from this point forward, because the only projects we are going to put money into are the ones that have expectations of very high returns."

I agreed with him, and he put the policy in place. He announced that there would be no dividend increases in the foreseeable future as long as they had superior returning projects. Guess what happened to the price of the shares? The shares went up dramatically. But, most interesting—and I find this fascinating—there was a change in ownership from small investors to institutional investors. Yet most managements, we are always told, think that institutions want dividends.

ASH: This is further evidence to what Michael was saying about the disparity between common perceptions and economic realities. And I find this evidence reinforcing some of my own suspicions about the role of institutions in pricing, and about the importance of dividends. It contradicts many of the myths that prevail in this investor relations business.

MIKE: John, the minority view falls to you.

JOHN: Well, let me comment on Joel's statement that a public company should be run as if it were private. We do a lot of financial advisory work with private companies and public companies. One of the first things we say is that how you operate is quite different when you are in the public market and when you are a privately owned company.

Now, let's take the case of a utility company. Joel, I assume you would tell a utility company to cut out all dividends?

JOEL: John, utilities are a most unusual animal. For two reasons. Number one: utilities do not receive the tax benefits of debt finance from their shareholders. So it doesn't make any difference whether the utilities borrow money or use equity financing. Their overall, risk-adjusted cost of capital is unaffected. The tax rebates on debt financing flow right through to the consumer in the form of lower rates.

The second reason why I would change my own mind about paying cash dividends to utilities is that the investor appears to be better off with dividends because of the political process. Because regulators seem to view dividends as a fixed charge to the company, they seem to be more willing to provide rate relief in response to unexpected increases in the inflation rate. So that more costs can be passed along, and utilities are allowed to earn higher total returns, than if there were no dividends paid at all. In other words I cannot trust the political process without dividend payments to provide an adequate rate of return.

I don't want to get too far off into this dividend business, except to say that if utility managers cared about giving the small investor exactly what the small investor needed, then the most efficient way to do that would be to have two classes of stock. You can then let the investor decide for himself what fraction of the total return should take the form of high dividend versus low dividend yield. That is, if you had two classes of stock, one paying a 6 percent cash dividend and one paying a 6 percent stock dividend, then you could take the weighted average of the two at fifty-fifty, and get a 3 percent cash yield if that is what you particularly wanted. So that way we wouldn't have to worry about what dividend policy was particularly right for somebody.

MORE ON THE ROLE OF INVESTOR RELATIONS ───────

STEVE: I would like to hark back to something that Michael brought up, but didn't really pursue. And that is the issue of stock price as an indicator of successful investor relations. (I do take issue, by the way, with the study he mentioned. We have studies that show that, over a period of time, price performance has been enhanced by retaining a financial public relations firm.) But if price performance is *not* an important measure of effective financial public relations, I am curious to know what everybody here believes the function of investor relations is. I know what management thinks it is.

JOEL: Let's assume for the sake of argument that the study that Mike mentioned is valid, and that companies that employed investor relations firms did *not* see a positive impact on their stock prices.

STEVE: But I know that that is an invalid assumption.

JOEL: Let's assume it is valid just for the sake of argument. Are there other functions that investor relations firms serve which would make them valuable to the company?

STEVE: They would be far less important. Far less important because if you asked managements what they ultimately seek in their financial investor relations program, I believe that they expect such a program to produce—over an extended period of time at least—a higher multiple for the company's stock.

JOEL: Michael, you are a competitor of Steve's. If the evidence that you've unearthed there in that study seems to indicate that managements do not do any better with or without investor relations firms, how do you justify the role that you play with the managements that you are selling your services to?

MIKE: How do I justify our usuriously high fees?

JOEL: You said that, I didn't.

MIKE: Well, you know, it ranges from the mundane to the sophisticated and arcane. Sometimes we get paid, in part, for reading and writing and arithmetic. We get paid for making sure that the vichyssoise is cold before the society meeting. We get paid to carry the bags.

JOEL: But does that justify the fee?

MIKE: In part it does. Damn right it does. At the other end of the spectrum, we sometimes encourage and participate in moves outside IR that are value creating—repurchase and restructuring, for example. In fact, after the first stage of the Dillingham deal, the arbitrageurs wound up with a lot of stock. So we suggested, "Here is a chance to do an interesting repurchase. The arbs can't sell it, which means we can buy it from them without a premium and shrink the capitalization." The question we had was whether there was going to be the same positive announcement effect on price that you normally get with "cap shrink." There wasn't.

And, like you, Joel, we have clients who ask us about the stock price implications of, say, an accounting issue—deferred taxes and pension fund accounting are two current issues, for example. And we pull out our "Joel Stern book" and we quote from it liberally. With attribution, of course. And from all the other research we follow.

JOEL: That will not be stricken from the record.

MIKE: But, Joel, as you know, there is a real value to being able to interpret or to project the likely market response to investment and financing decisions, and to the use of different accounting alternatives. It is important for management to understand how value is created and destroyed, and to understand how the market responds to management actions. That's where the best IR begins.

JOEL: Then what you are saying is that your investor relations firm acts as a financial advisor to the company on questions of valuation, capital structure as it affects valuation—the whole business?

MIKE: We advise companies on every means of communication, whether it be the annual report, dividends, stock repurchase, or restructuring.

JOEL: But in terms of the actual release of information, you are saying you don't believe that the quality of the information that is being released under the guidance of an investor relations firm is increasing the stock prices of those companies. Is that correct?

MIKE: Well, let's put it this way. I do not believe that a massive public relations campaign adds much value for stockholders. More business press clippings may make the stock more liquid, but it appears to have no correlation with higher stock prices. The only information that is valuable is that which is in some sense proprietary, not widely known—that which only the "lead steers" may share.

For example, John was talking about the value and necessity of the "road show" to market corporate securities. Well, we generally talk our clients *out* of doing "more" meetings. We try to talk them into doing "good" meetings with the most influential people. Typically, companies want to do New York and Boston, and then go right out to the West Coast and do San Francisco and LA. But we will say, "What do you want to do that for? Everything you have got to say you can say in New York or Boston. Then later, in six months or so, you can go to the West Coast when you have got new information."

JOEL: Are you saying that because if you announced it once or twice, the investment analysts in other places can simply read the *Wall Street Transcript* and get that information without you appearing there?

MIKE: They won't get it through the *Wall Street Transcript*. They will get it because the analyst in New York is going to cover it for his counterpart at Morgan Stanley in San Francisco. They will walk out of that meeting and say, "They said something new and here's what it means."

FABIANNE: It is going to be sent out over the internal wires.

JOEL: Over the internal wires? So would you then be saying that companies should not go racing all over the country doing these dog and pony shows?

FABIANNE: No, I think it's important to visit potential markets, especially those in which a company has visibility through an operation, for example. I have to step back a little because you have been talking all around this question of the lead steers. But, again, every company has its universe of followers. And they are not the same for every company, which I think is the claim you were making before. But you only can have so many companies that are followed by research analysts and portfolio managers, including the regionals.

JOEL: How do you know that?

FABIANNE: Because there aren't enough buy-side/sell-side analysts to follow every publicly held company. For instance, again, large institutions look for liquidity. If a couple of thousand shares move a stock price, an institution may be attracted to the stock the way an individual investor is. But the institutions can't get in and out.

JOEL: But many companies that trade on the over-the-counter (OTC) market with, say, a minimum of five or six dealers in their stock feel they don't have to list on the New York Stock Exchange (NYSE). In fact, many of the OTC companies I have visited have told me they would never list on the NYSE. They feel they have adequate liquidity with five or six dealers, and much lower listing and disclosure costs, when they trade on the OTC.

DIVIDEND POLICY AND FINANCIAL COMMUNICATION ___

JOEL: I would like to change the subject again, and I am sure John Childs is going to want to express an opinion on this one. Let us assume for the sake of argument that investor relations firms have become very successful in providing quality information. Then, if this is so, why do we continue to see a very strong correlation between major changes in dividends and stock prices? It is frequently claimed that dividend changes are used by companies to convey information about their prospects to the market. But, my question is, if investor relations firms are doing such a great job, why do we see such large stock price responses to dividend changes? Dividend changes should have become redundant announcements if management were consistently providing investors with high-quality information.

ASH: I don't see any change in the price of our stock when we increase the dividend. Increases simply validate already existing expectations. Behavior that violates expectations should be thought through carefully, and new expectations should be created *in advance* by effective financial communications.

MIKE: It is *unexpected* changes in dividends that cause changes in stock prices.

JOEL: Mike is right, companies will try to provide announcements to the market about the prospects of the firm through unexpected dividend increases. And, of course, when firms are *forced* to cut dividends, the market will interpret that, too. Now, my question is, why are managements using the dividend to convey their prospects to the market when they have also hired investor relations firms to carry their message to investors?

STEVE: Joel, you are overlooking that segment of the corporate community that is locked into twenty-five years of annual dividend increases. If a company does regularly increase its dividend, it is true that it may not get points for increasing the dividend when it is announced. But if they do not increase it, they may be penalized.

JOEL: Yes, Steve, but if investor relations firms perform a valuable function in communicating information, why does management feel the necessity of using a dividend change in order to cause a price change in the marketplace? Why not simply say, "We are expecting much higher returns in the future and we are going to spend lots of money to do it. We are going to increase our debt-equity ratio prudently to take advantage of great opportunities. And in view of these expectations, we think our shares are significantly undervalued." Why not simply say that, instead of increasing the dividends?

GARRY: Some companies would say that and get killed, while others could say it and benefit enormously.

JOEL: Why?

GARRY: Because there is an enormous difference between how some companies are perceived in the market and how others are. The relative level of credibility that any management statement would have is the result of an accumulated history of communicating objectives and achieving corporate performance that meets those objectives. And it is in that process of establishing and maintaining credibility that investor relations plays one of its most important roles.

ASH: Dividends are more powerful than managerial statements of intent simply because actions speak louder than words. There is a very profound difference in the way investors behave around words and around acts.

JOEL: It seems to me that managements could be communicating much more specific goals through announcements than through dividend changes. It would mean a great deal more to investors to hear words such as, "We have historically earned X percent on assets. But in the future we expect to earn X plus 10 percent on all capital investment." That would be a lot more specific than simply saying, "Oh, by the way, normally our dividend goes up by 5 percent each year. Now we are going to raise it by 35 percent." Don't you think that the first is a lot more specific about the prospects of the firm?

GARRY: When a dividend change is announced, that is an accomplished fact. It reflects a commitment by management, and that carries more weight than statements about future returns on investment. Second, there is no such thing as *information* about the future. There is only *speculation* about the future.

STEVE: Joel, you keep focusing on our function as releasing historical information. That is not primarily what we do. We do some of it. But that is only a small part of our function. Part of it is providing financial advice to our clients.

Another very critical factor in influencing lead steers is their view of management. We have talked about the structure of information, the information flow, the hot quote stream. But analysts' view of management, their direct confrontation and experience with management, also strongly influences their judgment.

JOEL: I agree with you. Well, let me ask whether you think it is helpful for managements to select a group of investment analysts and portfolio managers, and then invite them to cross-examine management about the company and its prospects?

ASH: If you ask analysts and fund managers, you will find they are very much influenced by their direct view of management, by the press-to-flesh contact with executives.

JOEL: Let's assume that that is the case. Then why is it that managements seemed to be interested in conveying additional significant information through dividend announcements?

MIKE: Joel, as one of your critics once wrote in the *Wall Street Journal*, you are "gamboling from the pinnacles of finance theory, while we practitioners below are slogging it out in the foothills of reality."

JOEL: What he meant was that he was *mired* in the bog of financial illusion. That was a letter to the editor by someone who was just about to be committed to an insane asylum.

MIKE: I treat my critics much more charitably than you do.

DENNIS: Joel has got a good point, though. We sit in the academic world and wonder why everybody does this. Because it doesn't make any empirical sense. Why go to the enormous expense of increasing your dividends to make an announcement instead of having someone say it? It suggests the investor relations function has achieved a very limited credibility. Communicating through dividends strikes me as an enormous penalty.

ASH: You know what I do every time we are going to do a dividend? I go talk to our principal owners and our potential owners, and I ask them what would they like. And they tell us that they want dividends. They tell us it is very important to them. Now if they all came back to me and said, "Look, Ash, forget the dividend. You really could use the funds much better because you are getting higher returns keeping the money in the business," I would be very much influenced by that. I am simply reacting to the expectation of the people who own the stock or could own the stock.

JOEL: Ashley, I have got a problem for you. I just finished addressing the senior management of a bank out west. And I made this comment: "Your debt-to-equity ratio is twenty to one; that is, deposits to shareholder funds. Historically you lend out 70 percent of that, although today it is higher than that. This means that about fourteen of every twenty dollars of deposits go to loans. Which means that for every one dollar in dividends you pay out, you could have made fourteen dollars more in loans. That is a higher leverage effect than any industrial company in the world of commercial finance.

"Now, at the Chase Manhattan Bank, they pay a $100 million a year in cash dividends. Which means they forgo $1.4 billion in loans every year indefinitely, forever. Unless, when they pay out the $100 million with the one hand, they turn right around and have an equity offering with the other—which is what they do. So why do they go through the charade of paying with one hand to only have to go back and ask for it with the other hand?"

MIKE: What did David tell you all those years?

JOEL: Well, what is interesting about this is that other firms which Steve and I know very well have never paid dividends—and they have declared their intention of never paying dividends—and they are very highly regarded in the market. In fact Henry Singleton's Teledyne has one of the highest of P/E multiples . . .

MIKE: Tandy is another good example.

JOEL: The reason I don't like to bring up Tandy is that Tandy is a high-tech–oriented company. And people tend to think that only high-tech, high-growth companies can get away with not paying dividends.

MIKE: Tandy has made more money with their financial policy than they have made running Radio Shack. They've bought back a lot of their shares at what have turned out to be bargain prices.

JOEL: But, anyway, there is no reason for banks, of all institutions, to pay such high cash dividends when they really need the money to make loans and to meet capital adequacy requirements.

MIKE: What if a company generating surplus cash can't find desirable reinvestment targets?

JOEL: Henry Singleton buys the shares of other companies, taking a minority position when he has excess cash. Why can't the banks do the same thing?

ASH: Joel, you keep avoiding the expectation of the investor. It seems to me that in this very, very competitive environment you have to pay some attention to people who are the ultimate decision makers of the buy or sell. Now if you can go out and campaign successfully to make them change their minds about dividends, God bless you. Because we would dearly love to keep the cash. I have no argument with you on the theology, if you will. It's the practicability that I have the problem with.

MIKE: But we should all remember that a lot of institutional money is tax-exempt. Give them a dollar in dividends, and they keep 85 cents.

JOEL: Well, we may be about to convince the first bank to do it. Their people said to me last week that they would like to find a way to get their dividend down to zero. And we think we have found a way for them to do it. But, do you know the problem we are going to run into if we are successful? I will just tell you in passing what I expect to take place. What is going to happen is that they are going to be successful. And then everyone is going to say, just as they do about Hong Kong and free enterprise, they are going to say, "But that is Hong Kong, that is not us, that wouldn't work here." So you will have to convince everybody by their own personal experience before you will get them to do it.

ASH: But why do the investors tell us they want dividends?

DENNIS: You may be talking about one of several possible investor subsets. Not surprisingly, the available evidence indicates that *some* investors want dividends and *some* investors do not. As an example, let me cite a study of dual-purpose mutual fund shareholders I recently completed. The general objective of the study was to provide evidence bearing on points of disagreement in the current dividend controversy. The data indicated that investors, at least those in our sample, do not have "either-or" return preferences. Income shareholders were found to have strong preferences for dividends, and would sell any securities that did not pay dividends. Capital shareholders, on the other hand, actively avoided dividend-paying securities. So there does seem to be a hard-core group of dividend fanatics out there— but I doubt that characterization applies to all investors.

ASH: These are institutional investors?

DENNIS: No, I surveyed individual shareholders. But I should note that dual-purpose mutual funds are not so peculiar as to be considered unrepresentative of return preferences in general. During the past few years, "tax-managed" mutual funds have become quite popular among investors. For example, I can point to the American Birthright Trust and the Colonial Tax-Managed Trust, both of which convert currently taxable dividends into long-term capital gains. The development of these funds suggests to me that we want to be a little cautious about asserting that investors want dividends.

ASH: No, but I am saying that we get an overwhelming, unanimous feedback from institutional investors that this is the way they want us to behave.

JOEL: Then I have a question for you: Why was it that when the Searle organization announced that they weren't going to increase their dividend anymore, the investors who came racing in were the institutional investors who you are now telling us want the cash dividends?

ASH: I am saying that we are one bank of many banks in a very well-defined industry group which has certain expectations built up around them. But I would be delighted to see some of your clients go out and kick the tires here and show us a new way.

THE VALUE OF INVESTOR RELATIONS

JOHN: Joel, I think you are wrong to pooh-pooh investor relations so much, and the usefulness of historical information. When you buy a company's stock, you face basically three risks. You have got a business risk, you have got a financial risk, and you have got an information risk. And if you get no information about the company, none whatsoever, you are not going to pay as good a price for that stock.

I can think of two particular companies to illustrate my point. One was Northern States Power. Years ago, they ignored the analysts and, as a result, the analysts totally ignored that stock. So the management was forced to take a different attitude. They talked to the analysts and did a very fine job (and I am not talking about giving out forecasts), and they eliminated that information risk. Another case was Allied Chemical. Years ago Allied Chemical presented only a balance sheet and income statement. Analysts would call and they would hang up. And the company was ignored. That, of course, has changed.

Mike, you mentioned that study showing no correlation between stock price and retaining an investor relations firm. Well, I don't think it's meaningful to compare the price of a stock of a company that has a good investor relations program with one that doesn't have a good program. Prices are sensitive to too many other factors. But let's take CBS as an example. Supposing tomorrow they decided that they didn't want to give out a bit of information. They hung up when the analysts called, and they merely supplied a balance sheet and an income statement. What do you think would happen to the price of the stock?

JOEL: Well, I have an anecdote of my own that suggests something quite different. In the 1960s Mr. Norris of Control Data told some Chase Bankers who were calling on the company (I happened to be at the meeting) that he had a policy of not saying anything to anybody. And if they didn't want to buy the stock, they didn't have to. I might add, by the way, that at the time Control Data was selling at eighty-eight times earnings. I might then ask you, "How did he get the price up so high by saying absolutely nothing?"

The problem with these kinds of anecdotes, though, is that they don't really allow us to draw general conclusions, general rules which could guide us in setting policy.

ASH: Let me make a comment on this. I have talked to a lot of our analysts, and we are one of the largest money managers in the world. We have a guy who used to follow Coca-Cola, and they didn't give out any information. And my analyst used to say, "I don't care if they never give out any information, as long as nobody else gets any other information. Because I can do my own homework and succeed as long as it is a fair and equal playing field." Of course this analyst I am speaking of went to the University of Chicago. So it all fits together.

JOEL: This is when Coca-Cola sold at twenty-five times earnings.

ASH: So what this tells me is that this is a very competitive environment. But perhaps Coca-Cola is a relatively unique company, and perhaps only they can get away with that. But if you are a company that is very much enmeshed in an industry group, for you to behave startlingly different from other leading companies in your own industry group might be more difficult.

MARKET EFFICIENCY ONCE MORE

ASH: Now, every year there is some $600 million swirling around out there, chasing information about securities, earnings estimates, etc. And this belies the notion of how fantastically efficient the market is in the short term, day after day, hour after hour. If this market were so efficient, there is no way that there could be that much economic value commanded by research analysts at Morgan Stanley or Bankers Trust or anyplace else.

JOEL: Yes, but as a percentage of the market value of all shares traded, that is a miniscule amount of money.

ASH: I know, but it is a lot more money than is spent in other information businesses. It is an enormous amount of money.

MIKE: Commissions totalled six and a half billion dollars in 1983. Much of this was compensation for equity research. That is more than the combined budgets of everybody I know, including the CIA. It is more than ABC is spending at Sarajevo. But it is still miniscule relative to the market cap.

JOEL: The question is: What percentage of the total expected return do we expect to earn as a result of spending the money on research? If we didn't expect this, we would stop spending the money.

ASH: This money is spent because people feel that they can make money with marginal competitive information. So that the challenge to this activity is in fact to deliver steadily and regularly valuable incremental information into this information system.

JOEL: Well, one possibility is that you are right, that there is some economic purpose being served. The other possibility is that we live in an evolving society, and that this is an activity that will ultimately die out because it does not provide an economic purpose.

GARRY: And Batterymarch [the index fund] is the profile of the institutional investment community of the future—one which will require no active portfolio management.

JOEL: It might fade away. But keep in mind that if you do not believe that you yourself can beat the market, it might pay to just try to replicate the market. Other people who see a special opportunity in trying to outfox the foxes might engage in that activity.

However, I do think that there must be too many analysts out there. The reason I feel this way is that I once wrote an article called "Fewer Analysts Please." And the letters to the editor about that piece alone saying bad things about me personally led me to conclude that there certainly are too many analysts.

MIKE: They know you too well, Joel.

STEVE: Well, Ben Graham consistently outperformed the Dow by 50 percent, from the beginning of the post-war era through the fifties and right up until the mid-seventies. Now your answer could be that there weren't that many institutions then. He was using fundamentalist principles of valuation which were refined by James Ray. And some of these principles probably led to the modern portfolio theory. But the fact is that today we have computers that go one hundred times faster than the best computers they once had. So there is no question that the statistical information will be readily available.

MIKE: Well, Steve, I just happen to have here a quote from Benjamin Graham himself, the man who made all that money using fundamental analysis to identify undervalued stocks. This remark was published in the *FAF Journal* in 1976:

I am no longer an advocate of elaborate techniques and security analysis in order to find superior value opportunities. This was a rewarding activity, say, 40 years ago when Graham and Dodd was first published. The situation has changed. Today I doubt whether such extensive efforts would generate sufficiently superior selections to justify their costs. I am on the side of the efficient market school of thought.

And I don't think there is a guy with more stature on the fundamental side of the equation than Graham.

DENNIS: A couple of bottom-line observations on efficient markets. Ash, I certainly agree with what you are saying, that a lot of money is spent on research, ferreting out information. But there is a little footnote in all the efficient markets literature that nobody ever seems to notice. And that footnote says that the only reason markets are efficient is that nobody believes they are totally efficient. They keep piling money into this research to make investment decisions, to trade stocks, and to make a lot of money.

So, I don't think you are going to beat the market over the years by buying most of the major stocks. You will get what you deserve given the risks. If you are going to beat the market, you will have to go elsewhere, away from the major stocks.

MIKE: I see a lot more money being "indexed," both in a direct and in a closet way. And I will never forget a turning point, years ago, in what I laughingly refer to as my career. I was walking up to a golf tee with a guy who is director of research of a major firm. And he said, "Oh, there is Jerry Martin. He runs CREF and they have some $15 billion under management." I said, "I want to meet that guy." But my friend replied, "Why bother? He is 80 percent indexed."

If you look around, you can see a tremendous amount of closet indexing out there. Take the banks, for example. With all due apologies, Ash, the banks have tried beating the market, and they have failed. They are losing assets and there has been a tremendous shift to a very defensive stance where they simply try to replicate the market portfolio in their holdings. Passive management strategies have meant lower management fees and lower transaction costs by creating so-called inventory funds. So in effect they are indexing. When they trade from one account to another they don't have a transaction cost. They simply have a paper entry.

OTHER MEANS OF FINANCIAL COMMUNICATION _____

JOEL: Mike, I would like to ask you this? Are there things other than the dividend announcement that companies do in a corporate finance sense that would affect stock prices through communication? I want to give you an example. Very often we used to find, and perhaps still do, that when companies announce they are going to sell common stock, their stock price falls. During the fifties and sixties, it was alleged, on the basis of the accounting model nonsense, that any new issue of stock would dilute EPS, and that was why stock prices are going down. Finance theory would argue, however, that as long as the stock is fairly priced and as long as management is expected to put new funds to good use (that is, invest in projects with positive net present values), then the stock price should not go down after a new equity issue—even if the stock is selling well below book value, causing dilution of EPS.

Recently, though, it has been suggested by finance scholars that one reason why stock prices fall on announcements of new equity offerings is that management possesses inside information about the prospects of the firm. And this communicates to the markets that the stock is, in some sense, overvalued. That is, the market may think management is trying to sell the stock before it falls back down to its intrinsic or fair value.

STEVE: That is fallacious.

MIKE: Well, the same thing happens in the case of leverage-decreasing exchange offers. Whenever companies reduce their leverage ratios, say, by exchanging their debt for equity, stock prices fall on average by about 7.5 percent. And the question is: What information is conveyed by the insiders, by management, through these transactions?

JOEL: That is the reason I am asking this group. Because, as investor relations advisors, you are supposed to be counseling the managements at the time they are considering these financing strategies. Mike, you said before that one of the roles your firm performs is that of an advisor to the company. Would you advise companies to consider selling new equity in order to raise equity before the stock price goes down?

GARRY: How does a company get to be "overvalued" in an efficient market?

JOEL: Well, very simple. The definition of an efficient market is one in which all relevant, available (and "available" here is the key word) information is reflected in share prices. Stock prices may be wrong because management knows something that the market doesn't. Just to use an example, let's assume a company is debt free. And, for the sake of argument, let's also assume that debt is cheaper than equity. But management is planning to borrow money for the first time and to keep that debt outstanding indefinitely. That is, they have a target debt ratio significantly greater than zero. Now the market does not yet know that, not even the lead steers know that. But as soon as management makes the announcement that, "Yes, we now have a target debt ratio greater than zero," then if there is a significant tax advantage from using debt rather than equity (and I believe there is at least a moderate tax advantage from a prudent use of debt), the market price should rise to reflect a new intrinsic worth. But that, to repeat, is not the result of any violation of an efficient market. It is just a difference in the information that is available to market and to management.

THE SUBSTANCE OF FINANCIAL COMMUNICATION _____

JOEL: There are, I think, three ways of viewing the market. There are some people—Fischer Black among them—who believe you don't have to tell the market anything. The market is so sophisticated that it already knows. The second view—and this is the one that I like to take—is that if you tell the market, the market will understand. Then there is the third view that seems to be very prevalent among the managements of firms; and that is, no matter what you tell the market, the market will never understand. And for that reason, the company needs to have an investor relations firm constantly pounding away at the market.

Now, the question I have been asking repeatedly is to what extent management relies on redundant financial tactics to accomplish what their investor relations firm should be accomplishing. It seems to me that dividend announcements are unnecessary. And I don't understand why, if financial communication is being done properly, the market systematically interprets new equity offerings and equity-for-debt recapitalizations as bad news. The function of the IR program should be to neutralize these market effects by explaining management's motives in undertaking such transactions.

JOHN: I see where you are leading. You are saying that stocks are affected by forecast. You are suggesting that the function of the investor relations group is to produce forecasts.

JOEL: Yes. Why do we substitute these wasteful, inefficient means of communication for words, for statements about our future projects, investments, profitability?

JOHN: Well, in the first place companies can't forecast much better than analysts. And if credibility is one of the most important goals of investor relations, and if they give out forecasts that turn out to be wrong, you can have a terrible disaster. I don't think management should be forecasting. They should just give the analysts what information they can, and let the analysts make the forecasts themselves. Forecasting is the analyst's job, not management's.

JOEL: I don't think I should have answered your question by saying that I believe in forecasting. I think I should have said that those companies that communicate effectively do not announce specific forecasts of earnings and dividends. They announce rather those financial principles that will guide their investments, and their methods of financing that investment. We like to give our clients an annual report put out by a company called Saficon Investments. They use their annual report to state their financial policies and objectives. For example, they will say, "Our objective is to earn rates of return on capital over time that exceed X percent." They do not announce what this year's earnings and sales are expected to be. Instead they talk about how much they plan to spend and in what kind of investments, what kind of ROI objectives they have set for themselves, what their target mix of debt to equity is, and what their dividend payout policy is likely to be. Now, why don't we see firms making these kinds of statements instead of issuing annual reports which focus attention on yesterday's results? There is almost never a section on tomorrow. Why don't we see this?

JOHN: Well, I know companies that do. I think Northwest Industries' annual report is an outstanding one for policy statements.

MIKE: Thank you, John. You are talking about one of my clients.

JOHN: I have no objection to policy statements. But forecasting earnings is terribly, terribly dangerous.

JOEL: I agree with you.

ASH: Well, why then do the analysts spend so much of their time driving Garry and me and other people like us crazy about earnings to the last nickel on this quarter's forecast? A large part of this $600 million going to research is trying to hit that quarterly earnings number on the head. Why do they do it? I'll tell you why. Because, in their perception, the buyers and owners of the stock want to buy that from them. And why do they want to buy those earnings forecasts? All I know is that the broker/dealer research staff wants to come up with the best earnings estimates they can. And they want this, I believe, because their clients (the institutions) demand it of them. The customers, more importantly, want to avoid surprises.

MIKE: Joel, you have been talking about lead steer *investors*, but what we haven't talked about is a concept of lead steer *companies*—companies that are extremely well managed and that communicate extremely well. You mentioned Northwest Industries and I couldn't agree with you more...

JOEL: Excuse me, Mike, but are any of the companies that communicate well *not* among your clients?

MIKE: Several, unfortunately. But, as you are well aware, Joel, there is a lack of understanding (and I don't mean this to sound pretentious) on the part of chief executives and boards of directors about how value is created and destroyed.

JOEL: In other words they don't see the idea of the lead steer and market sophistication at all?

MIKE: I will go further than that. I think that they are sometimes outright hostile toward the concepts that you espouse, Joel—concepts with which I am in substantial agreement.

JOEL: I often find that boards of directors and the management committees of firms do not believe that the market is sophisticated in the sense that it will understand what management has tried to convey and, as a result, the company will command fair value.

MIKE: The most recent *Business Week* presented the results of a Lou

Harris poll questioning chief executives about the "fairness" of the market in pricing their stocks. Almost two-thirds of the executives sampled said the market was undervaluing their stock. Only 2 percent thought they were overvalued. It is surprising.

JOEL: Michael, as I suggested earlier, if managements communicate poorly to the market about the prospects of their own firm, and management possesses information regarding those prospects and those prospects add value, it is entirely possible that in an efficient market many companies could in fact be undervalued. That is not to say that markets are inefficient or unsophisticated. It means that managements are not conveying the right information to ensure their current values reflect the intrinsic worth of the company.

MIKE: To put it another way, Joel, there can only be two explanations for an undervalued stock. Either the market doesn't understand the company or management doesn't understand the market. Both in a sense are communication problems; both are management problems.

GARRY: Isn't it possible that management misunderstands the intrinsic worth of the company?

JOEL: Yes, that is the other major possibility. And I suspect the truth lies somewhere between.

THE ANNUAL REPORT

MIKE: We have been talking about annual reports a lot today. And, correct me if I am wrong, but in surveys of what chief executives look to their internal and external IR people to do, they think of the annual report as their primary duty. Now, if you look at the typical annual report, it begins with the CEO's "Letter to the Stockholders." These are financial highlights. It is history. Then there is an operating review. It is history. Then there are the financial statements. These also are history. And then there are footnotes. These are gibberish. Then there is a management discussion. It is the triumph of the letter over the spirit of the law.

JOEL: So, Mike, you feel that none of this is likely to have any important effect on stock prices?

MIKE: Annual reports could. Two companies—Gulfstream Land and Esmark—have introduced sections called "Shareholder Value" into their annual reports. They say essentially this: "We understand what goes into creating value for stockholders in our company and in our industry and in this kind of economic environment. This is the kind of total return we have delivered to shareholders benchmarked against the S&P, benchmarked against the peer group."

JOHN: I don't believe there should be self-appraisal in an annual report. I think the appraisal should be left to the analysts. Give the analysts the information, but don't talk about how you beat the S&P. The next time the company's stock goes down, are they going to say, "Gee, the S&P beat the hell out of us?" You have got to be consistent.

MIKE: I agree that they must be consistent. If companies are going to talk about financial policies and objectives, and if things start to go bad, they should not change the policy statements. That is, they should not discontinue that section in the annual report or in presentations to security analysts because the company fails to meet certain standards in a given year. They should acknowledge their failure, explain why it happened, and what measures the company is taking to see that it doesn't happen again.

GARRY: What you say in good times you had better be prepared to say in bad times. This turns on the issue of credibility, and that is one of the critical objectives of investor relations.

JOHN: If you want a company which has done a fine job in presenting its historicals, you should look at Monsanto Chemical's annual report. They have a table showing what has happened from year to year in their business. I think it is a very valuable piece of information the way they have done it.

ASH: My feeling about annual reports is that nobody reads them anymore except maybe a couple of dozen specialists, and a few of us who create these monsters. And, as I said earlier, I really believe that stocks are sold, they are not bought. The selling is a verbal process. There is a whole verbal chain of information. That is what is happening on the individual side, where the broker is continually on the phone with his clients. On the institutional side, either the institutional salesman is in the door, the sell-side analyst is in the door, or an in-house analyst is being talked to.

The investment focus is increasingly on the short-term opportunities to get in and out of stocks. Billions of dollars are being run this way now. And this is being done through a verbal network.

CORPORATE RESTRUCTURING

JOEL: We have five minutes left, and I thought I would depart a bit from what we have done in the past. We have observers at our discussion and I would like to ask our editor, Don Chew, if there is any question he would like to raise that we may have not covered to his satisfaction.

DON: Yes, I am interested in hearing Mike Seely's explanation of the market's response to the announcements of these corporate restructuring programs. Why do you think these restructuring announcements have been so well received by the market? A company announces it is getting ready to divest certain divisions, and the market seems to respond almost systematically positively...

MIKE: The market's response has been predictably positive. I would emphasize "predictably."

JOHN: The price goes up because those companies have been doing so poorly in the first place.

GARRY: These announcements represent the acknowledgment of some mistakes in the past, as well as a promise that they are going to be better in the future.

MIKE: Well, it's not quite that simple. As a speaker at a recent New York Society of Security Analysts meeting, I counted eighteen reasons why companies go through these restructurings. But they boil down, generally speaking, to a very small list. Generally, these deals transmit value to shareholders in a tax-efficient way. A good example of this is what Boone Pickens is trying to do with Gulf: spinning off a portion of the assets into a royalty trust, thereby allowing for a tax-free distribution to the stockholders. Restructurings can also result in better allocation of corporate capital. By divesting its poor performers, a company can improve its return on capital. And the mere fact that management demonstrates that it is paying attention to its return on investment relative to its cost of capital may well tell the markets that capital will be allocated more efficiently in the future.

Restructurings also may allow the market to participate in something they can't own "purely" otherwise. I am not a believer in the conglomerate discount per se. But I certainly think there are such things as discounts for poor management.

JOEL: In the case of spin-offs, are you saying that management's incentives may be improved when divisions are allowed to stand alone, instead of being buried in the company's consolidated results?

MIKE: Management incentive compensation, as you know Joel, is a hot button in America today. We offer incentives to senior managements on the most irrational basis I can imagine. Total earnings, for example, or earnings per share are common yardsticks. They can be irrelevant to how management is building value for investors.

ASH: What about stock and stock options?

MIKE: Well, that may be the case in your operation. But that's not the prevailing practice at most corporations today. It is mostly annual bonuses based on current earnings.

JOEL: Yes, that's true. And, Ashley, I'm not even sure how useful stock options would be in a case like yours. If you have a man running your Tokyo branch, and he is going like gangbusters there, what if somebody in London is losing his shirt for the bank? The result is that the quality of Tokyo's performance has been diluted by the performance of somebody else. And the Tokyo man getting those stock options on Bankers Trust may not be getting the value he deserves.

My point is this: the more you can differentiate responsibility and accountability among managers, and then target your rewards as directly as possible, the better management incentives are, and the better the company will function as a whole. The reason why the spin-off idea makes some sense from the stockholders' viewpoint is that even though the overwhelming majority of the shares are retained by the parent entity, the fact that this individual unit now has its own stock price allows the management of that unit to be compensated with options on the stock of its own separate entity. And I believe that investors out there are not insensitive to the possibility that such a change in managerial incentives is going to create value for themselves, too. I think this is partly behind the market's favorable response to the spin-offs we've been seeing.

ASH: Well, Bankers Trust is a living example of the value of corporate restructuring. What really created value for Bankers Trust shareholders were the three or four years of divestitures—getting out of retail banking and sharpening our vision of our corporate strategy. It is the power of doing these two things together that created value for our stockholders over the past few years. And even if nothing else happened, our restructuring was done in an investment environment where you get more attention for these kinds of strategic moves. Investors begin to have more confidence that you know how to make money, that you understand how to create value in the future. Investors have clearly paid more attention to us because of this kind of restructuring.

DON: In this sense, then, these restructurings may be communicating what Joel has been suggesting that management convey more directly through words, through statements of policy. Restructurings may merely be an indirect means—though apparently a very effective one—of communicating changes in corporate policies to the market.

ASH: No, I don't believe in Joel's theory of words at all. The market is only paying attention to management's actions, not its words.

JOEL: Well, we have been told that Northwest Industries amongst others is an outstanding communicator, and this ability to communicate appears to have helped the company over time. They have been communicating by means of words and not by means of actions. They have announced their policy...

ASH: No, it was performance.

MIKE: I think Mr. Heineman has built up a feeling in the investment community—through actions and statements over a long period of time—that he was a value-oriented executive, committed to his shareholders. He wants to deliver value to stockholders. The market trusts him to find a way.

CLOSING REMARKS

JOEL: Fabianne, to give you the last word here, is there anything you have heard that you disagree with violently, or agree with overwhelmingly?

FABIANNE: No, however, I think there is another audience that we have probably overlooked. And it is, for example, at Morgan Stanley. These are the senior research analysts who follow the debt portion of companies and who interpret to investors the investment status of the company's debt instruments. The company's bond investors, like stockholders, want to understand the value of their investments, so that they can control and assess their portfolio's risk and volatility in relationship to its return.

Investor relations has become an essential corporate function because, as mentioned before, every company has its core of lead steers or followers who keep up to date and know it very well. But they may not be investors, or the same investors from year to year. A company has to communicate to many prospective and current investors to reach the players for its stock. At the very least, a corporation would be well served to have someone who can interpret and explain new developments and corporate news—someone who can pick up the phone and give a clear explanation of management's directions and policies.

JOEL: What if the study that Mike Seely mentioned is valid, and those companies that have investor relations firms working with them don't seem to improve their own stock price performance relative to their competition's?

FABIANNE: Well, stock price might not be the be-all and end-all of investor relations activity. For example, as Mike and I also said, the company may want liquidity. Or a new mix of investors. They may want to go more institutional. Or more individual, or geographically broader.

JOEL: Why would you want to do that if it would have no effect on the stock prices?

FABIANNE: A company may well decide to broaden its shareholder base to insure that it is less vulnerable to a surprise merger or leveraged buy-out offer, which would not need the approval of all its shareholders if its shares were closely held, or held by a limited number of investors.

JOEL: It sounds like a lovely idea for stockholders out there, doesn't it?

Okay. Well, I want to thank all of you very much for participating. I hope that as we got to know a little bit more about each other, we didn't become any less friendly. I think it is always enjoyable to have an exchange of ideas on subjects that we feel we know something about. I look at this as an opportunity to learn more about the subject so that I can become a better counsel to my clients. What you have done, though, is to give me pause—because I'm not sure I know as much about the subject as I once thought.

COMMENTARY:
HOW TO COMMUNICATE WITH AN EFFICIENT MARKET
by Bennett Stewart and David M. Glassman

A high stock price is a luxury few companies can afford to do without. It rewards shareholders, and where stock is used in bonus payments, management is compensated for a job well done. A higher stock price also allows companies to issue new shares to finance expansion at lower cost to current shareholders. Last but not least, a high share value is the best defense against an unwanted takeover offer.

How does a corporation achieve a high stock price? Of course, there is no substitute for good performance over the long haul. But when the value of management's forward plan is not fully appreciated by investors, effective financial communication can help to get tomorrow's stock price today. How? By carefully explaining the plans and policies that will guide the company's growth. What the market needs is not management's forecast, but their investment objectives, performance targets, and financing policies.

Perhaps the easiest way to highlight what constitutes effective financial communication is to describe what it most decidedly is not. It is not "financial disclosure": the packaging of historical accounting information in the most favorable light. Nor is it "financial hype": an attempt to increase demand for the company's shares through publicity directed toward investors. Both are powerless to raise a company's share price. To be really effective, financial communication must increase the expectations of sophisticated, price-setting investors about the company's fundamental, or intrinsic, value. This is a much harder, but unquestionably a more rewarding, approach to investor relations.

FINANCIAL DISCLOSURE

Proponents of the "disclosure" view of financial communication contend the stock market is dominated by investors who judge companies by their reported financial results. The essence of investor relations, they argue, lies in painting a record of steady earnings growth and glossing over any defects with creative accounting.

But is creative accounting an art form worth pursuing? That is, are earnings all that really matter in determining share values? A *Wall Street Journal* (*WSJ*) editorial entitled "The Market, Smart or Dumb?" (October 1, 1974) put the issue this way:

Unfortunately, a myth has grown up that the way a corporation maximizes its share price is to maximize its reported earnings. This is of course not entirely untrue, but it depends on what the earnings reflect. A lot of executives apparently believe that if they can figure out a way to boost reported earnings their stock price will go up even if the higher earnings do not represent any underlying economic change. In other words, the executives think that they are smart and that the market is dumb.

The same *WSJ* editorial went on to report the results of research undertaken by Shyam Sunder, an accounting professor at the University of Chicago Graduate School of Business. Sunder investigated what happens when companies switch from FIFO ("First-in, First-out") to LIFO ("Last-in, First-out") for inventory accounting. By making the switch in times of rising prices, companies report lower earnings on LIFO, but pay less taxes and, therefore, have more cash in the bank. This raises the question: Which affects the price of a company's common shares, the higher reported earnings with FIFO, or the better cash flow with LIFO?

Here is the answer the *WSJ* editorial provided:

Professor Sunder found 118 New York Stock Exchange Listed Firms that changed to or extended LIFO and 21 that abandoned or reduced it. The FIFO firms obviously reported higher earnings than they otherwise would have, but their stocks did not outperform the market. The LIFO firms reported lower earnings, but their stocks did outperform the market, over a two-year span centered on the public announcement of the change.

The research conducted on the question of LIFO versus FIFO has been replicated on many other accounting issues, including purchase versus pooling accounting for acquisitions, the introduction of FASB #8 for currency translation, switching from deferred to flow-through method of accounting for investment tax credits, and changing from straight-line to accelerated for book depreciation. In every instance the conclusion has been the same: the market is not fooled by accounting changes that inflate earnings without improving cash flow; and when the cash account is affected, stock prices follow the change in cash, not in accounting earnings.

The cumulative effect of this evidence is impressive. It strongly supports the view that the market is extraordinarily intelligent in seeing through accounting earnings to a company's underlying economic performance. As Ross Watts, one of the academic advisors to this journal, has written:

The message of the modern empirical research is thus fairly straightforward: Where earnings fail to present an accurate measure of cash flow performance, it is cash profitability—not accounting profits—that appears to be the market's dominant criterion for assessing economic value. As a consequence, the latitude allowed corporate managers in determining accounting methods does not represent a reliable opportunity to increase stock prices.[1]

Or, as the aforementioned *WSJ* editorial concluded in 1974:

The market is smart, apparently the dumb one is the corporate executive caught up in the earnings-per-share mystique. To us the lesson is clear: If the manager keeps his eye on the long-run health of the enterprise, the stock price will take care of itself.

SPEAK TO THE LEAD STEERS

Many corporate managers find this conclusion difficult to accept. After all, it seems that most investors are not sophisticated enough to understand the intricacies of accounting. Consequently, they are forced to rely on earnings as the most accessible measure of corporate performance. How is it, these managers ask, that earnings are not important when so many investors believe they are?

The answer involves understanding how the stock market really works. Share values are not set through a polling technique in which all investors have an equal say about what the price ought to be. Stock prices, like all prices, are set not by average investors; they are set "at the margin" by the smartest money in the game. The herd is led by influential investors—"lead steers" we call them. They care about cash flow and risk; they are not fooled by accounting illusion.

A few facts about the market may suffice to demonstrate that the importance of the retail investor is vastly overrated. In 1982, the number of trades on the Big Board represented by one hundred–share orders fell below 2 percent for the first time. Another startling fact is that exchange members trading for themselves now account for more volume than the entire retail public. Furthermore, institutional trading in blocks of 10,000 shares or more now makes up more than 40 percent of the market. And contrary to popular opinion, the absence of the retail customer on the American Stock Exchange and the over-the-counter market is even more pronounced than on the Big Board. Clearly, *the significance of the little investor has been exaggerated, and corporate financial communications may accordingly have been misdirected.*

If it is the lead steers who matter, how, then, do they acquire the information they need to properly price a company's shares? Do they rely upon an analysis only of a company's reported accounting results? It seems not, for if accounting statements were all that mattered, then stock prices would change just four times a year, that is, upon the release of each of the quarterly reports. The reality, of course, is that stock prices change, and often very dramatically, every business day. Prices change frequently because lead steers compete to be the first to ferret out new and potentially profitable information. They simply cannot wait until management releases the earnings because, by then, the news is so well-known that no profit can be made trading on it. Lead steer investors talk to customers, suppliers, and competitors to discover important developments, often before the company's management is aware of them.

An article taken from the pages of the *Wall Street Journal* illustrates how lead steers procure information. It is entitled "IBM Watchers Process Data on the Big Firm to Divine Its Program," and it chronicles how information on the computer giant is obtained in ways even IBM cannot prevent:

Computer users, competitors, stock-market investors, even some foreign governments want badly to know when IBM will bring out new products, how fast prices will drop, which new businesses IBM might enter and what its long range goals are....

With IBM so secretive—and its every move so important—an offbeat industry has sprung up to try to slake the thirst for information. IBM watchers from coast to coast question the computer company's customers, comb technical literature and study corporate statements like oracles examining entrails, striving to divine IBM's direction....

In a still more recent example, analysts already are able to estimate that IBM will ship up to 2 million personal computers in 1984 based on the company's orders for components. The anecdotes and the academic research both support the same conclusion: lead steers are uncanny in learning about corporate performance through channels other than published financial reports.

The implication for investor relations should be clear. Any attempt to influence investors to pay a higher price through accounting puffery is not likely to succeed. It insults the intelligence of the investors who really matter, who seek out important new information from many sources and quickly impound it into share values. Accounting reports matter little because they contain yesterday's score. The market is betting on tomorrow's contest.

A further implication of a market dominated by the lead steers is that when business judgment and accounting diverge, management should make the decision on an economic basis, and then carefully explain the accounting consequences to influential investors. The first principle of investor relations, then, is: Speak to the lead steer.

FINANCIAL HYPE (OR WHY SELLING STOCK IS UNLIKE SELLING SOAP)

Many senior managers believe that their common stock can be marketed just like any other product. Their business experience has taught them that profits depend on carefully selecting a target market, differentiating their product, and increasing demand through clever advertising. They see no reason why these same principles should not be applied to promote their company's stock, and increase its price.

To do so, public relations firms are hired, often at great expense, to tell the company's story through slick advertisements in business periodicals and on television. Senior management is encouraged to make frequent presentations to investment analysts to keep the company's name in front of those in a position to recommend purchase of the company's shares. And the annual report is carefully crafted to sell the company, its businesses, and its management to the investing public. In short, the company is hyped in the best Madison Avenue tradition.

Whether or not it is recognized as such, an important assumption behind these practices is that there are a fixed number of common shares outstanding, so that any increase in demand will require a higher stock price to allocate the available supply among potential investors. That assumption is incorrect. The supply of shares can expand or contract to meet changes in demand without changing the underlying stock price. In this regard, selling stock is unlike selling soap.

Suppose that as a result of an extensive publicity campaign, management is able to convince more investors to purchase the company's shares. Will this necessarily increase the company's stock price? No. So long as lead steers remain convinced that the company's intrinsic value has not changed, it is likely only to increase volume. Here's why.

As the new orders flood into the market, the increased demand will be met first by the stock exchange dealer who will sell shares directly out of inventory. The function of dealers is to satisfy just such temporary imbalances between supply and demand, and thus give the market continuity and liquidity. Of course, the dealer expects to replace the shares later at a slightly lower price. That's how they make money.

If the incoming orders exceed the dealer's supply, the price may inch up just enough to persuade other investors who hold shares to sell. Eagle-eyed investors constantly probe for opportunities to sell overvalued shares and to buy undervalued ones. It will not take much of a price move to command the attention of potential sellers.

But you may ask, "What recourse is available to investors who want to own the company's shares, but are prevented from doing so by the stampeding herd who just read about the company in Forbes and Barron's?" One strategy is to buy a mixture of riskier call options on the shares and less risky T-bills, and end up with essentially the same investment—even without directly owning the company's stock. A less precise, but equally satisfactory, result can be obtained just by buying the shares of companies of lower and higher risk, so as to match the company's risk in the portfolio. Of course, the simplest method may be to buy the shares of a close competitor. In the real world, financial repackaging is inexpensive, and this creates a virtually unlimited number of substitutes to satisfy investors' demand without changing price. This is an important difference between selling stock and selling soap.

It is also possible that some investors may be persuaded to sell the company's stock short, in essence, sell shares they do not own, in order to meet the demands of those who prefer to own the shares without regard for their price. In this case, the total number of shares owned by investors will exceed the number issued by the company, with the difference accounted for as shares borrowed in short sales. In this way, the supply of shares can readily expand (or contract) to meet changes in demand.

In summary, the smart money adjusts when the buying patterns of unsophisticated investors are swayed by the public relations artists. Lead steers compensate by selling the shares when they become overpriced, replicating their desired investment by combining positions in other markets and other stocks, and even selling short to create an artificial new supply of shares. This means that in a market dominated by forward-looking investors, shares can change hands without changing price.

The opposite chain of events presumably would be set in motion if all of a sudden a large new supply of shares were to be released on the market. In theory, this would prevent the stock price from collapsing.

Fortunately, whether this happens was studied by Myron Scholes in his doctoral dissertation at the University of Chicago. His research constitutes a critical test of which view of the market—the traditional "demand-supply" view or the "intrinsic value" view—is correct.

Professor Scholes examined the effect on share prices of sales of large blocks of stock offered through secondary offerings. According to the traditional view, the larger the block of shares to be sold (in relation to total float), the larger the price decline would have to be to induce ever-increasing numbers of investors to purchase the shares. By contrast, the intrinsic value view suggests that the stock price would be unaffected by the size of the block to be sold. It says that at the right place, the market would readily absorb additional shares.

The evidence is important and persuasive. Professor Scholes did find that stock prices decline upon the distribution of a large block of shares, but the price decline was unrelated to the size of the distribution. This means that the price discount is more correctly interpreted as a result of the adverse information communicated by a large block sale than as a result of "selling pressure." This interpretation is reinforced by the fact that the largest price discounts were recorded when the secondary sale was made by corporate officers and the company itself. (A further indication was the permanence of the price decline; the demand-supply view would predict a recovery after the selling pressure had abated.) Apparently once a new "right" price had been established for the company, a virtually unlimited pool of capital was available to purchase the company's shares. This is strong confirmation of the "intrinsic value" view of the market.

Probably the most direct evidence that the market follows intrinsic value and not demand-supply is contained in the day-to-day movements of the market. Advocates of the demand-supply view of share price behavior are fond of quoting "profit-taking" as the reason why stock prices fall after having increased for several days or weeks running. It conjures up images of men stuffing sacks full of money, hauling profits out of the market, and leaving it to collapse. But if the market opens in the morning down from its prior close, who took the profits out overnight? Even more difficult to explain using this line of reasoning is why stock prices increase. As we to believe that these same men haul the money back, unload the profits and put it back into the market? In other words, if it is "profit-taking" that sends the market down, is it "profit-giving" that sends it back up? Since when were investors so charitable?

The fallacy of the supply-and-demand description of the market is the assumption that money must enter or leave the market to send prices up or down. In reality, the market can close sharply up or down without any new money having arrived or departed. Lead steer investors simply agree to transact at prices that reflect a revised outlook for economic conditions. In "intrinsic value" markets, therefore, shares can change price without changing hands and, as previously demonstrated, can change hands without changing price.

The bottom line on financial publicity is that it is likely to increase volume, but not price. Sophisticated investors compensate for naive ones who are seduced by hype. The winners are Madison Avenue and the brokers; the losers are stockholders who foot the bill and managements who expect great things. The second principle of financial communication is: Madison Avenue can't help if your problem is on Wall Street.

INDIRECT FINANCIAL COMMUNICATION _____

When substantive financial communication from management is lacking, investors look to other signals as clues to management's intentions or expectations. This is not unusual. Recently, *Business Week* interviewed a group of Fed watchers—professionals who closely monitor the behavior of the Federal Reserve to learn about the future course of economic activity. They were asked why so much importance was attached to seemingly minor changes in the week-to-week money supply figures. The answer was that whatever the Fed thought was important became important as a clue to the future. If the Fed watched egg-salad production, the Fed watchers averred, they would also.

The same is true of lead steer investors. They look for something to hang their hat on. If management makes earnings the hook, that will grab the lead steers. But there is at least anecdotal evidence that this is not the right choice.

Mr. Malcolm Northrup, President of Verbatim Corporation, a maker of floppy disks for computers, told a group of security analysts that his company would experience a decline in earnings for the first time. The decline would not be caused by poor performance, but rather by costs incurred to open a major new plant. He stated further that he was not concerned with the earnings decline, and that if the security analysts were concerned, they were free to recommend other stocks. He claimed his management team was convinced the overall return on investment would be attractive, and for this reason the investment made sense regardless of what the near-term accounting impact might be. Following this emphatic statement, Verbatim's stock price climbed dramatically. Earnings, it seems, are important only when management makes them the sacred bull.

Other signals traditionally employed by management include increasing dividends and undertaking stock repurchases. Both, of course, are often associated with stock price improvements. The reason is that they suggest management's belief that performance will improve. Each, however, has an associated cost that could be avoided by communicating more directly and effectively with lead steers.

Because boards of directors are reluctant to reduce the dividend after it is increased, dividend payments resemble a fixed cost. And if management is averse to issuing new shares to "recapture" the dividend, the result will be a loss in financing and, perhaps, operating flexibility.

Stock repurchases accomplished through a tender offer express management's belief that the company's shares are undervalued. The problem, however, with this form of communication is that tender offers usually are made at a considerable premium over the current market price, thus representing a significant cost to non-tendering shareholders. It may also have the effect of unsettling the company's capital structure, or using cash needed in the business.

DIRECT FINANCIAL COMMUNICATION

Effective communication of the company's prospects should make these more costly signals unnecessary. In addition, it is likely to provide the following benefits:

- It makes the company's actions more predictable and, because investors pay a discount for uncertainty (never a premium), this by itself should improve share price.
- It boosts shareholder confidence in management's attentiveness to value-creation as the objective of its strategic planning process.
- It encourages a uniform framework of planning throughout the company. Because managers at all levels of the company become involved, internal as well as external communication improves.

What, then, is "financial communication"? Unlike financial disclosure, it concentrates on future economic prospects instead of dwelling on past or near-term accounting results. Contrary to financial hype, its purpose is to revise the expectations of lead steers, even if this seems to sacrifice appeal to the mass market. In short, financial communication greases the engine that drives stock prices.

The communication process should be the final step in a company's planning cycle, which includes the following stages:

1. Review the company's operating businesses to determine their past performance, strategic fit, profitable product lines, and minimum "hurdle" rates required to create value for stockholders.
2. Formulate operating plans consistent with the strategic direction established for the company.
3. Develop an overall financial plan that satisfies new capital needs without an imprudent reliance on debt financing.
4. Ensure that business goals and financial objectives are mutually consistent. Because a company's sources and uses of funds must balance, lead steers know that the company's financial plan must match the cash requirements of the business plan. All too frequently, the goals announced by management do not balance.

As part of an integrated approach to financial planning, we also recommend adoption of a management incentive compensation plan based on the factors that are critical to improving the company's share price. Communication of a plan that compensates managers handsomely only when the shareholders also benefit will reinforce investors' confidence in management.

THE CRITICAL FACTORS

Clearly, there are a great many variables that can affect the stock price of a company. But most of these can be captured in a model of valuation which reflects the expected levels, duration, and risk of future operating cash flow. This model, as presented by Franco Modigliani and Merton Miller in the late fifties, reduces the valuation process to essentially six factors. Four out of the six are directly under the influence of management, and should be discussed as the centerpiece of any program of financial communication. They are:

1. The current level of net operating (cash) profits *after* taxes, but before all financing costs (NOPAT). What is needed is not a forecast of the next year's NOPAT, but rather, the average level expected over a business cycle from capital already committed to the business.
2. The amount of new investment the company expects to make over the foreseeable future, where "investment" includes additions to working capital as well as capital expenditures.
3. The anticipated rate of return, in relevant cash-flow terms, over the lives of the investments.
4. The company's target capital structure. Because interest payments are tax-deductible, debt is cheaper than equity under all capital market conditions. Investors consequently need to be informed of the level of debt that management considers ideal so that temporary deviations will not be misinterpreted.

Less subject to control by management, but nevertheless important to lead steers, are the following two factors:

5. The degree of risk in each of the company's major lines of business. Along with the current level of interest rates, the level of risk determines the minimum return required by investors for each business activity, commonly known as the cost of capital.

6. The length of time investors expect management to have attractive new investments. After that time, investors believe competition will become sufficiently intense that management will find it difficult to find new investment opportunities that will yield a return in excess of the cost of capital.

While these six constitute the essential determinants of corporate value, there are other factors that should be made clear to investors. These include the following:

1. *Acquisition/Divestiture Strategy.* At a minimum, investors need to know what guidelines management has adopted in the search for suitable merger partners. Equally important are the criteria for disposing of non-competitive businesses.

2. *Management's Incentive Compensation Plan.* Recent evidence from the academic community has revealed that when management announces a bonus plan aimed at improving the underlying determinants of share value, the stock price increases. Investors then know that management will win only if they win. When bonuses are tied to earnings-per-share growth or other accounting measures, shareholder and management interests may diverge.

3. *Business Risk Management Policies.* Investors need to understand the exposure of the company to various business risks. Accordingly, management should disclose the nature of the company's contracts with its employees, customers, suppliers, and even franchise partners.

4. *International Performance.* Nowhere is accounting more misleading than in presenting the results of foreign operations. Management should attribute the FASB #52 adjustment to each major foreign country where the company has operations, and should indicate how much of the adjustment was due to translating liabilities and how much to translating assets. This will help investors to distinguish temporary from permanent exchange adjustments, and to better understand whether the adjustment is due to operating or financing decisions. The company's policy for hedging and financing its international operations should also be articulated.

5. *Financing Policies.* In addition to communicating the company's target capital structure, management should indicate the type of securities and financing vehicles it considers most appropriate. Management also should specify the company's dividend policy, and ensure it is consistent with the company's profit objective and capital structure target. Finally, investors should be apprised of the company's pension funding policy, including the assumptions used in arriving at the value of the pension fund liability.

CONCLUSIONS

It should be obvious by now that financial communication, to be really effective, must go to the heart of the company's planning process. As you might expect, many of the companies that have adopted this approach and reaped its benefits have been those where the quality of planning is superior. Investors know that management's decision to communicate, or not to communicate, along these lines says a great deal about how well they manage the company, how far they look into the future, and how much they are in control of their destiny. (We estimate that there are over 200 companies in the United States that now include such discussions in their annual report. In addition, many companies reinforce this with periodic letters to their shareholders and presentations to key industry analysts.)

Chief executive financial officers all too often miss opportunities to increase their company's stock price through effective communication with investors. More often than not, their discussions in annual reports are geared toward the "lowest common denominator," the least knowledgeable investors in the herd. These statements provide no relevant new information to the "lead steer" investors who really determine share values.

Companies that hype their stock will be disappointed by the results. Undertaking financial publicity to increase demand for the company's shares may increase trading volume, but such an increase in volume may well have little effect on transaction price. Lead steers will head off the stampeding herd.

To be successful, a program of financial communication must spur on the lead steers. They must come to expect more from the company year in and year out, on average and over the next business cycle. The most sensible way to do this is to cut them in on the company's planning process by announcing the operating goals and financial policies that will guide the company's growth.

NOTE

1. "Does it Pay to Manipulate EPS?," *Issues in Corporate Finance* (New York: Stern Stewart Putnam & Macklis, Ltd., 1983), p. 14.

II

Do Dividends Matter?
A DISCUSSION OF CORPORATE DIVIDEND POLICY

INTRODUCTION

Over the past fifteen or twenty years, the question of the effect of dividends on stock prices has been a controversial one. Until quite recently, in fact, the academic finance profession collectively had come up with no convincing rationale for corporate dividend payments. Up to this point, there were only two positions on the dividend question that were seriously defended by financial economists: (1) dividends are "irrelevant" (that is, whether companies retain their earnings or pay them out to stockholders is a matter of indifference to investors in aggregrate); and (2) higher dividends actually lead to lower stock prices because taxable investors pay higher taxes on dividends than on capital gains.

Of course, there has never been any doubt that large announced dividend increases are generally accompanied by increases in stock price, and that dividend cuts can send prices plummeting. But the reigning interpretation of this phenomenon has been that such changes in dividend policy convey information to the market *only* about the firm's future *earnings* power. The positive market response to announcements of higher dividends thus says nothing about a preference by investors for dividends per se over capital gains. And this "information effect" has accordingly been interpreted as being consistent with the dividend "irrelevance" proposition: namely, that investors in the aggregate care only about total returns, and the level of total stockholder returns is unaffected by management decisions to pay out part of that return in the form of dividends.

A third school, however, has recently proposed a positive economic rationale for corporate dividends by elaborating the role of dividends in providing information. Proponents of this relatively new line of reasoning observe that management often has significant inside information about its company's prospects that it cannot (or chooses not to) divulge to investors;

and the mere possibility of this information "gap" that inevitably exists between management and stockholders causes stock prices to be lower than they would otherwise be under conditions of perfect certainty. Corporate dividends, this argument goes, may be management's most cost-effective means of overcoming the investor uncertainty resulting from this potential "informational asymmetry." In periodically and predictably raising the dividend, management effectively binds itself to make a series of future payments to stockholders; and this commitment, which is costly in terms of management's future flexibility (we all know how reluctant managements are to cut the dividend), provides investors with the assurance that management is not sitting on some important piece of negative information.

A potential problem with this argument, however, is that it doesn't convincingly explain why dividend changes are the most efficient (least costly) way of communicating management's confidence. The fact that almost all successful companies pay dividends would suggest, at least to a "positive" economist, that dividends must have some value for investors that they don't get through capital gains. But, given that there are some very successful companies that have never paid a dividend, and have declared their intention of never paying a dividend, one is led to wonder whether investors really value dividends, or whether they have just been strongly "conditioned" by *management's* behavior to receive them. If the latter is the case, then presumably the process of market conditioning can be reversed by companies persuasively communicating their intention to put their costly equity capital (and the costs of issuing new equity, as new research suggests, may be higher than finance scholars have suspected) to more profitable uses.

In the "Roundtable Discussion of Corporate Dividend Policy" which follows, the dividend controversy is explored by two distinguished representatives of the investment banking community and two academics on the forefront of the research on dividends. The exchange offers an interesting and varied collection of views—not only on dividend policy, but on financial issues such as valuation, investment strategies, financing methods, and financial communication. In fact, this concentrated focus on the dividend controversy turns out to provide an ideal forum for investigating the workings of financial markets, the rationality of the investment community, and the process by which economic value is created. The position one takes on dividend policy, as becomes clear in this discussion, is necessarily determined by one's view of these fundamentals.

Thus, it is no surprise, for example, that John Childs, by far the most vigorous advocate in the discussion for the corporate practice of paying dividends, is also the most vocal in asserting the "irrationality" of stock market pricing. Childs, who advises primarily utilities for Kidder Peabody, quite sensibly argues that the dividend question must be approached on a firm-by-firm basis. High dividends, he maintains, while not appropriate for high-growth firms, are desirable for large industrial companies, and "absolutely necessary" for banks and utilities (which are said to appeal to a wholly different breed of investor).

But, as Bob Litzenberger (of Stanford University) repeatedly points out, this by no means implies that such investors really value dividends more highly than capital gains. The unspoken assumption behind this conventional prescription for dividend policy is that management's dividend policy is really being "driven" by its investment decisions. That is, profitable growth companies tend not to pay dividends because they have better uses for their funds; whereas low-growth firms in mature or regulated industries appear to be rewarded by markets for paying out their profits instead of reinvesting them in unprofitable projects. Dividend payments, in the latter case, appear to be an effective means for management to promise its investors that the company will not destroy shareholder wealth by reinvesting earnings in unprofitable operations or pursuing a strategy of growth for growth's sake. (This also appears to be a plausible explanation of the role of stock repurchases in the recent wave of restructuring activity.)

The real crux of the dividend controversy, however, comes down to the final question considered: Does management dare cut the dividend to provide equity capital for funding profitable growth? And furthermore, if it can be done, how should this strategy be communicated to the market? At the time of this discussion, there was no academic evidence bearing on this question (although the recent cases of Gould Inc. and Litton Industries, as well as some new research by Randy Woolridge of Penn State, suggest that the answer to the first question may be yes); and none of the participants was willing to stick out his neck very far. Joel Stern, however, proposes a hypothetical case in which management announces, eighteen months in advance, that it is ceasing all dividend payments to fund profitable growth opportunities. This amount of advance notice allows the pro-dividend "clientele" among the company's investors sufficient time to sell out in an orderly fashion; and the company's stock is thereby supported, if not actually increased, by the announcement of a new capital spending plan, which brings about an influx of a new clientele of investors seeking capital gains.

The question we are left to contemplate is: Do such things really happen in the "real world"? As Bob Litzenberger closes the discussion, "I would agree with Joel . . . that there should always be bargain hunters keeping share prices fairly valued, even when a dividend is cut. . . . The problem . . . is the difficulty of making a substantial reduction without the market interpreting this as negative information. I'm not sure it can be done and there is no way to test this without actually trying it. The farthest any companies have gone in this direction is to (1) cut back on the rate of growth in dividends or (2) hold the level of dividends paid out constant so that the payout ratio declines over time. Bill noted that these actions represent giant steps so I guess there is no reason to believe we will see companies go beyond this to substantially cut the level of dividends, unless they are really in trouble. Until they do we can only speculate."

DHC

DO DIVIDENDS MATTER?:
A DISCUSSION OF CORPORATE DIVIDEND POLICY
January 6, 1982

JOSEPH T. WILLETT, MODERATOR: I would like to welcome the participants and guests to this discussion, the subject of which is Corporate Dividend Policy. The general questions we want to address are these: Does dividend policy matter? And if so, why and how does it matter? Certain people argue that the theory of finance, combined with the treatment of dividends under U.S. tax law, would suggest that low dividends benefit investors. Others argue that because of the demand by some investors for current income, high dividends benefit investors.

In the presence of these widely held views, I think it is fair to say that most carefully executed research has revealed no consistent relationship between dividends and share prices. From these studies, the market collectively appears to be "dividend neutral." That is, while individual investors may have preferences between dividends and capital gains, the results suggest neither a preference for nor an aversion to dividends. Which, of course, doesn't satisfy either the pro-dividend or anti-dividend group.

Amid all this confusion, one observation stands out: nearly all successful firms pay dividends. And, furthermore, dividend policy is an important concern of most chief financial officers and financial managers generally. These facts of corporate practice, in light of all the evidence on the subject, present us with a puzzle—one which has continued to baffle the academic finance profession. In a paper written in 1976, entitled "The Dividend Puzzle," Fischer Black of MIT—one of the most widely respected researchers in the field—posed the question: "What should the individual investor do about dividends in his portfolio? What should the corporation do about dividend policy?" His concluding response to both was: "We don't know."

With that as a backdrop, I would like to introduce our distinguished group of participants, who bring us a variety of viewpoints and experience:

JOHN M. CHILDS is Vice President, Kidder Peabody, and widely known in the field of corporate finance as an advisor and lecturer. John is the author of several books, the most recent of which is *Corporate Finance and Capital*

Management for the Chief Executive Officer. He is a member of the New York Society of Security Analysts and the New York Bar Association;

PATRICK J. HESS is Assistant Professor of Finance at the College of Administrative Sciences, Ohio State University. Pat has contributed articles to the *Journal of Financial Economics*, the *Journal of Finance*, and the *Journal of Business*. Most of his recent work has concerned the effect of dividends on stock prices;

WILLIAM J. KEALY is Partner & Director of Research for Goldman Sachs & Company, with whom he has been associated for the past fifteen years. Bill is a CFA and a member of the New York Society of Security Analysts;

ROBERT LITZENBERGER is COG Miller Distinguished Professor of Finance, Stanford University. Bob is a member of the Editorial Boards of the *Journal of Finance* and the *Journal of Financial Economics*. His study on dividends (co-authored by Krishna Ramaswamy), which attempted to demonstrate an adverse tax effect on stock prices, has become one of the most potent empirical arguments for the "anti-dividend" school of thought;

JOEL M. STERN is President of Stern Stewart & Co., Corporate Financial Consultants and Economic Forecasters. Joel is the author of *Analytical Methods in Financial Planning*, and his numerous corporate finance articles have appeared in the *Wall Street Journal*, the *Commercial and Financial Chronicle*, and the *Financial Times* in London. He is also a rotating panelist on the television program *Wall Street Week*;

JOSEPH T. WILLETT, formerly Vice President of the Chase Financial Policy Division of the Chase Manhattan Bank, now works on the Treasury staff at Merrill Lynch & Co., Inc.

I should point out, both to the participants and to the audience, that this discussion is not intended to be a formal debate, but rather an open exchange of ideas. "Free-for-all" might be an appropriate description. At some point in the session, however, we want to address the following issues:

- What is the relationship between dividends and share prices?
- Why do companies pay dividends?
- Should companies pay dividends?
- What factors should companies pay attention to in setting, or changing, dividend policy?

Joel, you have a fairly extreme—or, at least, a well-known—position on dividends . . . one that might be classified by some people as extreme. So it might be a good way to start for you to describe, briefly, your views on dividend policy.

THE MODERN FINANCE APPROACH TO DIVIDEND POLICY

JOEL: I'd like to start by pointing out that the major reason why people like Fischer Black believe they don't know the answer to the question of the appropriate dividend policy is this: the evidence that has been accumulated in the academic community by serious researchers—by people that we have a lot of respect for, who are on the faculties of the premiere business schools—almost without exception, these academics find that there is no evidence to suggest that investors at the margin, where prices are set, have any preference for dividends over capital gains. This supports the point of view that the price-setting, marginal investor is "dividend-neutral," which means that a dollar of dividends gained is equal to a dollar of capital gains lost. That means that investors would care only about total return, while being indifferent how that return was divided between dividends and price appreciation.

There is a second point of view, that has been expressed recently in research, which shows that investors who receive dividends cannot undo the harmful tax consequences of receiving that dividend. And, as a result, the market is actually "dividend averse," marking down prices of shares that pay cash dividends, so that the pre-tax returns that investors earn are high enough such that, post-tax, the returns are what they would have been had the company not paid cash dividends in the first place. But there is no creditable evidence that I am aware of—none that has been accepted by the academic finance community—that shows that investors prefer dividends over capital gains.

If the evidence that has been published to date says that investors are dividend neutral or dividend averse, then how is it that somebody with the esteem of Fischer Black can come along and say: "We don't know what the right dividend policy is." The problem is that he is what we call a "positive economist." That doesn't mean that he is an economist who is positive about things. It means that he says the job of the economist is to account for what we see around us. He believes that markets behave in a sensible fashion at the margin; that under the guidance of the dominant price-setting investors, the market behaves in a rational manner, making the right choices for itself. Therefore, he is saying that there must be a reason why almost all companies for all time have been paying cash dividends. If a few companies paid dividends for all time, or almost all companies paid dividends only occasionally, then one could make the case that it is possible dividends are really not important. But, if we find that almost all companies pay dividends for almost all time, there must be a good reason why they are paying the dividends. Therefore, who are we, as financial advisors, to say to a company, "No, don't pay cash dividends. After all, it won't harm you very much despite the fact that almost all companies are paying cash dividends"? That wouldn't make very much sense.

THE ANTI-DIVIDEND POSITION _____

JOEL: So, then, where do I come up with the position I take, which really *is* an extreme position? My position is this: I don't believe that any company, at almost any time, should pay cash dividends, even if it has no projects in which to invest the money where there are expectations of high rates of return. How do I account for my position?

The answer is to be seen, I think, in a kind of theoretical discussion initially, and through a set of examples—which admittedly provide only anecdotal rather than scientific, statistical evidence—that follow. Let's start off the discussion by assuming a world, which we are admittedly saying is artificial, in which there are no personal income taxes, and there are no transactions costs. Then also assume that a company has three possible sets of projects: one in which the returns are expected to exceed what investors can otherwise do with their money; the second, in which the returns are equal to what investors can otherwise do with their money; and the third, in which the expectation is that the returns will be inadequate compared to what the investors can otherwise use their money for. My argument is that if the company can do better than its investors with the funds, invest it inside the company. It would be better for investors, and for the company, to leave the money inside than to take it outside. If they need money on which to live, if they have "current consumption" needs, they can always sell off their shares. As for the second category, where the company has the same expected rates of return as what investors could otherwise do with their money, I would argue that it wouldn't make any difference whether the company invested the money or the investor took the money and invested it himself. As long as we are assuming no transactions costs and no tax consequence, it wouldn't make any difference whether the company reinvested its earnings or paid dividends. In the third case, where the company is expected to do worse on projects than the investor might otherwise do outside, there the argument would be in favor of 100 percent dividend payout. In fact, in this case, one could argue that you should hire a very good mechanical engineer so that you wouldn't even have to reinvest the depreciation to maintain the plant. And then, just before the plant falls in, you get all of the people out.

But humor aside, I'm saying if you can do better with funds, then no dividends. If you're doing the same as the investors can do with the funds, you're indifferent. And if you do worse than the investors, then you pay it all out. But once you relax the assumptions about the no transactions costs and the personal income taxes, things seem to change. In the finance profession, the argument has been made that there is a "clientele" of investors that prefer dividends, a clientele that is neutral, and a clientele that's even averse. The preferences, or the indifference, of each of these "clienteles" would reflect mainly the tax consequences: that is, investors' tax rates on dividends or ordinary income, relative to the taxes they would pay on capital gains. Another important variable is the transactions costs that the investor would have to pay in selling his stock, instead of receiving dividends, to get current income. And, on the basis of these two offsetting considerations—

the tax consequences of receiving dividends and the possible transactions costs from being forced to sell shares—the theory says that investors tend to "sort themselves out" by holding stocks which satisfy their own dividend preferences. High-dividend stocks, as the argument runs, will attract a clientele of investors different from low-dividend stocks.

But once a company establishes a particular dividend policy, notice how it begs the issue. Once you establish the dividend policy, you are stuck with the clientele who wants the policy that you've got. So it's like the person who says, "Don't tell me what's in my best interests; I know what's in my best interests, and that's why I'm here. So don't change the policy." The problem with that point of view is that the evidence does not seem to favor the view that you can't trade one clientele for another. That is, it is possible to change the clientele without incurring a significant cost to the shareholder base. And one clientele seems to be as good as another. So because the evidence seems to indicate that dividends and capital gains are treated about equally in the market, we can be effectively dividend neutral—despite the fact that there are clienteles.

Now the question is: Why do I come out against dividend payments, in view of the theory and the evidence? Professor Eli Shapiro maintained, in a recent *Wall Street Journal* letter, that the reason corporate dividend payments were rising in the year 1980 was that companies were earning inadequate rates of return; and, therefore, the money was being paid out to the investors. I have a problem with that, and the reason is (as I know from my experience, and the anecdotes could probably go on for as many as 400 different companies I have worked for over the last fifteen years) that once the company's Board of Directors raises the dividend, it will only be a calamity that will get the dividends back down. Now is Professor Shapiro willing to say that when the company raises the dividend payments, it knows with a high degree of probability that not only are current returns expected to be inadequate, but also returns in the indefinite future? It doesn't make sense to me. Because the Boards of Directors of companies treat the dividend as a fixed cost. Once they raise it, they will not cut it. Thus, increasing the dividend effectively reduces the flexibility of management in raising capital under what they would consider to be the most favorable terms.

And even if a company does have excess cash that cannot be profitably reinvested, managements have another option superior to paying out cash dividends. We know for a fact that there are companies that are retaining their excess cash in the business and building an investment portfolio for their shareholders. Teledyne is the most obvious example. So that we have an operating company on one side, and an investment company on the other. What that company is doing is maintaining a well-diversified portfolio at a far lower cost than what the investor would otherwise have to incur, because they buy the shares at lower cost. Any dividends that are still being paid are being collected 85 percent tax free inside that corporate entity.

And the company can also borrow against the value of the portfolio, thereby shielding the rest of the dividend income from taxes. Essentially what I am saying is that, given the world in which Boards of Directors will not reduce dividend payments, and where there is also the prospect of profitable projects in the future that are not yet obvious today, most companies should become their own banks, retaining and reinvesting excess cash in their own investment portfolios. Mr. Willett, it's all yours.

JOE: Okay, let me summarize very quickly what I think you said. First of all, the evidence suggests that there are no preferences collectively on the part of the market for dividends. The harmful effects of dividends to the corporation are that (1) dividends are viewed as a fixed cost, reducing management's financing flexibility, and (2) dividends potentially increase transactions costs. Let's consider the first point, now, which is that the market exhibits, apparently, neither a preference for nor an aversion to dividends. None of the research has been interpreted as demonstrating a preference for dividends. What is the panel's view on that contention?

DIVIDENDS CONVEY INFORMATION _____

PAT HESS: Well, I think the case has been stated a little strongly, at least from my point of view. It seems to me that it is not really clear whether the market has an aversion or a preference. In fact, there is no particularly easy way to summarize the evidence. I think there are a lot of problems associated with some past empirical work; and there are almost inherently some problems in general of trying to detect if there is a preference for or aversion to dividends—or neutrality. The reason for that, I think, is that dividends may not be an important causal variable. What I mean is that dividends may be telling investors something else about the company— about its earnings prospects, its rate of future investment, and so forth. So to control for all the things that might go wrong is a very difficult problem in terms of doing the research. And for this reason, I think there's a little bit of overstatement on Joel's part to say (and this was also stated in the introductory remarks) that the market looks "dividend neutral." I don't think you can make that strong a case. I don't think you can summarize the market's position on dividends in a single word, whether it be "neutral," "averse," or "preferring."

JOEL: Could I ask you a very quick question? When you say that the evidence is a bit muddy...

PAT: Yes, quite muddy.

JOEL: ... it reminds me of something that Dick Roll [Professor of Finance, UCLA] said; and that is: "I don't agree with the empirical framework of the capital asset pricing model. But, conceptually, I certainly do agree with it." In other words, he says there is something wrong with the empirical work; but conceptually he accepts the practical implications of what it tells us. Would you say that, based on your reading of the research and the studies, you would recommend to a company that they pay or not pay cash dividends for any particular reason?

PAT: Quite honestly, I would have a very difficult time, intellectually, making a recommendation. If someone told me, "Look, if we increase our dividends we're going to upset our shareholders; induce them to engage in some large portfolio adjustments, and there is a real cost there," I could easily end up agreeing with that. But I think that it's going to come down to some *real* issues, such as the company's investment policies and earnings prospects. And not to the merely *financial* issue of whether stockholders want their returns now as opposed to later through capital gains, or whether the company, by paying higher dividends, has to go out and raise external equity.

JOEL: Some people have said that some companies pay cash dividends because they are trying to convey information to the market about the prospects of the company, so that they say, "When we raise or lower our dividend payments, we're telling you something, not only about the near-term prospects of the company, but the medium- to distant-term prospects too. If we are not doing well in the short run, we'll still try to maintain our dividend policy because we want you to be aware that the prospects are only temporarily impaired, and not for the long run." Would you subscribe to that being a sufficient case for public utilities, for example, paying cash dividends? You wouldn't think it would make a great deal of difference there, would it?

PAT: Well, actually, I've always been a bit dubious about that view because there should be so many alternatives to signalling through the dividend. Although one does have to admit there is this particular pattern in dividend announcements, I've always been puzzled by the presumption that they really use dividends *just* to signal their prospects. Certainly, dividends do appear to have some information content. But I'm not particularly satisfied with that explanation. So, I guess the answer to the question is that the utilities present a paradox. Why would utilities have this big incentive to signal, if signalling is the explanation. Why don't we see them using other signals—more direct ones?

BILL KEALY: One of the problems, from a practical point of view, of looking at this question of dividends as information signals is that there is a difference between those people who merely own equities, and those people who tend to be the price-setting participants in the marketplace. What I'm talking about is the spread between institutional ownership of the bulk of stocks, and their percentage of transactions, as compared with the considerably smaller percentage of transactions accounted for by individuals, despite their large ownership. I agree with the theoretical literature to the extent that I understand it. I agree with this "indifference" concept. The problem when you look at the real world is that if you eliminate a dividend, there is a body of individuals who won't understand the signals. They are not sophisticated investors. But if they become the price-setters, if they leave this theoretical "throne of indifference" with respect to dividends, you will see a very different reaction in the marketplace from that predicted by the indifference theory. Institutional investors understand payout ratios, retention rates, investment priorities, investment alternatives. They understand the signals embedded in changes in dividends or dividend policy. If the individual investor, however, who happens to dominate the ownership class but not the transaction class, and who is not generally setting prices—if these investors are disturbed inordinately by a change in dividend policy—if you eliminate, cut the dividend, or do something drastic which affects their perception of their net worth—they then may become the price-setter. They then become very active and aggressive in the marketplace.

BOB LITZENBERGER: I would like to respond to a couple of points that I disagreed with. Now the evidence suggests that *unanticipated* changes in dividends do have an impact on price. That should not be interpreted either as an aversion to or a preference for dividends per se. Such price changes should be interpreted merely as an "information effect." As Joel said earlier, because corporations generally try to maintain a stable dividend policy, they are very reluctant to cut a dividend once they announce an increase. So that when a company's management announces an increase in the dividend, it's telling the market that the future level and stability of earnings is going to be sufficient to maintain that dividend. We do observe stock prices responding positively to unanticipated dividend increases, and negatively to unanticipated decreases.

Now the trouble with that "information effect" argument is that it is almost an argument for inertia, for doing nothing, as opposed to choosing a policy. This argument also implies that it is very difficult to radically change your policy. It also doesn't answer the question of a new firm: Should they pay dividends or not?

JOEL: You mean a company going public for the first time?

BOB: Yes, going public for the first time. Also it doesn't answer the question: "Well, even with some inertia, can we slowly drift to a new policy without actually cutting the dividend?" You could perhaps decrease the rate of increase in the dividend without conveying substantial negative information. Joel touched on public utilities. The only industry where we see very large dividends and, at the same time, very large equity flotations is the public utility industry. So you might say, from that perspective, utilities seem to be the biggest paradox.

Now going back to an earlier point, I think if you look at the research in finance, it's fairly clear now that most research—including Pat's own research—shows that there *is* some hidden effect. That is, when you attempt to measure the effect of dividends on stock prices, you're probably not looking at a major causal variable. Dividends are probably saying something about more fundamental variables—about investment policies, for instance.

They could also be a proxy for some measure of risk that has not been controlled for by the model. We know, for example that high dividend–paying companies tend to have lower risk measures than low dividend companies. Focusing on my evidence, though, if you rule out this "missing variable" explanation, it's consistent with an *aversion to dividends.*

There are two explanations of my findings: one possible interpretation is that there are "clientele" effects. Now the one problem with that explanation is that studies that have actually looked at holdings of people in different tax brackets show that there is certainly no strong tendency for the actual holding of high dividend–paying stocks to be associated with people in low tax brackets, and for low dividend–paying stocks to be associated with people in high tax brackets. So the actual holdings of investors don't seem to correspond with this clientele explanation. A second explanation of my findings is that there are investors in the market who are dividend averse because of their tax consequences. But, by the same token, there are corporations that would find high-paying dividend stocks attractive because of the 85 percent dividend exclusion; and their actions in the market would have the effect of essentially eliminating the adverse tax effect associated with high dividend–paying stocks.

Two things happen when a firm changes its dividend policy: if it increases its dividend, then it's paying out more of its earnings in the way of ordinary income versus capital gains—that is, paying more dividends instead of accumulating cash, reinvesting in projects, or doing share repurchases. Normally, we would expect a negative impact on price because it would force investors to pay higher taxes on their return. However, such a change might attract a different clientele of investors—investors within lower tax brackets. So that perhaps the corporation might be able to accomplish a kind of "tax arbitrage"—exchanging a higher-taxed clientele for a lower-taxed clientele—which would keep the negative response of high-taxed, dividend-averse investors from hurting the company's stock price. To the extent that changing dividend policy would lead to this kind of interchange of clienteles, the negative tax impact of increased dividends would be neutralized. But for other companies in different dividend-paying ranges, this kind of "tax-arbitrage" would not be effective. In these cases, increasing the dividend payout ratio could lead investors to raise their required pre-tax returns (to keep their after-tax returns constant), and this would cause the stock price to fall. So that's one interpretation of my evidence: that the tax effect of dividends on investors has a negative impact on stock prices.

DIVIDENDS AND SHARE PRICES

JOE: John, you've been around public utilities for a good many years.
JOHN: About thirty-five or forty.

JOE: Why do you think that utilities have such high dividend payout ratios?

JOHN: They're raising dividends so they can raise capital. We are constantly advising utility companies. We are the second biggest underwriter of utilities, and the reason I advise these companies to pay out high percentages of their earnings is strictly so that they can raise capital.

JOEL: John, when you say "to raise capital," do you mean in order to keep investors satisfied?

JOHN: To keep investors buying their stock.

JOEL: Just for the sake of argument, if utilities were to stop paying cash dividends, the share prices—aside from the informational effect—would not necessarily fall, because those people who were dividend averse would actually come in. And second, if those investors wanted to take a higher risk position than what the public utility would offer because of its regulatory nature, they could get a higher risk by simply leveraging their portfolio. The share price would not go down because investors are leaving—because the supply of investors willing to buy the utilities exceeded the demand. What we're saying is that there are other investors who are waiting for profit opportunities. It's like the argument that, around the end of the year, there is a lot of tax-loss selling; and thus share prices go down around Christmas time. There must be people who are bargain hunters who are waiting for that opportunity.

JOHN: Joel, remember when the sixties ended, the utilities were no longer growth stocks. All the institutions moved out of utility stocks, and it became a market for individual investors. That's what I'm saying. I'm sure if you would talk to syndicate people in an investment banking firm, you would find that they're not selling utilities to institutions. Now what you're saying is that if the company drove all the individuals away, then the higher growth rate because of the retention would bring the institutions back. I say that's absolute hogwash.

JOEL: We are not saying that the investors are coming to the security because they expect to earn anything other than what the underlying returns are supposed to be. All I am suggesting is that, if the shares were to drop below their perceived fair value, there would be bargain hunters waiting to take advantage of them who would boost the share price back up to its fair value. If you don't want to call them institutional investors, you can call them wealthy investors, or you can call them high risk investors. Anybody who feels that the shares are being undervalued is going to come racing in, in order to bring the share price back—after the informational content has had its temporary impact.

BILL: Why would anybody assume that the shares were undervalued if the functional attractiveness of your equity was, at that particular moment, impaired?

JOEL: Because we were told that if the company were to discontinue their dividend payments, and you remove the dividend signalling effect, the price of the shares would drop because those dividend-conscious investors were the only ones setting the price of the shares. Suddenly, there was an excess supply of shares relative to the demand. I am simply saying that that is not a significant issue.

JOHN: That is a major issue. If you take the dividends out of utilities today, you'll never sell another share of stock. That's how important it is. In fact, if a few major utilities (with no special problems) cut their dividend, small investors would lose faith in the utility industry and that would finish the sales of utility stocks. You ought to talk to the syndicate people who have to sell these. Go out to the brokers who have to sell them. And say, "If they cut the dividend, you'll find somebody else to purchase the stock." Who will buy it? This is nonsense.

PAT: What Joel is saying is, assuming there is no change in the *operating* side or the investment decisions of the company, it doesn't make very much sense to argue that a purely *financial* change like cutting the dividend will have a permanent impact on the value of the firm. Simply because there will always be investors waiting on the sidelines to pick these bargains up.

BILL: But don't people rush into "undervalued" equities only because they think the undervaluation is going to be soon eliminated by a set of circumstances?

PAT: They are presumably the ones that do it.

BILL: But they don't do it. I think I understand the argument that you are making, but what I can't get through my head is: Who is that first investor who is going to step up after the dividend has been cut? Even if he recognizes the argument.

My point is that if you question a supposedly rational investor on an issue like dividends, you won't necessarily get rational responses. I'm not sure that the irrational investors won't take over when you cut the dividend. There is no way to test this short of doing something considered anathema by that silent ownership group—and then see what the heck happens. I think the answer would be something you wouldn't like if you were sitting in a corporate financial officer's chair.

BOB: But is this price or is this flak? If we don't believe there is an information effect, and we don't believe there is a tax effect, or a clientele effect, what is the reason that somehow dividends are supporting stock prices? If companies' operating earnings are independent of dividends, why would paying dividends help companies to be able to raise capital and maintain their stock prices? You can't say there is no impact on stock prices and say it helps you raise capital. *Dividends themselves create a need for raising additional capital.* Unless there is an impact on stock price, which we could interpret reasonably through an information effect, there is no way it's going to help you raise capital. So that's more in the way of a question.

THE PRO-DIVIDEND POSITION _____

JOHN: I would agree with that completely. Do you want me to take a whack at it? We have the practical problem of doing dividend studies for companies.

When a chairman of a company calls up and says: "Would you come out and talk to my board?," we've got to have some answers. And our approach is this.

First, the stockholders like dividends. I don't care if they're crazy or not, they like dividends. Now if you've done any advisory work for a privately owned company, you will find that if the founder has died, and the stock has passed on through a number of generations, there are still some very wealthy stockholders. And there are also some stockholders that are not so wealthy. One of the jobs we get from such a company is to determine what dividend policy the company should follow. "The smaller holders," management will say, "are pestering us for more dividends." Now if people didn't like dividends, why would the less wealthy stockholders in a privately owned company want dividends? Why would they want more of them?

JOEL: I would say one reason they would want them is because they have no influence over their holdings. In the public markets, they could always sell their shares if they were unhappy and wanted to do something else.

JOHN: Let's take a closely held company. There is a public market and the stockholders could sell their stock. You've got the same situation and the same evidence. You've got the wealthy founder who doesn't want dividends because of the tax question. You've got the other relatives who are still holding some of the stock, may not want to sell it, but they want dividends. There is no question that they want dividends. If you want another indication of who wants dividends, consider that there are two groups of stockholders: individuals and institutions. The individuals are wealthy or moderately wealthy; the institutions include corporations with an 85 percent dividend tax credit and tax-exempt charitable institutions.

Now, if you want to find out whether the institutions want dividends, for God's sake, go out and call them up and ask them! I have done this and here are some of the comments I got. I'd say it was a very sketchy survey, but it's certainly some indication. Here is the reply from a large private pension fund: "Companies should pay dividends except for those in high-technology industries. Stockholders have a right to dividends." Here is what another fund said: "We want dividends." A moderate-sized pension fund: "Interested in total return, but pay no taxes and dividends are a bird in the hand, therefore, dividends are very important." Life insurance company: "Want income and, therefore, dividends are important." Personal trust department of a bank: "90 percent of the personal trust funds want dividends because income is necessary for the life of the beneficiaries." Mutual savings banks: "Dividends are extremely important. Generally have to have a dividend record in order to buy a stock." State and local retirement fund: "Funds are managed by outsiders, but stocks, in order to be legal, must pay dividends for five years."

Let me give you another example. In selecting a mutal fund, individuals have complete choice as to whether they buy a growth mutual fund, a balanced mututal fund, or a cash mutual fund. The evidence I looked at a while ago showed that the cash fund had the greatest amount of money in it at that time. The second largest was the balanced fund—dividends plus market appreciation—and the smallest was the fund that had just appreciation. Investors were not forced to make that choice. They did it because that is what they wanted.

General Public Utilities is another good example. In 1968, General Public Utilities, which had been paying a 40-cent dividend every quarter, decided to cut out three quarterly dividends, and pay a stock dividend in place of those three quarterly dividends. When they announced this policy, I can't remember exactly what the stock went off, but I think it went off a couple of points. In other words, here you have a company that was going to eliminate its cash dividend and give a stock dividend in its place. They got such a protest that the company had to call the idea off.

Let's take another example. Lowes Corporation is one of the outstanding companies in the country. This would be one of Joel Stern's companies that has a high rate of return, and shouldn't pay any dividends. They did a survey of the stockholders; and 39 percent said that they wanted both dividends and appreciation. Now, you can't tell me that investors don't like dividends. I think there is only one group that doesn't like dividends and that's the very wealthy group.

I seriously object to these theoretical studies that say dividends have no effect. Because what they do is to throw in all kinds of different companies together; and I wouldn't expect you to get any noticeable effect from dividends with such statistics. In order to measure the effect of dividend policy on price, you have to have everything else constant. You have to use the same types of companies, with the same rates of return, the same debt-to-equity ratios, etc. This way you're measuring the one thing that you would like to know, and that is the dividend effect. If you made a study of the dividend effect on price today of all the banks, and you throw in the New York banks, the Florida banks, the Texas banks, and the suburban banks, of course you couldn't see the effect of dividend policy.

I have a study here that Kidder Peabody puts out. It shows the correlation between dividends as a percent of book, and market as a percent of book. If you make a selection of these utilities that are the same in every respect— and you can do it in the utilities because there is enough uniformity so that you can get utilities which have basically the same debt ratings and rates of return—then you would find out dividends do affect price. We use this study all the time when working on dividend policies. And there is a very close correlation between dividend to book and market to book.

Let me just give you a couple of cases. Illinois Power, Northern State Power, and Con Ed, all earning a 13 percent return on book equity. Now I'm giving you one year, and this is a spot study. If I was going to give a detailed study of this I would make a comparison of this company with other utility companies over five years to make sure that I was making the companies comparable. Consider Illinois Power: Dividends-to-book—11.61 percent, and market-to-book—98.9 percent. Northern State Power: Dividends-to-book—8.88 percent, and 89 percent market-to-book. Con Ed: Dividends-to-book—6 percent, and market-to-book—69 percent. Now Con Ed is not a comparable company, but the picture is interesting. If you take comparable companies with comparable rates of return, and then study the dividends-to-book and market-to-book, you will find there is a direct correlation. Now to say there is no evidence that dividends affect stock prices means you don't want to look at the evidence on the basis of companies which, except for their dividend, are comparable.

What you are trying to do with the dividend policy is to enhance and strengthen the natural interest of investors in your company. The type of stockholders you will attract will depend on the type of company you are. If you're a Genentech, or something like Genentech, you are going to attract the type of stockholders which have absolutely no interest in dividends. In fact, you would hurt the stock if you paid dividends. On the other hand, you go over to the other extreme such as the utilities' and the yield banks' stocks—there the stockholders are extremely interested in dividends, and there dividends have an effect on market price. In between, there are different types of companies.

We say that there are five dividend policies for five different kinds of companies: (1) a zero dividend policy; (2) a 5 to 10 percent payout ratio, which is "nominal"; (3) 30 percent, which is "low"; (4) 40 to 50 percent, which is "average"; and (5) 70 percent which is "high." Let's take the case of Lowes. It certainly isn't in the fifth category. It certainly isn't average, because we say when a company can earn a high rate of return like 20 percent, they ought to have a low payout. We don't think it's nominal either; and that's where Joel and I would disagree. We would suggest a good sound policy of 30 percent, which is a low dividend payout policy. Now, could they create higher earnings growth by paying no dividend? Sure. But would Lowes have more appeal overall, a better stock price, if it paid out less dividends? Well, I think you've got to look at that survey in which they said 39 percent of their stockholders want some dividends.

In advising companies on dividend policy, we're absolutely sure on one side that the investors in companies like the utilities and suburban banks want dividends. We're absolutely sure on the other side that Genentech and the high-technology companies should have no dividends. For the high earners—the ones that have a high rate of return like 20 percent, or more than their cost of capital—we think they should have a low payout ratio. We think a typical industrial company which earns its cost of capital—just earns its cost of capital—probably should be in the average range of 40 to 50 percent. This is our approach, and we have a practical problem of talking to companies regularly on the subject.

THE EMPIRICAL EVIDENCE

PAT: The issue I think that we perhaps need to focus on is: At the margin, is there a preference for dividends? In other words, could a company increase its share price by changing its dividend policy in a particular way?

JOHN: If you agree with my evidence on this ...

PAT: I would have to look at it very carefully. I have my suspicions, but that would be a matter of looking at it. There are two important issues you raise. One is regarding careful studies. It is true it can be difficult to make comparisons. But, after all, that is what careful studies are about. You don't, for example, select specific samples and try to generalize those samples. I certainly wouldn't recommend to anybody that they generalize from, say, New York banks about the effect of dividends. What I'm really suggesting to you is that I doubt seriously even if you look at utilities, you can make an unambiguous statement about the effect of dividends.

JOHN: OK. How have you studied it? Have you taken the utilities that are comparable, or just run them all in together?

PAT: Well, let's make sure we understand some part of what's being done here. The model itself controls the parts. The statistical model itself controls for differences by grouping stocks of like risks into portfolios.

JOHN: No model is going to control if you throw stuff in that has no comparability or where there is no causal relationship. For example, Tampa Electric is different from most utilities.

PAT: Well, if you're saying we can't generalize, then we're in serious trouble. Not just in this field but in general. The only way we can pursue knowledge is presumably to make some useful generalizations and specifications. If our conclusions were based entirely on a method which simply relies on presenting one example after another, we're going to be really confused about everything.

JOHN: Well, you've confused me.

JOE: Bob, you had something to say?

BOB: I just want to make a point. I think that if you are just looking at a simple correlation between market-to-book ratios and dividend-to-book ratios for utilities, you have a certain problem in that other characteristics of utilities are not the same. So you try to get them comparable. But no group, or course, is perfectly comparable. The approach that some studies take is to ask the question, "Why are they not comparable?" And if companies do have different growth opportunities and different rates of profitability, these studies attempt to account for effects of the differences.

One study that specifically examined electric utilities was done by [Merton] Miller and [Franco] Modigliani in 1966. They explicitly tried to separate the impact of dividends on stock price from another effect: the impact of dividend policy on the market's expectations of the company's future earnings, growth, and level of profitable investment. Basically, their finding was that once you remove the sort of informational impact of the dividends on the market's perception of the company's future earnings prospects, the level of dividends per se had no relation to the companies' market-to-book ratios. As a matter of fact, the variables were in exactly the same form as in John's study, because the dependent variable was the market-to-book value ratio. In their model, they accounted for the differences in growth of different firms. Now you might say that study is out of date, but why did they find that back then...

JOHN: What year was that?

BOB: 1966.

JOHN: Ask me what has changed! Do you understand what the utility industry was like in the sixties?

BOB: Oh, I understand very well, that...

JOHN: Well, what is the difference between then and now?

BOB: But why should there be a different impact by the dividends? That's what I'm asking. I understand the impact of profitability...

JOHN: Because the utilities were bought as growth stocks back in the sixties. Today, they're bought as yield stocks and that is a major, major, major difference.

BILL: Usually when the stock is selling below book, it is dilutive, and it wasn't dilutive back then.

BOB: That is a very good point. If you have two firms with different dividend-to-book value ratios, that probably means—when selling equity is dilutive and thus unlikely to be done—that there is another important difference between these two companies: namely, their investment policies. The utility with the higher dividend-to-book ratio—to the extent that it is not relying on external financing—is probably investing less. And it may be investing less because it doesn't have to invest as much to maintain a given level of operations, production, revenues, earnings, and so forth. If a higher dividend policy is really the result of a lower investment or reinvestment policy, which in turn may be the result of more efficient or profitable operations, this will have a favorable impact on price. Did you account for differences in investment rates among those firms?

JOHN: Well, I try, when I do this type of analysis, to take companies with the same rates of return.

BOB: No. Your rate of return is not the investment rate. We're not talking about the ROE, we're talking about their rate of investment. What I'm saying is that if the market-to-book is below one, it's an indication that the company's investments are undesirable, no matter how they're financed. And if a higher dividend-to-book value ratio means a lower investment rate, then the higher dividend-to-book should have a positive impact on price... for reasons having to do *not* with the dividend per se, but with investment rates and profitability. It's really saying those firms that are paying out more are essentially investing less. Now you can't be sure of this because there is outside financing. But you may really be just showing that it's optimal for the utility to try to control its growth as much as possible.

I guess my basic point is that I think it's admirable to try to come up with a sample of firms that are as similar as possible. That's absolutely valid; but you know no two firms are identical. And you still have this problem which I think is very important: the more the market-to-book ratios differ from one another, the more crucial it is to try to account for differences in investment rates among the firms.

JOEL: I would like to raise another issue concerning John's evidence, and that is I think that the technique that he has used to perform his tests is structurally unsound. The dividend-to-book ratio, which is being correlated with market-to-book, has two components: it can be broken down into the dividend payout ratio (dividends/earnings) multiplied by the return on equity (earnings/book). The hidden correlation in this kind of test is between market-to-book and earnings-to-book, or return on equity; and thus it is profitability, and not the dividend payout, which is really driving the correlation with market values.

Several years ago, we plotted these ratios ourselves and we found no relationship whatsoever between the dividend-to-earnings ratio (that is, the dividend payout ratio) and the market-to-book ratio. And yet there was a very strong correlation between the market-to-book ratio and the return on equity.

JOHN: Well, Joel, I gave you a couple of examples, and there are dozens of others which you can find if you want to look.

DIVIDENDS AND FINANCIAL COMMUNICATION _____

PAT: Let's step back and take Fischer Black's point of view. What we have to discover is why dividends are being paid, and once we know why that is going on, then we can perhaps make some other statements.

JOEL: Well, let's take a look at the history of it. I would say that Fischer Black's position—which is the position of, I would say, most very good economists—is that we have to account for what we see and that markets make the right choices. Let's go back in time. The first corporations in the United States were single project firms. They built the railroad across the United States or they had a mine and they had a stake and that was it. They had single projects and they had the returns coming in on those projects and could pay it out in the form of cash dividends.

Now why was that optimal then? Mainly because there was no income tax at that time. This was the nineteenth century. The income tax didn't come in until the second decade of the twentieth century. Not only that, taxes were not exorbitant in the United States until well into the 1950s. So it didn't make a great deal of difference until well into the twentieth century.

BOB: That's really not true. There was progressive taxation and it's not the average tax that's helping the bulk of the shares. So that's a little deceptive, because you can argue that the impact of institutionalization—savings and pension funds—would be offsetting that.

JOEL: Exactly the point though. The point was that it appears as if the institutionalization of the market, from a tax-free position, came about when personal income tax rates became onerous with the receipt of cash dividends.

JOE: Joel, how can you simultaneously accept the dividend neutrality argument, and say that dividends are harmful to investors because of the tax argument and the reduced financing flexibility? In other words, if, in fact, dividends are harmful to investors, shouldn't that show up in the share price?

JOEL: I am suggesting there is a reason why dividends are being paid, regardless of which of the two academic arguments you subscribe to: dividend neutrality or, the stronger argument, dividend aversion. And that is the informational content of the dividend. By and large, managements have chosen not to make specific statements about the prospects of their company. They choose instead to use the dividend policy to communicate their prospects. Now we have been advising companies that there is a better way. That is, they can cut down or eliminate dividend payments and improve their financial communication by making certain key statements. These are not forecasts, but statements announcing long-range objectives, which is what the dividend policy was designed to do. I believe that we are in a period of transition. That is, corporations are about to learn how to go about improving their financial communication and thereby rely far less on dividend policy for communicating the same objective.

BOB: I think the problem with that argument is that the credibility of dividends as a signal depends on there being a cost to management, in the form of reduced future financing flexibility, from raising the dividend. If there weren't this cost, dividends wouldn't have the same information value. But there is a cost to management, and that's precisely why this information—you know the old adage, "Talk is cheap"—might have credibility to investors. If the signal were free, then management could simply be lying.

JOEL: Absolutely. I'm not suggesting for a moment that managements cannot lie about this. But there are also ways for managements to be lying through dividend increases, and that is to finance the dividends by borrowing more.

BOB: But there is also some cost to them from doing this.

JOEL: There is, but there is also some cost of lying when communicating directly to the investment community. In which case, going back to the market the next time around will be difficult. One of my past clients, a chief executive of an equipment manufacturing company, made statements that appeared to the market to be untrue; and from that point forward, the estimates of the prospects of the company seem to have been almost permanently reduced for as long as he has remained with the company. So there are hidden costs associated with misleading the market. I'll be the first to say it. But because of these other costs—especially the reduced financing flexibility—we think there is a good reason why companies will want to change their method of communication. Until now, the managements of companies have associated a great benefit to them from signalling to shareholders through the dividend policy. I think that they are becoming aware, in a kind of evolutionary process, of the alternative methods that could be used where statements would replace actions—actions which have harmful consequences to companies and stockholders.

BILL: Let me ask a question, Joel. You made the point about managements being unaware of alternative methods for communication other than through the dividend policy. That doesn't strike me as being reasonable or rational. There are numerous alternative communication approaches. There are presidents' letters in annual reports, presentations to security analysts, specific earnings forecasts, interviews in the *Wall Street Journal*, and quarterly releases to shareholders. I don't really understand why you say companies don't know of alternative forms. I think they know full well. And they know that unhappiness is expectation unfulfilled. They are not about to create unrealistic expectations through optimistic earnings forecasts, capital project expectations, return forecasts. They are often just not willing to engage in the forms of communication which are in fact available to them and have been for many, many years.

JOEL: But you are referring to vehicles rather than the content of what they say.

BILL: Even with respect to content, try to get companies to establish explicit goals with respect to capital project return levels. Forget about where they do it, through an annual report, through some publication required either by the SEC or by the stock exchange. I don't care about the form; the substance of what they say is often constrained.

JOEL: I am suggesting that *policies* can be effectively spelled out, rather than specific numbers. There are companies announcing that, for example, they do not undertake projects with the expectation that the rates of return (measured on a cash-flow basis and adjusted for the time value of money) will be less than X percent.

BOB: But now, what happens when, say, costs of capital change, and they want to change their policy? Any policy that you reannounce every year, every quarter, doesn't convey a lot of information unless you say the policy is: "We won't accept anything that isn't 2 percent above the long-term interest rate." But if you say "subject to reevaluation," that might be effective.

JOEL: The point is that managements are trying to say to their shareholders with dividend signals, or with these announcements: "We have certain prospects based on current economic conditions, and there are certain minimum rates of return that we are setting for ourselves. We expect to take on projects of a certain magnitude over, say, the next three to five years." They are announcing the amount of planned capital expenditures. "We review this periodically in case economic conditions are altered, so as to make some of our projects unacceptable. We will keep you informed." In fact, one of the companies we work with has announced that: "You will learn any relevant financial and investment policy changes from us first—not from any other source." That's a very important statement.

CHANGING THE DIVIDEND POLICY ——————————————

JOEL: I'd like to give two examples, if I may, that we really haven't gotten into very much. In one case, we had a situation of a client coming to us and saying: "We have been in a business that has not required much cash." I'd rather not identify the company or the industry, for obvious reasons. But the nature of the business suddenly changed, requiring enormous capital outlays. And one of their major competitors, which had been privately held, went public paying no cash dividends. Their company was paying sixty percent of their earnings out in cash dividends. They came to us and said: "What do you think would be the best dividend policy for us?" We said to them, "Why don't you make believe that you are going public today for the first time? What are the prospective returns on the projects that now require your capital investment, as compared to before?" They said: "The returns we expect are going to be very high, as they are for our major competitor." I said: "Then what would be the right dividend policy for you?" They said: "Well, if we were going public today, we would pay no cash dividends." I said: "Then the question is: How are you going to go from sixty percent down to zero, correct?" They said: "No! One of our directors who has a large equity stake doesn't want us to reduce the dividend because he thinks it will have a detrimental impact on the price of the shares."

Now what is the right policy in a situation like that? It's not a utility, I agree. The prospects of return are very, very high. And the company is saddled with an inflexible series of fixed payments that are enormous relative to the size of the company.

BOB: In that instance, would they be forgoing the very profitable projects in order to avoid external financing or additional financing?

JOEL: They were trading on the New York Stock Exchange.

JOHN: What we would do in that case is this. The company is able to get equity money at a reasonable price, not less than book value, right?

JOEL: I don't think that makes a whole heck of a lot of difference.

JOHN: I think it makes a difference.

JOEL: You think that if the company is selling below book value, it should not raise new equity with a new share offering? If its prospect of returns is very high on the projects?

JOHN: I didn't say that, I'm just saying that, in this particular case, does it have easy access to the equity market?

JOEL: It's trading on the New York Stock Exchange.

JOHN: Well, all right. Could they sell enough equity to get all the equity needed for their investment?

JOEL: Any company could, if it can convince the markets that its expected returns are high enough.

JOHN: When we have a company that has too high a dividend, we think that any precipitous move, say cutting it from 60 percent payout down to zero or down to 30 percent, is the wrong thing to do. What we would do is to recommend holding the increases down, and let the earnings go up and get to a new level this way. I think that is a very practical approach.

PAT: But Joel's point is that if you do that, you're hurting yourself by presumably paying more flotation costs.

JOHN: Are flotation costs going to be greater than what you are going to do to your stockholders? I think not.

BOB: I sort of agree with John on changing the dividend gradually. No matter what your statements are, it's hard to make a substantial change without the market interpreting some information content. Perhaps, if more corporations stopped using dividends as signals, then maybe the gradual approach wouldn't be necessary.

BILL: Wasn't this a perfect example of an instance where circumstances did, in fact, change for a company which has an established policy? And that if the theory of zero dividends for this company is the rational policy for the future, then this is probably the perfect test case for that change?

JOEL: Would you suggest, perhaps, as to how it might be done?

BOB: That's my question; it's really one of feasibility. The situation in which a firm has an established dividend policy. And given its new set of investment opportunities, and the high cost of floating new equity issues, the company feels it wants to move to a drastically lower payout. Now do you think it would be possible for them to announce drastic cuts—even with their new profitable opportunities—without having a negative impact on price? I haven't seen instances like that.

JOEL: The technique that I recommend that a company follow to get its dividend down is this: to announce that they are ceasing all dividend payments eighteen months from now. Not right now, eighteen months from now. The reason is that over those eighteen months, they are expecting to show continued good performance. So that investors would see that they are not cutting the dividend down to zero because "they can't afford to pay it," but because they do have the projects. Second, those people who are "cash now" advocates, as opposed to calling them dividend lovers, will have plenty of time to move into other investments. They won't knock each other over trying to get out, nor will the dividend-averse people knock each other over coming in. They will have plenty of time to come and go as they choose, in which case the company will be able to adopt a new policy without having a major impact presently on stock price. In fact, there may even be a positive impact on price because you would be, in effect, announcing that we've got the projects; and in cutting the dividend, we're making a strong statement about the high expected profitability of our future investments.

BOB: Unfortunately, this has to remain at the level of a conceptual argument because there is no evidence on those types of firms.

DIVIDENDS AND INVESTMENT POLICY _____

JOEL: From 1975 to 1977 companies were being told by their investment bankers and brokers that there was a very high correlation between higher dividends and higher stock prices. So that if you wanted to get your price up, you should raise your dividend payments.

BILL: Those recommendations were coming not just from the investment bankers and the brokers; they were coming from those shareholders that John has been telling us about.

JOEL: How did the managements find this out? I'm not sure that I understand this. The chief executive, the senior management group, at the annual meeting, is persuaded by one vocal stockholder, maybe five stockholders...

BILL: I think the information flow comes from selected investment professionals visiting the management, and saying to them: "We want dividends." I don't think you can argue that that was something foisted on the investment community by the investment banking profession and/or the brokers. I think there was a manifestation of interest in dividends by stockholders precisely at the wrong time. Precisely before the price of capital was about to go through the roof—the replacement cost, that is—and when companies were going to need that means of financing, that source of funds. So, the 1977–78 experience came precisely at the wrong time. But I don't think that it was a figment of the vivid imagination of the investment banking community. I think the interest in dividends was broad in the land.

JOEL: But how did the companies do who were not paying any dividends at all? The Digital Equipments, the Datapoints, and so forth. How were they doing during that market when the allegation was being made that higher dividends and higher stock prices go together? In fact, it turns out that the companies that were increasing their dividend payments very substantially during that market decline fell every bit as much as every other company.

BILL: I'm not saying that the argument for dividends was correct. In fact, I'm stating that the argument, at the time, was incorrect. It's just the origin of the argument. The rising inflation rate focuses interest on current income and current returns. And investors collectively demanded higher yields.

BOB: I would have another interpretation of the higher dividends during the 1977–78 period. During that period, market-to-replacement cost ratios were substantially below one. Now admittedly, that's on *average* investment. But it wasn't at all clear that investors were perceiving that it was above one on *marginal* investments. And thus, the demand for higher dividends by investors may have stemmed from their perception that corporations were earning inadequate rates of return on new investment. The point I'm trying to make in all this is that you can't simply look at a change in the dividend and its impact on stock price, and then say it is the dividend and not the implicit decision about investment. In paying higher dividends, companies may actually—in cases where expected returns are substandard—be choosing disinvestment to help their stockholders. And that's what stock prices may be reflecting.

JOEL: I have a question for you, Bob. If this information flows into the investment community from the shareholder community, why does it flow with the words: "Give me more cash dividends," rather than "Reduce the amount of investment you are making"? Because if you take a look at what the companies were doing, it is true that they raised the cash dividends in that 1977–78 period. But they also went out and borrowed a lot of money to take on those same projects that would otherwise have been financed through retained earnings.

BOB: But very few companies or industries, it seems to me, are paying high dividends and, at the same time, relying on large amounts of external equity financing. So that might mean that some companies' decisions to pay high dividends are conscious decisions to move toward a more highly leveraged capital structure. Or implicitly, they are making some statement about their investment policy.

PAT: Do you think firms are passing up good investment opportunities instead of cutting dividends?

JOEL: I'm convinced that paying high dividends is forcing some companies to forgo profitable projects. Let me tell you about our experience with how companies make their investment decisions. The man who is running a major operating unit and who is in the process of selecting internal projects has had to deal with the fact that the company will not sell new shares to finance new investment. What I'm talking about is the growth that does not have an earnings string attached to it—it will reduce the EPS from what it would otherwise be. Consequently, the amount of cash available for capital investment in that year is limited to retained earnings and what the company will likely borrow to maintain a target ratio of debt to equity. And thus, the projects that are likely to come up for acceptance are going to be limited by that. This has been my experience not only in advising companies. But also when we have our sessions with companies where the heads of the operating units are present, I have often made that statement; and there is almost always a nodding of heads. I am a director of three companies, and in each case, that is exactly the limitation on new investment. There is not even the slightest thought to raising outside capital for those purposes. And, so I think that profitable investments not undertaken because of capital rationing should be counted as one of the costs, in practice if not in theory, of increasing the dividend.

BOB: That's an important point because most companies don't rely on external equity financing. Whether they should or not is another question. So, this way, when they're talking or thinking about dividend policy, they're probably often really thinking about investment policy.

CONCLUSION _____

JOEL: There is an argument in favor of cash dividends, really two arguments: one is that a bird in the hand is worth more than one in the bush; the other argument is that shares sell on a dividend yield basis. Bill, could I ask your opinion about these arguments?

BILL: The bird in the hand argument makes no sense to me. I think a total return is a total return and how it is distributed between current and future returns is a matter of indifference to the investor, provided he gets his X percent. The second point, about stocks selling on a yield basis: there are stocks which demonstrate certain kinds of characteristics through specific moments of time. To say that an oil company that started 1981 with a yield of 7 percent and ended 1981 with a yield of 9.5 percent demonstrated "defensive characteristics" because of its higher yield is clearly absurd. At the same time, however, AT&T and other utility stocks performed particularly well in 1981, and might have started in some cases with yields not that different from the yield levels that were typical of other "defensive type" securities.

There are a lot of embedded truisms which have become part of the general market lore. One of these truisms is that utility stocks and other relatively high-yield stocks are "interest rate sensitive." And the fact of the matter is that certain groups of stocks do perform well when there are general expectations of falling interest rates. Those groups performed well, for example, in 1981. To say that a utility is interest rate sensitive, trading on a yield basis, by that historical observation, is true. Again, I don't disagree with the theoretical premise that yields and dividend policies shouldn't matter, and that the market should exhibit some magical indifference to dividends and yields. The problem is you are here in the 1980s; dividend policies have been long established. You are not back in 1900 about to establish a rational policy for changing tax laws and changing ownership versus yield.

JOEL: As an investment advisor to a company, let's assume it has a large amount of capital requirements, and you are convinced by the management that its expected rates of return are more than adequate; that is, they are equal to or greater than the cost of equity capital. Would you say that that company should invest the available funds in the business?

BILL: Yes.

JOEL: In other words, you would not be encouraging that company to be conveying lots of information by means of higher dividend payments?

BILL: Absolutely not. I would be encouraging them to retain the earnings in the business and reinvest. If the marginal return on equity exceeds the historical returns, and those historical returns have been competitive, I would not recommend that they increase the dividend.

BOB: If the expected returns are higher than the cost of capital, would you advise them to cut the dividend?

BILL: Much more difficult question. Again, the information content associated with cutting the dividend would be the problem. So, in theory I would say "yes"; in practice, I would say "no." There are no heroes—or, at most, very few—in a capitalistic system. The reductio ad absurdum is an easy trap, and the theoretical answer is: "Yes, you should cut the dividend because the marginal return is higher than what the investor can get for himself." The practical fact of the matter is that the companies who have done nothing more drastic than reduced their payout ratios go through all kinds of soul-searching. Last year Electronic Data Systems announced that they were cutting their payout ratio but not their dividends, and they went through . . .

JOEL: Electronic Data Systems was one. A second one was Tom Roberts' company, DeKalb AgResearch; and the third one, a few years ago, was G. D. Searle & Co., when Donald Rumsfeld announced, henceforth, there would be no dividend increases. He kept the absolute level of dividends constant. And I remember asking him the same question. I said, "How about a slight cut in the dividend." He answered exactly the way you did, "No."

In the case of G. D. Searle, there were principally large numbers of small investors who liked the company's paying a very large dividend. The dividend yield was relatively high when the policy of maintaining a constant dividend was put into effect. Over a four-year period, there was a change in clientele, and the stock attracted, of all things, the institutional investors. The same investors who, we were being told, are dividend conscious. As a result, the price of shares did not suffer to any extent.

BILL: But that's, again, the information problem. How many other things was the company also doing? They were disposing of businesses which didn't meet return requirements. They were, in fact, disinvesting during that period of time. I think that investors were attracted to the scent of an entity that was about to go through a change, not the fact that there would be no dividend growth.

JOEL: What we are trying to do during this discussion is to separate the dividend-signalling issue from the price issue. When you knock out the information issue, the question is: If the price drops below its fair value, then what will happen?

BILL: That is a very difficult issue.

BOB: You see, one thing's true, what Joel started out with. Talking about Fischer Black, he said that people who believe in positive economics don't assume that anything that happens is irrational. They strain their imaginations for ways of rationalizing policies that we observe, and Joel's unwilling to do that on the dividend question.

Now John, on the other hand, has more business experience than any of us. He seems absolutely certain in his policy recommendations that dividends make perfect sense in some industries, but not for, say, high-technology companies.

I think the rest of us are a bit more cautious. I would agree with Joel, and I think Pat would also, to the extent that there should always be bargain hunters keeping share prices fairly valued, even when a dividend is cut, but provided the information effect can be eliminated. The problem, as Bill has just observed, is the difficulty of making a substantial reduction without the market interpreting this as negative information. I'm not sure it can be done and there is no way to test this without actually trying it. The farthest any companies have gone in this direction is to (1) cut back on the rate of growth in dividends or (2) hold the level of dividends paid out constant so that the payout ratio declines over time. Bill noted that these actions represent giant steps so I guess there is no reason to believe we will see companies go beyond this to substantially cut the level of dividends, unless they are really in trouble. Until they do we can only speculate.

COMMENTARY:
WHY PAY DIVIDENDS?
by Donald H. Chew, Jr.

If you take a close look at the stocks that have consistently outperformed the Dow Jones Industrial Average over the years, many of them pay little or no dividends. A number of these stocks are over-the-counter (OTC), high-growth, high-technology stocks; and we all know that such companies can get away without paying high, if indeed any, dividends. But consider the cases of more staid companies like Capital Cities Communications and the Gleason Company. Capital Cities, which recently acquired ABC, pays a dividend of 20 cents, offering an effective annual yield of less than 0.1

percent. It is in a very old business: publications and other communications. The Gleason Company (formerly Gleason Works) manufactures auto parts and pays no dividend. Do such companies, and their investors, suffer from management's decision to retain earnings rather than paying them out? The answer coming from professional researchers at premiere business schools appears to be a forthright "No."

Over the past fifteen or twenty years, the question of the effect of dividends on stock prices has become a controversial one. Among finance scholars today, there are only two positions on the dividend question that are seriously defended: (1) dividends are "irrelevant" (that is, whether companies retain their earnings or pay them out to stockholders, is a matter of indifference to investors in aggregate); and (2) dividends are actually harmful to taxable investors, because such investors pay higher taxes on dividends than on capital gains.

DIVIDENDS ARE IRRELEVANT _____

The smart investor—and there are plenty of them around—is concerned not just about the dividend yield, but about his total return: dividends plus capital gains. Although some investors need current income to pay their bills, the investors that dominate the market—those that move the market and set stock prices—are really concerned only about total return. (They are also, of course, concerned about how those returns will be taxed.)

As long as there are efficient capital markets, those stockholders requiring income can get their hands on cash simply by selling shares. Investors, on the whole, should not be willing to pay higher prices for high-dividend shares just because they provide a slightly more convenient means of getting cash.

This means, setting tax consequences aside for a moment, that a dollar paid out in dividends is simply a dollar lost in capital gains. This principle can be seen at work when companies trade on the ex-dividend date: when the shares go ex-dividend, their stock price typically falls by an amount roughly equal to the dividend-per-share paid out to investors.

From corporate management's point of view, the dividend payout is really just another means of liquidating the company's assets. If the company pays out a very high proportion of its earnings, it will only be able to finance future growth by raising more money through a new debt or stock offering. For this reason, unless a company is repeatedly announcing new debt or stock issues (like AT&T, for example, which is about to go through a new growth phase), you can interpret a high-dividend yield as the sign of a mature, if not indeed, stagnant company.

Public utilities, for example, have the highest dividend yields going, and there are good reasons for it. Their rates are set by state commissions, which are designed to allow them to earn a "fair" rate of return on invested capital.

But no more. Companies grow rapidly only when they face prospects of highly profitable returns. Utility companies, because so regulated, do not offer the promise of abnormally high rates of return on capital. Therefore, their incentive is not to retain their earnings and invest in expansion, but instead to distribute their earnings to stockholders.

Utilities are thus a low-risk, low-return investment. You will never get rich investing in utilities. If consumer causes restrict utilities' ability to raise their rates, you may indeed lose, although probably not a lot.

It is a mistake, at any rate, to think that utilities are less risky *because* they pay high dividends. If you think this way, you are failing to consider that it's the total return—dividends plus capital appreciation—that should matter. Utilities, as you've probably noticed, resort more to new stock and debt offerings than companies in any other industry. This is not because they are contemplating new investment. It's because they have paid all that cash out to investors, and now they have to retrieve it. They are simply recycling cash. And as anyone who has held utility stocks over the past ten years will confirm, the process of recycling does not add greatly to stockholder wealth.

This does not mean, however, that utilities *should* not pay high dividends. It simply reflects management's judgment about the prospects for utilities in a highly regulated environment. Rather than invest large amounts of cash in projects, like nuclear power, where the risks appear to greatly outweigh the rewards, utility executives seem to have determined collectively that it is better to distribute earnings to investors, who can then *choose* to reinvest, or place the cash in more promising investments—with a better risk-reward trade-off.

In this sense, then, a company's *refusal* to pay a dividend may actually signal management's optimism about the future. They are saying: "We have good prospects, and we need the funds for growth. You, the investor, are better served by allowing us to keep your money than by returning it to you to stash in a money market fund."

We also know, of course, that announcements of dividends cut or passed are not well received by the market. But this is not because of dividends per se. The negative response to dividend reductions is really in response to the negative *information* released by such announcements. Reduced dividends means diminished earnings prospects for the future.

DIVIDENDS AND RISK

What this boils down to, then, is that although *changes* in the dividend matter to the market, the *level* of the dividend does not affect stock prices. It can be used to provide a fairly reliable, though not infallible, guide to the relative risk of investments in companies. This is because risky companies—those whose earnings, and stock prices, fluctuate from year to year—tend to pay out a significantly lower percentage of earnings than their less risky counterparts.

Risky companies do this for a good reason: to the extent that management refuses to cut the dividend, dividends really represent a fixed cost of the business. Risky businesses are already risky because they have a large proportion of fixed to variable costs. So that when the economy, the demand for their products, and thus their revenues turn down, their costs remain high, squeezing profits. Such companies wisely restrict the dividend.

But it is important to recognize that higher dividends do not *cause* lower risk, they simply *reflect* the level of corporate risk. They are not the reason why the proverbial "widows and orphans" typically hold shares of public utilities. The risks of utilities, and indeed all companies, are determined by how vulnerable their earnings power is to changes in the economy. Risk is not affected by management's decision to pay out or reinvest earnings.

It is true, of course, that dividends are more predictable than capital gains. They are subject to the control of management, not the vagaries of the market.

This is the popular "bird in the hand" argument. It says in effect: "Well, even if the market goes down, at least I'll have a stable return from dividends over the lean years." The flaw in this argument is the failure to recognize that a dollar paid in per share dividends means that the stock price will have fallen a dollar lower than otherwise. Dividends are paid out of earnings, and it's earnings, or the expectation of future earnings, that drive stock prices.

DIVIDENDS CAN HURT _____

The only serious challenge to the dividend "irrelevance" proposition comes from those who believe dividends hurt. The main argument of the "anti-dividend" school of thought is, as suggested initially, a tax argument.

The marginal rate of tax (for most individuals) has a negative effect on stock prices. Dividends received by investors are taxed as ordinary income and, until recently, could be taxed at rates as high as 70 percent. That rate is now, of course, 50 percent. Capital gains, because of the 60 percent exclusion, have a maximum marginal tax rate of 20 percent (40 percent x 50 percent). And capital gains can also be deferred indefinitely simply by holding the stock indefinitely.

Thus, at the extreme, dividends are taxed at a rate 50 percent higher than capital gains. To illustrate the argument with a very simple example, assume there are only two companies available to investors. They have identical earnings prospects. Company A is expected to pay out all its earnings in dividends forever. Company B will never pay a dividend, but will distribute its earnings to stockholders in the form of non-taxable stock repurchases. Assume also that all investors are taxed at 50 percent on dividends, and (as in many countries) pay no taxes on capital gains. In such a world, Company A would be worth exactly one-half of Company B. Or, to view it a little differently, Company A would have to earn twice as much as Company B in order to sell at the same price.

Going back to the real world, this example means that investors, in order to earn the same return after tax, must expect to earn a higher total return (dividends plus appreciation) on high-dividend than on equivalently risky, low-dividend stocks. And, in order to offer a higher total return, high-dividend stocks must sell at *lower prices* than otherwise.

Finance scholars have attempted to test this argument by measuring the total returns of high- versus low-paying stocks over time. And though there are some remaining problems of method, all the tests provide at least some support for the anti-dividend argument.

With the fall in the ordinary income tax rate, and the increasing domination of the market by large tax-exempt institutions like pension funds and insurance companies, tax considerations are probably not as important. And investors can avoid taxes on dividends by offsetting this income with interest on borrowings, or other tax shelters.

TOTAL AFTER-TAX RETURN IS WHAT COUNTS _____

The long and short of dividends, then, is that they don't really matter. They are merely one way of slicing the pie of a company's market value. It is true they can be used as a guide to management's intentions, and to the risk of your investment. But this is because managements have based the dividend not only on past earnings, but also on the future earnings and investment prospects of the company.

The total return, nonetheless, is what counts. The value of the corporation is determined by profits, expectations of future earnings. Dividends are merely a means of distributing the proceeds. And if investors are not successful in neutralizing tax effects, dividends may actually be shrinking the size of the corporate pie—by cutting the government in.

III

The Market for Corporate Control
A DISCUSSION OF CORPORATE MERGERS AND ACQUISITIONS

INTRODUCTION

One of the most controversial topics, both on Wall Street and in academic circles, concerns the pricing, and thus the profitability, of corporate mergers and acquisitions. In an efficient market—one in which current stock prices reflect an unbiased estimate of companies' values—how can we explain the large acquisition premiums over market that are being paid? Furthermore, do mergers and acquisitions contribute to the net wealth of the economy? And if so, how are these economic gains divided between the shareholders of the buying and the acquired companies?

The available academic research suggests that, on average and over the years, mergers and acquisitions have proven a profitable investment of corporate funds for the buying companies—though acquired firms appear to have received the lion's share of the gains. The research also documents that acquired companies tend to have *underperformed*, and acquiring companies *outperformed*, the market over the years *prior* to acquisitions, suggesting that the market for corporate control functions as a means of channeling assets to more efficient users, or higher-valued uses.

What these statistical averages conceal, however, is that many acquiring companies have paid too dearly and, in the process, materially harmed their own stockholders. A study by Peter Dodd of the most recent merger wave (1979–82) suggests that both mergers and tender offers appear to have resulted in significantly *negative* returns, on average, to stockholders of buying companies. The frequent negative market reaction to *buying* firms, together with what appears to be an unprecedented resistance by target managements to "unfriendly" takeovers (or, at least, an astonishing proliferation of new anti-takeover strategies) suggests that the market for corporate control may be undergoing some fundamental changes. Critics of the takeover process charge that the spectacle of managerial empire-building is provoking the no more defensible response of managerial entrenchment, all apparently at the expense of stockholders. And thus the call for more regulation is becoming ever more shrill and insistent.

In the following "Discussion of Mergers and Acquisitions," the takeover controversy is explored by three distinguished M & A specialists from the investment banking community and three academics conducting research in the field. The discussion offers a classic confrontation between the perspectives of theorist and practitioner. Although there are important areas of agreement, there nevertheless remains a pronounced difference between investment bankers and researchers in the level of sophistication ascribed to capital markets. And this in turn leads to significantly different assessments of (1) current stock prices as guides to the fair value of companies; (2) the validity of using stock price reactions to judge the success of acquisitions; (3) the value of *ownership* versus the value of *control* of the corporation; (4) corporate diversification as a motive for mergers and acquisitions; (5) the proper role of target management in responding to tender offers; and (6) the desirability and effects of tender offer legislation.

To get a sampling of the flavor of this discussion, consider this exchange early in the discussion between Steve Friedman, who runs Goldman Sach's M & A Department, and two academics, Bill Schwert (of the University of Rochester) and Dan Fischel (of the University of Chicago Law School):

STEVE FRIEDMAN: Incidentally, I am a little bit shocked by the trend of this discussion...I had always thought the only people more short-sighted than American businessmen were investors in the stock market... I am amazed to find out that, in the academic community, you are measuring the success of an acquisition by how well it does for the stock in the short run. The enlightened management that we deal with are certainly interested in what the stock market's reaction is going to be. They are also interested in what the impact is going to be on their credit ratings and on other things. But they regard these *only* as cost factors...

DAN FISCHEL: But you are assuming that creditors and shareholders are all acting irrationally. You are saying a transaction that is a good deal economically—that is, it increases the long-term value of the firm—will have the effect of making the firm's credit rating worse off, and cause investors to lower their estimation of the value of the firm. That doesn't make any sense to me, unless you're assuming that both creditors and investors will act irrationally.

STEVE FRIEDMAN: I am not assuming they are acting irrationally. Once again, you have loaded the statement. I am assuming that reasonable men can disagree about the long term, or even the short term, and that people are paid for taking contrary points of view at times. It is only you folks who are imputing total rationality and, indeed, correctness to the stock market.

BILL SCHWERT: We are not asserting that management never makes decisions that turn out to be right, even though the market reacts negatively in the short run. What we are saying is that the market's reaction to an announcement of an acquisition has no systematic bias; that is, on average, it neither understates nor overstates the value of that acquisition to a company. This means that, *on average* (though not in every case), the market's immediate reaction to an announcement of an acquisition can be viewed as an objective assessment of the value of that acquisition. The judgment of managers about the long-term payoff may be better than the market's in some cases. But when investors collectively think an acquisition was a bad deal, and the market price drops to reflect that, investors are going to be right more often than they're wrong. And they're just as likely to overstate the value of an acquisition as to understate it.

So, when you argue that you can only measure the success of an acquisition several years down the road, well, okay, in a sense that's true. But this statement can only be made *ex post*, after the fact. From our point of view, if you see companies bidding for target firms and their stock price drops, they probably made a mistake. So, we are very surprised to hear that management would ever undertake a transaction which they knew in advance was going to cause their stock price to drop.

STEVE FRIEDMAN: Oh, no, management will sometimes be sure

JOEL STERN: You mean they assume the stock price will drop, and they still go ahead with the deal?

STEVE FRIEDMAN: Yes. They feel the stock price will only reflect the market's short-term outlook. But is it the short term that the management is paid to consider? No, it's the intermediate, the longer term.

BILL SCHWERT: What I can't understand is: When we're talking about a major acquisition, how great can the difference be between what management knows and what the market knows? If management thinks the acquisition is good for the company, it should have a strong incentive to try to convince financial analysts and pension fund managers that the acquisition is in fact a good deal, not a bad deal. I don't understand why there would be this large disagreement between management and the market about the long-run effects of an acquisition on a company's profitability.

This fundamental disagreement about the validity of market pricing, which makes the discussion contentious (and lively) throughout, also becomes especially focused when questions arise about the large premiums over market paid by acquiring companies. The investment bankers assert that, even in cases where the market is not "undervaluing" assets, there is always a significant value to securing *control* over corporate assets—a control not available to the average, passive investor. As the academics point out, however, such control would be worth a significant premium over market *only* if the current management were not committing corporate resources to their highest-valued use. And, in such cases, that very failure by management to put assets to their most valuable use (which, in some cases, might mean selling them off) would explain why many companies sell at a stock price well below the liquidation value of their net assets. But, predictably, the suggestion that widespread corporate mismanagement may be behind much of the corporate takeover activity predictably unleashes another round of controversy, point and counterpoint.

DHC

THE MARKET FOR CORPORATE CONTROL: A DISCUSSION OF MERGERS AND ACQUISITIONS
February 24, 1983

JOEL STERN, MODERATOR: On behalf of all of us associated with the *Midland Corporate Finance Journal,* I would like to welcome both participants and guests to this discussion. While the topic of mergers and acquisitions will provide the main focus, we would like to cover a number of issues that fall under the more general rubric of the "market for corporate control."

Let me start by giving a brief overview of the issues we would like to explore:

1. Virtually all academic studies of mergers and tender offers show most of the gains going to target stockholders. The stockholders of acquiring companies appear to earn only normal rates of return, on average. And in many cases, judging from the market's response, there appear to have been sizable losses to buying companies' stockholders. The evidence also shows that bidding wars are especially harmful to bidding companies' stock prices, and that large companies have been the worst offenders.

   One of the questions we have for you, then, is do the test results square with your own experience and intuition? Or are the statistics failing to pick up something important? If the tests confirm your intuition, then why do companies continue to pay such large premiums over market to acquire other companies? Why are such premiums becoming ever larger? Is the market systematically undervaluing corporate assets, or is there some value to gaining control of companies that we would not expect to be reflected in stock prices?

2. How do companies determine the price they are willing to pay for an acquisition? Do they typically discount expected cash flows to determine a net present value? Or do they use more subjective, qualitative criteria? Is EPS dilution still a major concern, so that acquirers only acquire companies with lower P/E's in a cash purchase transaction?

3. The theory and evidence of modern finance suggest that domestic diversification by large public companies seems to be penalized rather than rewarded by the market. Is diversification per se an important motive for acquisitions?

4. How should managers respond to takeover attempts? What are their legal responsibilities? Are such responsibilities consistent with shareholder interests? Has tender offer legislation helped target stockholders or hurt them? What is the net

effect both of tender offers, and on the regulation of tender offers, on the efficiency of the system as a whole?

5. We seem to be seeing a lot more "negative merger" activity in recent years. What are the corporate motives for, and the market consequences of, divestitures and spin-offs?

With this as background, I would like to introduce our very distinguished group of participants, who bring to the table a variety of viewpoints, experience, and achievement. They are:

JEFF BECK heads the Mergers and Acquisitions Department at Oppenheimer, and is also on Oppenheimer's Executive Committee. He holds an MBA degree from Columbia University;

PETER DODD is Associate Professor of Finance at the University of Chicago's Graduate School of Business. Peter received a Ph.D. in Finance from the University of Rochester, and is the author of numerous studies and articles on mergers, acquisitions, tender offers, and, more generally, on issues of the market for corporate control;

DAN FISCHEL is Assistant Professor of Law at the University of Chicago Law School. He has authored numerous articles on the market for corporate control, including "Corporate Control Transactions" (in *The Yale Law Journal*, 1982) and "The Proper Role of a Target's Management in Responding to a Tender Offer" (in *Harvard Law Review*, April 1981). Dan also teaches a course in corporate finance which, interestingly, has become part of the Chicago Law School curriculum.

STEVE FRIEDMAN, who has been a Partner of Goldman Sachs since 1973. Steve heads both the Mergers & Acquisitions and the Private Financing Departments. He is also a member of Goldman Sachs' Management Committee. Steve holds a law degree from Columbia University.

JUD REIS has been a Managing Director of Morgan Stanley since 1976, and is a member of its Mergers and Acquisitions Department. Jud holds an MBA from the Harvard Business School;

BILL SCHWERT is Associate Professor of Finance at the Graduate School of Management, University of Rochester. Bill is an Editor of the *Journal of Financial Economics*, which is preparing a special issue summarizing academic evidence on those issues which we discuss today. Bill holds a Ph.D. in Finance from the University of Chicago.

Before we begin, I want to lay down the ground rules. This discussion is not intended to be a formal debate, but rather an open—and reasonably friendly—exchange of ideas. There will of course be some points of disagreement. When these arise, you can go after each other. But, I will try to maintain some semblance of order by waving my hands in the air so that you know that I recognize you—even though you will probably be on top of one another before I get the chance to stop you.

I'll start with the first major topic. And if you don't mind, I'll start by asking Bill Schwert the first question, because it has to do with this particular issue of M & A research that Bill is very familiar with. Could you summarize, Bill, what the research findings are telling us about the prices companies have been paying to consummate acquisitions and mergers? Mike Bradley's study of tender offers, for instance, seems to find that if there are "abnormal" gains at all for buyers, they appear, on average, to be negligible. Why would it be in the interest of buyers to engage in this activity if there is very little value left over for the buyer?

BILL SCHWERT: Well, Joel, I believe the statement you made is a fairly accurate summary of a large part of that literature. There has been a lot of work done recently on mergers and tender offers: Mike Bradley's dissertation, subsequently published in part in the *Journal of Business*; Peter Dodd's dissertation on mergers, published in the *Journal of Financial Economics* (*JFE*); the Dodd-Ruback paper, also in the *JFE*; and there are a number of papers that are coming out shortly in a special issue of the *JFE*. All these studies look at the market's reaction to announcements of mergers or tender offers, and their results are all very similar. Most of the abnormal gains go to the target firms; bidding firms tend to earn just normal rates of return, on average. That is, they tend to do no better or worse than the market when consummating a transaction.

But there is a problem in interpreting these results for the bidding companies. The stock price change for bidding firms in mergers and tender offers tends not to be very large—not at least when compared to the size of the premiums over market value paid for the target firms. On the other hand, the size of the bidding firms is usually orders of magnitude bigger than the size of the target firms. Because of this great difference in the size of buying and selling companies, it may not be meaningful to compare the buying company's *percentage change* in value (which is bound to be relatively smaller because of the larger size of the base against which it is measured) with the seller's.

However, Paul Malatesta has written a paper—coming out in the special issue of the *JFE* Joel mentioned—which tries to get around this problem. He actually calculated the *dollar* losses and gains to both bidding firms and target firms, and came to the conclusion that the dollar orders of magnitude were actually fairly comparable.

JOEL: Comparable in what terms? Are you suggesting that when the buyer bought the target company, there were gains to both parties?

BILL: The estimate of the gains to bidding firms was comparable to the estimate of the dollar gains to the target shareholders. This means that it is not quite so clear that the targets get all the abnormal gains, and that the bidders earn only normal returns.

PETER DODD: There is one thing that I would like to add. Although the average gains, measured in dollars and not as returns, are shared *on average* fairly evenly between buyer and seller, these averages hide the fact that there is a surprisingly large proportion of negatives, or losers, among bidding firms, whether measured in dollar values or returns. That is, there are a great many cases where the bidding firm's value falls as a result of consummating the transaction.

JOEL: Would that imply, then, that companies were bidding too much, or overpaying for acquisitions?

PETER: Well, some companies are, but not on average. If you look at the mean or average case, then it appears to be a "fair game" situation. On average, buyers get what they pay for. The prices paid for companies seem to make them, on average, a zero NPV-value investment.

JOEL: Which means it would be a matter of indifference to the buying shareholders whether the deal was made?

PETER: That's basically right. But you have to be careful drawing that conclusion because the cross-sectional averaging method employed by these tests can be a little misleading.

JUD REIS: Peter, what time period did these tests measure?

PETER: The last twenty years, going back to the sixties and...

JUD: No, I mean in terms of when you measure the gain or loss of the buying companies.

PETER: Well, that is an important issue. If you assume that capital markets are efficient, and the company's current stock price represents an unbiased estimate of the future value of the company, then the only way you can do it is to go back to a time when the offer was unknown to the market. Okay, so in cases...

JUD: But do you measure the gain a week after the deal, a year after the deal, five years after the deal...

PETER: We start measuring from a point in time before the first announcement—usually ten to twenty days before the first public announcement of the offer. This allows us to pick up any sort of leakage—anticipation, or whatever you want to call it. Some of the studies begin measuring the market's reaction the day after the announcement of a successful bid. Other times they go through the complete transaction, from days before the first announcement until the thing is finally completed. But it is interesting that the results don't vary much with the difference in testing periods. They are very much the same from test to test.

JUD: But you never measured, for example, two years later.

PETER: Well, if you do it that way, then all you're measuring is the *ex post* realization.

JOEL: Wait a second. The point Peter is making is that if markets behave in a reasonably sophisticated manner, today's stock price is supposed to reflect the capitalized value of the potential benefits of the acquisition. What Jud is implying is that it takes two or three years to determine whether these gains are really going to materialize. My question, then, is: Wouldn't it have been in the interest of one or both of the parties engaged in the transaction to somehow communicate those longer-term prospects at the time of the transaction?

JUD: I think some of the parties would feel that they did. What I think we have seen, particularly in some of the larger acquisitions, is management of the acquiring company making what they believe to be a very long-term decision, a strategic decision. They have decided that the acquisition is the most economical alternative they have of getting into another business in a significant way. And they are willing—whether they are right or wrong— to take the chance that the market will be proven wrong. What has been driving them is this long-term strategic decision they expect will take time to pay off.

I think it is fair to say that a lot of shareholders, for whatever reason, have a much shorter-term point of view. And what drives them is an immediate premium, or very near-term performance. So you have a difference in perception between the shareholder base making the market day to day, and the market for corporate control which has a longer-term outlook.

JOEL: Dan, what do you think?

DAN FISCHEL: This is one of the classic points of contention between academics and the people who are involved in the transactions themselves: that is, the extent to which stock prices reflect long-term values as well as short-term values. One of the reasons commonly given for restricting the ability of firms to make acquisitions in the first place is that the threat of tender offers forces target managers to focus only on short-run earnings, and thus ignore long-run prospects. Firms will ignore positive net present value projects which will only pay off in the future if there is a possibility of being taken over in the interim. Similarly, people attempt to justify transactions where the bidder appears to lose—that is, their stockholders appear to lose a lot of money on the announcement—by saying that the payoff will come in the future.

Well, both these arguments are based on the assumption that stock prices do not reflect long-run prospects. The academic literature, however, would suggest that if there is really going to be a big payoff two years down the road, or five years down the road, then the present value of that payoff would be reflected in the acquiring company's stock price soon after the acquisition. For this reason, it is not very convincing to argue that negative returns to bidding shareholders at the time of the acquisition will be positive down the road. Because that assumes again, in effect, an irrational stock market. Those stockholders selling out on the announcement would be systematically making the wrong decision, systematically losing money, by doing so. I don't think there is any evidence to support that.

JUD: Well, my experience has been that quarterly performance is very important. You may think you have a stock that is terrific and will make a lot of money two, three, four years down the road. But you may not have the account if you don't perform the eight quarters before that. So I think there are some pressures on people who, on the margin, may drive the price of the stock one way or the other. It may not be entirely rational, but it reflects the pressures of the world they are in.

PETER: Yes, but why is the announcement of an acquisition or tender offer any different from when IBM or Kodak announces a brand-new technology? The stock price reacts very quickly in those cases to reflect the long-run implications for value. I think most of us would agree that in those cases stock prices jump straight away. Now why is it any different in the merger case, which, like the new technology, also may take three or four years to show its real contribution to profitability?

STEVE FRIEDMAN: I suspect that the advantage of the Kodak or IBM products is that analysts think they can quantify those effects relatively well. I don't believe that, in the case of acquisitions, even the chief executive, who has a strong feeling that there are going to be synergies, is ever really as confident that he can quantify them. You talk about communicating the prospects. He certainly is not able to communicate this to the public.

JOEL: No, there have been examples of successful communication. Ben Heineman of Northwest Industries, as I recall, was running full-page advertisements in the *Wall Street Journal* announcing that if projects did not meet certain minimum criteria of performance (including discounted cash flow rate of return requirements of something like 12 to 15 percent after tax), he wouldn't take them on. Then, when he acquired Coca-Cola Bottling in Los Angeles for $205 million, he repeated his statement that even though the book value was only $30 million, and the market price had been $60 million, the $205 million he paid for that company had not violated his principle. He intended to earn 15 percent after tax on that $205 million. Interestingly enough, the stock price of Northwest Industries did not decline on the announcement that he was paying $205 million for a company whose market price had been $60 million.

ACQUISITION PREMIUMS

JOEL: There is another matter I would like to bring up at this stage. Haven't you detected, Steve, that the premiums being paid above the current market price have increased dramatically in the last four to five years compared to, say, ten to fifteen years ago? At one time it used to be 20 to 25 percent over the market. Now it is up to 100 percent or more.

STEVE: Well, sure. For one thing, you have the function of inflation, with the underlying assets appreciating substantially in value. And until earlier this year, you also had a terribly depressed stock market. So you had an enormous disparity between the underlying values of the stocks and the liquidation value of assets.

BILL: Maybe so, but you're still assuming that somehow the people holding the stock of Conoco or Cities Service don't understand the underlying value of the assets—and that DuPont or Mobil or some other company has a much better understanding of that underlying asset value than the people who already own the shares of Conoco.

It seems to me that DuPont's management, when they made a tender offer for Conoco, should have had a strong incentive to disclose information that would have kept their stock price from dropping a lot. In fact, the stock price dropped substantially.

JEFF: How is anybody going to know whether the DuPont-Conoco transaction made sense unless you give it a long period of time?

JOEL: What we are trying to point out is that stock prices today are supposed to reflect the market's best collective judgment of the expected future results of that acquisition. When the actual results come in, they will affect people's expectations at that point going forward as well. The market price two years down the road may not be reflecting the success of the past acquisition. It will be looking at the prospects further down the road. You can't use future stock prices to measure the effects of today's announced merger because the prices are always looking into the future.

So, at any one time, on any given day, the market is taking a gamble on the outcome. And the question is: What information is being used, and who is processing it? Now we like to say that there are "lead steers" and there are "average steers." And if you want to find out where the herd is going, you don't have to interview all the steers to find out. You try to find out what the lead steers are doing. The concept here then, Jud, is that the market is made up of all kinds of people who have all kinds of judgment and so forth. We only care about what we would call this lead steer, or marginal investor, because he is going to have the greatest effect on the stock price.

But the question still comes back to how you can justify premiums of say 50, 60, 100 percent now versus 20 to 25 percent earlier. Steve, you were saying that the inflation rate would account for some of this. If that is the case, how come the stock price doesn't reflect those gains in asset value caused by inflation?

STEVE: Well, wait a minute. You have got to focus on what your share ownership entitles you to. If your share ownership entitles you to get dividends from a company and to vote for its management, and if the earnings and dividends are not really rising commensurately with inflation, maybe you are only willing to pay a certain price for a thousand shares. On the other hand, you can be told with absolute confidence by a group of leading experts that if you buy control of this company, the markets are such that we can turn around and sell those underlying oil reserves for a price substantially in excess of the price of the stock. Because that is what people are bidding for oil reserves. Then people say to themselves, "By God that stock is at $40 and they are telling me I can get $80 for it—and putting in a margin of safety for inaccuracy, I am sure I can get at least $70."

That may not fit with your tidy notions of the way the world should operate, but the guy buying the thousand shares can't sell those reserves. The guy buying 51 percent can sell them.

DAN: Are you implying that the company is mismanaged when it is not being liquidated, because the going concern value is that much less than the liquidation value?

STEVE: I am not implying that at all.

DAN: When you say the market is depressed, it seems to me there are two possible explanations. One is you are saying that the market prices do not reflect the going concern value of the firm—in which case you are saying the bidder is a superior stock picker to everybody else in the economy. You're saying this, remember, about a world where empirical studies have shown that institutional investors do not generally outperform the market. In that case, however, you have to ask why the cheapest strategy for identifying undervalued securities is to pay a large premium for them. Why not simply buy a lot of shares in different undervalued companies at their market prices and have a corporate portfolio of securities?

STEVE: Because then you can't get your hands on the assets.

DAN: No, wait a minute. The other possibility is that market values accurately reflect the going concern value of the firm and, for whatever reason, the going concern value is less than the liquidation value. If the difference in value is significant, that implies that the firm is being mismanaged by continuing to operate.

STEVE: I think if one felt that the spread between the liquidating value and the market value was going to last for a lengthy period of time, it would indeed be mismanagement not to capture that value. Like everything else, though, it is relative. If you think the spread is 20 percent, and it is going to last for a year, that is different than if the spread is 100 percent, and in your view it is going to last for five years. Some managements clearly made the judgment that the liquidating value of the assets was going to stay higher than the stock price for a long period of time. In these cases, it wasn't the buyers who put the company on the market. The managers or owners put the company on the market themselves by giving us, or one of our competitors, the assignment to sell it. Others looked at it and, as reasonable men, said, "Sure, we would increase our shareholders' wealth by X percent over the short term if we liquidated today. In the intermediate to longer term, though, we think the business is going to resurge, and that stockholder values are going to be higher by holding onto the stock."

DAN: I think that is implausible because the possibility of the business resurging in the future is incorporated into the market price today. And if you can sell the assets and make a liquidating distribution for a significantly greater amount, then the company is not being managed in the best interests of stockholders.

STEVE: You have a profound faith in the market's judgment.

THE ROLE OF THE INVESTMENT BANKER _____

JOEL: Steve, I have a question for you. Does Goldman Sachs or any other investment banker, to your knowledge, review the assumptions that were made periodically in formulating transactions that were allegedly based on under- or overvaluation by the market? Let me give you an example. Recently Sohio bought Kennecott Copper. The price of copper was so low in the United States that some companies were actually closing down their operations and buying copper on the open market to fulfill contractual arrangements. The price of Kennecott was in the high $20s or maybe around $30 at the time of the deal. And Sohio paid something like $65 a share for Kennecott.

Are you suggesting that the market price of Kennecott was not based on the spot price for copper, but on a future price for copper which was not reflected in today's stock price? Or were the people at Sohio willing to gamble against what sophisticated commodity traders were estimating the future price of copper to be, in order to say that the price of Kennecott was being systematically undervalued in the marketplace?

STEVE: The Sohio management made a judgment about where they thought future copper prices were likely to be. The price they were willing to pay was based on that estimate. They recognized that it was a judgment that was not necessarily going to be immediately popular with the stock market. I think they also recognized that they would be proven right or wrong somewhere down the road.

JOEL: Well, when your advice to a company is based on assumptions that appear to be contrary to what currently is impounded in the price of the shares, do you keep a record someplace to evaluate whether the position that your firm took was in fact borne out with the passage of time?

STEVE: No, not in the sense you are talking about. In this particular case, our assignment was clearly not to give them our views on the future likelihood of copper prices. They had tapped what they felt was a broad range of expert opinions and they had their own views on future copper prices. In that transaction our views were solicited on how to execute the deal. They also wanted to know our opinion about the likely market impact, which—we were candid with them—was not going to be favorable. They recognized it wasn't going to be favorable and I think that they took a courageous point of view.

Incidentally, I am a little bit shocked by the trend of this discussion because American business has been criticized for being too short-term oriented. I had always thought the only people more short-sighted than American businessmen were investors in the stock market. They may be the only people who are more short-term oriented than the press, who tend to evaluate things based on how good it looks in the next quarter.

I am amazed to find out that, in the academic community, you are measuring the success of an acquisition by how well it does for the stock in the short run. The enlightened managements that we deal with are certainly interested in what the stock market's reaction is going to be. They are also interested in what the impact is going to be on their credit ratings and on other things. But they regard these *only* as cost factors. At times, of course, the cost factor may be so substantial that they can't really do something that they would otherwise feel would be a good thing to do down the road— because they can't afford to lose their single A rating, or they can't afford to lose their equity financing ability by having the stock drop X percent. But other times they look at it simply as a necessary cost of an otherwise sound transaction: "The stock will be down several points, but we think we will be vindicated by the results and that is what we are paid for—to make decisions."

DAN: But you are assuming that creditors and shareholders are all acting irrationally. You are saying a transaction that is a good deal economically— that is, it increases the long-term value of the firm—will have the effect of making the firm's credit rating worse off, and cause investors to lower their estimation of the value of the firm. That doesn't make any sense to me, unless you're assuming that both creditors and investors will act irrationally.

STEVE: I am not assuming they were acting irrationally. Once again, you have loaded the statement. I am assuming that reasonable men can disagree about the long term, or even the short term, and that people are paid for taking contrary points of view at times. It is only you folks who are imputing total rationality and, indeed, correctness to the stock market.

BILL: We are not asserting that management never makes decisions that turn out to be right, even though the market reacts negatively in the short run. What we are saying is that the market's reaction to an announcement of an acquisition has no systematic bias; that is, on average, it neither understates nor overstates the value of that acquisition to a company. This means that, *on average* (though not in every case), the market's immediate reaction to an announcement of an acquisition can be viewed as an objective assessment of the value of that acquisition. The judgment of managers about the long-term payoff may be better than the market's in some cases. But when investors collectively think an acquisition was a bad deal, and the market price drops to reflect that, investors are going to be right more often than they're wrong. And they're just as likely to overstate the value of an acquisition as to understate it.

So, when you argue that you can only measure the success of an acquisition several years down the road, well, okay, in a sense that's true. But this statement can only be made ex post facto, after the fact. From our point of view, if you see companies bidding for target firms and their stock price drops, they probably made a mistake. So, we are very surprised to hear that management would ever undertake a transaction which they knew in advance was going to cause their stock price to drop.

STEVE: Oh, no, management will sometimes be sure.

JOEL: You mean they assume the stock price will drop?

STEVE: Yes. They feel the stock price will only reflect the market's short-term outlook. But is it the short term that the management is paid to consider? No, it's the intermediate, the longer term.

JEFF: Absolutely. No question about it.

BILL: What I can't understand is: When we're talking about a major acquisition, how great can the difference be between what management knows and what the market knows? If management thinks the acquisition is good for the company, it should have a strong incentive to try to convince financial analysts and pension fund managers that the acquisition is in fact a good deal, not a bad deal. I don't understand why there would be this large disagreement between management and the market about the long-run effects of an acquisition on a company's profitability.

DIVESTITURES

JOEL: Jeff, in your experience with divestitures, do you find that the senior managements of companies that are divesting do so not so much because they think the returns on those businesses are inadequate—but rather because they feel that if they were to sell off all or a part of the company, it would have a tremendous impact on their own stock price?

JEFF: No, I don't think studies have shown that about the divestiture and corporate restructuring announcements that we are seeing. We did a study of fifty or sixty different announcements of corporate restructurings. And if you knew in advance that management was considering restructuring their company, and if you had invested in all those companies, for every dollar you invested you would have had a return of *four*.

JOEL: Well, I find that a little puzzling. Because if you were to ask Bill Schwert or Peter Dodd what the serious researchers have found about the values of companies, it is that those values are equal to the sum of the values of the parts of companies. If managements don't believe that, and they feel that they're undervalued because the market cannot value their component parts, they might want to sell off a portion of a company and have that trade separately. They will then provide as much information on that spun-off unit as a prospectus and an annual report will require. They would do this because they felt that the sum of the parts, trading individually, is greater than the whole.

My problem with this strategy is as follows: If management is willing to provide all that information, why not provide it as part of the existing company, instead of selling off an operating unit in order to have its fair value recognized by the market?

JEFF: Well, that is an argument. But, it's hard for me to say, because we are not usually called in to make value judgments on twenty-five different divisions. My experience has been, though, that companies sell off divisions because they do not meet their expected return requirements. Or it doesn't fit with the strategy of the corporation that owns it. They typically find a buyer who is in the same business, and the buying company expects to do better things with that division. The buyer buys something he sees has been an ignored division, one which fits with his strategy. He is an incremental value buyer. He wants the business, he understands the business, he wants to grow the business, he knows how to manage the business better than XYZ corporation. So there are economic advantages to both parties, buyer and seller.

PETER: Jeff, you said that the evidence shows that the market responds very favorably to these announcements of divestitures and restructuring plans. Okay, this means that the capital market seems to work fine in the case of divestitures. My question, then, is: Why doesn't it work fine in the case of acquisitions? The market seems to be looking at the *long-term* effects of a restructuring, and rewarding managements that are improving long-run profitability. The restructuring transaction presumably increases the value of the firm, and the capital market recognizes that. But now why isn't the market capable of making the same kind of long-term judgments when it comes to responding to announcements of acquisitions?

STEVE: In a divestiture, you have got immediate publicity of the loss that you have eliminated, immediate publicity of the cash-flow drain you may have done away with. The benefits are obvious. Whereas, in the case of acquisitions, things are much less clear, much more open-ended.

You are all saying that an enlightened manager will inform the stock market of all the pluses of the acquisition. And, indeed, within whatever limitations the SEC imposes, you would try to do this. But if you sat down with corporate managements and asked them: "Why do you feel good about this particular deal?," you know you will get certain imprecise, unquantified responses, like . . . "I really feel that we can help them with their plans for such and such business. We understand their business." But, if you ask them to quantify the benefits of an acquisition, they are not good at that. I think, intuitively, they are probably wise enough to know that they are going to get a substantial number of surprises. But they are confident enough in the general thrust of it.

PETER: But surely that kind of analysis has to be quantified at some point by somebody in the company. They would have to arrive at a price they are going to be prepared to pay. So presumably they have done *some* analysis. Sure, they may be more uncertain about those cash flows and the effect of synergies on profitability. But regardless of how formalized or sophisticated, management must have done some cash-flow analysis.

JEFF: On the divestiture side, though, management has typically lived with these divisions for ten or fifteen years. So how can you possibly expect the quality of information on a new acquisition to be the same as the quality of the information on a divestiture?

PETER: It may be easier for management, and the market, to value the gains from divestitures. But in mergers and acquisitions, the principle is the same. The market tries to evaluate those events in the same way.

DIVERSIFICATION

JUD: I think it is harder to communicate this kind of acquisition analysis to the market. I think analysts are more skeptical about it. You say the market is unbiased, but I don't think it is. Bill, you made the point that managements know more about their businesses than the market. But they also know their own skeletons. They know the problems they are having, which they are loathe to publicize for reasons that are understandable. And when they look at another business—say, a steel company considering getting into the oil business, they may say, "If I don't do something, diversify out of the steel business, we may be headed straight down." They may be more aware of their own problems than the market. The only alternative facing them is diversifying into a business that seems to have better prospects. Stockholders may be better off with that decision.

STEVE: That happens to be a very crucial point. Winston Churchill once observed that the problem with criticizing events made in the course of history is that you never know what the alternative would have been. I think that many corporations that come to us and want to do sizable transactions relative to their own market capitalization are essentially saying not necessarily that they are frightened about their future, but rather that their own growth has leveled off. They are concerned about trends in their own business, and they feel there is some virtue to diversification. I think it would be very interesting to do a study of companies that have failed to diversify during the period of their maturity—when they were still able to do it— and then to watch them some years later when they are no longer able to do it.

JOEL: The problem with diversification, though, is that the dominant investors in markets—the large investors who really set stock prices—are already well diversified. Why is it in their interest to have the corporation diversified when they themselves can do it?

STEVE: That is their choice as investors. The management of a company views its responsibility differently. Corporate management is totally unpersuaded by the notion: "You stay as a 'pure play.' Maybe ten years from now you will be an obsolescent 'pure play,' but for the portfolio managers of America that is irrelevant." No, the manager does not buy that. He feels his job is to keep his entity viable and thriving.

JOEL: Okay, but it's only the synergistic aspects of an acquisition that can justify my paying a premium over market to buy that company in a different industry. Only the synergies, or new efficiencies, add value to the enterprise. Diversification for diversification's sake does not add value; and if you overpay, and there are no synergies, you are penalizing your own stockholders.

Let's assume I am acquiring a company that is unrelated to my basic business. On what basis, as an advisor to a company, can you say to me, "You are justified in paying a premium above the current market price"? If the current market price reflects the prospects of the company under the existing management, and there is not going to be anything that we can really add to this because it is a pure, unrelated diversification effort—then why are the buying company's shareholders better served by using corporate cash to diversify than instead—I hate to suggest it to you—do you ever suggest to the company that they might instead pay out a liquidating dividend to their shareholders with the same cash they would have used to make that acquisition?

STEVE: Certainly we raise the possibility of using excess cash to buy their own stock, which is a partial liquidation. Certainly we do.

JOEL: But, I mean, how would you justify the diversification argument where the proposed acquisition is totally unrelated to their basic activity? There is no possibility of adding significant value in that case.

DAN: The important point is that diversification is available to the firm's shareholders at almost no cost. So how can there be any benefit to them from management's paying a huge premium simply to diversify? It is just a much more expensive way of achieving for investors the same effect as buying shares in a mutual fund. The party that really benefits from acquisitions undertaken to diversify is the managers themselves. Because they can't diversify their human capital. So, if they are in a failing business, managers benefit from diversification. But they benefit at the expense of their own stockholders.

I should point out, though, that the evidence on mergers and acquisitions does not suggest that diversification is a primary motive for corporate acquisitions. The evidence shows gains, on average, going to *both* bidding and target companies' stockholders. If diversification per se were really a widespread motive, then you would simply have a wealth transfer from the bidders to the target stockholders. So that what the stockholders of the target gained as a premium would be offset exactly by a loss to the bidder's stockholders. We do see this in some cases. But the majority of transactions show gains to both parties. So that suggests there is something more going on than pure diversification.

JEFF: Yes, but what are we paying the managers to do? According to your theory, the guys are just sitting there, passively. They have no concept of an ongoing enterprise. At some point in time, you're assuming they are just going to say: "Okay, things don't look good, let's liquidate." Managers don't behave that way. They are there to grow the company, aren't they? And one of the ways of growing the company is to acquire other companies, whether the acquisitions are synergistic or completely outside their own line of business.

DAN: What about just making sound capital investments in their own businesses?

JEFF: There are a lot of alternatives. But you can't sit around in the real world. You can't theorize that the guys running these corporations don't have any concept of an ongoing enterprise. The managers are there to grow the firm.

BILL: To grow the *size* of the firm, or grow the *value* of the firm? That's an important difference. You can get a lot bigger and still hurt your own stockholders in the process. Just because your EPS goes up every year by 15 percent doesn't necessarily mean you're helping your stockholders. You may actually be reducing the *value* of the firm at the same time. There's a big difference between profitable growth and unprofitable growth.

ACQUISITION PRICING

JOEL: How do you go about setting the price of an acquisition for the buyer? Jud, how does Morgan Stanley go about placing an upper limit on the price? Do you say to your clients: "Should the price go above the following number, we would no longer recommend that transaction to you because we just feel there is no value left over for your shareholders"?

JUD: Absolutely. That is something we are often asked. You can look at that question on the basis of the information you have about what the present value of the expected return is. At some price that return becomes unattractive.

Returning to your question about the large premiums, though, I think that a strong, if not a complete, case can be made that the premiums really are almost a mathematical "fallout" of the acquisition process. Companies are being priced using different forms of analysis, whether using net present values or expected internal rates of return. They obviously look at the premiums paid in comparable transactions. But there is also liquidation analysis, which may give the same answer as present value analysis if you have a sufficiently long time horizon. If there are management efficiencies or synergies resulting from the business combination—again those benefits will not be reflected in cash flows until a few years out. They don't happen instantly.

All these different kinds of analysis translate into a whole range of values that you might be willing to pay for a company. When pricing an acquisition candidate, you put that range of expected values against the stock price and the premium, if you will, "falls out." Really, the way we look seriously at the question of acquisition premiums is not so much in terms of observed premiums on comparable transactions. We don't say to our clients, "You can buy a company in the oil business at a 20 percent, or a 50 percent, or a 100 percent, premium over market price." What we say is, "After you have done your analysis, and the premium falls out, we will offer our judgment about what is necessary to give the deal a chance at being successful. Stockholders are used to looking at premiums in a different way, and we can tell what may be necessary to excite them."

JOEL: Can I ask this question, then? If you are using a very sophisticated valuation model, such as DCF, that has built-in *long-term* considerations, do you mean to tell us that you are advising your clients on the basis of sophisticated tools when you believe the market prices are set by people who are relatively unsophisticated?

JUD: We are advising our clients with the use of the most sophisticated tools we can get our hands on, yes. You can be assured of that. I think the hardest thing, though—and probably the most important thing—any investment banking firm can do for its clients is to tell them when you think they are paying too much. And that can be a function both of our judgment about the value of the property they want to buy, and of the client's financial wherewithal to make an acquisition of a certain size—even if the price is right. They may do such damage to their own financial structure that the acquisition won't have been worth it.

JOEL: I remember many years ago when Xerox announced the acquisition of CIT Financial, Xerox was selling at 88 times earnings. When they announced they were going to buy CIT for 55 times earnings, their own stock price fell very dramatically. The chairman—the late Joe Wilson—made the statement, "I think the market thinks we overpaid." I thought there was no doubt about it. My question is: How come the investment banker was not standing there saying, "Look, Xerox, the reason you sell at a high multiple like that is that your prospects are just fabulous. And CIT does not justify a 55 times earnings multiple"?

STEVE: I don't know who the investment banker was. I don't know whether he said it. But I also think that not only do you folks have a faith in the stock market beyond what I have. I also think you have an exaggerated faith in clients' willingness to take investment bankers' advice at all.

JEFF: Steve is right. We are not running these companies.

STEVE: You know there is this notion that investment bankers create these mergers and force the deals down the throats of companies. But I have to tell you something. The companies regard us as a resource as they do their lawyers. If you are an aggressive and reasonably tough-minded investment banker, you will sometimes say to companies, "You have asked me this question. Here is the answer. But I don't think that you asked us the right question. Here are two other questions that I think you ought to have asked, and here are the answers." And there are times when a strong-minded management will say to an investment banker, "We are very appreciative of your advice but, notwithstanding, we are going to go forward."

JOEL: I appreciate that. But there is still one major problem. The investment banker's fee is subject to the deal being consummated. Is there not a conflict of interest there? How often are you going to be able to tell the management of a bidding company not to bid a higher price?

JUD: This is the short-term versus long-term disagreement we are having. If you are in business as an investment banker for the long term, you probably aren't going to be there very long if you give your clients bad advice. You must have a consistent record. I would pass up a fee by giving the client the right advice because I want our reputation to survive.

JOEL: You are saying that you wouldn't give them bad advice. Yet, at the same time, you are telling all of us that you would not judge the success of an acquisition according to what happens to the buyer's stock price after the deal is consummated. So, if the price goes down afterward, then you say, "I am sorry in the near term," and that's all right?

STEVE: Within limits. Within limits.

JOEL: And if you wait for a long enough period of time there certainly will be other factors that will affect the stock price that have nothing to do with the transaction. So how, then, is the client to judge the quality of the advice he is getting from his investment banker?

STEVE: First of all, we judge the quality of our advice by the accuracy of what we predicted to the client. We may predict to the client the stock will stay where it is. We may predict it will drop a couple of points. We may predict that it will drop by 10 percent. Whether that thwarts his zeal to go ahead is a wholly separate question.

Life just doesn't work out neatly enough for a dissertation. It is unfortunate. You have loaded the question, and they are going to catch on to you academics. You see, I didn't go to business school, and I have stumbled into this thing with a great deal of naïveté. Now I've discovered what a ruthless group you are.

MORE ON THE ROLE OF INVESTMENT BANKERS _____

JOEL: I'd like, if I could, to get back to this issue of companies paying large premiums over market to get into unrelated businesses. Picture Sohio, for example, ready to acquire Kennecott. The copper price is low. The futures price of copper is low, and copper companies are losing money. Kennecott's stock price is in the high twenties and Sohio says, "We are going to pay $65 a share for Kennecott." They have come to you, Steve, and said, "What is your advice about us paying a premium of well over

100 percent for a company whose prospects, the market says, are quite poor, and where the futures price of copper is also quite low?" Are you coming to them to justify the acquisition at $65? Would you say to them, as an advisor, "It is our judgment that the price of copper is likely to rise substantially, even though the commodities' futures market just doesn't see it our way"?

STEVE: Well, I think part of your question arises from misconceptions about what the investment banker's role is in these things. One item of advice we give a company is that if you're planning to buy a commodity business—whether it is oil, timber, copper, whatever—and if your decision is profoundly based on what your investment banker thinks the likely trend of future prices is going to be, our strong advice is, "You don't know enough about this business to be in this game, get out. You are a dilettante and you shouldn't be in this business." The people in the commodities business might hire us and they might say, "We very much want your *execution* talents on this transaction. We are also interested in your opinion—or the opinion of the analysts you know in this area who we think well of—about the outlook for certain commodities. We know you have a number of clients in this business, and we would like your opinion. But basically, Goldman Sachs, we're going to be a little joint venture and, with all due respect, we at Weyerhauser think we know more about timber than you. But if you didn't know more about execution we wouldn't be hiring you, and so that is going to be the basis of our partnership." And that seems to me pretty sound.

JOEL: So you are saying that a company typically comes to Goldman Sachs and says, "We would like to do this transaction (even if the price is 100 percent above market), and what we are calling on you for is your ability to execute the deal."

STEVE: Well, companies come to us for a broad range of things. The purest situation is where the company comes to you and says, "We have just announced that we are acquiring XYZ Company for $50 a share—it was on the tape ten minutes ago. We are not asking you to do anything other than come in and give an opinion as to whether you do or don't think this is a fair price. Your fee will be X dollars whether you say it is 'fair' or 'unfair.' " At this point, you are put into the purest exercise whether you do or don't think it is a good deal for the stock.

PETER: Do you ever get involved in setting the prices, or the premium?

STEVE: As Jud said earlier, we don't set "premiums." We don't think in terms of "premiums." We ask ourselves, "If you are the seller, then is this the best price you can get for the business? If you are a buyer, is this a good deal?"

PETER: Is it a premium over the market price, that's all I'm asking?

STEVE: Okay, but you are putting too much emphasis on this notion of a premium. If your company was for sale and we were hired to represent the buyer, I would feel perfectly comfortable valuing your company while *pretending you were a private company* all the way up to just five minutes before the conversation with the client. We would say, "Don't tell me what the quote is for the stock, I don't want to know." Running all the figures you can, looking at everything you can think of, we then ask: "What are the price levels at which you continue to feel the buyer has done a good job, and will be a better company for going through with the transaction?"

DAN: Can I ask a question? Let us say somebody comes to you, and they say, "We want to make an acquisition for a company we feel is a very good company, it has very good managers. We don't want to change a thing after the acquisition. But we think this is a very good investment for the future." Would you perform the same analysis to determine whether the market price of the target firm is less than the valuation that you would place on it if it were a private company? And if it was, would you recommend going forward with an acquisition where you are going to pay a premium over the market price to get control of the firm, *when absolutely nothing is going to be changed*? Would you be willing to say that is possibly a beneficial transaction for the acquiring firm?

STEVE: If we thought that it would make sense and was a sound move, and that they would be a better company after, of course we would. You see, once again, you are in my humble opinion a prisoner of the preconception that the market has correctly discounted the future potentials of that company, so that company X is only worth what the stock price is. And if there are no synergies to be plugged into the deal, then you are overpaying. Does that state your argument correctly?

Okay, we do not buy that argument. We do not accept the notion that the stock market encapsulates company values with that precision. I think we have all seen moves in and out of industries.

Let me turn that around and look at it another way. We have all been focusing on the buyer. If any one of the three bankers here is hastily summoned to the board room of a client who has just become a target of a tender offer, and the client says, "You know, my stock price is at $20. These bastards in so and so just offered me $25 a share for the stock, and they said they are going to do a tender offer to the stockholders at $25. Even with present depressed stock prices, I can get the most conservative oil engineers to say that I can sell my reserves for $30 plus." By the logic of your question, the investment banker would have to say, "Hey, sell it. The present value of your company is $20 a share. We know that to be a fact because we can look at the New York stock table today. (Now, of course, two weeks ago the value was $15 because we see the range for the year.) But, you have got to sell it."

If we gave that advice—"Hey, grab it because you know $25 is higher than $20, thank you, we will take our check and go home"—we would be lynched!

UNDERVALUED ASSETS

PETER: Let's go back to the oil companies. The oil company case interests me because you said before that you don't use the timber market prices as a guide to the future. Timber firms are easy to value because they have got commodity markets and futures prices. But we see these oil company take-overs, where the buyers say, "We are buying because the market price doesn't reflect the true value of the reserves." But there you have got proven reserves and the market has got plenty of information about it. There are plenty of sophisticated traders in the oil and oil futures market. Given all this information, then how can the market be systematically undervaluing those assets?

STEVE: Have you ever seen 100,000 shares in control of a company?

PETER: No, that argument doesn't work.

JUD: Peter, the best example of that, if we want to get to practicalities, is to look at Belridge Oil, which had a very slight trading market for its shares. But you did have a trading market. At the time Morgan Stanley was hired by Belridge, if you took the stock price and multiplied it by the number of shares, it was worth about $450 million. Not long thereafter, we sold it for over $3.5 billion.

PETER: Well, let's take the Conoco case. It is the cheap oil story there. I want to know why U.S. Steel and DuPont are buying cheap oil. How does that make any sense?

JUD: Let me take that to the next step. You get a broadly traded stock, where instead of trading by appointment twice a week, you trade several hundred thousand shares a day. The second market is going to be better than the first because there are more buyers and sellers, it's true. But it is still ignoring the most important buyer that we have seen for some of these companies lately—and that gets back to the point all three of us have made. It is the guy who can get his hands on those assets and do something with them. The thousand-share shareholder, or even the million-share share-holder, can't do this.

I want to talk about Conoco for a second. I was on the Conoco side of that. When Dome Petroleum offered $65 for Conoco when it was trading at $45, we told the Conoco board the Dome offer was "grossly inadequate." I am sure all of the academics said, "You know, you dumb sons of bitches are just in there for your fee, or you are doing something else foolish."

JOEL: There were some of us who thought that way.

JUD: Yes. And yet several weeks later, if you followed our advice or the board of directors' advice instead of your own instincts, you would have gotten $98. Now I don't know what the theory is that justifies that. But we get paid for giving the advice as we see it.

RESPONDING TO TENDER OFFERS _____

PETER: I think we have concentrated too much so far on the few examples where there is obviously a bad stock price reaction to the bidding firms. The evidence which Bill started off with a long while ago says that, on average, the bidding firms are responded to favorably by the market *when the deal is first announced*. Now, though we don't know what the source of the synergies or benefits is, we know that, in the majority of cases, there is no evidence of this short-run, long-run problem that you have been talking about. In over half the cases, the market immediately said, "These are legitimate transactions and good decisions by management." They were good decisions both *ex ante* and *ex post*. So let's not concentrate too much on these others.

JUD: Let's try to explain part of this another way. First of all, there are going to be tax considerations. There may be better tax consequences from paying out corporate cash to buy part of a company than from distributing it directly to the shareholders. So that buying another company, instead of liquidating capital, may add value or, in effect, save shareholder wealth if you are a controlling shareholder as opposed to a liquidating shareholder.

As a practical matter, it may be very difficult for an existing management to consider liquidating their company. Just because they have been trained to think in other ways, or because there are human or emotional aspects to it. That may explain some of the differences between stock prices and underlying asset values. If you have a newer, more flexible management—one less tied to the company—then there is a higher likelihood of liquidation, and that should be reflected somewhere in the value—in a higher stock price.

BILL: We have some interesting evidence on unsuccessful tender offers and mergers which might confirm what you're saying. The exact kind of example you were talking about—Dome Petroleum throwing in a bid for Conoco that was unsuccessful, even at a big premium. The evidence we have suggests that unsuccessful target firms end up with permanent changes in stock price that are higher *only* if they are subsequently taken over. And if they are not subsequently taken over, the stock price goes back to where the market thought it was beforehand. That may confirm your theory, Jud, that market values are influenced by the possibility of liquidation.

JUD: But there are examples the other way.

BILL: I understand there are other examples. But I am talking about an average result across large numbers of cases. What typically happens, I'm saying, is that following an unsuccessful tender offer, two things can happen. One is that it's unsuccessful because management thinks there is going to be a better tender offer down the road. Because you can eventually liquidate, but at a higher price. The other possibility is that you hope for another tender offer, and you are wrong. And in most of those cases, the stock price of the target goes back to that $20. *Ex post*, you gave bad advice to say, "Don't take $25."

STEVE: But, you know something, that $25 is always there. Indeed $30 is always there.

JOEL: If there is a belief that there is a possibility of $25, then why would the stock price go back to $20?

BILL: That is the whole point. The evidence says it *doesn't* go back to $20 if there really is $25 or $30 out there.

STEVE: I am saying the $25 is always there. Because if you choose to put the company on the block, we can tell you with a high degree of confidence that we can get you that $25, and indeed higher. As a matter of fact, when companies call us in in this kind of situation, we do not say to them, "That price is fair." We don't care whether that $25 is fair or unfair. It may be a "fair" price in the sense that a reasonable man who really wanted to sell would do it. We really say to them, "Based on the following things, it is our best judgment that we can get you a higher price." Now, having heard that, they can be comfortable because they have not chosen to turn down something that is so wonderful that their stockholders are being put at a disadvantage. And we are very careful about giving those opinions. We have never given one that, when called upon to justify it, we were not able to do so.

STOCK PRICES AND LIQUIDATION VALUES ⎯⎯⎯⎯⎯⎯⎯

STEVE: May I just ask one thing of Peter? Did I hear skepticism on your part about whether liquidating values really were in many cases—in the case of natural resource companies, for example—substantially above the stock prices?

PETER: Yes. Earlier you made the comment that, in the timber industry, there are a lot of people sophisticated enough to know the value of those reserves. But suddenly, when we come to another commodity market, which I think has equally sophisticated investors who value these proven reserves in spot prices and in the futures market, then you tell me a different story. Why is it that the stock market can value the company's reserves in the timber industry, but in the oil industry it can't?

STEVE: I didn't say that there was a difference in the markets' ability to appraise the values. I just said that during long periods in the 1970s and the early 1980s, the stock market's valuation of a thousand or a hundred thousand shares in the going concern was substantially less than what you could have sold the sum of the parts for.

PETER: No.

STEVE: Well, you say no but this isn't a question of opinion. You just saw countless cases where you could sell the such and such reserve for X and the so and so basin for Y. And when you put X and Y together, it is worth a hell of a lot more than what the stock price was selling at. That is an empirical fact.

BILL: Yes, but you're leaving out one of the important reasons why that was true. One reason is the implicit partnership between those companies and the federal government in the form of different taxes or price controls that are going to be imposed. You can't sell off a going concern, and just sell off all its assets and not its liabilities.

STEVE: I am talking about *net* asset values. Is this something empirically that anyone disagrees with me on?

BILL: Yes, but what your net asset value doesn't reflect is the possibility of future government taxation and regulation of those natural resource companies. I am talking about liabilities that the market knows about, but that are not recorded on any balance sheet. The market expects them to show up in the form of reduced earnings down the road.

STEVE: But, on the other hand, there are also times when the market is higher than the liquidation value because people have an enormous faith in companies' exploratory talent. There are times when you can't sell the company for as high a price as the stock price, because someone has gone off into fantasy land about their exploration prospects in some area.

ACQUISITION PRICING

STEVE: Let me ask you this. Does it trouble the academics in this group at all that the people who live in the financial world are telling you that you have a world scheme which is not predictive of how people really act? Is there an implicit assumption that corporate managements are acting irrationally? Because I think what we are all telling you is that you are wedded—indeed, I would say "bonded"—to certain hypotheses which really are totally at odds with the way people think who have to make their living in the world.

PETER: The fact that none of you thinks this way really doesn't affect the predictive power of our theory. And what you said about our assumptions is not true. I look at the way markets work from the outside. What I am trying to get from you people is explanations for why these things happen—things that, to us outsiders, seem irrational. I don't assume that people are irrational. In fact, I assume the opposite. I start by assuming that investors and management are rational. On average, they have good economic reasons for the decisions they make. That's where our theory begins, and that's where its predictive power comes from.

STEVE: You seem to have a faith that, somehow, the irrationalities in the market are equalizing one another, that the process somehow works out, and the market value is right.

PETER: I observe transactions where the market price of a firm suddenly becomes far greater than it was valued before. And all I am trying to work out, as a scientist, is this: What is this new information about the value of that firm which we didn't have before? I have a lot of trouble with some of the explanations that you people and the managements are giving us for these things.

STEVE: One of the things that you are leaving out—you keep on talking about valuing the firm—is that the market value of a given firm can be very different depending on who the buyer is.

PETER: Yes, there are efficiencies that can only be taken advantage of by certain other companies. Synergies.

STEVE: But you are talking about the premium. You keep on talking about the premium. How can you say there is a premium? That particular premium might be exorbitant for company X, and might be a bargain for company Y, for a variety of reasons.

JOEL: There is no question that value is in the eye of the beholder. The question that is being raised is different. What we want to know is: what makes the same company worth such different values to individual investors, to certain bidding companies, and to other companies? What kind of gains do companies expect to get after they pay these premiums? Are the gains coming from the strategic fit, synergies, efficiencies?

STEVE: It's not efficiencies.

JOEL: But how, then, do you justify some of the premiums that we see? I see, for example, mining companies being acquired at absolutely wild premiums above the current price. And I say, "Well, how can we justify that?" The spot price is one thing. We don't think that is terribly important. But we certainly think the futures price is very important. And yet that doesn't seem to justify the price. The argument being used is: "We should be in that business. It's part of our strategic plans." My response to all this is: "OK, but at what price?"

STEVE: How far out do the futures prices go that you are looking at?

PETER: I presume they go out to—in the limit—to infinity. When people are pricing firms . . .

STEVE: This is not a rhetorical question.

DAN: The current stock price contains an implicit futures price. And that implicit futures price has, in effect, an infinite time horizon.

STEVE: Okay. But the people buying metals companies would be guilty of all the sins that the journalists accuse them of—thinking only of the short-term—if they were only looking at today's futures prices. Those people are basing their price on expectations looking out well beyond that.

JOEL: Let's go backwards instead. Let's assume that you were using discounted cash-flow analysis. If you took the existing stock price and went backwards to figure out what the implied price for a commodity would have to be to justify today's price, that would give you some idea how the market is pricing commodity-based companies. When we advise corporations, we often say to a company, "Let us have your forward plan, and we will convert that into a current market price using an acceptable model." We sometimes find that our estimate of the company's current market value (based on the forward plan) is much higher than the existing stock price. We then say to management, "We think you may be making some assumptions that are unrealistic, especially when set against what the market thinks about the outlook for your business."

STEVE: Well, let me say something about this business of projecting cash flow. I deal with two kinds of situations. One is the typical industrial company where you are going to be very hard put to get them to predict with any degree of confidence their cash flows beyond a certain period. The other is the commodities business where anyone can look at some of these metal companies and say, "Look, I know exactly what your capacity is, and if the copper prices are X cents a ton, then you are going to make this. If they are Y cents a ton, you are going to make that." You can do a very neat cash flow based on your projections.

Well, I have found one thing about copper prices. I know as much about it as anyone in America because I have dealt with the experts, and they will all disclaim any predictive ability—zero. And the estimates of those experts range all over. So we are all in the same damn boat.

JOEL: There is one easy way to judge whether companies really have confidence in their predictions. And that is, when you see these companies stop making new capital investments in the copper industry until they see a change in the copper price. You can tell me all you like that the buyer of a Kennecott Copper foresees tremendous improvements in copper prices, and that is what justifies the premium paid. But if that really is the case, how come he is not investing in huge capital expansion once he takes over Kennecott Copper? Why wasn't Sohio operating to expand their business rapidly if they thought the copper price was about to go up? After all, if higher prices are just around the corner, they better have a smelter ready.

STEVE: Maybe they thought they had sufficient capacity onstream already.

JOEL: No.

STEVE: What do you mean no?

JOEL: They stopped it overnight. They just cut everything off. They stopped expanding. Zero. No investment at all.

JUD: Maybe a financially stronger firm can take that risk where a financially weaker firm can't.

JOEL: A financially weaker firm can always issue new shares if they have got new investments which the market knows have good prospects.

STEVE: The point I was trying to make is that you will get a range of prognostication about copper prices. One analyst could predict 80 cents, another $1.60. And you could take any kid in the tenth grade with a computer and come back with a good cash flow just plugging in those prices. But that doesn't give you any more certainty about where copper prices are going to be. Establishing the value of those commodities is really a highly subjective matter.

JOEL: There is one bit more of certainty that you *can* get, and that is by observing whether or not people are willing to buy and sell at a particular price. If you happen to think that the price is going to be a lot higher, and the current stock price does not reflect that information, you will be a buyer of that stock until it gets to the level where you would just about break even. My point is that current stock prices of copper companies reflect a certain outlook for copper prices. If you believe that your outlook is different, fine, then go out and buy the company. But when you go out and buy that company, it will be interesting for us all to be told that the reason you're buying Kennecott is that you think copper prices are going to turn around—when the market doesn't think so.

STEVE: Wait a minute. You didn't need to be told that. No one was buying copper or oil stocks without believing that there was going to be a resurgence in prices.

PETER: Wait, this is very different from what you said before. What you said before was that you bought because the *current price* doesn't reflect the value of those assets *now, today*. That is different from saying that the value is going to be higher in the future. Now, you're just saying that the bidding companies want to get that oil or copper before the price goes up. That's different from what you said earlier.

JUD: No, but their view of the stock has to reflect their view of the basic price of the commodity.

PETER: If you tell me they have better information about the supply and demand in that market, and thus about future prices for the commodity, that is fine. I can accept that. But don't tell me they buy it because it is undervalued *given the current information*. That is a very different argument. And that is what we were hearing earlier today.

STEVE: I would accept that the current value of a copper company should logically be a discounted stream of expected future earnings, and that calculation could be fairly simple. But when you start looking five years out over the next cycle, and then you start factoring in all the political questions, like the regulation of mines in less developed countries and so on—what I am telling you is that you can get an enormous range of "guesstimates" as to where copper is likely to be selling. So, I am saying rational man X can take a conservative point of view, and rational man Y can take a much more optimistic view. And someone else can say, "I am willing to buy based on my in-between kind of appraisal." But this price may still be appreciably higher than the conservative estimate built into the current market price.

DIVERSIFICATION REVISITED _____

JUD: You see an interesting phenomenon in some of these conglomerate acquisitions or mergers—the ones undertaken for diversification. And I don't know what the ultimate impact on value is. But one of the interesting side questions from DuPont and Conoco is: Who follows the stock now? If the answer is that both the chemical analysts and the oil analysts will follow only their segments of the company, then it is much more cumbersome to write their research reports.

JOEL: Jud, are you suggesting that because the analyst that follows the company may not be well versed in all of the company's operations, the company's stock price may not be right? The problem with that view is that it is then possible for somebody else to come along, develop the skills necessary to value both kinds of operations, and make a lot of money for his clients. The process itself would eventually force the prices right back to their fair value. The argument that things are too complicated for the market to be able to price them correctly means that all that is necessary to make huge amounts of money in the market is to improve on the quality of the information. That seems like a very low cost to companies to allow them dramatically to improve their stock price.

JUD: What I was saying is that there will be some confusion in research departments, some reorientation as to who is going to follow the company. It may now require two analysts in two different disciplines to follow the same company. Coordinating their work to come up with a joint recommendation could be more difficult.

PETER: Yes, but that brings us back to our earlier question. It is hard for academics like us, people on the outside, to understand what the possible efficiency gains from those combinations are. The two analysts who follow that stock much more carefully than I do, and know the stock much better than other people—if they have trouble seeing what addition to value has been made, then how are we to understand the reason for these conglomerate mergers? I don't accept most of the explanations given by management.

JUD: One possibility we haven't talked about at all—I raised this analyst thing as sort of a side point—is management's measure of the risks in their business.

PETER: Measure of risk, or their preference for risk?

JUD: Both. Let's consider the DuPont-Conoco transaction (and although we were on the Conoco side of this deal, we have done a lot of work over the years for DuPont and still do). From DuPont's point of view, one could make the case—though I am not making it—that management wanted a more secure source of raw material, one that was less subject to the very cyclical pricing of that raw material. They might have decided that is a better long-term way to run their business than to be at the mercy of a raw material that was in short supply, or subject to very volatile price swings.

Perhaps for other structural reasons, those price swings could not be passed through into the price of the final product, thus making their bottom line very unstable.

BILL: Couldn't they sign a long-term contract?

JUD: But that is different than having the direct access to supplies.

DAN: Yes, but that is just the diversification argument in a slightly different form. Why do the shareholders care if the earnings stream is irregular?

JUD: I am not sure I know, but they seem to.

DAN: Well, you see, that same shareholder can buy a share in another company. By buying a lot of different stocks, he himself can even out the earnings stream of his portfolio of combined companies at a much lower cost—without having to pay this premium to do it.

JUD: And yet analysts and portfolio managers tend to like companies that don't show volatile earnings, that show steadily growing earnings. And, though I am really out of my element here, that is, on how stocks perform from an analyst's or portfolio manager's point of view—I nevertheless think those stocks that an analyst or a portfolio manager feels have a higher degree of predictability over time will probably do better than the sum of the two cyclical stocks over that same period of time. They will view it as a less risky investment.

OWNERSHIP AND CONTROL

STEVE: Let me ask Peter a question. We spent a lot of time on oil, but let me just go back to an example there. Let's say you had the opportunity to invest in a company where management said, "The company is owned by a philanthropic trust. This trust will not be liquidated. This company will not be sold. We can establish to your satisfaction that we have $100 million worth of reserves. All cash flow from these reserves will be reinvested in exploration in perpetuity, and you will never receive a dividend. Every single cent in cash flow will go into growing assets." That is case A. In case B you can invest in the exact same company and management says, "We are economic men. We are going to invest every cent in developing assets, but we are going to tell you that no later than the seventh year that if we see really fantastic ebullience, overoptimism about oil prices, we are going to liquidate the company between now and the seventh year." Which one would you pay more for?

PETER: Well, the way you put the question, I would always pay more for the second because that option to liquidate is always valuable. But, that is too simple a . . .

STEVE: You see, I have learned a lot here. I can load hypotheses with the best of them.

PETER: That is the part that worries me. But, to return to case A, where they will never pay a dividend . . .

STEVE: I meant that. There will never be a dividend. I am taking cash flow out of it. You are building wealth that you can't get your hands on. I am trying to take a pure case. In the other case, case B, you are assured the assets will be sold, and the proceeds distributed. What I am suggesting to you—and this is obviously an extreme form—case A is obviously what you face, though in a less extreme form, when you buy 100 shares of a stock. Case B is the case if I, as an entrepreneur, buy control of that company. I can lay my hands on that wealth.

JOEL: Are you implying, then, that the managers of these companies really don't act in the interest of their shareholders?

STEVE: No. I think they believe that they are acting in the longer-term interest of the shareholders. But what I am trying to say is that the enhanced ability to get your hands on the underlying wealth leads to an enormous premium in the value. You folks keep on talking about "premiums," but people will in fact pay more for control. Forget the public market. If it is a private company...

JOEL: Yes, but they must be willing to pay more only if they expect that their returns on their outlay are going to be worth paying those premiums to get control, correct?

STEVE: The returns, or the potential returns, or the degree of control. If you forget a public market, and you say, "Jud, you go sell 49 percent of this company," or you say, on the other hand, "Jud, I will give you the choice of selling 49 or 51 percent, where are you going to get me more on a pro rata basis?" The answer to that question is very easy.

PETER: That is an important issue. I happen to believe that the market for corporate control is one of the essential elements that makes the corporate system survive—your ability to buy and sell shares and ownership in companies. If you set up the corporate system such that there is this perpetual management which can never be changed or influenced, then buying corporate shares would be a very different investment. You would have very different pricing and very different supply and demand conditions in that market. A competitive market for corporate control gives managers a strong incentive to look out for the interests of stockholders. That is a very essential and reassuring business.

STEVE: We all agree on that. I am just trying to overcome your reaction as I earlier perceived it. Now I am trying to say that control, as opposed to ownership, of a corporation has an enormous, quantifiable value. There is a hell of a big difference between what can you get for 51 percent, and what can you get for 49 percent.

PETER: That doesn't explain the premiums we see. At every point in time, there are potential bidders coming in to take over control of the company. And the price should reflect that possibility. The fact that actual bidders don't always materialize doesn't explain to me why the price, as you claim, is undervalued. Because someone else can take control. There is always a potential every day for somebody else to come and take control. And that possibility—the existence of this market for corporate control—should ensure that, on average, the price is not undervalued. Only the possibility of synergies or efficiency gains can make the company more valuable to the bidder than it is to the market at large.

STEVE: Say it is a private company. You own 51 percent and I own 49 percent. There are no bidders that are going to come in. Either you are going to sell, or I am going to sell, or we both are going to sell. You know there is no bidder, there is no public market. You are going to get a hell of a lot more than the 2 percent difference for your 51 percent than I am going to get for my 49 percent.

PETER: Only if I can get much more than 2 percent more of the future cash flows from the firm than you can.

STEVE: No, no.

PETER: If I am restricted by law to pay everything out equally.

STEVE: Absolutely not. No, that is not so.

PETER: Tell me how you get more than me.

STEVE: This should be intuitively obvious. If a potential bidder has the option of buying your 51 percent or my 49 percent, it is true that the buyer of your 51 percent is only going to get 2 percent more of the dividends. But he will also have the ability to decide three years on what he wants to do with the business. He has the choice, the right to make decisions. He might, for example, think there is a wildly exaggerated view of the prospects of oil companies. And he might want to sell this business. He might not want to drill on such and such basin. He has the right to say, "I don't like deep sand, I like shallow sand. I want to stop exploring, I want to start paying the dividends." The crucial difference is that the extra 2 percent gives him control, and that is worth more than just 2 percent of the cash flow.

JOEL: Yes, but that's because you're assuming that your decisions will create more value than the ones the existing management is now making. That is what makes the difference. It's not the *right* to make the decisions, it's the *quality* of the decisions themselves. If you can't improve on the existing management's performance, then you would have no reason to bid a premium for control. The control, in that case, would not be worth any more to you than to existing management. And the value of existing management's decision-making capability is reflected by the stock market every day.

INVESTMENT BANKING FEES _____

JOEL: I would like to turn to one final topic because I know Jeff has to leave. As long as we have got three of you in the room, I find one thing that really bothers me a great deal. I am very concerned about the form in which investment bankers get compensated for these transactions. (Incidentally, I expect to look very different after we get finished talking about this.) I would like to understand better why, in the investment banking business, success essentially pays for the failures. That is, if you don't execute a transaction, the bulk of the fee does not get paid. But if you do execute the transaction, the fee can be quite enormous. How does that arrangement serve the interest of the shareholders in those companies? Why shouldn't you simply be saying, "Our time costs us so much, and we will bill you on an hourly basis, I don't care what kind of transaction it is"? Does it actually cost you more to do a $200 million transaction than to do, say, a $5 billion transaction? Why should the fee be determined by the size of the deal?

The reason I say that to you is that I have an attitude, frankly, with regard to my dentist. I don't know anything about what is going on in my mouth. So when I go to my dentist, I say, "Murray, I have got a deal for you. I will pay you $500 a year. It is much higher than you would expect to get otherwise. I want you to take care of anything that goes wrong in my mouth for $500. But, Murray, I want you to know that after each visit, I go from you to another dentist. And if he finds there is anything wrong with my mouth, you are in big trouble. So take good care of my mouth." Why shouldn't that be the attitude that is used by investment bankers on M & A?

JEFF: It is very simple, Joel. Very simple. It is an outcome of our free market system, of arms-length negotiations between us and our clients.

JOEL: How can you afford to tell the client, "We think Marathon Oil is a crazy transaction. It is not worth it"? Because it will hurt your fee if you don't do the transaction?

JUD: Joel, you're taking a very short-run view of your mouth.

STEVE: How could someone who has such a touching faith in markets be so cynical about investment banking when you know that it is a very competitive business, with a number of very, very efficient and capable investment banking firms? And, remember, they are dealing, in every case, with clients who have far superior bargaining power. So if they are not happy with the relationship—and believe me there are no questions you are raising that all of us don't hear a number of times a month—if, in their minds, they were not satisfied that there was enough integrity in the firms they were dealing with to argue with them when they thought they were doing something wrong, there is no scarcity of people down the street they can go to.

DAN: I am with these guys. I don't believe in regulation of fees.

STEVE: Since you agree with me, Dan, and we haven't agreed on anything yet today, I think I had better reexamine my position on this.

DAN: I don't believe in regulation of fee-setting at all. I think if you can get somebody to pay whatever you are asking, and they do it voluntarily, that is far better than when there is some kind of government control over what you can charge.

JOEL: Dan, I don't disagree with you. I am simply trying to understand why the fee structure has tended in this direction instead of a flat fee.

STEVE: They want to pay for results. They know they have their ultimate finger on the trigger. They have no fear that we are going to cram something down their throats. And, face it, they happen to be dealing by now with a firm that they are convinced has integrity.

DAN: The rationale for this fee structure may have a lot to do with the fact that there are, on average, large gains in these transactions, for buyers as well as sellers. Therefore, somebody who can facilitate these gains taking place on a contingent basis deserves a higher reward than somebody who, for whatever reason, screws up and the deal falls through. And I also agree with what Jud and Steve said on this. The long-term reputational interest of the firm, in terms of repeat business, is a sufficient guarantee against the moral hazard problem of recommending terrible deals in order to get fees. As you say, you won't be on the street very long if you do that.

TENDER OFFER LEGISLATION _____

JOEL: Dan, since you are our representative from the Law School, I want to ask you a specific question about the new legislation of tender offers. What is your impression of the new SEC procedure on two-tier tender offers?

DAN: I think it is hard to analyze these questions without having a theory of what tender offers accomplish and what regulation of tender offers accomplishes. The position that I have taken in a number of papers is that the situation that existed prior to the passage of the Williams Act was the most desirable from the perspective of investors as a whole. That was, in effect, a world of pure freedom of contract. Then you could say, "I am offering to buy X percent of the shares of your firm." I could set the terms, I could set the time at which people had a chance to sell. I could say it was on a first-come, first-serve basis. I could say if people didn't sell in the first hour, the price the second hour would be one dollar less, and it would decrease one dollar per hour. That situation is, in effect, no different from what now prevails in the real estate market, or any other commodity market. We don't have regulation of bargaining terms there.

Now, the reason why I think that is desirable is the following. We have a lot of empirical evidence that tender offers and mergers create gains, create value, for investors. What regulation does, in effect, is to impose a tax on those gains. And as a result, as with any tax, the result of that regulation is that there will be less desirable activity taking place than without the tax. This problem is compounded by the ability of lawyers and investment bankers, during these waiting periods, to also take a share of the gain in these negotiation processes. From my perspective, that is a pure deadweight loss to society. It serves no allocative function whatsoever.

BILL: My impression is that the average premium has gone up substantially since the Williams Act. One interpretation of that is only the really profitable transactions occur now. The ones that would have been profitable before are not profitable now, and thus don't occur.

STEVE: I think the market has a unique perspective. Did it occur to you that the size of those premiums might have something to do with the direction in which assets were going, and the direction which stock prices were going most of the periods since then?

PETER: They have been going in the same direction.

STEVE: Would you be interested if someone told you empirically that people talking about making tender offers really do start out with a notion that they want to buy this company?

BILL: They are not paying more for it than they think they have to. They are not going to pay a higher premium for it than they absolutely think they have to, to actually engage in a transaction. You are not going to tell them to pay $65 if they could buy it for $50.

My point is that, if you didn't have to go through all this costly legal rigamarole, maybe you wouldn't have to pay so much to buy the company. You could get it for $50 instead of $65. It means that when tender offers take place, a lot more of the gains are going to go to the target shareholders, and a lot less to the bidding company shareholders, than before the regulation.

And if you have to pay $65 instead of $50 to buy that company, well then, a lot of companies are just not going to make tender offers. There will be less tender offers than there would have been otherwise. And that means that a lot of companies that might have been taken over are not going to be. And that makes the values of a lot of those companies *less*, not more, than they would have been. You've just made the market for corporate control that much less efficient by regulating tender offers, and the net result to society is that stockholder wealth is *reduced*, not increased. Stock prices are lower, not higher, because tender offers are less profitable for the buying companies. And those investors that you think you're trying to protect are actually worse off, on net, because of this legislation.

JUD: I think there is another explanation for these higher premiums, one other than the Williams Act. It is more sociological than rational. But that is something that markets factor in, too. Ten years ago, for whatever reasons, and maybe they were irrational reasons, a lot of companies wouldn't make hostile tender offers. They just didn't think it was right. It wasn't an accepted way of doing business. You got thrown out of your country club. Your friends wouldn't play golf with you. There was a human factor there.

JOEL: How do you spend your time now?

JUD: They let me back in a couple of years ago, because the number of people willing to make hostile tender offers is a lot greater than it was in 1973.

PETER: In fact, in the fifties you didn't find any at all. It emerged only in the last twenty years as a way of changing control of the corporation.

STEVE: It is more recent than the last twenty years. And much of it was after the Williams Bill. If the Williams Bill had a chilling effect, you wouldn't have seen this profusion of tender offers since 1968.

PETER: No, you can't say that.

STEVE: Why not?

PETER: Bill's point is that you don't know how many tender offers there would have been in the absence of the Williams Bill. The rise in the average premium might indicate that many of the less profitable tender offers under consideration never occurred. So that an even larger number of tender offers would have happened if the Williams Bill and similar state regulations had not been part of the law.

EPS DILUTION

JOEL: I want to ask you all one last question on a different subject. One was given the impression in the 1960s and early 1970s that the tools being used to evaluate mergers and acquisitions were based on an accounting-oriented model of the firm. More specifically, on earnings per share, and effects on EPS. When a high P/E bought a low P/E company, the EPS went up and that was good. If a low P/E bought a high P/E company with an exchange of shares, the EPS went down and that was bad. That was called "dilution" of earnings per share.

PETER: Boot-strapping.

JOEL: Yes. Earnings leverage and all of that stuff. What was interesting is that when A bought B, that was good. When B bought A that was bad. Somehow it seemed to escape the detection of these analysts that AB and BA were the same company after the transaction. So it appeared that the structure of the transaction was very important, and that we should carefully manage the EPS effects of the deal. Do you think that that was ever true? Do you think it is true now? Or do you think that the economic value of the enterprise is what matters, the discounted cash-flow analysis that most companies now use? Jud, what do you think?

JUD: Well, I entered this business seventeen years ago. The first three or four years I was buried in a bunch of statistical stuff and really did not have the opportunity to see how decision makers were making their decisions. But certainly the literature and the press at the time seemed to say what you were saying. There was a lot of acquisition activity. And it seemed to be driven by the desire to increase reported earnings per share. I don't think that the analysis of some of those acquisitions was as sophisticated as it is today.

JOEL: There were certain accounting opinions that seemed to have been put in place by pressure from potential target companies. For example, if you do a deal using something other than common equity, you will have to amortize goodwill. Purchase versus pooling. That seemed to have come in during the heyday of these acquisitions. Many people, frankly, were afraid of being acquired, and they thought that if they could put an accounting stumbling block in the way, that would stop it from taking place. Now, if amortization of goodwill is a non-tax, non-cash expense and what matters is how much you pay for something, but not how you record it afterwards, that impact should have been negligible.

JUD: Well, I think, in the real world, accounting has an impact. People look at an earnings per share number, a net income number, and they take that number as an indicator of value. They run with it, if you will. Others might look behind it and say, "Well, gee, this guy's earnings have a higher quality than this other guy's for these reasons."

JOEL: The big question is whether or not the lead steer is looking at EPS, or real underlying economic value—cash profitability.

JUD: But I would say that structure—how you put A and B together— does have an impact on the value of that company as an ongoing concern. Because if you do it in the wrong way, it is not just an accounting issue. It is really a matter of financial strength and capitalization. How is cash flow going to be used, and what kind of cash flow is available for financing? Is the company overcapitalized or undercapitalized after the transaction? Those all can affect the value of the firm over time. It may change the risk profile.

JOEL: I am not talking about whether the transaction is financed with debt or equity. One may be less expensive than the other for whatever tax reasons are involved, and hence the method of financing may have a real economic impact. I am talking about those transactions that were designed for the purpose of achieving a certain EPS effect. Those where management says, "We will not use common equity to buy that company because we are paying a P/E higher than our own. However, if we use cash that was raised by borrowing money, and it helps our EPS (ignoring all tax consequences), we can do it that way. Otherwise we cannot do the transaction at all." That is the issue I want to address. Do people still think this way?

JUD: Dilution is an issue because people are concerned that the market is going to look at it. But it is not the key issue. The time frame for dilution is important. Important questions include: How soon an acquisition will earn out? and, if there is initial dilution, when does it end? and what are the future positive earnings benefits?

STEVE: No, Joel, you have much too simplistic a model. Fundamental economics, I think, have assumed a much greater role than perhaps they did twelve or fifteen years ago. I think there were, and still are, some accounting and financial approaches which, to me, make no damn sense at all. This whole dilution thing is a good example. It took years to get someone to understand that, when you have preferred convertible stock that could be converted at any second, fully diluted earnings per share was a more meaningful concept than primary earnings per share. But people persisted in this supposedly rational market—persisted for a long time in looking at primary EPS. I agree with you totally about this accounting principle making them amortize the goodwill. To a much greater extent, people have moved away from those oversimplistic views.

It is also simplistic, though, to say that it is a dilution-driven analysis. Dilution is a fact of life. We talk to the head of our research department, and we ask, "What is going to be the impact on their stock if they do this?" We have cases where they said to the buying company, "You are going to need a 20 percent pickup in earnings per share for your stock price to stay even because this makes so little damn sense to the market. That may be the price you have to pay to consummate a good deal."

JOEL: You are saying that the company will have to improve EPS by a certain amount to overcome the dilution of the transaction?

STEVE: The accounting numbers are used to form a judgment about how the market is going to respond to the announcement of the acquisition. In the case I just cited, our research said that a 20 percent pickup in earnings per share is going to give you a "break even" of stock price. We have another case where we looked at the earnings per share dilution, and what is of profound importance is what the analysts think is going to be the "break even" *time*—that is, how long will it take for the dilution to go out of the system. Indeed, you must be assuming that this target company is going to grow faster than you, otherwise why would you be paying way over your own multiple for that company?

JOEL: I don't like to describe it that way. I realize that M & A people talk about growth as opposed to earning adequate returns on investment.

STEVE: Yes, we are talking about growth. You have to look at a whole range of things. So permit me to concentrate on the one that we are addressing at the moment which is...

JOEL: But if you are using DCF analysis, the value of that growth is accounted for. There's no need to even talk about growth in EPS; the value of growth—provided it's profitable growth—is reflected in the DCF calculation. That's all taken into consideration.

STEVE: Wait a minute. We are talking about looking at a whole bunch of different things. And one of the things you want to form a judgment on is what the stock price is going to be. That should be of tremendous importance to *you* because you are putting even more emphasis on it than we are. And what I am trying to do is diminish in your mind the importance of dilution. I am taking one case in which, even if you have an 18 percent pickup in EPS, we are saying your stock will still suffer. I will give you another case—a real-life case—where we had a 16 percent dilution in the trailing twelve-month earnings. It was a case where we had important relations on both sides of the transaction. One side had us swear on blood, "We think your stock will hold steady because we think people will be willing to give you credit for the company's growth prospects. (And, yes, Joel, those growth prospects back into higher return on investment. But that is a different, though related, question.) We think this will actually cause your stock to appreciate as people gradually take the fudge factor out, and become totally convinced of it." So, obviously, considerations of dilution are not the major factor driving acquisition and merger activity.

JOEL: Yes, but there is another problem. Consider the case of a Hewlett-Packard, which sells at a very high P/E ratio. And suppose that your stock sells at, say, nine or ten times earnings. Is it true, then, that the M & A people would never seriously consider a Hewlett-Packard because it commands a high P/E—because of the effect on EPS?

STEVE: Wait a minute, Joel. I have just given you an example where that was not true. By definition, if our client acquired someone in a pooling that diluted its trailing twelve-month earnings by 16 percent, it had to be paying a lot higher multiple than its own.

JOEL: Why are you looking at the *trailing* anything in the evaluation of this company?

STEVE: Well, you are not only looking at the trailing. The trailing happens to have the virtue of being the most recent earnings per share number about which you can be certain. Once you start going out forward, you get an increasing degree of uncertainty. But, obviously, you don't look only at trailing earnings, because they would say to you, "Why does your analysis shut off there?" So you have to be looking at two lines: Where does your EPS break even compared to where you would have been if you hadn't acquired the company? And, then, how certain am I that the lines are going to cross because the acquired company has a higher expected growth rate? How long will it take for those two lines to cross? These are the major considerations.

JOEL: I was reading in the *Wall Street Journal* that a firm called Morgan Stanley discounts the net cash benefits to the buyer over time back to a current value. That number is called the "estimated fair value of the transaction." If you do it that way, it seems to me that the so-called EPS or accounting issues are essentially irrelevant.

STEVE: Would you still feel the same way if Morgan Stanley's research department said, "You know, we are sorry to have to say this, but a great many pension fund managers are not yet sophisticated enough to buy this theory. They are still operating on a voodoo kind of stock picking mode, and the stock is going to fall 25 percent because of the dilution of earnings per share"?

JOEL: Peter Dodd would be especially uncomfortable about that, and I will tell you why. Because the research findings that date back only about fifty-six years seem to indicate that markets were quite capable—even fifty-six years ago—of looking at the underlying economic value of a transaction. That is, they looked at cash as opposed to accounting, bookkeeping entries. The market was just as sophisticated then. That is not to say that many people are not unsophisticated. Just that there are enough people with enough wealth who are sophisticated enough so that transactions take place on a sophisticated basis.

The fact is, you happen to be engaging in transactions where you are saying to yourself, "We better be careful about the accounting implications because the market out there may be unsophisticated." Are you ready for the last surprise of all? The people who have been supporting the research of these academic scholars and their colleagues for about the last twenty-five years have principally been the investment banking firms and the brokerage firms.

STEVE: Would I be able to understand the calculus in these research reports?

JOEL: Once a year, representatives of the firms who support the research are invited to a research center—whether it is MIT or Carnegie Mellon or Chicago or Stanford—and the academic scholars review for them, in non-technical terms, the results of their research. Why do they do that? Because they want to continue receiving funds, and they know if Jud and Steve don't understand what they are doing, they are unlikely to vote at their firms to continue funding the research. Therefore, you can be darn sure the people understand the research findings. And you know what is fascinating, no matter what the research findings seem to show consistently over time—research by Peter Dodd or Eugene Fama or Bill Schwert—it seems to be contrary to the advice that merger and acquisition specialists are giving their clients about what the engine is that drives share prices.

STEVE: Well, you know we have an advantage that you don't have. We have the record of the advice we have given clients about the likely impact on their stock prices of particular transactions. Very often, when we say to our research people, "Now look, there are certain things that we know, and that our client knows, about the likely future course of these two companies. But, for SEC and other reasons, we are not going to be able to tell the market all these things. So we don't want to tell you either because, to use our phrase, we don't want you to be 'more knowledgeable' than the market. Because if you are 'more knowledgeable,' then your predictive abilities will be no damn good." And we have found if the research people know more than we are able to tell the market, it does influence their opinions. But by telling him essentially what we are able to tell the market—and with whatever arcane techniques they use, very few of which are as sophisticated as the ones you are talking about—our research people tend to have a very good feel on whether the stock prices are going to go up or down, and by how much.

PETER: I want to comment on what Joel said. We have strong evidence that accounting numbers *do* convey information. They are a strong proxy for underlying cash flows, and the things we use to value firms. Accounting does matter.

But the dilution question is a very different issue. Your research people at Goldman, Steve, seem to be assuming there is this "functional fixation" on the EPS number. That is, the market will mechanically and uncritically take this EPS number and assign a standard multiple to it. And that is a very different statement—one that I find very hard to believe.

STEVE: Yes, but I'm not completely disagreeing with you on this. We are telling you that the markets are most sophisticated now than they were in the late sixties. The markets are more willing to tolerate dilution if they see sensible underlying reasons for it. Therefore, we are saying to our clients, "Here is our prediction. Here is what we think the market will do." At the same time, we are saying the market will be more tolerant of dilution if there is a sensible reason for it.

JOEL: Some years ago I had the opportunity to work closely with the senior management of Litton Industries. And they were kind enough to provide me with memos that dated well back into the early sixties and late fifties on the evaluation of their investment opportunities—their mergers and acquisitions. It turned out that there were two things going on simultaneously with Litton's acquisitions, either of which may have helped their stock price to rise the way it did. One, they expected to earn very high rates of return on these projects based on the price they were going to pay. And, two, the fact that they were a high P/E company buying a lower P/E company meant an automatic increase in EPS.

The reason I think Litton Industries sold at forty times earnings then was not because of the EPS effect, but because they demonstrated a consistent ability to synergize, to energize the assets they acquired. That is what led to their high P/E. True, they bought low P/E companies. But, why were the companies selling at low P/Es? Because they didn't have the same quality management. And when Litton Industries took them over they improved it. So, from examples like Litton, many analysts looked at this spurious correlation between artificially higher EPS and higher stock prices, and they concluded that the market mechanically responds to the EPS number. And, from the same kind of evidence assembled by the unaided eye, people concluded, "Well, if you want to have a high stock price and a high P/E ratio, don't you ever buy companies that have a high P/E going in—because that will hurt your EPS."

STEVE: Joel, before we close, can I make a suggestion about why these people fund this research, and then never listen to it? I have a little story to tell that I think has something to do with this.

When I used to dig wells in the country, I would hire a dowser. And he would come with his two birch rods...he would walk around like so...

Now, did I deep down really believe it was going to work? No. But he was such a silver-tongued devil that I just thought he might be worth the $150 I shelled out for him.

JOEL: What you are really saying is that his entertainment value to you was very high.

STEVE: Well, you learn how to price your product...You know the other thing he told us that was just fascinating? He said you will find water here...at between 195 and 200 feet. And I was amazed at the touching faith he had in that precision.

JOEL: How close did he come?

STEVE: We found water at 300 feet.

JOEL: Well, there it is. I want to thank you all very much for coming.

COMMENTARY: HOW TO VALUE AN ACQUISITION, OR DON'T GIVE AWAY THE STORE
by Joel M. Stern

Overpaying for an acquisition is one of the most reliable methods of reducing a company's stock price. One classic example was the $5 fall in the price of DuPont's stock when the acquisition bid for Conoco was announced. Another was the $3 fall in the price of Xerox stock following the announcement of the bid for Crum and Forster. Had these and other companies understood how the market responds to acquisition pricing, and had these managements known the potential loss of wealth they were inflicting on their shareholders, perhaps the acquisition price would have been lower or the deal turned away.

While the immediate response of the stock market to an acquisition, as measured by the change in the stock price of the acquiring company, may seem to some a rather short-sighted method of judging an acquisition, there is good reason to rely on the market's "snap" judgment. Sophisticated market players evaluate the total value received by the acquiring company and weigh that value received against the total value paid. And the values paid and received are based on the market's best guess of the long-run performance of the merged companies. The market is taking a view of future performance and placing a value on it today.

While some acquisitions which the market judges as value-damaging do become successful in the long run, others that the market judges as value-enhancing are not successful in the long run. This does not mean that market evaluation of the acquisition should be ignored. Academic research indicates that the market is an "unbiased predictor" of the success of an acquisition. That is, the market's initial response to an acquisition is a fallible evaluation, but not one that is prone to consistent over- or underestimates of future value. Furthermore, the market's initial evaluation reflects the interplay of many sophisticated investors putting their money on the line. A stock price change provides a measure of the acquisition's value added (or value lost) that managements ignore at their peril and that shareholders, certainly, cannot ignore.

The focus of this article, then, is to examine how to value acquisitions so that one can anticipate whether the acquisition will result in an immediate gain or loss of wealth for the shareholders of the acquiring company. Even in the face of a potentially severe fall in their stock price, some managements will undoubtedly decide to go ahead with value-damaging acquisitions, betting against the market. But prudent managements will make an acquisition bid only after they have carefully considered the likely response that the stock market will inflict on their shareholders if they are perceived to have paid too much.

VALUE RECEIVED MINUS VALUE PAID

In a straightforward manner, the stock market's response to an acquisition bid is nothing more than its assessment of whether the total value received by the acquiring company exceeds the total value paid. If the value received fails to measure up to the value surrendered, then the stock price of the acquiring firm falls.

Conceptually, the value received may be divided into two components: (1) the stand-alone value of the target company and (2) the anticipated value added by the financial and operating benefits of the merger, often known as "synergy." The value paid also can be divided into two components: (1) the current market value of the target company plus (2) the premium paid over the market value. Net Value Added (Lost) is merely the difference between value received and value paid.

(1)   Net Value Added (Lost) = Value Received − Value Paid,

or,

(2)   Net Value Added (Lost) = Stand-Alone Value + Synergy
                                                  − Market Value − Premium

From the arrangement of terms on the right side of equation (2) one can see that value can be created in either of two ways. First, one could identify acquisition targets for which the stand-alone value exceeds the market value. Second, one could seek target firms in which the expected synergies are greater than the premium required.

The first of these methods essentially requires the buyer to discover an "undervalued" company and acquire it without giving the value away in the premium paid over the market value. A whole host of sophisticated investors are constantly searching for such companies, and rarely does the market so misprice a company that large premiums can be paid and still leave the acquiring firm with any value added. We would be skeptical about such "bargain hunting" as a acquisition strategy. We prefer to begin with the premise that the stand-alone value of the target firm equals its market value, unless a strong case can be made to the contrary. Stated another way, we accept that the market has fairly valued the target company as a stand-alone entity.

Given this assumption, then a value-adding acquisition is one in which the expected synergies exceed the premium paid. Thus, the critical part of evaluating an acquisition is placing a value on the expected synergies. In general, synergies can be divided into two categories: (1) financial synergies, which include tax and leverage benefits; and (2) operating synergies, which may result from more efficient operations due to scale increases, to improved management, or to other business benefits resulting from the merger.

VALUE FINANCIAL SYNERGIES

There are two primary sources of financial synergy that deserve explicit treatment. They include (1) the value of changing the capital structure of the acquiring and the acquired firms, and (2) tax benefits to the acquirer from changes in plant and inventory valuations in the target firm.

Recapitalization Benefits

The structure of an acquisition deal, whether by an exchange of shares, by a cash payment financed by debt, or by some mixture of debt and equity, generally results in a new capital structure for both the acquiring and the acquired firm. This has an immediate impact on the value of both firms separately and on their value as a combined unit.

Capital structure, as embodied in the choice of debt versus equity financing, is an important element in the valuation of a firm because the interest on debt is tax deductible. The prudent use of debt provides a tax shield that saves cash and adds value. That is, within limits the use of debt financing effectively reduces the total cost of capital to the firm.

There is, however, a reduction in the firm's financial flexibility that comes with the increase in the debt-to-equity ratio of the firm. Firms operating in stable businesses can often carry more debt. Firms in high-risk businesses, on the other hand, find that as leverage increases, the financial risks that are added are not worth the benefits of a higher tax shield from the use of debt over equity.

Recognizing the role of capital structure in the valuation of a firm leads to several issues in analyzing an acquisition. First, an acquisition may result in a change in the capital structure of the acquiring firm. The acquisition is the motivating force to which the company is responding when it alters its capital structure, but the capital structure could have been changed without the acquisition. The value of the firm would be affected in either case. Second, the acquired firm also may have its capital structure changed after the acquisition. And again, value is affected.

In the first case, where the acquiring firm's capital structure is altered, the value change must be viewed as independent of the acquisition. That is, there are other ways to change a capital structure than by an acquisition financed with debt—share repurchase, for example. Whatever value is created from the capital structure change should not, therefore, be credited to the acquisition.

For example, take a company with 20 percent debt-to-capital and a current cost of capital of 14.5 percent. Such a company might decide to alter its capital structure to 25 percent debt. Two adjustments must be considered to see the effect on the value of the firm, everything else remaining unchanged. First, the financial risk of the firm is increased, and this may result in a lower bond rating and a higher interest rate on the firm's new debt. Second, the greater use of debt will save on tax payments. In this case, assuming the company is in a low-risk business, the tax benefits are likely to outweigh the financial risk disadvantages by a wide margin, and typically might reduce the cost of capital to 14 percent from the original 14.5 percent. For a firm valued on the stock market at $1 billion, a reduction of fifty basis points in the cost of capital could result in an increase in total value of over $30 million.

When a relatively unleveraged company makes a large acquisition financed by adding debt, the change in the capital structure of the firm can easily be more dramatic than the previous example. And, if the immediate change in the capital structure is viewed as a permanent change, then the stock market will reflect the full value of the increased use of debt. This value should not be attributed to the acquisition, since the capital structure could have been altered without making the acquisition. To do so would incorrectly mix the financing decision (capital structure) with the investment decision (whether to make the acquisition).

The second recapitalizing effect is felt on the value of the target firm. If this recapitalization creates value, then this value can be appropriately used to justify the payment of a given premium over market value for the target firm.

When the target is acquired, it will come under the umbrella of the acquiring firm. Essentially, the target firm is recapitalized with the new debt structure of the parent firm. If a company uses debt to acquire a target, and the use of debt, including the consolidated position of the target, takes the company to a 25 percent debt-to-total capital ratio, then the target company must be revalued using the 25 percent ratio. This holds regardless of what the capital structure of the target company was before it was acquired.

If the target company's stand-alone use of debt stood at say 10 percent, less than that of the acquiring company's new capital structure, then the new value of the target company is likely to exceed its old value. Suppose the target company moves from a 10 percent to 25 percent debt structure. If the original cost of capital for the target was 15.0 percent, the increase in the debt ratio will lower the cost of capital to 14.0 percent. If the target was worth about $250 million in stand-alone value, then the recapitalization benefit would be around $20 million. This is an example of financial synergy that is properly included in the acquisition evaluation.

As an aside, what may be happening when the target company is recapitalized at a higher debt ratio is that the acquirer is using the debt capacity of the target firm to finance the acquisition. Hence, a corollary point is that to avoid a takeover, a potential target firm should maintain a high debt load.

Tax Synergies

In most acquisitions tax synergies are very important, and in leveraged buy-outs they are critical. Benefits to the acquirer arise because the target firm's inventories and plant and equipment can be revalued to save cash through tax reductions.

By writing up the value of inventories of the target firm, the acquiring firm reduces the taxable income that results when the inventories are sold. In some industries this can be a very substantial benefit. Also, the plant and equipment of the target company can be revalued at fair market value rather than at the historical costs as carried on the books of the target firm. This write-up of plant and equipment values then leads directly to higher depreciation charges, saving cash taxes. Depending on the form of the acquisition, these write-ups may also trigger a recapture tax liability, but generally the benefits outweigh the costs.

These tax benefits are not available to the target firm as a stand-alone entity. But at the time of the acquisition, the acquiring firm can allocate a portion of the premium it is paying to writing up the asset values. For example, in the case of the Brown-Forman acquisition of Lenox, the tax synergies represented around $29 million. As can be seen, tax synergies can be very substantial.

OPERATING SYNERGIES

Compared to the financial synergies, which can be calculated in a straightforward way, the operating synergies involve extensive judgment. The judgment comes in selecting the forward plan of the target company on which to place a value.

The market has placed a value on the target firm as a stand-alone entity. But the acquiring firm often feels that through economies of scale, improved management, increased marketing strength, or through any of a variety of operating factors, the target firm will produce a higher cash flow in the years after the acquisition than was possible as a stand-alone entity. The value of these increased cash flows represents the value ascribed to operating synergies.

In many cases, it pays to work backwards from the price of the acquisition to determine the implicit value being placed on operating synergies. For example, an acquiring firm may offer a 50 percent premium over today's share price to acquire the target firm. Based on relatively well-defined financial synergies, as described in previous sections, an offer of a 30 percent premium can be justified. The remaining premium must be justified by operating synergies. And if it is not, then the stock price of the acquiring firm will decline when the acquisition is announced.

In other words, one can calculate just how well the target firm must do in coming years for the premium to just equal the value received. That is, the forward plan that must be achieved just for the acquisition to break even in value terms can be examined to see if it is possible to achieve. And of course, if the operating synergies just equal the required amount, then the stockholders of the acquiring company are neither hurt nor helped. The stockholders of the target company get all the gains.

Operating synergies, because they involve the most judgment, are the prime areas to scrutinize before making an acquisition. In almost every case, there are substantial financial synergies for the acquiring company. But a healthy premium is paid to the target company's stockholders. Operating synergies must exceed the difference between the two previous factors, which are relatively "hard" numbers, before value can be created for the stockholders of the acquiring firm.

Calculating what is required in future performance by the target firm to justify a given premium can help immensely in avoiding value-damaging acquisitions. If the numbers look reasonable, then the acquisition may make good sense. But in many cases, the implied forward plan appears much too optimistic for the stock market to bear, and the immediate result is that the market writes down the value of the acquiring firm.

DON'T GIVE AWAY THE STORE

By comparing the total value received to the total value paid, the acquiring firm can make an educated guess as to the effect of an acquisition on its share price. Even where the financial synergies look compelling and operating synergies seem obvious, the deal will harm the shareholders of the acquiring company if the premium paid exceeds the value of the financial and operating synergies. What has happened is that all the benefits of the acquisition (plus some) have been captured by the shareholders of the target firm. There is nothing left over, in terms of value added, for the shareholders of the acquiring firm.

It does not have to be this way. For example, when GTE acquired Sprint,

GTE's stock price rose, as did the stock price of Southern Pacific, the seller from whom GTE bought Sprint. The acquisition made good business sense, and the deal was arranged so that both the buyer and the seller shared the benefits.

In the case of Heilemann Breweries acquiring Pabst, again, the share price of both the buyer and the seller rose after the announcement of the merger. The operating synergies made business sense and the value added was split between the buyer and seller.

Acquisitions are not generally zero-sum games. Value is created, but the question is who gets it. If the acquiring company get caught in a bidding war and allows emotions to rule, then the target company's shareholders may get all the benefits and then some. The shareholders of the acquiring company must shoulder this burden.

On the other hand, if the acquiring company makes an objective evaluation of the financial synergies and avoids an acquisition price that implies a terribly unrealistic forward plan for the target company, then the acquirer will know when to drop out of the bidding and let the deal collapse. To add value for the stockholders, management cannot allow itself to give away the store.

COMMENTARY:
IS BUYING BIG BAD?
A REVIEW OF 1984's BIGGEST M & A DEALS
by Timothy M. Koller

In 1984, thirteen U.S. companies made acquisitions valued at over one billion dollars each, spending an aggregate of $45.5 billion. Most of the major business periodicals have published year-end review articles describing the deals. These articles generally skip the economics of the big deals, however, to talk about the intrigue and personalities associated with the transactions. For example, *Institutional Investor* reported that Mobil's president William Tavoulareas, when in pursuit of Superior Oil, once registered in a Dallas hotel as "Mr. Brown"; a few days later he registered in Houston as "Mr. Taylor."[1]

As fascinating as this material is in its own right (and we were disappointed, incidentally, at not being informed of the names of the hotels housing Tavoulareas), our goal in this article is to examine a different issue: Did the deals make sense for the acquiring companies? For the most part, the answer coming from the stock market was "no." As a result of these thirteen acquisitions, the acquiring firms' shareholders saw the combined market value of their shares drop by $2.1 billion, or almost 5 percent of their prior value. Only two of the thirteen deals were favorably received by the stock market: Texaco's purchase of Getty Oil, and IBM's purchase of Rolm Corp. The market rejected the other eleven.

Of course the market is not always right, but it is right much more often than it is wrong. The preponderance of evidence shows that market prices are set by the interaction of sophisticated investors with considerable knowledge about the firms they are investing in and substantial amounts of their wealth tied to their investment performance. For this reason, we feel that executives of acquiring companies who systematically ignore the stock market's signals are probably not acting in their shareholders' best interests.

METHODS AND ACADEMIC FINDINGS

Before discussing the results of our study in more detail, let us describe our method. Simply stated, we evaluate an acquisition by looking at the acquiring company's share price reaction to the announcement of the deal. (This is the standard technique employed by academic researchers studying various economic events.) If the stock price goes up relative to the market, the acquisition adds value to the buyer. If the price declines, the acquirer overpaid.

The major assumption underlying the method is that the immediate stock price reaction to the announcement of the acquisition reflects the market's evaluation of the *long-term* effects of the transaction on the value of the acquiring company. In other words, the market is efficient in that all known information about the future prospects of the firm is reflected in the current share price. For example, when an oil company announces a major offshore oil discovery, its stock price will rise immediately, even though more than a decade of development work will probably pass before any oil can be sold from that well.

From reading the popular financial press, one would get the impression that the stock market cares only about the very short term, particularly next quarter's earnings. According to this view, an acquisition that reduces the accounting earnings of the acquirer in the short run will cause the acquirer's share price to decline even if the acquisition promises to be profitable over the long run. For example, in a recent *New York Times* article, the reporter dismissed the fall in Occidental Petroleum's share price upon the announcement of its proposed acquisition of Diamond Shamrock as follows: "No particular significance was attached to the price drop because the stocks of acquiring companies typically decline immediately after such announcements."[2] On the contrary, most studies have shown that, on average, the stock prices of acquiring firms *increase* upon the announcement of an acquisition. For example, the share prices of the following companies rose upon announcement of their major acquisitions: General Foods' purchase of Entenmann's, GTE's purchase of Sprint, and Heilemann's purchase of Pabst.[3] In a study of 161 successful tender offers, by Michael Bradley of the University of Michigan, 59 percent of the acquirers experienced price increases, while only 41 percent experienced price declines.[4] The results of most academic studies are consistent with Bradley's results.

Furthermore, the price reaction to the acquisition announcement is not transitory but permanent. In other words, on average the market's initial assessment of the value of an acquisition is correct, and the acquiring firm's share price does not return to its pre-announcement level (adjusted for overall changes in the market and the riskiness of the acquirer). Peter Dodd of the University of Chicago and Richard Ruback of the Massachusetts Institute of Technology studied the stock prices of acquiring firms for five years *after* the announcement of their acquisitions.[5] They found that an investor who had invested in these companies immediately after the announcement of the acquisitions and held for five years would have earned only average returns—the same return as investing in a random portfolio of stocks. This leads us to the conclusion that the market's first guess about the value of an acquisition is an "unbiased" estimate (that is, neither consistently too low nor too high), if not indeed an accurate one.

THE RESULTS

Exhibit A contains the list of deals in our study along with the value added or lost on each deal. The deals in our study were all consummated in 1984, were valued in excess of $1 billion, and the acquiring firms were all publicly traded U.S. companies. Each deal is evaluated based on its stock price reaction over the five-day period beginning two days before and ending two days after the announcement of the acquisition. This time period was chosen because of the difficulty of identifying the exact announcement date. The stock price reaction is measured as a percentage change relative to the change in the S&P 500 index, adjusted for the riskiness, or beta, of the company. For example, assume the acquirer's stock price rose 5 percent upon the announcement of the acquisition, while over the same time period the S&P 500 rose 2 percent. Assume also that the acquirer's risk level is the same as the S&P 500. In this case, the abnormal return is about 3 percent ($[(1 + .05)/(1 + .02) - 1]$). The stock rose 3 percent more than expected given the overall market movement. The value added or lost on each deal is simply the abnormal return times the total market value of the acquirer's common shares just prior to the announcement.

From Exhibit A, you can see that the average acquirer's shares lost about 5 percent during the period surrounding the announcement and that the acquirers' shares lost a total of $2.1 billion in market value. While this loss is enormous it is probably understated for two reasons. First, some of the transactions were being planned for some time prior to the first public announcement of the deal, particularly the negotiated deals. It is likely that, by the time of the announcement, the stock prices already incorporated some expectations about the deals due to rumors or leaks. Second, upon

Exhibit A

Acquirer	Target	Annce. Date	Trans- action Value ($MM)	Buyer Share Price Before Annce.	Dollar Change −2 to +2	Abnormal Return	Value Added (Lost) ($MM)
Chevron Corp.	Gulf Corp.	Feb 29, 1984	$13,400	$37.50	($2.25)	−6.97%	($894)
Texaco Inc.	**Getty Oil Co.**	**Jan 6, 1984**	**10,120**	**36.00**	**1.75**	**3.87%**	**359**
Mobil Corp.	Superior Oil Co.	Mar 12, 1984	5,700	30.25	(0.88)	−3.88%	(477)
Beatrice Cos.	**Esmark Inc.**	**May 21, 1984**	**2,710**	**30.63**	**(2.50)**	**−6.30%**	**(175)**
General Motors Corp.	Electric Data Systems Corp.	May 17, 1984	2,600	63.88	(1.63)	−1.16%	(233)
Champion Intl. Corp.	**St. Regis Corp.**	**Jul 31, 1984**	**1,830**	**19.13**	**(1.13)**	**−11.53%**	**(121)**
Phillips Petroleum	R.J. Reynolds Inc. (Energy Opers.)	Sept 20, 1984	1,700	41.75	(2.88)	−5.85%	(374)
Manuf. Han- over Corp.	**C.I.T. Financial Unit**	**Sept 24, 1983**	**1,510**	**43.88**	**(3.88)**	**−8.76%**	**(154)**
Dun & Brad- street Corp.	A.C. Neilson Co.	May 18, 1984	1,340	55.25	(4.75)	−5.93%	(185)
IBM	**Rolm Corp.**	**Sept 25, 1984**	**1,260**	**123.75**	**1.63**	**0.57%**	**430**
American General Corp.	Gulf United Corp. (Ins. Operations)	Mar 30, 1983	1,200	22.38	(1.33)	−6.85%	(102)
General Electric Co.	**Employers Rein- surance Corp.**	**May 10, 1984**	**1,075**	**54.88**	**(1.13)**	**−0.13%**	**(32)**
Texas Eastern Corp.	Petrolane	Jun 21, 1984	1,040	31.50	(3.38)	−11.29%	(93)
Total/Average			**$45,485**			**−4.94%**	**($2,052)**

the announcement of the deals, it is generally not certain that the deal will be consummated; and often not all of the information about the deal is available. Therefore, the reaction may only be partial. For example, in General Motors' acquisition of Electronic Data Systems (EDS), there were three significant announcement dates, with each successive date bringing new information to the market. On May 17, 1984, the existence of merger discussions was acknowledged; on June 28, the agreement on terms was announced; and on September 19 the proxy materials were registered. On each date, GM's stock price went down further relative to the market.

Exhibit B shows the results in graphic form. The graph represents the average cumulative abnormal returns to the thirteen acquiring companies over the period extending from ten days prior to ten days after the acqui- sition announcements. Day "zero" on the graph represents the announce- ment date. Since the graph is an average over different companies and different time periods, we would normally expect the random elements affecting the companies to net out, resulting in a straight line at zero. This is, in fact, what we find over the periods prior to and after the acquisitions. Right around the announcement date, however, the companies experience

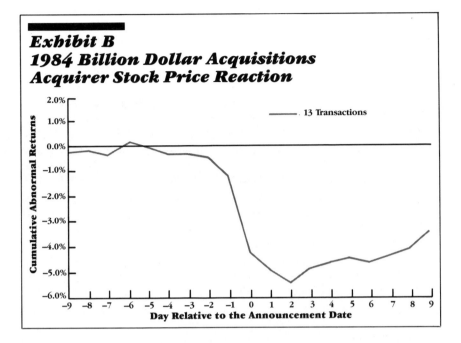

Exhibit B
1984 Billion Dollar Acquisitions
Acquirer Stock Price Reaction

large negative returns. These negative returns are not offset by positive returns in the next few days, and the line stays at a level of −3 to −4 percent. (To satisfy skeptics, we intend to revisit these thirteen companies in one year to see if the line returns to or even surpasses zero.)

While the overall results of our study are clear—these acquisitions did not add value to the acquiring firms—caution must be exercised in evaluating specific transactions. It is impossible to know exactly when the market first learned of an acquisition. Our rule of thumb is to assume the market assimilates the information the first time the transaction is mentioned on the Dow Jones newswire or the *Wall Street Journal*. Further, other company or industry-specific events may be affecting the acquiring firm's share price at the same time as the acquisition. We minimize the impact of other events confusing the results by limiting the time period to just a few days around the announcement date. As a result, our measurement of the impact may be understated, but the direction is unambiguous.

THE OIL DEALS

Given the small sample, it is difficult to make any generalization other than that most of these companies paid too much. We do not claim that the deals did not make good business sense. There were probably large synergistic benefits; however, most of the expected benefits appear to have gone to the acquired companies in the form of the large premium over market they were paid. For example, the consolidation of the oil industry, reflected in the fact that five of the thirteen deals involved energy businesses, probably makes good economic sense. The oil companies have been spending too much on unprofitable exploration and refining projects over the past several years. Further, their staffs, insulated by the enormous profits of the 1970s, became too large and inefficient. These acquisitions will result in lower aggregate capital spending and smaller staffs. The industry and the economy will benefit, but some of the purchasers' shareholders have lost out because their companies overpaid. That is why Texaco's shares rose upon announcement of its acquisition of Getty while the others fell. The market did not think that Texaco overpaid. Interestingly, Texaco's deal was structured almost overnight before any competition could bid up the price.

One of the arguments advanced by the acquiring oil companies to justify their purchases was that the target (and oil companies in general) was undervalued by the market. First, given the sophistication of the market, that seems unlikely. Second, if the oil companies as a group were undervalued, it would make more sense to buy a portfolio of oil companies at the undervalued market price than to pay a substantial premium over market for one company. It is possible that the assets of the oil companies *under current management* are worth less than they might be under somebody else's management. That is not the same, however, as saying that the stock market has undervalued the company. Unless management is changed, the potentially higher value of the firm will never be realized.

IBM AND ROLM

The only deal other than Texaco/Getty to receive a favorable reaction from the market was IBM's purchase of Rolm Corp. This acquisition gives IBM an important advantage in integrating computers and telecommunications. We would also like to point out that, like the Texaco deal, this transaction was negotiated away from the marketplace. There was no competitive bidding.

We might tentatively conclude that it is easier to strike a deal fair to the shareholders of both the acquirer and the target in the absence of competitive bidding.

GENERAL MOTORS AND ELECTRONIC DATA SYSTEMS

GM's shares lost about 1 percent of their market value upon the announcement of the EDS acquisition. Given the difficulty of measuring and interpreting such a small change, we cannot decisively conclude that the deal was bad for GM. In fact, the GM/EDS deal appears to be one that would make economic sense. GM has massive communications and data

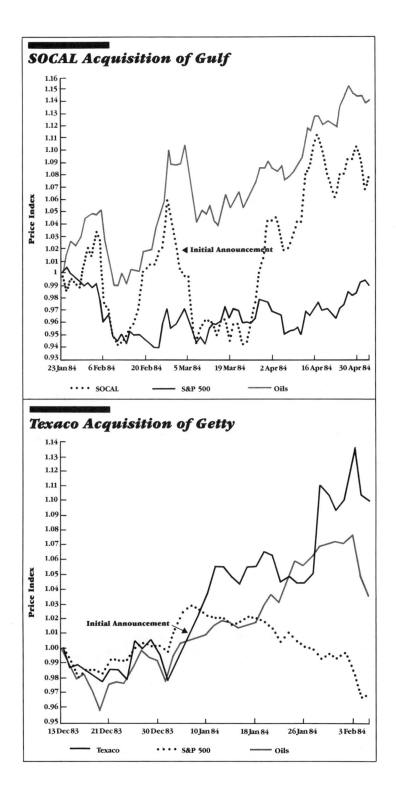

SOCAL Acquisition of Gulf

Price Index

1.16
1.15
1.14
1.13
1.12
1.11
1.10
1.09
1.08
1.07
1.06
1.05
1.04
1.03
1.02
1.01
1
0.99
0.98
0.97
0.96
0.95
0.94
0.93

◄ Initial Announcement

23 Jan 84   6 Feb 84   20 Feb 84   5 Mar 84   19 Mar 84   2 Apr 84   16 Apr 84   30 Apr 84

•••• SOCAL   —— S&P 500   —— Oils

Texaco Acquisition of Getty

Price Index

1.14
1.13
1.12
1.11
1.10
1.09
1.08
1.07
1.06
1.05
1.04
1.03
1.02
1.01
1.00
0.99
0.98
0.97
0.96
0.95

Initial Announcement ↘

13 Dec 83   21 Dec 83   30 Dec 83   10 Jan 84   18 Jan 84   26 Jan 84   3 Feb 84

—— Texaco   •••• S&P 500   —— Oils

processing needs. EDS should be able to help GM find solutions to those needs. On the other hand, GM paid about $2.6 billion for EDS, which prior to the acquisition had a market value of only $1.7 billion—that is a premium of over 50 percent.

BEATRICE AND ESMARK

The market was betrayed by Beatrice's acquisition of Esmark and, as a result, the market value of Beatrice's shares fell by about 6 percent. In February 1983, Beatrice announced a massive business restructuring. The company's chairman, James Dutt, said that Beatrice would divest itself of fifty companies, consolidate its remaining businesses, step up marketing, and emphasize internal growth over acquisitions. The market rewarded this announcement by increasing the market value of Beatrice's shares by about 11 percent. Then about a year later, Beatrice announced the acquisition of Esmark, leading the market to believe that Beatrice is returning to its old ways.

CONCLUSION

Is buying big bad? Not necessarily. Acquisitions are not generally zero-sum games. Value is created but the question is: Who gets it? In this brief study we did not measure the change in the value of the targets' shares. It is quite likely that for many of the transactions the increase in the target's value exceeded the loss in the acquirer's value. For example, while GM's shareholders lost about $200 million, EDS's shareholders gained about $900 million. The net value created was $700 million. In cases like this the acquisition made sense but the buyer overpaid. Buying big is not bad unless you overpay.

NOTES

1. "M&A Deals of the Year," *Institutional Investor*, January 1985, pp. 211–26.
2. Robert J. Cole, "Occidental, Shamrock Study Link," *New York Times*, January 5, 1985.
3. Heilemann's agreement with Pabst was effectively cancelled by FTC action before it was consummated.
4. Michael Bradley, "The Economic Effects of Acquisition by Tender Offer," *Issues in Corporate Finance*, Stern Stewart Putnam & Macklis, Ltd., 1983, pp. 63–71. Peter Dodd found that the stock market response was insignificant or positive in only about 40 percent of the cases. See Peter Dodd, "The Market for Corporate Control: A Review of the Evidence," *Midland Corporate Finance Journal*, vol. 1, no. 2, Summer 1983, Stern Stewart Putnam & Macklis, Ltd., pp. 6–20.
5. Peter Dodd and Richard Ruback, "Tender Offers and Stockholder Returns: An Empirical Analysis," *Journal of Financial Economics*, vol. 5, pp. 351–74.

IV

The Restructuring of Corporate America
A DISCUSSION OF THE REVERSE MERGER MOVEMENT

INTRODUCTION

In recent years, and in the 1980s especially, we have seen an unprecedented wave of "reverse mergers." The increasing number and size of divestitures, spin-offs, and leveraged buy-outs are bringing about striking changes in the product mix and organizational structure of American corporations. This massive "redeployment" of corporate assets has received considerable attention in the popular business press. In the academy, however, finance scholars have only recently begun to turn their attention away from mergers and acquisitions and toward these relatively new corporate phenomena.

The results of the academic finance community's initial explorations in the field of corporate restructuring suggest that we may be witnessing a new phase in the evolution of the public corporation into a more efficient vehicle for building and storing stockholder wealth. The market's early endorsement of this restructuring also suggests that some forms of corporate organization—most notably, the large, sprawling conglomerate—may now be under serious challenge from increasingly activist investors, perhaps even in the earliest stages of obsolescence.

Gailen Hite, one of the academic spokesmen for the growing body of new research, views these developments as part of a "general corporate trend toward more streamlined, decentralized, entrepreneurial organizations." He suggests, furthermore, that

a new kind of arithmetic has come into play. Whereas corporate management once seemed to behave as if 2 + 2 were equal to 5, especially during the conglomerate heyday of the 60s, the wave of reverse mergers seems based on the counter proposition that 5 − 1 is 5. And the market's consistently positive response to such deals seems to be providing broad confirmation of the 'new math.' ("The Restructuring of Corporate America," *Midland Corporate Finance Journal,* vol. 2, no. 2 [1984].)

Some observers have argued that "reverse mergers" like divestitures and spin-offs increase stock values by enabling analysts properly to evaluate divisions otherwise buried within a conglomerate structure. Such an argument, of course, partly contradicts the academic conception of an efficient market. And academics have accordingly expressed skepticism about this popular argument for spin-offs, suggesting that the market's positive response is more likely based on expected improvements in managerial accountability and incentives from separating unrelated businesses units. Spin-offs, for example, besides often providing divisional management with greater decision-making authority, also result in much more visible evaluation criteria (including a separate stock price) for the spun-off entity. Significant improvements in profitability may be expected from a more direct linking of managerial rewards with performance.

Similar expectations of improvements in managerial incentives and performance also seem to underlie the recent proliferation of leveraged buyouts. Management's willingness to pay their own stockholders large premiums (that on average exceeded 50 percent of the pre-proposal price) to take their companies private raises two important questions: What are the expected benefits to going private? Furthermore, what do these multi-billion dollar leveraged buy-out proposals suggest about the efficiency of the public corporation as a form of business organization?

Recent developments in finance theory—most notably, Michael Jensen and William Meckling's formulation of "agency" theory—have drawn attention to the potential loss in the value of public corporations caused by the conflict of interest between management and its stockholders. Most finance scholars, including Jensen and Meckling, have concluded that the "agency costs" of separating ownership from control in the public corporation cannot be very great for two reasons: the existence of a market for executive labor should curb the natural tendency of corporate managements to pursue their own interests at the expense of their public stockholders, and management incentive contracts are designed to mitigate this potential conflict of interest. But the recent flurry of ever larger leveraged buy-out proposals may be telling us that the "agency costs" of public equity ownership may be far greater than finance scholars have suspected.

The popularity of going private no doubt reflects, in large part, the large tax and regulatory burden imposed on the public corporation. But it may also suggest that management compensation committees of public corporations could be doing far more to strengthen management incentives to perform—or that the legal impediments to adopting more effective management compensation schemes in public corporations are very great. For, besides providing significant stock ownership for a number of key managers, leveraged buy-outs often strengthen managerial incentives by designing compensation agreements that tie management bonuses more closely to increases in a company's profitability (often measured in terms of cash flow rather than accounting earnings). In addition, the large amounts of leverage supported in these deals contain the suggestion either that some public companies may be significantly underleveraged or that the private corporation per se has considerably more debt capacity than its public counterpart—perhaps because of the improved management incentive structure, but also because of the intermediation of reputable third-party professional investors between management and lending institutions.

The following "Discussion of Corporate Restructuring" features a distinguished group of investment bankers and academics. In this discussion, which proved to be a mutually educational exchange of ideas and experience, the perspective of the investment bankers provides a valuable complement—mainly supportive, but in some instances conflicting—to the academics' theoretical view of restructuring. Leveraged buy-outs (LBOs) are clearly the subject of greatest interest, and accordingly receive the most attention. Although the suggestion is raised that LBOs might be a "fad," the consensus that seems to emerge—among investment bankers and academics alike—is that the LBO phenomenon is a legitimate response by managements both to increasing government regulation and taxation of the public corporation and to severe limits on the public corporation's ability to reward and thus motivate management.

In dealing with the question of the market's response to divestitures and spin-offs, the investment bankers show some inclination to doubt the ability of investors to assess the values of conglomerates—especially in the case of public companies with valuable real estate holdings. (In fact, they seem unanimous in agreement that real estate companies themselves should be run as private companies!) But, at the same time, this suggestion of market inefficiency is tempered by the expression of a competing view: namely, that the market's endorsement of "reverse mergers" in part reflects analysts' perception that conglomerate organizations are difficult to manage well. Stated more forcefully, this view also suggests that much of this dismembering of conglomerates may reflect management attempts to forestall stockholder activists' charges of corporate mismanagement.

Whatever uncertainties remained about the cause of the market's positive response, however, there seemed little remaining disagreement that such restructurings, on the whole, are conferring large benefits on corporate stockholders.

DHC

THE RESTRUCTURING OF CORPORATE AMERICA: A DISCUSSION OF THE REVERSE MERGER MOVEMENT
June 13, 1984

JOEL STERN, MODERATOR: I would like to welcome everybody to this roundtable discussion of corporate restructuring. Our main focus will be on the corporate motives for, and the stockholder consequences of, all the so-called "reverse merger" transactions: divestitures, leveraged buy-outs of divisions or subsidiaries of public companies, and all the varieties of corporate "spin-offs" and "split-ups" that we have been seeing.

In the course of this discussion, we would like to come up with some answers to questions like the following:

1. Is there some broad economic rationale for the recent wave of divestitures? Is this simply an unraveling of the M & A waves of the sixties and late seventies— an acknowledgment of failure by conglomerates? Is it a response to undervaluation by the stock market? Or are there other strategic motives behind this trading of divisions among companies?

2. Why do selling companies' stock prices consistently go up on announcements of divestitures? Is it because of some kind of "conglomerate discount" caused by the failure of analysts to understand complex structures? Or are corporate managements incapable of managing conglomerates efficiently?

3. What exactly are spin-offs? How do they relate to the other deals with which they are often confused: split-ups? split-offs? limited partnerships? partial public offerings—why, incidentally, would stockholders want to hold a minority interest in such a deal?

4. What explains the market's consistently positive response to announcements of spin-offs? Market undervaluation? Tax-free distributions to stockholders (and if so, how long will the IRS allow this)? Avoidance of regulatory constraints? What about the improvement of management accountability and incentives?

5. Why are so many and such large companies going private, and why are managements willing to pay such high premiums over market to get there? What do leveraged buy-outs say, if anything, about corporate debt capacity? Does changing ownership structure by going private itself create more debt capacity? Or is there a strong suggestion that many public companies are grossly underleveraged?

6. In view of the concern expressed about the amount of leverage in these deals, how have those companies fared with all that debt? Are the management incentive contracts of private companies structured much differently from those of public companies? What are the real benefits of being a private versus a public corporation? What, if anything, does all this suggest about the efficiency of the public corporation as a form of corporate organization?

7. If the possibility of divestiture isn't there, what about the partial or wholesale liquidations of corporate assets? The market's consistently positive response to the total liquidations suggests that many companies may be worth more "dead than alive" to their stockholders. Are there many companies whose stockholders would benefit from such liquidations?

With this as an overview of the general issues, I would like to introduce the very distinguished cast of characters we've assembled here. As I'm fond— perhaps too fond—of saying to my colleagues, we don't want .300 hitters, we want .350 hitters. Well, we have all .350 hitters here today. So let me say a little about each of our panelists:

CARL FERENBACH is a Managing Director of Thomas H. Lee Co., a firm specializing in the arrangement of leveraged buy-outs. Carl was formerly head of Merrill Lynch's M & A Department;

GAILEN HITE is Associate Professor of Finance at Southern Methodist University. Gailen has published a number of studies on divestitures, liquidations, and spin-offs;

MICHAEL JENSEN is LaClare Professor of Finance and Business Administration and Director of the Managerial Economics Research Center at the University of Rochester's Graduate School of Management. Mike is the co-originator, along with Bill Meckling, of the "agency cost" theory;

JOSIAH LOW III is Managing Director of Merrill Lynch's Corporate Finance Department. Joe has served Merrill Lynch in a number of capacities for the past twenty-three years. He has been involved in the financing of oil and gas deals, and presently runs the "emerging growth" group;

DAVID SCHULTE recently formed his own merchant banking firm, Chilmark Partners, based in Chicago. He was formerly a Senior Vice President at Salomon Brothers, where he created the Corporate Reorganization Group. He managed, among other cases, the reorganizations of Chrysler and International Harvester;

JAMES SCOTT is Chairman of the Finance Department at the University of Columbia's Graduate School of Business. Jim has also worked at McKinsey & Co. and in the Corporate Finance Department at Goldman Sachs & Co.;

MICHAEL SEELY is President of Investor Access Corp., a financial communications firm in New York. Mike organized a very successful conference on the subject of restructuring two years ago, and has published the conference proceedings in a volume called *The Guide to Corporate Restructuring*; and

MICHAEL SHERMAN is Senior Vice President and Chairman of Investment Policy at Shearson Lehman/American Express. Mike has been involved in analyzing securities, managing money, and giving advice to investors for over twenty years. He has also spoken at a number of conferences on how corporations can use restructuring techniques to build shareholder value.

JOEL: I would like to begin the discussion by turning to Gailen Hite. In the past, we have generally started things off by asking the corporate practitioners what they think they have been doing in these deals. After we have had a chance to hear their version, we then turn to what I call the "serious researchers," the academic scholars, and try to get their views on what we see going on here.

Today, I would like to do it the other way around. Let me ask you, Gailen, about the research you have done on the subject. What does it tell you about what the practitioners appear to be doing? Do you think that these corporate restructuring transactions are benefiting the shareholders of the companies who are initiating the deals?

GAILEN HITE: Well, over the last ten years or so, most of the academic research on restructuring has been devoted to mergers and acquisitions. The issues there have been whether or not those transactions create value, and how that value gets split between the stockholders of the targets and the bidders. But while we have been concentrating on the acquisition decision, there has been a lot of so-called "reverse merger" activity—attempts to get rid of, or at least separate, corporate assets. It is only recently that we have begun to look seriously at these kinds of transactions.

In particular, we have started to examine the stockholder effects of divestitures—that is, corporate sales of divisions or subsidiaries or product groups to other corporations. Another transaction we have looked at fairly closely are the spin-offs—the ones where you create a separate corporation out of a subsidiary, and then give the shares in the new corporation to your existing stockholders. We have also been looking at total liquidations of corporations—those cases where corporate assets are sold off in parts and the entire proceeds are then distributed to the existing stockholders. And then, finally, we have started to look at going private transactions—at both the pure buy-outs by management, and at the leveraged buy-outs involving outside investors.

What we find in virtually all of these transactions, at least in terms of the broad averages, is that the total market value of the companies that engage in these restructuring deals increases. I interpret these results to mean that corporate assets are going to higher-valued uses, or to more efficient users. Also, as product markets and other things in the economy change, the optimal organizational structure changes. For this reason, we may be seeing the evolution of new corporate forms. We are certainly seeing changes in the corporate product mix and in the mix of assets that corporations are holding.

LEVERAGED BUY-OUTS

JOEL: Some people have attributed the wave of leveraged buy-outs to favorable tax consequences and to expected improvements in managerial performance from stronger incentives. If there were no tax consequences, do you think it would be desirable for public companies to stay public and simply change their incentive compensation program? Or do you think it is impossible to do that within the public corporation?

GAILEN: Well, first of all, let me say something about the tax motives. You sometimes hear that a major benefit of leveraged buy-outs is that they allow you to write up the assets of the firm, and start from a new higher basis to depreciate those assets. But there is another side of that story: there are also taxes which are going to be paid by the investors who are selling out. To assess the real size of the *net* tax benefits, you have to look at both sides of the transaction, at the extra taxes that are paid by the sellers as well as the additional tax savings when the assets are written up. Now there probably is a net tax gain from leveraged buy-outs, but it is not all a free lunch. Somebody else is going to wind up paying for those write-ups.

The other tax argument has to do with the tax savings from the interest payments from using a large amount of debt. But that also gives me some problems. For one thing, it is not clear to me why the firm didn't previously take advantage of this tremendous tax savings—if it does in fact exist. In addition to that, if there are these tremendous tax savings, why is it that the first thing the company does after going private is to pay down the debt? That is, if it is optimal to have this large amount of debt which generates these tax savings, why would you get rid of it right away after you have put it in place?

So, the motive for leveraged buy-outs I find most plausible is the restructuring of the incentive plans. Now your question was: Why couldn't they just do that as a public corporation? And I agree with you. I don't understand why they couldn't provide stronger incentives in the public corporation.

CARL FERENBACH: For management, going private means the difference between being an owner and just being a manager. As a general manager, you are running your life from an income statement. When you become an owner, you run your life from a balance sheet. And that is an important difference. Also, the tax consequence of ownership to you personally is 20 percent—versus 50 percent on ordinary income through bonuses or whatever.

JOEL: Wait a second, Carl. There is a company that we know in the Chicago area and they went private through a leveraged buy-out. I asked their president what motivated him to do it. And he said his reason was that he didn't "have to manage for earnings anymore." He was now going to manage so as to maximize the cash-generating ability of the company.

CARL: You are addressing a different subject though, Joel. You said that one of the driving factors is incentive compensation. In most leveraged buy-outs that are organized by third-party professionals, incentive compensation falls into two categories: direct cash compensation and a percentage of the company that management owns. Typically direct cash compensation doesn't change much. But the ownership is a significant motivating factor.

JOEL: Why couldn't a plan be designed that would essentially mimic or replicate that process in a publicly traded firm without having to go through the leveraged buy-out routine?

CARL: Well, management can buy into the equity of a leveraged buy-out company relatively cheaply. And if they do a good job of managing that business, the value of your investment will increase much more rapidly than in a public firm.

MIKE JENSEN: But you can give managers phantom stock. Or stock appreciation rights. A full range of substitutes are available in a public company.

CARL: But, in terms of the whole, these substitutes aren't meaningful enough to be strong motivators.

DAVID SCHULTE: I think the answer to Joel's question is that public companies could do this, if they set their minds to it.

JOE LOW: Well, in fact they have. There is an example of a well-known company where the chairman and the board of directors voted the chairman a very significant stock option plan. Those options would have increased his ownership from approximately 5 percent to 25 percent, if he chose to exercise them. That meant that the plan had to be announced in a proxy statement.

The public stockholders' reaction to this announcement was that that particular individual was raping the company for his own benefit. This individual spent the next year defending his position in this option. A number of us went through the depositions in his defense, and it was not a pleasant experience. So, I would say, retroactively, that providing management with significant equity ownership or incentives is very difficult to do in the public marketplace.

MIKE SEELY: I would argue that people like Teledyne chairman Henry Singleton have in fact accomplished what leveraged buy-outs do. Mr. Singleton has levered his company and shrunk its capitalization around his equity position, so that over time his equity interest and that of other key managers have increased proportionately. He has in fact done a series of going "less public" transactions. This has had two consequences: the public shareholders have been able to sell their stock at a premium to the market and the insiders have enlarged the terminal value of their stock in the company.

JOEL: I think that Gailen is telling us, though, that he doesn't understand why these companies are going private—because the incentive structures that private companies set up can presumably be duplicated by public corporations.

JOE: Time, I think, is a very important consideration. These changes can be executed very quickly and neatly in the mechanism that has been devised by the marketplace. And leveraged buy-outs, incidentally, are not a new phenomenon, they just happen to be used a lot more in today's marketplace than ever before.

Going back to Gailen's other point, though (and Carl knows this much better than I), he reason you have a repayment of that debt stream is that if you look at the going-in valuation on an LBO, there is an expected terminal value which is given considerable weight. In order to achieve that terminal or "selling out" value, you have got to restructure the company so that either through sale to another company, or through a partial or complete public offering, you can achieve a portion of that terminal value to get your return on investment. If you leave it highly leveraged, you may well reap the benefits of the cash-flow stream during that period of time. But the big benefits are down the road when you refinance that animal.

JOEL: What do you think about that, Gailen?

GAILEN: Well, in the meantime, you are using the funds generated by the business to retire the debt. Presumably those funds have alternative uses. For example, why couldn't you just pay a large dividend? You would get part of your value then as opposed to at the end. All you are doing is using a dollar's worth of operating cash flow to retire a dollar's worth of debt. Now what is the benefit from doing that?

JOE: I can show you a mathematical equation that demonstrates that, at least initially, you are better off repaying debt rather than extending it. You are effectively deciding whether you would rather have X dollars today, or blank times X at some point in the future. And you make either a conscious or an unconscious decision as to which of those you want.

CARL: When a manager can invest a dollar in his own business, or I can invest a dollar in his business, my expectation is that over a five-year period my internal rate of return is going to be 50 percent or better. Whether as a manager or a third-party professional in a leveraged buy-out, I am confident I can do that when I am running (or investing in) a business that has got a record—when I know the business well, when I have seen it work. In these cases, your expectations for the future can be reasonably and confidently based on past performance. Consequently, your expectation of achieving those rates of return is reasonably certain. Needless to say, there aren't many of these opportunities around. The promise of these high returns is the only reason for doing a leveraged buy-out. And it is a compelling reason from the investor's perspective.

GAILEN: Are you saying that taking a dollar to pay off a dollar's worth of debt creates more than a dollar's worth of value?

CARL: Yes, if the company is profitable. If its cash flow is sufficient to service the debt and still generate profits, then clearly higher leverage will raise the level of those profits.

JOEL: Why, in your opinion, are lenders willing to put debt-equity ratios of five or ten to one onto a company, when they weren't willing to lend that kind of ratio before?

CARL: Several reasons, I think. First, they are lending to businesses they know something about, so there is not a large discomfort level. Secondly, lenders have gotten smarter—or at least they think so. And their ability to analyze and evaluate companies' creditworthiness has been enhanced by the information revolution. They can look at thirty-six different alternatives in their little computer, and they can understand the risks better from a financial standpoint. They are also more deeply staffed so they can do a more complete "due diligence." And, in the final analysis, they are also making a bet on the groups that are organizing the buy-out and on the management itself.

JOEL: The question I would then ask you is this: If that is the case, what do you find the banks doing for companies that compete against the companies they have just put those high debt ratios on? After they have allowed companies going private to lever themselves up to eight-, nine-, or ten-to-one debt-equity ratios, do the banks then permit those companies' *public* competitors to have similar leverage ratios?

CARL: If those companies asked for that kind of leverage, I think the banks would give it to them. But public companies don't typically ask for that. And the banks do not initiate it. They don't say, "We have just leveraged a Hyster, so let's go to its nearest competitor and suggest to them that they go the same route." They will lend on an if-requested basis.

JOEL: Mike, what do you think about that?

MIKE JENSEN: I am puzzled by all this leverage. I see some sense to the argument that leveraged buy-outs may create value by improving incentive compensation. We have just gone through a period in which we have seen great political sensitivity to the large numbers that show up in published records of executive compensation. I agree with what Joel was saying. But it goes beyond just the problems of the stockholders and the lawsuits. It goes to the political system. People like Nader, Green, and Brock—and other representatives of special interest groups—will use those numbers to bring political intervention and interference. And for this reason alone, going private may well be required in order to give management the right set of incentives.

JOEL: What is your interpretation of the capital structure discussion you have just heard?

MIKE JENSEN: I don't know. I just don't understand how private companies can support so much leverage, or why they do it. However, I think there is more than a little chance that there are going to be some people finding out that they overbet—that they were too confident—very much like what happened in the energy business in the late seventies. It may well be a mistake, but time will tell.

JOEL: How would you account for the differences in debt ratios for competing companies in the same industry, when you have an eight- or nine- or ten-to-one debt-equity ratio for one company and then you don't see anything like that for the competing companies? Carl said that the banks, if asked, might do it. But, remember, the banks are competing hard to sell loans to good credits. Why do you think banks would not be as willing to offer very high debt-equity ratios to a competing public company?

MIKE JENSEN: Well, one of the reasons Carl gave was that the banks have confidence in the management and in the operations of the company that has evolved over a long association. They may not have that confidence with their competitors. But I still don't understand it.

DAVID: I think the real explanation of these leveraged buy-outs has much to do with fad and fashion. It may be that, from the academic perspective, you have trouble incorporating fads into any systematic explanation of behavior. But it is a very real phenomenon. The Esmark situation recently was an interesting example. There is probably no way that the management of Esmark could have borrowed $2 billion to finance their business. I don't believe they could have raised that kind of debt. Yet, a couple of guys from Madison Avenue called Kohlberg Kravis, the wizards of the day, appear and suddenly $2 billion of debt financing is available. Remember, after the company goes private, operating management remains precisely the same, the company is precisely the same. The lenders and outside professionals are making an investment that doesn't increase operating earnings one jot.

So I believe we are going through a fad cycle. Now it may be that the institutional financiers, the people who are taking the mezzanine, the "funny paper," at the bottom of these leveraged buy-outs (and this "funny paper" is essential to their financial structure)—it may be that these lenders realize, at some subliminal level, that they are really buying equity. They are people who for years have gotten slaughtered buying long-term fixed income securities. I always think of that great line of Warren Buffet's in Berkshire Hathaway's annual report two years ago. Buffet said—with echoes of Polonius to Laertes—that his recent experience had taught him "neither a short-term borrower nor long-term lender be." A lot of these institutions have been long-term lenders and it hasn't done well for them. It may just be that what these institutions are now buying in leveraged buy-outs is equity "in drag."

And these things can tip over. If and when they do, the existing equity layer is wiped out in a flash, and the lenders will own the company. Perhaps the financiers are willing to take that risk. Otherwise I can't make sense out of it.

MIKE JENSEN: But you know that prospect of bankruptcy clearly involves looking at huge costs. The loss of product markets, the loss of managers. The bankruptcy process can be very expensive.

DAVID: Why does it have to be a bankruptcy process? It doesn't have to be bankruptcy. It can be a work-out process.

MIKE JENSEN: I see. You are saying that because it is a private company, the renegotiations will all be much smoother, much less costly to accomplish. Well, if that's what happens, that is a plausible argument.

DAVID: The other day one of the major banks brought me a leveraged buy-out that had gone sour. It had been done at a debt-to-equity ratio of eighty-to-one. They had one million dollars of equity. And now, lo and behold, because the marketing plans didn't mature, they needed $25 million of new equity.

So they are now going to capitalize the company properly. And that $25 million of equity is going to command a major proportion of ownership. It is going to be done out of court. It is going to be a sensible recapitalization. What that really means is that the ownership structure on the date of the first closing won't necessarily be the ownership structure for all time.

MIKE JENSEN: Roughly how long will it take to accomplish this reorganization?

DAVID: Well, if they are lucky, they could probably get that done in two or three months, unless people don't like the product outlook. In that case, they might never get it done. But it generally doesn't take that long to do a refinancing.

JOE: Mike, step back in history for a minute and take a look at the other side of the coin. Take a look at that investment theory that prodded all of the top investment advisors in this country to buy the "favored fifty" stocks at multiples of sixty to eighty times earnings. I would guess that, if you could quantify it, the risk of making a return from those stocks at those P/E ratios was less than the risk of those investments that the banks are now making in these leverage buy-outs.

So, like David, I think leveraged buy-outs are a fad. The pendulum swings, and it swings not in small amplitudes, but in amplitudes that are far too great for any of us to explain rationally. But they happen.

CARL: I think that that is a little overstated. I don't think the risks are as great as everybody has made them out to be. You don't see very many of these companies in trouble. Of course, the test will come when we have a real downturn in the economy. But typically, you know, when the economy does turn down, companies liquidate working capital and generate cash. So their ability to service debt is not significantly impaired. And if they then manage their growth on the asset side, they shouldn't have much trouble servicing the debt during the growth cycle. So, the argument that leveraged buy-outs are impending disasters has, I think, been greatly exaggerated.

I think you also have to remember to differentiate a little bit among the kinds of companies doing LBOs. The visible, highly publicized portion of this marketplace are the large public companies. But the vast bulk of these transactions are really divestitures of divisions and private companies who are transferring ownership to other investors through the leveraged buy-out process. In the majority of these deals, the leveraged buy-out provides a means for bringing in new investors and regenerating management processes, and other kinds of real economic changes.

JOEL: To what extent do you think that the debt ratios of companies are being reduced after leveraged buy-outs because the companies' financial advisors tell management that they can not go back into the public market with debt-equity ratios that high?

CARL: I think that's important. I think the debt ratios come down quickly for two reasons. One is that when a company is leveraged up at seven- or eight- or ten-to-one, management's total focus is on the debt. Which means that it is distracted from its ability to invest in the company's future. The first priority is to service the debt. And management's incentives are usually geared directly to that priority. So they are going to get that debt down to a workable level as quickly as they can.

JOEL: To what extent do you think these leveraged buy-outs are taking place because the managements of the companies, and perhaps their directors, feel that the market is not giving them fair value the way they are currently capitalized and the way they are currently run? Perhaps they say to themselves, "If only we were private, we could do something valuable for the company—something which the public market would not appreciate, not at least over the interim period when this value was being created."

CARL: I think there is some of that sentiment in public companies—that they are not getting much recognition from the market, that they are being partly ignored because of the tremendous amount of competition for institutional investors' attention. There are, I think, a limited number of institutional investors chasing certain stocks, and companies must compete for their attention.

JOEL: You are saying that the shares are not being fairly valued.

CARL: That is what managements think in many cases.

MIKE SEELY: In two out of three cases, according to a recent Lou Harris poll.

JOEL: What do you tell these companies?

CARL: I am a buyer, I am not an advisor. I care about price, and about what it costs me to finance. I can tell you, though, that when I was an advisor, I had the good fortune to be dealing with a stock market that was trading around 800. The market was broadly undervalued then, and a lot of companies wanted to do deals under those circumstances.

THE ROLE OF THE LEVERAGED BUY-OUT SPECIALIST ____

MIKE JENSEN: Carl, what can you tell me about the role of the outside investors in leveraged buy-outs? What role do you and the Kohlberg Kravises play in these deals?

GAILEN: Could we expand that question just a little to see what the role of the buy-out specialist is—not only in terms of engineering the deal, but in contributing to the ability of the firm to handle these nine- or ten-to-one leverage ratios?

CARL: There has been quite a proliferation of buy-out groups, and each may have somewhat different motives and capabilities. The investment banks, whose primary business is an agency business, are in leveraged buy-outs, too. But the private buy-out groups tend to be motivated by the same things—usually ownership and its benefits. You have to understand where we begin. We have a fund of institutional money, which we invest along with our own money. We buy only common stock in leveraged buy-outs, which we organize around a management team. So we are at the bottom of the heap when we buy common stock. Our interest, therefore, is in owning corporations.

To do a deal, first we must agree with a seller on a form of purchase. Once we agree to buy, our next job is to finance the deal. We typically arrange financing through banks, insurance companies and other lending institutions. When the deal has been structured and the financing done, our job then will be to worry about it a lot. In the course of structuring the company, we not only have to structure the debt, we also have to worry about the management's participation and its compensation; and about establishing a shareholders' agreement to govern the company's owners' rights. We also have to think about how we and the other investors are going to get our investment out in the future. You got in, but you got in with the intention at some point of getting out. There must be some foreseeable, achievable plan there, whether it is through a public offering or selling the company or bringing in other leveraged buy-out groups.

Most buy-out groups serve as an active board of directors. Operating management gets involved in buy-outs because they know they are going to have the control they want and need to operate. Through the board, the buy-out group has a lot of direct contact with management, and expresses its concern about financial and other policy matters. Most buy-out groups are made up mainly of financial types. We are a little different in that we have two operating partners in our group, and we do focus on operations. Nonetheless, like other groups, our primary focus is on how are we doing with our debt service, and how are we doing in terms of our long-term strategy.

MIKE JENSEN: What is the frequency of the management turnover after the buy-out occurs when this monitoring is going on? Do the buy-out specialists get rid of them very often?

CARL: Like all boards, we probably tend to wait too long. Changing management is an unnerving process for the buyer management. Particularly when they own 5 or 10 percent of the company. By firing them you are in effect terminating their opportunity for wealth.

But the answer is yes. If things aren't going well and you are not going to be able to service your debt or to deal with your junior security holders, you may have to do something drastic.

MIKE JENSEN: Now when you go into these things, do you have a buy-out provision for terminated management?

CARL: Typically you have a shareholders' agreement and a management contract. And in one or both, you will specify what happens to management's stock in the event of termination.

MIKE JENSEN: Is it normally bought back?

CARL: Typically it is.

MIKE JENSEN: Do you think top-level management is terminated under these kinds of arrangements more frequently than in public companies?

CARL: I don't have much of a basis for saying this, but I think the frequency of terminations after leveraged buy-out deals is probably less than in public companies. Hopefully, you have done your homework on the management in advance. The consummation of a buy-out is about a six-month process. And it entails at least half a dozen fairly intense negotiations. In the course of that, you get to see a guy under fire. And if your discomfort level gets high, you know you have got to stop the deal from going through.

DAVID: Well, Carl, isn't the incentive structure also so much more direct for management after a buy-out, so that you probably have a much greater likelihood of getting good performance? Take someone who has been managing a piece of a big company. Let's say he accounts for 5 percent of the corporate earnings, and he has stock options in the parent company. The fact is, this guy can hit home runs or bunt or hit singles—and it won't matter. There is no direct linkage between how well he does his job and his equity reward.

MIKE JENSEN: The data just don't support your statement. We have now got some good data on the relationship between changes in stock prices and changes in the wealth of top-level executives. Two colleagues of mine, George Benston and Kevin Murphy, have collected data for large publicly held firms showing that when the price of a company's stock goes up or down by more than 30 percent, changes in the value of management's direct equity ownership swamp their annual income—by a factor of three to five times on average. It may be that they hold a relatively small fraction of the organization, but the individual executives' total wealth changes are enormous. Thus, the popular notion that top-level executives' compensation is independent of stockholder returns is false.

JOEL: But David may be referring to operating division managers, not just the presidents and chief executive officers your studies talk about.

DAVID: Yes, Joel is right. Take the people who ran Gibson Greeting Cards. They have probably made several thousand percent more as participants in that leveraged buy-out than they would have made as part of RCA or any public corporation. And they made out because the deal "flipped," because the company went public again. But most LBOs have not flipped yet. So we can't know yet how much managements are earning through leveraged buy-outs. But compared to what those people were making with RCA stock options, the leveraged buy-out proved to be a gold mine.

MIKE JENSEN: But this seems to me to be an argument for taking a division public—either partially or in its entirety—through a spin-off or a public offering. You are now arguing that that is why we should take the division private.

DAVID: No, no. What I am saying is that the taking private is an interim step. Forgive me, Carl, but the going private is a promoter's chance to step into the process—a process in which the division ends up becoming a public company, or part of a public company, once more. Instead of going public directly, someone buys them out first, owns them for a while, builds in the benefit of financial leverage, but then sooner or later (and this goes back to what Joe said before about the terminal value), a leveraged–buy-out player is going to sell a piece or the whole of that company. He does not buy and hold forever.

MIKE JENSEN: But in the interim how does he solve the problem of the compensation of division managers?

DAVID: This is the point. He gets them to pull for the long term because the long term is not that far down the road.

MIKE JENSEN: Do they have an equity interest?

DAVID: Oh absolutely.

MIKE SEELY: To paraphrase "Love Story," going private means never having to ask for a raise.

MIKE JENSEN: How far down in the organizaton does this go?

DAVID: Well, it depends on what company you're talking about. Where was Gibson in RCA? It was a small entity buried in the pile somewhere. It was a secondary or a tertiary business, as far as senior management were concerned. Maybe the one or two top guys in Gibson were lucky enough to have options in RCA. Now, if you buy Gibson out, there are maybe nine or ten guys you can identify as the key players. So you give them all stock in the new company.

JOEL: Why wouldn't you design a compensation package at Gibson so as not to lose Gibson? If there is a tremendous gain in value that is passed along to people other than the immediate management, why shouldn't the board of directors of RCA see the sense behind changing the compensation for people at Gibson so that the shareholders of RCA participate in this value?

CARL: Joel, I think you are right. It is an important management issue in this country now—that is, why are so many of these businesses doing so much better independently, after they are bought out, than as conglomerate appendages?

MORE ON LEVERAGED BUY-OUTS _____

JOEL: I wonder if I could steer the discussion toward Mike Sherman. Mike, you must advise companies on leveraged buy-outs. My guess would be that you are dealing with people who are at the senior executive level of an RCA-type company. When they ask you these questions, do you ever come back to them and say, "Hey, look, you don't have to go through all of that. Why don't you retain the value change for the RCA shareholders and simply change the method of compensating the people at the divisional level?"

MIKE SHERMAN: Well, I should tell you that Gibson was our deal.

JOEL: I didn't know that.

MIKE SHERMAN: I personally was not involved in RCA's decision making on that one.

But, to return to this issue of leveraged buy-outs, I sense that a couple of points are being missed here. A leveraged buy-out is a way of inside management, or a group of investors together with inside management, becoming very, very rich and taking some large personal risks with their reputation. But, in truth, there are not many financial risks relative to the expected gains—because the loans are non-recourse loans. You have money in your estate outside of the company. There is no way for the insurance company or the bank to get at that money. So what you are doing by leveraging up the company is this: you are putting your reputation on the line with the lenders as a means of getting control of *all* of the equity of the company (as opposed to the small part that management typically owns in a public firm).

JOEL: But the issue of the leverage apparently is not that important. We are hearing the argument that the immediate objective of a private company with a high debt ratio is to drive that debt ratio down. So the change in value must be taking place on the asset side—from expected improvements in asset management.

MIKE SHERMAN: The lenders are the ones that put the repayment provisions in these deals. There are all kinds of leverages, tiers of leverage. Some of the lenders have a participation in the equity. In fact most of the buy-outs are structured as follows: bank debt comprises about 30 percent of the capital structure; straight debentures held by insurance companies are another 20 percent; insurance companies' convertible debentures, or with warrants, are another 30 percent; and then, at the bottom of this, is 10 percent of straight equity.

JOEL: I guess the question I am asking you is this: What kind of advice do you give directors and senior management of firms like RCA when they are considering a leveraged buy-out? They may have an operating unit that may not be doing well. One of the reasons I ask you this question is that one of our clients in New York told me that they have about 30 operating units, all of which are probably going to be sold. They said, "It is our objective to get them out of here as fast as possible." I said to the chief financial officer, "Why don't you change the method of compensating the people at the operating units?" He said, "Because even if they improve their performance tremendously, it will still be quite inadequate." So I said, "Yes, but if they still improve the performance dramatically, won't the price you get when you sell it be a lot higher? So why don't you wait a year or two? Put a new incentive plan in there and see what happens." But he said to me, "We just want to get rid of it." Now that may have more to do with the fact that I don't have much of a reputation to offer compared to somebody like you. But I am wondering whether, when you are presented with that situation, do you suggest that companies put that incentive plan in there, hang onto the business for a while, and see what happens?

MIKE SHERMAN: No comment.

JIM SCOTT: Let me say something about compensation. One of the points we have been making about leveraged buy-outs is that they are a good way to compensate managers. But it seems to me that a lot of these deals are now, in an important sense, "plays" on interest rates. If I am the management in one of these companies that gets bought out, and interest rates fall, the stock market is going to go way up. My options are going to become quite valuable. We can go public and I will make a lot of money. On the other hand, if interest rates go through the ceiling and I have got a lot of floating-rate debt, then I have an incredible amount of headaches. And even in spite of my best efforts, the company may go under.

The problem with the argument about new compensation packages is that much of the rewards have nothing to do with how good a job the management of these spun-off companies do. It is just what Mother Nature does with respect to interest rates that really determines the size of the payoff.

JOE: But you are missing a major point, I think, and that is the importance of the return of the entrepreneurial spirit. Those people want to take those risks. They really want to return to that.

MIKE SEELY: And in very important ways, the same systems that perpetuate professional managements discourage that entrepreneurial spirit and creation of shareholder value. The incentive systems are really compensation delivery systems that fail to link the interests of management and shareholders.

JIM: In a sense I am underlining Joel's point that maybe we can come up with a better compensation scheme that will reward management according to their effort, and the success of their effort, rather than according to what happens to rates and where we happen to fall in the business cycle.

JOE: Well, you may be right. We have an individual sitting right here whose career is a prime example of the failure of public corporations to create an entrepreneurial environment. Carl Ferenbach was a very productive man at a major U.S. publicly traded corporation. But, within that organization, top management couldn't design a compensation package that could keep Carl away from doing what he did. And his case is a perfect microcosm of what we are talking about.

JOEL: I have a question for you, then. Would you say that the firms that are engaged in compensation advisory work—firms like Towers Perrin, Hewitt Associates, and Hay Associates—have simply failed their corporate clients in designing compensation packages? And that, for this reason, corporations are forced to go the route of the leveraged buy-out to compensate their middle people?

CARL: Joel, you know how hard it is to change a compensation system in a big corporation.

JOE: I am not sure the corporation wants to hear that. Nor am I sure that when it hears, it will act upon the advice of those advisors.

JOEL: Well, the question is: How many Carl Ferenbachs can our public companies afford to lose?

JOE: And they are losing them.

DAVID: It happens, Joel. I have worked with Towers Perrin, and what all those people begin by doing is to anchor the compensation system with the chief executive at the top and then work down. The fact of the matter is this: I don't know what Carl is making at Thomas Lee, but I would be prepared to bet you blind that over a five-year period he expects to outearn every chief executive in American business. So if that is what is at stake, if that is the size of the expected gain from getting outside the form of the public corporation, then there is little wonder that management buy-outs seem to be springing up everywhere.

You see, the problem with the public corporation is that, in the world of public disclosure and proxies, there are practical limitations on how much top corporate people are going to get. *The great thing about the going private move is that it all happens completely out of public scrutiny.*

CARL: There is also a sociological factor contributing to the number of leveraged buy-outs. The guys running the businesses tend to be in their early fifties. Their kids are out of the nest—they are either being educated or have finished their education. And most of these people are looking at a longer career cycle than historically was the case. They feel good, they are energetic. They are dying to do something, and they are looking at ten or fifteen more years of the same thing if they stay where they are. The opportunity for these division managers to get control of their businesses and really have a lot more to say about running them is extremely enticing, and it is driving an awful lot of them to take the bull by the horns and do it themselves.

JOEL: How do the senior managements and directors who attend annual meetings respond to shareholders—say two, three, or four years after a management buy-out—when they hear how well some of these buy-out companies have done? What do the shareholders then say to these management committees who are sitting up there? How could you let something like that get away? What has been your experience in that?

CARL: Well, that is what Mike Thomas said in a *New York Magazine* article on RCA and Gibson Greeting Cards. I haven't been to many annual meetings in the last couple of years, and I don't know how many shareholders are really putting management's feet to the fire on that question. But it is probably not very many.

JOE: It doesn't work that way. The annual meeting is another anachronism. Nothing ever happens. Management is never put to the test. And if they are, they have got a pat answer that they all agree on and they hold hands and give the answer. And it goes away.

JOEL: Mike Seely is in the financial public relations business. Would you tell us a little bit about what your experience has been?

MIKE SEELY: Well, my position on annual meetings hasn't endeared me to my corporate marketplace. It is simply that *anybody who can make annual meetings seem interesting could also make celibacy look appealing.* So we concur with Joe on that subject.

As for this whole LBO phenomenon, the best explanation I have heard of it is not my own, but that of Arthur Taylor, the former president of CBS. He approached me at a cocktail party a few months ago. He said, "Mike, I have finally figured out what LBOs are about. They are a way to *inventory* companies." By that I think he simply meant that the availability of capital facilitates a "going private" transaction, which is done with an eye toward a public takeout at a later date. You can get your bait back and are left with a residual equity position of some significance. And in many cases your only value added was financial expertise—you knew where to go for the capital.

DIVESTITURE

JOEL: How would you account for the observation that the share prices of selling companies go up after big divestitures? You know, a company has a division, perhaps a good LBO candidate, something that apparently was not performing as well as you would like to see it, but maybe peforming adequately. That division is sold off, and the value of the company's remaining assets is suddenly higher. In the 1960s people promoting conglomerate takeovers used to tell us that two and two is five. Now we are hearing that five minus one is still five.

MIKE SEELY: Well, Gailen made the observation that a good deal is a transaction which moves assets to someone to whom they are worth more. And that sounds plausible to me. Also, a business unit can have a negative value to the company—it can be worth less than nothing. That's a point that many managements miss.

JOEL: But why does that add value to the company that doesn't have the assets any longer? All they have is cash.

MIKE SEELY: They were paid a premium over the values.

JOE: And it is assumed that they are going to do something with that cash that will benefit the residual company.

JOEL: Okay, but after the divestiture, the parent company has one asset less and they have got cash that needs to be put to work. If they have received a premium on the sale of those assets, then they have a lot of cash. If they are not going to pay that cash out to the shareholders, then they are probably going to make another acquisition, and they are going to have to pay a premium to get in there. Now, how does that whole process benefit stockholders?

DAVID: The cash may find its way to stockholders through dividends or stock repurchase.

MIKE SEELY: Or it may be redeployed in existing businesses with a higher rate of return than the one divested.

JOE: Or in something that will increase the multiple. You may have a situation that is sold that doesn't fit the parent company. And it may be 20 percent of the company and dragging down the P/E because the analysts can't understand it.

JOEL: Oh? . . . Is that right? [Laughter]

JOE: Yes, sir. Is it time to take a break? [More laughter]

JOEL: Everything was just going along just fine until I heard that last one. Do you *mean* to tell me that the market is unable to properly value some of these companies and that is why these sales are taking place?

JOE: I don't think I said that. That is a *very* strong inference.

JOEL: I have been in meetings of companies that are in a variety of industries. And I have been told that the problem is that the analysts can't understand what is really going on there. If that were the case, why wouldn't the managements of those companies have substantial incentives to hire people like Mike Seely to get a better story out there? This way the market would understand and companies wouldn't have to sell off valuable assets to somebody else to trade at fair value.

JOE: You would think they would do that.

MIKE SEELY: Would you elaborate on that point, Joe?

MIKE SHERMAN: This is a different point. But I think we're getting the story the wrong way around. I think it's the analysts who believe that management doesn't understand what is going on in those conglomerates— the ones with lots of different businesses. And, therefore, the analysts' expectation is that management, by getting rid of some of the businesses, can better manage the remaining ones.

JOEL: That is why I am curious about what kind of advice you offer the management committees of the firms you advise. When you walk in there and you take a look at a firm that is not being well managed in your view . . .

MIKE SHERMAN: We never say that.

JOEL: So what is your selling advice? What do you say to them as to why they should get rid of an operating unit?

MIKE: I am on a different side of the business. I don't get involved in that.

JOEL: Does anybody want to comment on this business?

JIM: I have looked at some companies considering divestiture. And when

I think about my experience, I think about the Boston Consulting Group's matrix, with the "dogs" and the "cows" and the "stars" and whatnot. The old idea was that your "cows" financed your "question marks" and your "stars." It was a very corporate-centered view of the world. It was not a view of the world that necessarily took the shareholder into consideration. The aim of the strategy was to make the corporation grow larger by providing an internal funding mechanism—as if capital markets did not even exist.

But I think one of the things that is happening more frequently now is that people are paying closer attention to the old corporate finance notion that individual investments should earn adequate rates of return. You don't worry about cows funding this and that. The problem with the Boston Consulting Group (BCG) strategy is that some companies—instead of having the "cows" finance "stars" as BCG recommended—were having "cows" finance "dogs." And these "dogs," the substandard businesses, later became LBO candidates.

I think one reason for the market's positive response to many divestitures is that sometimes corporate managements find it easier to stop making negative net present value investments by divesting the unit, than by going through the internal politics of saying, "Well, we are going to cut off the money from this division. We are not going to finance this thing anymore." Instead they get rid of the whole thing. Often it is a positive development.

MIKE SEELY: Let me add two footnotes, Jim. Any mention of BCG should include Bruce Henderson's great dictum about where companies are in their "life cycle" and their management orientation. "A growth business needs a risk-taker," he'd say, "a maturing business needs a caretaker, and a no-growth business like steel needs an undertaker." We have a lot of dead businesses, but few effective undertakers and fewer managements that grasp where their companies are in terms of life cycle and value creation or destruction trends.

My second footnote concerns a Fortune 100 forest products company that invited us in a few weeks ago. After recounting with some pride their lavish capital spending program, they asked what it and other strategies had probably done for shareholders. I said, "You've probably destroyed $5 billion in value over the past five years!" Ten people looked shocked and the final chap—the senior person around the table—nodded sadly and said, "At least that much."

MIKE SHERMAN: My impression is that the reasons the senior management of XYZ are divesting subsidiaries are all over the lot. They can range from having the Boston Consulting Group do a thorough analysis of the company and propose a strategic approach to the future, down to just saying, "We are doing a lousy job with this. We can't figure out how to fix it and let's get Mike in here to sell it for us. We don't want him to ask us why, we just want him to go out and get us the best price." It can be complex, but it can be simple.

JOE: I would also suggest here that you don't make the heroic assumption that public companies are run for the benefit of the public stockholders. And if you will accept that, then I will go on to say that I and others on our side of the business often do proffer the advice that perhaps divestiture makes some sense from the shareholders' point of view—that a certain segment of the business doesn't fit, doesn't meet the returns that Wall Street thinks it ought to meet, doesn't fit in the product mix, or doesn't help the research community follow the stock. All of these might be well and good. But there may well be some other reason, perhaps something to do with the owning family's preferences.

In some cases, I don't know why some divisions are *kept*. But they are kept. And I guess I am like Mike. I stick my head up a couple of times. And when it gets shot off, I learn after a while. That's how I lost most of my hair. (It's growing back though, Carl. Did you notice?)

DIVESTITURES, SPIN-OFFS, LBOS, AND MANAGEMENT COMPENSATION

MIKE JENSEN: What do you do when management calls you in after deciding that a division or business just isn't working with them. Somehow they would like to get rid of it. Now on what basis is the decision made to take it the LBO route versus a spin-off versus an outright sale to another company?

JOE: Well, when we are asked that question, it then becomes a question of value to the corporation. Once the decision is made to get rid of it, the question is then: How can you get the most for it?

MIKE JENSEN: So you look at all those things?

JOE: Sure.

MIKE JENSEN: And how do you value the spin-off, the situation where you just distribute shares in the entity to the existing stockholders?

JOE: That is hard. For our purposes, we look at spinning it off and value it as a separate company. Then, theoretically, in your own mind, you buy back your own stock with the proceeds to get an evaluation technique set up. Or you can be the beneficent corporate owner, the Boone Pickens, the new Robin Hood of the day, who is going to distribute the corporate proceeds, and thus give value, directly to the shareholders.

MIKE JENSEN: Who knows? That might work. It might create value.

DAVID: If you are doing that analysis on a particular division of a complex company, wouldn't you wind up valuing the spin-off by assessing the probable trading value of that division with normal capitalization? If you did that, wouldn't you find that the leveraged buy-out community (if it was the kind of deal they would have an appetite for) would almost always pay more for the same operation, because they are working on pretax cash flow?

JOE: Yes, that's right.

DAVID: You see, Joel, earlier you kept saying the leverage wasn't an important part of these deals. Horsefeathers. I think the leverage is enormously part of it. LBO companies can support higher prices because they are working on about twice the cash flow the public market is. This is because they have a risk preference for leverage very different from what the average manager is going to subject the average public company to.

JOEL: But why can't the individual take on that additional leverage by himself on his own personal portfolio?

DAVID: The corporate manager is not going to play under the assumption that that is what the investor is going to do.

MIKE JENSEN: Well, it is true that the LBO puts together the leverage position with the manager's own control. He is betting on his own future, so to speak. If he were simply buying a diversified portfolio and leveraging it to the hilt, then he is really betting on what Volcker does with the money supply or the success of other managers.

JIM: He is still betting on Volcker a bit.

MIKE: I didn't mean to say that the business climate is not going to affect the performance of these leveraged buy-outs. But more of the poker game is under his control.

JOEL: I am still puzzled, though, about why it is that when companies consider selling off an operating unit, they don't put in a changed incentive compensation plan before they sell it off. This way they might benefit from that value change expected from strengthening management incentives. And if this doesn't work, *then* they can sell it off.

MIKE JENSEN: I agree. As somebody said earlier, there is good reason to suspect that compensation plans in public companies have not been very innovative. They have been very restricted. It is the problem with the CEO serving as an upper bound to what anybody else in the organization can make, independently of what the performance is. And that generally is not going to be very sensible system.

CARL: Senior management has created a precedent. You know, if you give one division a certain comp plan, then you almost automatically limit the plans of all the other businesses to looking like that one.

JOEL: But, if Mike is right that these senior managements have stock option plans of their own, then it would seem that *they* would have tremendous incentives to make sure that these values are created at the operating units—*before* they are sold. I find it very puzzling that the change in compensation does not take place first. Because they lose a great deal if the numbers are as large as...

JOE: You are saying, really, that the leveraged buy-out firms of the future ought to be the existing parent—the parent company that fails to realize the value of its subsidiaries.

MIKE JENSEN: But, wait a second. I think we are being too hard on the firm managers, Joel. It wasn't more than a month or two ago that I listened to the CEO of Esmark, who was at Rochester giving a talk. He argued that one of the reasons Esmark was taking parts of various subsidiaries public was exactly what we are talking about here. They found that having some fraction of those subsidiary companies outstanding gives them a market value, which in turn enables the parent company to measure performance much better, and thus to institute compensation plans at the divisional level that are much more effective.

MIKE SHERMAN: I think this compensation proposal sounds sensible. But it is not "real world." Let's take an example. Let's assume that you are Roger Smith of General Motors, and last year you made $1.4 million up from $800,000 the year before. You are among the most highly paid executives in the United States. You have got stock options, but they haven't been worth much for a long time.

Now, let's say you reach down into the Delco division of GM, and you say, "You know that little division would do a hell of a lot better if we really paid those guys what these LBO guys are getting paid. So let's set up a package for them and make this guy rich." So the designers come back with the package which allows us to compete with a similar LBO—same size, same deal as an LBO someplace else. But then Smith looks at it and says, "Gee, this is terrific. The guy is going to make $20 million by the time he retires. Meanwhile, I'll be sitting here making a million and half a year, half of which goes to Uncle Sam, and my options will be worthless."

JOEL: Why will his options be worthless?

MIKE SHERMAN: Because I am running a $50 billion public corporation. I can't leverage it up the way he can. I can't manage it the way he can. There is an implicit stewardship cost for management in a public corporation that does not exist in a private corporation.

MIKE JENSEN: But you have just given an argument why that large organization ought to be broken up into smaller pieces. And this seems to be exactly what is happening.

MIKE SHERMAN: No, I am giving an argument why, in certain cases, corporations which don't need constant access to capital can be much more rewarding for the people who run them, and the people who own them—which are the same people in this case. That is why public corporations are going private.

MIKE JENSEN: But one of the major advantages that you lose by taking something private is the tremendous economies available in risk-bearing in public capital markets. There is no doubt in my mind that is the major advantage that the public corporate form has over all other forms of organization; the benefits are huge. For this reason, I don't understand the proposal to take a huge company like Getty private. It boggles my mind. It doesn't make any sense.

MIKE SHERMAN: An LBO average company is basically a company in the process of liquidation. The minute you take it private you are now in liquidation. Cash flow is increasing because the dividend is eliminated, and depreciation tax shields are enlarged. You are no longer making grand investment decisions about what your assets are going to be over the next three years. All this because there are going to be large debt payments over the near term.

So the people who own the company are in effect bleeding it of its future growth potential. They can do that only so long. Their bet is that the market they are going to resurface in is going to be a better market, and they will then resell equity at a multiple of what they took it in at. And it will be all their equity and not the stockholders'.

JOE: You can also take what Mike just said and apply it to what Carl told us earlier about his expected rate of return. Recall that Carl said that he looks for an internal rate of 50 percent a year. On the low end of the spectrum of investments, you can buy what we call "Tigers," which are U.S. government–backed zero coupon bonds with an implicit internal rate of return of, say, 13 percent. They are risk-free, if you buy the assumption that the U.S. government will pay off on its debts. Now, if Carl is looking for 50 percent, and if everyone around this table shares the assumption that there isn't that much risk in an LBO, then you see how attractive these deals look. (But at the same time, of course, the fact that these deals are being bought with the expectation of earning a 50 percent IRR shows you that there still must be a substantial amount of risk-bearing.)

MIKE JENSEN: Yes, but there is something in this process more than just the added risk-taking that increases value. The fact that somebody like Carl was willing to pay such large premiums suggests that something else in this leveraged buy-out process is expected to create value.

JIM: Yes, that is interesting because this compensation story that we have been telling is completely opposed to the liquidation story Mike Sherman just gave us. I mean if the liquidation story is right, then we are not getting a lot more effective use of resources through leveraged buy-outs, and economic value is not really being increased.

CARL: Let me go back to Mike Seely's comment that leveraged buy-outs are really a way to "inventory" companies. It would be very foolish for a manager in his fifties to put most of his wealth into the stock of a company if he were just planning to liquidate it. Unless he was completely confident he could get out, his hedge would be to continue that operation as a viable business—to create value by continuing to cause the company to develop.

Now, how does he do that? He has to go through the company's operations and really tear his cost structure apart. He has to reexamine the way his business has been run for years. He has got to ask, "What can I do without and what can

I really develop?" What he tends to find is that he shortens his line of communications. He eliminates redundant people. He spends more time directly with his customers. He spends more time with his suppliers. He is much tougher in labor negotiations because he has to be.

These are all things that American businesses have been criticized for not doing for the last fifteen to twenty years. And the leverage gives someone a tremendous incentive to do that. Because if he doesn't, he is then going to have to do what Mike Sherman said is the purpose of an LBO: he is going to have to liquidate his company.

MIKE JENSEN: Well, it isn't just the leverage, then, that is adding value in these LBOs. It is the change in management's interest; it's the change in management compensation, incentives, and performance.

CARL: Yes, that is what I am saying.

GAILEN: How can you make the assumption though, Carl, that it doesn't make more sense to liquidate a lot of companies? I am not just talking about disaggregation, but literally selling out the interest.

MIKE SEELY: In fact, liquidation is the clear choice for many companies. So is repurchase. But a management that lacks a significant equity piece is more likely to reinvest, even when that reinvestment destroys value by magnifying negative spreads between the cost and the return on capital. All these restructuring alternatives are unspoken alternatives—as remote from institutional investors as they are from the public—known really only to the handful of very aggressive capitalists out there who go by the names of Bass, Steinberg, Sigeloff, etc.

THE RESTRUCTURING OF CORPORATE AMERICA: A MACROVIEW

JOEL: I wonder if I can turn here to Mike Sherman and ask a question about an article he is alleged to have written called "The Restructuring of America." I am told that it attempts to explain all this corporate restructuring activity by looking at some broad changes in our political and economic system.

MIKE SHERMAN: Well, let me redirect this a little because that article was written two years ago, and it seemed very good at the time.

JOEL: You have been carrying it around with you for the last two years?

MIKE SHERMAN: It has held up well with age, Joel. It attempts to explore some issues relating to LBOs and stock repurchases and some other corporate changes. And it asks: What economic forces are causing all this corporate restructuring? And why now?

Well, I think these changes—especially the LBO—are kind of the "end game" of a series of economic and tax policies that have been imposed on this country by government for decades. The fact that we have a corporate tax makes the public corporation a less than desirable method for building wealth. Because we end up with double taxation on dividends, corporations have been forced over the years to retain earnings and make investments in areas where they did not have much skill. And when you combine this with rising inflation and a huge increase in government spending as a percentage of GNP, what you have is a tax structure that is heavily biased against the public stockholder. Inflation and government spending have also crowded out the corporation from outside equity capital.

This combination of events and pressures has led governments to provide what amounts to "backdoor" financing for corporations through investment tax credits and accelerated write-offs. In fact, today, I would say that about 25 percent of the S&P 400's corporate earnings are not accounted for. In other words, if you took the deferred taxes on the income statement of the S&P 400, and added them back into that income (which, by the way, you should do, if you want to get a better picture of corporate profitability), I believe you would increase that number by 25 percent. These are government incentives at work—through the "back door" to business.

In effect, then, the government is out there crowding the credit markets; and, at the same time, they are writing a tax rebate check to GM for the 1981 tax act. So when you put this all together with the corporate tax and the tax-deductibility of interest payments, you have a national economic policy which encourages leveraging. We have had good experience with leverage over the past three decades. By and large, it has been a big winner because of inflation.

And when you take all those elements together, the whole thing appears to come together into a nucleus called the "LBO." The LBO involves the maximum use of tax credits, the maximum use of the corporate tax to shelter your cost of debt, and the maximum use of leverage, which is really part and parcel of a general inflationary psychology. What I mean by "inflationary psychology" is this: I don't think that people who are now going into these things are saying to themselves, "Boy, I think the rate of inflation is going to be 10 percent." But they don't think it is going to be zero either.

They are not threatened, however, by a macroeconomic policy which says there will be no inflation. They assume that the conditions in the economy will remain relatively programmed. And these conditions will be fostered by the Federal Reserve and the government. So therefore the risks of carrying all this leverage don't seem as large as these debt ratios would suggest.

MIKE JENSEN: One part of your story which I find very interesting, though I'm not sure I understand it very well, is the tax argument. The data indicate that the effective corporate income tax, as a fraction of corporate cash flows, reached a peak in the Korean War period of around 40 to 45 percent. It has since declined systematically, and fairly rapidly, to the low to mid-twenties, if I recall correctly. It hasn't increased.

MIKE SHERMAN: That is the effective tax rate. That is not the tax at the margin.

MIKE JENSEN: I understand. The tax on the margin has actually gone down a little, too, to the 46 percent level. We get this continual passage of new tax subsidies that reduce the effective tax rate. So, other than from the leverage, I don't see where there are any other unique tax benefits from a leveraged buy-out. You don't get around the corporate income tax by going private.

The corporate tax *could* be an argument for doing some other things. Going into a mutual form, for example, or a cooperative or a non-profit form are all ways of avoiding the corporate tax. So, if taxes were as important in LBOs as you're making out, then it seems to me we would see more of these other forms of organization. But the fact is, we don't.

CARL: The problem with pushing around the numbers like this is that the guys who have been working the tax codes themselves have been doing the same thing. Those tax reductions are going to be made up somewhere. For example, you have the accelerated depreciation "recapture," which adds to the purchase price. Some of the assets you can use ACRS on, some you can't. But when you go through this process of calculating tax savings, and you finish pushing the numbers all around, your IRR on the asset write-up turns out to be not so good. So the only big shelter you get is from the debt.

MIKE JENSEN: The write-up is clearly not going to give you more than dollar-for-dollar of tax benefits.

MIKE SHERMAN: Not if your actual tax rate is in the twenties, when the marginal rate is 46 percent.

GAILEN: Then, when you do the buy-out, why don't they keep the debt if it is so valuable to have it? Why do they pull the debt right back down?

MIKE SHERMAN: Well, they get it down to a point where they can resurface as a public company.

MIKE JENSEN: The only story that makes sense to me is that, in these leveraged buy-outs, the reorganization itself—by changing management incentives or whatever—creates a lot of value that is not reflected on the balance sheet. It reminds me of what Sohio did in the early days of the Prudhoe Bay field. It was then less than a billion-dollar company. But in a period of less than five years, it obtained something like $5 billion more of capital from the capital markets. One billion of that was common equity; the rest of it was all debt. And they hadn't gotten one dime's worth of cash flow out of the field. They finally turned the faucet on. But in the interim, what happened of course was that the leverage ratio skyrocketed by normal book measures. But everybody understood that these book measures didn't make any sense.

So, my argument is that if the leveraged buy-out thing is real—that is, the conjecture we made earlier about it being a fad or a balloon is incorrect—then this reorganization must be causing a real increase in value. This value is not reflected in the book values and on the balance sheets, and this means that the leverage isn't really as high as it looks. But the fact that they pay that debt down indicates that something else is also going on.

JOE: Well, you are missing one point. Remember that terminal value. In a leveraged buy-out, you are always thinking about the time that you can sell out. Let's assume that your objective is to sell off enough equity in a primary offering so that the company on a pro forma basis will carry itself in the public marketplace. You want to do that as soon as possible so that you can take your invested dollars and reinvest them again at 50 percent. Because, at some point, the company matures and you cannot get 50 percent out of it at the margin.

So, as investment bankers, we always look forward to an initial public offering. We look at the company on a pro forma basis, with the intention of getting the debt down so that we can make an offering and have the company stand on its own two feet.

CARL: Yeah, but the reason the banks and people at other lending institutions give for paying down the debt is that the companies can't tolerate the level of leverage. There is an initial repayment schedule and . . .

MIKE JENSEN: That was my next question. Is there a repayment schedule?

CARL: There is on the debt and the lenders always want it. And if you have an incremental dollar beyond your schedule, the chances are that they may also require you to use that dollar to pay off debt.

MIKE JENSEN: What that amounts to, then, is a monitoring device. It says that the lender requires you to show evidence of this value increase by making the following profile of payments. We are going to make you bond your promises to us by paying us back in installments. It's like the function of a sinking-fund schedule. And if you can't make those payments we are going to take over.

CARL: That's right.

MIKE JENSEN: That makes sense to me.

MIKE SHERMAN: You just said, "Why can't public companies do the same thing? Why don't they do it?" But they do. Some have done it. Sohio did it.

MIKE JENSEN: Well, that is a case where there was a big increase in value.

MIKE SHERMAN: What was the promise at Sohio? The promise was that this money was going to be used to develop the known resource, which was the oil. And in the time period, they were going to use this money— they would pay no dividends for it. There would be no other capital spending of any kind.

And I imagine that most public companies could get that kind of debt if they could "ink out" that kind of an opportunity to ignore their shareholders and eliminate the dividend and eliminate other kinds of capital spending.

MIKE JENSEN: Yes, but the bottom line on this Sohio story is that the benefits weren't coming from the leverage. They were coming from 15 billion barrels of oil—or whatever it was—on the North Shore. That leverage was simply a way to get there. There is an interesting question about why they chose to finance it one way as opposed to another. But the debt was merely a means for financing the investment. The investment, the oil, was creating the value which allowed that kind of leverage.

What is materializing for me, then, is a story that makes a lot of sense. The leveraged buy-out story, it seems to me, is really based on organizational inefficiencies in a large firm. It isn't just because of management incompetence, by any means. It may not have anything to do with that. It may have to do with all kinds of constraints that are placed on the management of a public firm by public shareholders—the kind of thing that Joe was talking about earlier. Gailen Hite and other academics have looked at leveraged buy-outs and also offered this kind of explanation. And, from a distance, it has sounded very hypothetical to me. But from what you people are saying, this explanation is beginning to make a lot of sense.

The explanation for the increased leverage in LBOs is, I think, the expected increase in value from going private—from the increased organizational efficiencies that you can bring about by having closer monitoring by third-party professionals and investors. And right behind them, obviously, are the banks and the debtholders, who have no small amount of financial expertise. And there is much more flexibility in structuring the compensation contracts, and in changing the rest of the organization. This would also undoubtedly include the ability to close plants with far less interference.

It would be fascinating, I think, to see exactly how one of these things actually works.

JIM: When you talk about organizational inefficiencies, it's not just the change in the compensation package that's important. The change in ownership structure may also dramatically improve the intracorporate allocation of resources. It is a way to cut off making bad decisions, to stop making investments in substandard businesses. Spinning a company off could also have the same effect.

MIKE JENSEN: Yes, the spin-off could accomplish many of the same changes.

GAILEN: I think that this is where the buy-out specialist comes in—that is, as the intermediary between the lenders, the managers, and the equity participants and their funds. In some sense this huge amount of leverage sets up certain incentives to take advantage of bondholders. And yet the fact that the buy-out specialist wants to come back to that market in the future allows him to function as a credible monitor on behalf of the banks and on behalf of the outside equity participants.

So that the debt itself is more part of the mechanism of getting to this new structure than anything really inherent or valuable in the debt itself.

LBOS AND THE WORKINGS OF THE CREDIT MARKETS ___

MIKE JENSEN: I want to go back to something that came up earlier. It is something which I think is going to be very important in whether this system works. The way I see it is this: when you go from being a public firm to a private firm, the major thing you give up is the enormous economies associated with specialization in risk-bearing. That is just huge. By going private, you concentrate that risk in a small number of hands—and even you guys have limited wealth. So you begin to worry about that, and that is one of the things that push you to have these high required returns in leveraged buy-out deals.

One way to get back part of those economies of diversification is through limited liability—through the non-recourse loans and a high leverage ratio. This places a large fraction of that risk—much larger than you would find in a publicly owned corporation—back onto the creditors. Now if that is going to work, it has to be that the costs of losing on that bet have got to be much less than the costs we observe in normal bankruptcy proceedings.

Now, you were saying earlier that those costs really aren't very high in the reorganization of a leveraged buy-out that has gone bad, or in a private reorganization. Do you all agree with that? You guys who have practical experience with what is going on out there in the world? Because if it is true, then it really begins to make sense to me.

CARL: You see where people exercise their rights. You know the banks come first and they, as a consequence, will also be the first to say, "Gee, this is a problem. We have got to do something about it now."

The junior creditors, because they are subordinated, really have some incentives to wait things out. They have to have confidence in management. And the guys at the bottom are really trying to mediate it all to avoid a "workout"—because the typical result of the "workout" is to reschedule debt into equity in some form, thereby reducing the benefits of that leveraged equity, assuming there are any left.

MIKE JENSEN: So, in this case, what is really going on is that the LBO specialists that end up taking a chunk of the equity are really financial experts who promise that they are going to stay around. It is not going to be a one-hit thing. They are going to monitor this whole thing and negotiate with the lenders and handle the whole mess.

And I suspect that the reputation of the buy-out specialist must be important in such a deal because that is what is being sold to the banks and the debtholders. You bond your reputation by putting up your own bucks.

CARL: That is correct. And if your company gets in trouble and you walk away, you will never do another deal. That is the point.

MIKE JENSEN: Yes. That is the point.

GAILEN: Your reputation also has to be very important with the outside equity people—those people who put the money in the pool that you are working with.

MIKE JENSEN: That further leverages your reputation because if you burn them a couple of times, then you are all done too.

MIKE SHERMAN: Wasn't there somebody who walked away from a deal?

CARL: I don't know who the investor group was.

MIKE JENSEN: Let me pursue this just for one moment. Somebody walked away from a deal?

MIKE SHERMAN: Yes, that is my recollection.

MIKE JENSEN: And has it affected their future?

GAILEN: Well, we don't now seem to recall who they were. So apparently it has.

MIKE JENSEN: The theory predicts that they would have a tough time getting back in the market. But your gut feel is that you would have a tough time doing another deal.

CARL: Right.

MIKE JENSEN: Well, does anybody know how and when these leveraged buy-outs got started?

CARL: They've been around for many years, but I think Kohlberg launched the modern era at Bear Stearns around fourteen years ago.

MIKE SEELY: Less publicized ones go back to the fifties. Dyson-Kissner pioneered this approach to deals three decades ago.

MIKE JENSEN: So there has been time—time and recessions enough for things to shake down.

CARL: There have been some workouts. I was involved with a situation that had to be worked out.

MIKE JENSEN: But it didn't involve huge costs? Not the kind of thing you see in a public bankruptcy?

CARL: No. Certainly not. It involved a lot of anguish, though, a lot of difficult negotiations.

MIKE JENSEN: I mean there are certainly going to be lawyers involved because of the conflicting interests of the parties.

CARL: Yes, absolutely. But it was strictly a negotiation between the junior lenders, the senior lenders, and the equityholders. And the equityholders, of course, ended up sucking hind tit and bearing most of the costs of the renegotiation.

MIKE JENSEN: What about the buy-out specialists, the promoters? I mean there is obviously going to be pressure on them to put up more bucks to bail some of these people out.

CARL: Every situation is different. But there is usually big pressure for the banks to reduce their rates, and for the junior lenders to convert some of their debt into equity or warrants. And there is pressure for the preferred stockholders to give up a dividend. Of course, they can convert some of it into common stock. But the process will result in a much more substantial number of common shares, and then everybody's interest is significantly diluted. Then, hopefully, the reorganized company goes merrily on its way.

PRICING LBOS

JOEL: Gailen, the comment was made that when the stock market is low, a lot of these deals seem very attractive because of the so-called upside potential. Do you think that is the case? Do you think the level of stock prices really matters? The stock market last year was up above 1200, and we seemed to see a lot of these deals being done. And today the stock market is a lot lower, and the deals are still being done.

GAILEN: Well, in 1979 the market was down, and we saw LBO deals totaling about $600 million. In 1983, after the market run-up of the previous year, we saw deals of about $7 billion. If your general assertion is correct, then we would expect more of these deals when the market seems low and companies appear to be trading at "bargain" prices. But in fact, it appears that we are seeing a lot more and bigger deals now that the market is relatively high. So I don't think that the relationship is important.

JOEL: Is the price, or the negotiation process, of a leveraged buy-out affected by whether it is an entire public company that is being bought out or just a division of a company?

CARL: In the case of a public company, because of the time it takes to complete an LBO, the acquisition marketplace is the deal. You and I might agree on price. But it is then going to sit out there for 90 or 120 days while we obtain financing, and if it isn't right, somebody else may come along and top it, saying, "I don't think you paid enough."

With a division, it is almost totally dependent on process. If you hired an investment bank and told them to get the best price that they can get, it would be a high price. But if you said, "I like my management team and I am going to try to negotiate a fair deal with them and get somebody to tell me it is a fair deal," then it won't be such a big price. Under those circumstances, though, you are at the mercy of the seller.

JIM: How many of them are the former and how many the latter in the situation where you are spinning off a division?

CARL: More and more managements are hiring professionals to get them the best deal they can get.

MIKE JENSEN: Does that have an effect on the price you pay?

CARL: Yes, it forces the price up.

MIKE SEELY: Hasn't there been a proliferation of people in this game, too? Hasn't that also forced prices up?

CARL: Yeah, there are more people willing to pay to play.

MIKE SEELY: And more capital available.

GAILEN: Let me ask a question about the case where you are taking the entire company private, as opposed to the case of a division, through a leveraged buy-out. We have been talking about restructuring the debt, restructuring the set of contracts. Yet the impression we've been given here is that the idea is eventually to bring the company back public. Now, what I am confused about is this: If public ownership is getting in the way initially, then five years later when you bring that company back public, aren't you going to run into all the same problems that made you go private in the first place? Or is the restructuring so permanent that when the company comes back public those problems are gone for good?

CARL: Well, that is an interesting question. When you are looking at this deal from the front end, you are asking the question: How am I going to get out of this? The public market is one of your alternatives. Selling the business is another. And sale to another buy-out group is a third possibility. It all depends on what looks most advantageous when the time comes to take that action. It will also depend on the feeling of the other investors, on what *they* want to accomplish. But, if one of your objectives is to grow the business and your sources of private capital are limited, then you probably will need to use the public equity markets. This balances the company back into more traditional financial shape, and allows you to continue to build.

A perfect example of this was a company called Guilford Industries. It is a growing company that sells fabric for open plan office systems. It is a textile business and it is capital-intensive. It owns a lot of machinery. Guilford's business was growing at an extraordinary rate—nearly 40 percent a year. They went into a buy-out essentially in order to transfer ownership from one generation to the next, and they needed to get a new group of owners to facilitate that process. But really the only way to enable them to continue to take advantage of the enormous growth in that market, and the share they had in it, was to turn around and raise equity capital in the public markets.

GAILEN: But how, when they come back public, are they going to avoid the problems of public ownership that led to the buy-out in the first place?

CARL: Only by better management.

MIKE SEELY: That is a deal that I really admired. But as I recall, you guys bought it as a textile company at a single-digit multiple. Then you put it out to the public and public investors valued it like a play on open offices, the "office of the future." That was a double-digit multiple. And, therefore, all the stuff we have been talking about is irrelevant to the value-creation that occurred at Guilford. Correct me if I'm wrong.

SPIN-OFFS _____

JOEL: Can somebody help us understand what the differences are between things called "spin-offs" and "split-ups" and "split-offs" and so forth.

It sounds like a real mouthful to me. Gailen, would you like to give this a shot?

GAILEN: Well, I have heard the term "spin-off" used here a couple of times. I have defined a spin-off as the kind of transaction where you separately incorporate a division or a subsidiary, and then distribute the shares of the subsidiary to your existing stockholders. Then the two firms operate as separate entities.

Now, there is another form of spin-off that comes up quite often where instead of distributing stock to your stockholders, you make a public offering—an initial public offering—of stock of a subsidiary.

JOEL: How big a percentage do you offer?

GAILEN: Sometimes the entire thing, sometimes only a fraction. Then, at a later date, you might spin off the rest of it to existing stockholders. The Trans World Corporation did that with TWA. I think they sold 15 to 20 percent in the public market and then distributed the remaining fraction to their existing stockholders. But the difference there is that you do have money coming into the parent corporation when you sell part of it to the public. Whereas with the pure spin-off, there is no infusion of funds.

Now, the "split-up" is where you have a corporation that divides its businesses into two or three separate corporations. The parent company dissolves, and the shares in the different entities are then distributed to the existing stockholders. Finally, the "split-off" is where some of the stockholders exchange their equity interest in the parent for a piece of pie. An example that comes to mind was the deal whereby Dome Petroleum gained ownership of Conoco's Hudson Bay oil and gas fields. Dome purchased an equity interest in Conoco, and then eventually traded that stock for the particular Conoco assets they were looking for. In that case, you don't have this pro rata split-up. You take a specific set of assets, and you go your own separate way. It is essentially a way of making a tax-free sale of assets from one company to another.

MIKE SHERMAN: I think there are three basic kinds of spin-offs that sort of cover the waterfront. One is the spin-off of the losing corporation to bring out the value of the parent. The TWA spin-off is a good example of this.

The second kind is the spin-off of two disparate organizations. That was Olin and Squibb. Two totally different companies each had to go their own way. Olin's spin-off worked very well, and created a new value in the marketplace for the company.

The third kind is to release the value of a subsidiary of a major corporation so that the market can recognize its value. The classic one of all time was Ogden Shipyards' spin-out of Syntex in 1958 at $2 a share.

JOEL: Are you suggesting that the market didn't realize the full value of these two companies when joined together?

MIKE SHERMAN: I make no imputation whatsoever.

(Laughter)

JIM: There is an interesting anti-diversification argument for these spin-offs that has some theoretical soundness. When we talk about mergers, we say, "If you merge A and B, and if there are no business synergies, then nobody is going to be any better or worse off." But there is a fair amount of theory about what is called an "incomplete market." In an incomplete market, so-called "pure plays" may be valuable. Pure plays are companies investors would like to buy, but they can't find those securities simply because they don't exist. So, if you have a corporation that is made up of a series of "pure play" candidates, and you spin off some of these corporations, it is perfectly logical that the sum of the values of the spun-off companies could exceed the value of the original company—without any kind of changes in management efficiency or taxes or anything.

MIKE SEELY: In other words, you create a security that doesn't exist and its scarcity has value.

JIM: Right. It didn't exist. Investors wanted to invest in this business and couldn't do it.

MIKE SEELY: There were two of those "pure play" deals right where I live in Greenwich. CONDEC spun out part of its Unimation subsidiary when everyone was getting excited about productivity and robotics companies. And, when the market interest in defense plays was peaking, Clabir spun out a minority interest in General Defense. Both deals generated low-cost capital for the parent company.

Also, in the area of consumer electronics retailing, there are really only a couple of companies, and they have done quite well. They did well in the recession. So conglomerates with their own consumer electronics divisions are probably looking at the success of these two "pure plays." They are trying to decide whether to buy Sony or RCA. Their participation is attractive to industry. So clones are now coming out. Four of them are in registration right now.

JOEL: I don't understand something. Why does that benefit people from the standpoint of diversification? Am I missing something?

JIM: It is an anti-diversification argument. We all don't have the same expectations, so we all don't buy the same portfolio of securities. I happen to think this industry is going to do very well. The problem I have in buying into that industry is that every time I find a business in the industry, it is part of a great big conglomerate. So I have to buy the whole conglomerate. I don't know if I want to do that. So if the conglomerate spins off the division, it creates a package of securities that fits my preferences better and I will pay for that.

MIKE JENSEN: The "incomplete markets" story can explain a once-and-for-all value increase from such a spin-off. But it won't explain the Syntex kind of thing. It doesn't have any implications for the growth rate of the new entity afterwards. That has to come from some kind of organizational benefits.

JIM: Right, but it could explain some of the things that Gailen is finding about the market's response to spin-off announcements.

MIKE SEELY: But the benefits would go only to the first companies providing the new security. Just as the first issuers who put out zero coupon bonds were the main beneficiaries.

MIKE JENSEN: That is exactly right.

GAILEN: Another reason we found given for spin-offs gets back to some of Mike's points about government regulation. There occasionally are times when the regulatory environment changes and you have a subsidiary—say, a bank or a public utility—that is regulated. That may bring the entire organization under some influence of a regulator—especially in the case of public utilities where, in some states anyway, it appears that the regulators have attempted to tax profits of unregulated businesses to subsidize the rates for consumers on the public utility services. In those cases, management said, "The hell with it. We are going to get rid of this unit, and then the rates will not be set on the basis of the subsidies coming in from the other businesses. They will be set solely on what the utility is doing." So, in some sense, I think there are other reasons for spin-offs. And eliminating outside interference from regulators is one of them.

JOE: This was also true of spin-offs in the oil and gas world. Southern Union Production Company was spun out of the Southern Union Company. It was the third one that was spun out of that utility. They spun out Aztec and one other before that. And those companies went on to be very successful public companies; they were bid for and were purchased by other companies.

MIKE JENSEN: And the spin-offs got them out from underneath the regulatory burden?

JOE: Absolutely. They created value in and of themselves. In your vernacular, though, I guess this deal was technically a "partial public offering" of the unregulated subsidiary's stock. The rest of that subsidiary was later divested and merged with another company.

MIKE SHERMAN: Well, I would like to go on record here as saying that the worst form of this spin-off business is when the corporation takes 20 percent of a subsidiary and sells it to the public. I say this because they usually do this when they think they can "arbitrage" the public sentiment, so to speak, with a subsidiary. At the same time, they want to keep 80 percent so that they can consolidate it for tax purposes.

But when they let go of 20 percent, then all of a sudden they create two problems. One is that the public becomes a minority shareholder. And the actions of the parent can diverge from the interests of that minority shareholder, and they frequently do. The second problem is, if they were so damn smart to sell 20 percent of it to the public, why didn't they sell it all? So, inevitably, you look back and these decisions look horrible, almost every single one of them.

CARL: They could buy them back if they wanted.

MIKE SHERMAN: Yes, they can buy them back. But that would probably compound the problem.

GAILEN: Well, let's take the case of Mesa Petroleum. We talked about Pickens. He did two spin-offs into the oil royalty trusts, one in '79 and one in '82. Now, at the time of each of these spin-offs, he said his reason was that there were tax advantages to having the royalty trust. But he recently announced that he was going to buy back the first one.

MIKE SHERMAN: These were total spin-offs?

GAILEN: Well, the properties are still managed by Mesa, but the royalties go into a trust that is then paid out to the stockholders of the trust—that is, the original stockholders. This allowed Mesa to bypass one level of taxation.

Now if he was doing that to bypass the corporate level of taxation, then why is he now buying it back and subjecting it to corporate taxes?

CARL: He's doing this to increase his reserves. Otherwise, according to his own statement, he would have to sell the company.

GAILEN: Couldn't he engage in long-term contracts with the trust to provide him with the reserves?

CARL: Joe knows a lot about these trusts.

JOE: You can't link these transactions. Don't make that mistake. If you look at them as separate transactions, the spin-out of the first Mesa royalty trust was a very creative move. It bypassed that one level of taxation and it was a great benefit to the shareholders. It got cash flow in their hands.

MIKE JENSEN: Didn't it also do one other important thing? It guaranteed stockholders that those cash flows, or some part of them at least, would not be dumped down more dry rat holes.

JOE: Well, it did several other things, too. It also provided Pickens with a smaller base on which his exploration efforts would be measured, which was an important factor in his decision.

Now, the current transaction should be looked at completely separately. Let's look at it from Pickens' point of view. If, as Carl said, he wants to increase his reserve base—for whatever reason—then he should look to the cheapest way to increase that reserve base. You can either explore or you can find those particular reserves on the balance sheet of traded corporations. And after reviewing traded corporations, Pickens decided that the cheapest way to purchase these reserves was to buy back his own royalty trust.

But by linking these separate deals, you confuse yourself in this whole thing.

MIKE SEELY: A question, though. My understanding, Joe, is that an important feature of these contemplated trusts was the tax comfort they got up front from the IRS. You could then get a letter from the IRS that made clear what your tax situation would be. But the people who followed in Pickens' footsteps have not been able to get that assurance. And today the IRS is saying that future deals might not be allowed to escape taxation at the corporate level; it may be a taxable event on distribution.

JOE: Actually, I think that there have been several tax rulings, involving both Mesa and the subsequent royalty trust. Houston Oil's was a different type of a trust distribution than was Mesa's. And then the Permian Basin's was different from either of these two. Southland Royalty's was a taxable transaction. Boone's was not a taxable transaction. It was an adjustment of basis and it was called a grantor trust.

GAILEN: But isn't Pickens undoing this favorable tax ruling that he got in the first place?

JOE: As I said, you have got to separate the transactions. The shareholder who received the Mesa Royalty Trust now has an option. He can hold that trust and receive the benefits, or he can capitalize the present value of those expected cash streams and sell it back to Pickens for $35 per share.

JIM: Isn't the market saying, though, that the oil isn't worth that much?

JOE: You mean that the present value of the stream is not worth that much? Yes, that's true. But isn't Pickens by the same token saying that it is? So don't you have a classic confrontation where you have got two different people saying what the values are?

JIM: Perhaps, perhaps. But if it is the same market...

JOE: Or any other market.

JIM: Well, except that it is not exactly the same if Mesa is a publicly traded corporation—because the same group of shareholders who are valuing the royalty trust include those who are valuing the corporation.

JOE: Not necessarily the same. They started out the same. But they are not necessarily the same.

JIM: Well, let's say Mesa were a private company, and you told me that the CEO had different expectations about the future price of oil than the market. And, for that reason, the CEO is buying those resources. That makes sense to me. But it's very different if the CEO is the steward for his public shareholders, and if shareholders are saying through the way they price the royalty trusts in other oil companies that they don't think that the oil is worth that much. In this case, it is not clear to me that Boone Pickens ought to be out there paying more to acquire oil than what stockholders think oil is worth.

JOE: In his defense, I would say that he is the steward and he has made the decision that he will stay in the reserve generation business. He wants to have a base of reserves. Once you accept that as an assumption, you then have to look to the best place to purchase those assets.

JIM: That is true. All I am saying is it looks like the market is saying you shouldn't be paying more to buy oil than these royalty trust shares are selling for—because we don't think oil is that valuable.

JOE: But I think that the royalty trust shares trade on a yield basis. You do not have speculators now in royalty trusts.

REAL ESTATE SPIN-OFFS

JOEL: Many financial advisors claim that some companies would realize large values by spinning off their real estate units. Gailen has done a study of two different kinds of companies: real estate companies spinning off real estate units and industrials spinning off real estate units. Can you summarize your results for us, Gailen?

GAILEN: We found that when real estate companies announced they were spinning off their real properties, their stock prices were virtually unchanged, on average. But when industrial firms announced spin-offs of their real estate assets, we found a roughly 9 percent increase in value at the time of the announcement.

JOEL: Were you able to differentiate between cases in which there were basis step-ups and those in which there was none? Are there any important tax, and thus cash flow, differences between these two kinds of deals?

GAILEN: Well, you don't get that in the spin-offs that we were looking at. You place the real estate assets in the new corporation, and then the shares in that new company are distributed to existing stockholders. So, since there is no cash involved or no sale of those assets, there isn't a step-up in the tax basis. In fact, it may carry over the basis from the parent corporation. At least, that's my understanding of the way it works.

DAVID: Did the spinning-off corporation have the same amount of leverage on the real estate that real estate companies usually have? Or were they underleveraged?

GAILEN: I don't know. We didn't look at that.

JOE: My guess is that sample is a tough one, too, because the majority of real estate–oriented companies are not typically publicly held companies. So you get all sorts of aberrations.

MIKE JENSEN: Why is that? Do you have any conjectures?

JOE: Well, the earnings streams are different from those of a public corporation. A real estate company creates value in a different way. Look at the problems the Rouse Company (which I consider to be a very good company) has had in convincing the investing public that earnings don't make any difference. Every year they pay Landauer a quarter of a million dollars to come in and do an updated appraisal. And that appraisal is based upon the pre-tax cash flow generated by their properties. They try to get you to understand that that is the way that company ought to be evaluated.

MIKE SEELY: And yet I would guess it is very undervalued. Here I think you have to make a very strong distinction between the kinds of real estate companies. There is the guy who just builds buildings and gets a depreciation shield on his asset. And then there is the builder who owns large tracts and builds out these properties over time.

My contention is that the market does not pay managements for hoarding valuable assets. Drawing attention to the value of hidden assets which are not generating much cash is a very tough case to make to the market. And all the appraisals in the world won't do it.

Getting third parties to affirm the new higher values of corporate assets isn't new. They are required in Australia, where the new estimates move stock prices very clearly. They are encouraged in the United Kingdom, where they seem to affect stock prices. But they don't work at all here. Appraisals of value will not convince the market that the assets are worth paying huge premiums for—that is, not as long as management uses those assets in a way that produces low explicit rates of return.

MIKE SHERMAN: A successful real estate company has no business showing any earnings. If you are an outside shareholder, why the hell would you want to be in a public real estate company—unless they had plans to liquidate their holdings at some point?

MIKE SEELY: Exactly. That is the same argument I think they made.

MIKE JENSEN: I don't understand this argument. They can hold the real estate privately. So why won't they hold it publicly?

MIKE SEELY: Because the capital spreads look lousy.

MIKE JENSEN: What do you mean by capital spreads?

MIKE SEELY: The spread between the cost of the capital invested in the company's assets and the reported, bookkeeping rate of return earned on that capital and those assets. For most real estate companies, those spreads look awful.

Take the case of Gulfstream Land & Development. It has a book value of over $20 per share and a much higher liquidation value. As it is, their historical reported return on equity is on the order of 10 to 12 percent. That is a few points below the S&P average. If the market was convinced that management would quicken the absorption rate or otherwise liquidate the assets, the stock would go up. We've found it hard to convince the market to factor into the stock price the appreciation in the value of undeveloped acreage, though it is significant. It seems that there is no way to convincingly make that case.

JOE: Mike's point is right on target. If you go out and try to sell a real estate company, you'll find the broad-based buying public will say, "Give us yield." But, in fact, that is the last thing that investors in real estate should want. So you defeat your purpose.

Two years ago I created a real estate company out of Dallas—Lomas and Nettleton has them—and we bought garden apartments with equity dollars. We spent 10 percent of our capital every year in giving people a return. But if that money had been kept within the corporation and reinvested (as it should have been), it would have earned a 20 percent IRR over a fifteen-year life. When I tried to market this idea to investors, however, I couldn't sell share one. I had to beat the sales force to sell $50 million worth.

JIM: How much leverage did you have?

JOE: Zero.

JIM: Good grief!

MIKE SEELY: Gulfstream Land is the same way. They have a squeaky clean balance sheet today, but the market was very antagonistic to the deleveraging they did. And perhaps with good reason.

JOE: In our case, they were worried about the real estate being too highly leveraged. The real estate world in a public marketplace gets very confused about what they want.

MIKE JENSEN: So does that mean that partnerships specialize in turning out these highly leveraged real estate operations?

JOE: They are tax-oriented. It's a very different animal.

MIKE JENSEN: You mean that they are marketing to a different group of investors?

JOE: Absolutely.

MIKE SHERMAN: The same guy who buys a tax deal, an apartment tax deal, won't touch a real estate stock.

JOEL: So why should you ever own a real estate company in the form of a public corporation? Your arguments suggest that you ought to take them all private, so you can manage for after-tax cash flow and not worry about earnings or yield.

For example, take a company that owns and operates commercial properties. If those properties were bought or developed some time ago, why would it make sense to own those properties in a corporate form? Instead they could form a limited partnership, buy the properties, and get a tremendous step-up in the tax basis. And you could change the depreciation schedule from forty to fifteen years. The tax benefits would be enormous.

JOE: Turn the machine off. Let's do a deal.

MIKE SEELY: I'd like to quibble with some of Gailen's findings. Some asset-rich real estate companies have in fact separated the asset part of the company from the development part. The development organization added value, was not capital-intensive, and made good rates of return. The asset part was more or less passive. Cenville Development is a good example. Their deal resulted in significant gains to their shareholders.

JOEL: Koger is a good example of a company which spun out its income-producing properties. So it effectively became two companies: one is the developer, the other is the ownership company. The developer develops the properties and then sells them to the ownership company, and neither of them pays any taxes because of the interest deductions and the depreciation. And that seems to be working very well.

JOE: Well, there is another interesting case of this. Centex builds and then owns for a while. It takes the tax benefits from the real estate, and it spreads them over its oil and gas and its cement businesses. So the three different companies blend together and, theoretically at least, the tax benefits accrue to all. Although I should add that they are now spinning out the oil and gas operation.

JOEL: I have another question. I read some of the statements by management explaining the motives behind these spin-offs. And the statements often say, "The market doesn't really understand the two kinds of businesses when we combine them. So we are going to separate them so the market can see what we are doing." Now, my question is this: Is that really the motivation, or is it really a tax-based argument which management obviously doesn't want to state publicly?

JOE: No comment.

MIKE SHERMAN: Well, let me try to answer this last part of the question you raised. That is, when industrial companies spin off real estate units there seems to be a net benefit. It gets back to this notion of an efficient market. My question is: Do investment analysts truly know the total value of the assets of a corporation if they are not listed? Certainly, appreciation of corporate real estate is not listed on the balance sheet. Second, do investors really know how management might create value out of these assets? Remember when IC Industries sold off its air rights over its station in Chicago? Who would have thought of that? *After* they did it, you would have thought of it. Everybody did then.

JOEL: Well, once management makes the statement that they recognize that value and they are willing to translate that into something which is of value to the shareholders, then the market may respond to that. Especially if it is an asset that nobody is talking about it. Nobody is going to give them credit for it. Because there is no expectation that management is going to make use of it.

DAVID: The 20th-Century Fox acquisition a couple of years ago was very much a case in point. They were sitting with an enormous piece of real estate, and they had no particular intention of liquidating and translating it into value. So it was there, but it wasn't reflected in the share prices. In fact the value of the real estate was enough to finance the whole acquisition. The value of the real estate was equal to the acquisition price, and all the rest of the company came for free. But a stockholder buying one hundred shares had no way of getting at that.

THE EFFICIENCY OF THE PUBLIC CORPORATION AS AN ORGANIZATIONAL FORM

MIKE SEELY: One suggestion that somebody made which fascinated me—and nobody touched it—was that maybe the modern corporation is a terribly flawed mechanism for creating shareholder value. Many corporate managements seem to have a very poor idea of the value-creation opportunities they have in their existing businesses, much less a clear idea about how to exploit them—whether by a divestment procedure using an LBO or spinning out a higher P/E business unit or whatever. I would be very interested in hearing what everybody thinks about this: Is the public company a really efficient vehicle for creating shareholder value? Do managements really understand the potential they have to wrest more value from their existing businesses? And what do these other forms of restructuring have to say about those opportunities?

MIKE SHERMAN: I think the evidence is fairly clear that most corporations have made the wrong bet at the wrong time. They have failed to learn from our history of cycles.

My favorite story about this is the inflation in forest products—the inflation that took place in woodlands in the United States over basically the last fifteen years. Most of the corporate managers who had the job of managing those assets took it as a matter of course that the increases in the value of their real estate would continue forever. They not only became so entranced by this great increase in value of their holdings, but they felt the need to go out and acquire more of it—even though they already had a lot of it. They wanted more because this increase in values was the best thing they had going. It was much better than building a paper mill or developing a distribution system downstream. That would take talent and planning. This way, all you had to do was just to go out and buy a big hunk of it. Remember the bidding contests that took place on one piece of property that went up and up and up?

Well, the whole rationale for expecting that increase in value of those properties to continue was this: One, there was a general inflation. Two, there was a specific policy by the U.S. government to limit the cut. And, of course, we had to go by the government because it owns over half the forests in the country. And, therefore, that limit forced the market to go only to the commercial operators.

Well, when the Reagan administration got in, they opened up public forests, and the price spiral just collapsed. Now, we are talking about the flawed corporation, and I will tell you this: While this was happening, I remember approaching a company which had a $600 million market value. It had received a bid for $1 billion for its forests, which were producing only about 20 percent of its earnings. We suggested that they sell off their forests for a billion dollars and buy back their stock. But our proposal was turned down by management... because they were operating people. They didn't want anything to do with fancy stuff like selling off a good asset like timberlands.

So, maybe the LBO *is* a response to widespread corporate mismanagement. Or, at least, a widespread failure to create stockholder value.

CARL: What you are saying is that management wasn't thinking like stockholders.

MIKE SHERMAN: No, they weren't thinking like stockholders. They were thinking like a professional entrenched management. The only rationale in their life was having more assets under management. They did not care about the rate of return they were earning on those assets.

MIKE JENSEN: Well, wait a minute. I think you have got to keep all this in perspective. If you look back more than a few years—even the last decade or two—I think it is absolutely clear that the corporation is just an incredibly productive social invention. In terms of what it has contributed to human welfare, it must rival something like the invention of the steam engine. Who knows, maybe even the wheel. It is impossible to get dollar estimates of what it has contributed.

That doesn't mean it is perfect. But you have to step back and realize that the corporate form of organization has got to compete with all other possible forms of organization, including the "closed" corporation (which is what I call these things that you create through LBOs), the pure proprietorship or partnership, mutuals, and non-profit organizations. And what we observe, if you look across this spectrum, is that the corporation dominates throughout the free world. First of all, it overwhelmingly dominates in large-scale, complex, non-financial activities. And it does so in spite of these very large tax and regulatory disadvantages that exist in almost every country. There are huge real taxes put on the corporation that are not imposed on other organizational forms.

You guys should certainly understand this because you are in the business of creating some of the competing forms. Non-profit institutions, for example, can compete in this business, and sometimes they do. But in most business activities they don't. They have organizational flaws that have caused them through time simply to find other niches: they generally dominate in cultural and religious and educational activities. Private partnerships tend to be in professional activities like law, consulting, public accounting— although the corporate form is also having some interesting tests there now. But the corporate form just doesn't work as well in those activities. The financial industry mutuals have done very well, and for reasons that we can identify.

That doesn't mean, as I said before, that the public corporate form is perfect. It can have all kinds of problems. And one way to think about this LBO phenomenon is that it represents rising competition from another major organizational form. The bottom line will be whether this movement proves that somehow the corporate form is permanently or deeply flawed— and whether the new taxes and regulations that are continually being imposed by government on the public corporation are going to bury it.

We are not going to get a complete answer to these questions until we find out how these LBOs work themselves out. If they are worked out by taking them public again at the end of the line, then the LBO movement has only been a transitional phase, a reorganization that really is not indicative of a flaw in a particular form, but only a particular manifestation of the species, so to speak. You are merely improving the "gene pool" by taking companies private. But if they stay private, if they stay closed, then that indicates that a larger part of the public corporate sector is going to move over.

MIKE SHERMAN: They can't stay closed.

MIKE JENSEN: Then what you are saying is that the corporate form is not really flawed—not terminally flawed.

MIKE SEELY: Some of the greatest fortunes ever amassed were done via private companies: Ludwig and Onassis—they were running highly leveraged private organizations. I wouldn't dispute with you, Michael, that the modern public corporation does wonderful things. Viewed collectively as an institution, public companies are probably the most just and strongest part of our social fabric. But judged simply by the standard of: do they create wealth more efficiently than other forms?, the record is mixed and that's a factor behind the LBOs.

It seems to me that all you do in an LBO is to recompose the shareholder base. You get rid of the public guys and you bring in a small group of highly motivated stockholders and quasi-stockholders. They then may lose some of their attractiveness in an institutional sense—minority employment, corporate philanthropy, etc.—but they probably will create more total wealth. It's Adam Smith's "invisible hand" at work.

MIKE JENSEN: But the point is that this fundamentally changes the nature of the organization. Legally these things have the same form; they are both called corporations; they are taxed the same. But from an economic standpoint, they are different organizations. And the economists are beginning to treat them as different organizations.

They differ in this sense. The "open" corporation, as I want to call the Fortune 500, has residual claims that are unrestricted in the sense that anybody can own them. The closed corporation has a set of residual claims that are restricted to a small set of people who often are also major decision agents in the firm. You can't sell your right to be a partner in a law firm. Non-profits don't have residual claims. They are the extreme form of this kind of thing. The mutuals require their residual claims to be linked to the customers of the organization. These are all very different organizations.

MIKE SHERMAN: There is a hybrid form of organization in the world that is both a public and a private corporation. It is the average corporation in Japan. They rarely raise money in the equity market. Their source of funds is the plowback of earnings plus tremendous leverage from the banks. They have a very close relationship with their banks. Their bank loans frequently represent 50 percent of their capital.

It is changing, though, as we go through time. But in that situation, the professional managers of these corporations did not get their rewards through enormous leverage off the equity. They got their regards from enormous status within the society. But you know, there are parallels elsewhere for these very close relationships between financial institutions and industrial corporations.

MIKE JENSEN: This is limited in the United States by Glass Steagall, and all kinds of other restrictions that come from the anti-trust laws as well. If there is anybody that knows about the Japanese system, I would like to know more about it. My conjecture is that it works as follows: groups of organizations form around a major trading company, and there will always be a major bank involved. The interesting part of that structure is that they have figured out a brilliant way to solve conflicts of interest in a private way without involving the courts or the state. It is my understanding that banks in Japan are not subject to the same set of constraints that the banks in the United States are with respect to the ownership of equity.

MIKE SHERMAN: As a matter of fact, in order to get business from a Japanese industrial corporation, a bank will request permission of that corporation to buy a certain percentage of the stock.

MIKE JENSEN: That is just what I wanted to hear. This means that, in the Japanese system, the banks can hold an approximately unlevered position in each of the organizations that make up this group. The bank is then in a position to be a private enforcer of contracts. So when conflicts arise between these organizations, as they inevitably do, the bank is in a position to take the correct view of the situation—that is, one that chooses the resolution of those contractual disputes that maximizes the value of the complete pie. And how do the banks enforce the contracts? They enforce them through future decisions they make with respect to providing debt and allowing companies to stay affiliated with this group.

When you have that kind of low-cost enforcement process, you can have a much richer set of exchanges across organizational boundaries. For example, if one of the firms—even a major firm—gets in trouble, my understanding is that labor will move out to other firms on a temporary basis and then be brought back in. How is all that accomplished? It is not accomplished just because they are friends, it is accomplished because there is a contract-enforcement mechanism—and I don't mean legal contracts that are written down. I believe that the Japanese banks play a major role in keeping intercompany disputes out of the courts and out of the political sector.

This is very different from what goes on in the United States. We are handicapped in the United States. American industry in the financial sector is prevented from doing these kinds of thing by anti-trust laws. Even though adopting such a system would increase the efficiency of our economy, this would not play well in Washington and with the Nader types. In this country, we have a penchant, as individuals, for using the political sector to cut our own throats. For example, certain segments of the financial community don't want the banks involved in these kinds of things and vice versa. And what this artificial segmentation does is to cripple the entire system.

JIM: But I think there are some things going on in our system now that are mitigating this problem. You mentioned that corporate operating people don't care that much about managing for the stockholders. But I think that one of the things that so riled people in the oil business was that Boone Pickens was very aggressively taking a shareholder-wealth maximization perspective. He was challenging the conventional corporate notion that "this is the way we run an oil company, and to run an oil company we have got to be fully integrated: we have got to have marketing and we have got to have distribution and all this sort of thing." Whether you agree with the point or not, he was saying, "Look, there are certain parts of the oil business that are negative net present value activities. And if we are going to run this thing to maximize shareholder wealth, we ought to split these companies up and change the way that they are operating."

One of the interesting things we have been seeing recently is that a lot of very large American corporations are under pressure now to stop looking at their business from the old conventional point of view—to stop saying, "this is the way we run an oil company." They are being forced by these incredibly large takeovers, by LBOs and by a new stockholder activism to ask, "Well, what do we have to do to maximize the value of the corporation?" So, although we don't have the flexibility of the Japanese system, it seems to me that some of these recent developments are encouraging.

COMMENTARY:
WHY RESTRUCTURING WORKS
by David M. Glassman

In the last several years, headlines describing corporate restructurings have become so familiar as to seem routine. What is different about recent restructurings, however, is that instead of using acquisitions to change their mix of businesses, a large number of companies are downsizing. Spin-offs, divestitures, leveraged buy-outs, asset trusts, partnerships, and even liquidations have been used to change dramatically such well-known companies as Atlantic Richfield, Allied-Signal, Union Carbide, Gulf + Western, Beatrice, TRW, and Phillips Petroleum, to name just a few. Additionally, such strategies have been accompanied by major financial structure changes. Stock repurchases, often at a premium to the market price, have been used to return capital to investors and have resulted in much more aggressive use of financial leverage.

What is particularly interesting is that, unlike the large acquisitions of recent years, spin-offs and divestitures have benefited stockholders. Evidence accumulated by financial markets researchers clearly indicates that many, if not most, recent acquisitions have at best resulted in no significant gains for stockholders of the acquiring company. Spin-offs and divestitures, on the other hand, have often resulted in considerable gains, even though they are often accompanied by large accounting write-offs that make the company's earnings appear particularly dismal.

THE WRONG REASON

In explaining this trend many analysts and other "experts" have offered a broad array of dubious, often simplistic rationalizations. One of the most common, often used by the restructuring management itself, is that the market doesn't understand the value of a company that has diverse operations. A corollary is that investment analysts specialize along industry lines. This means that a company like W. R. Grace, which participates in several industries, will not have a well-informed following and will therefore sell at less than its "true" value. This reasoning is so prevalent it even has an abbreviated notation, the "conglomerate discount."

When offered by management this rationale is self-serving. Portfolio managers, analysts, and other investors have tremendous incentive to understand the operations of even the most complex company. While one can perhaps believe that investors, when taken in the aggregate, fail to understand a few select companies, the claim that the market cannot make fair estimates of *any* (or even most) diversified companies' operations is particularly doubtful. While it is a palatable explanation for management, there is little evidence to suggest that we should take it seriously.

THE RIGHT REASONS

Why, then, do these kinds of restructurings seem to work? Interestingly, many of the same reasons that explain this also account for why acquisitions often result in lower stock values. It often appears that investors don't believe management fully understands all the businesses they oversee. And with good reason. The results of oil company forays into unrelated activities have been well documented. The pairings of Sohio and Kennecott, Arco and Anaconda, Exxon and Reliance Electric, Mobil and Montgomery Ward, have all been disastrous for stockholders. Similarly, Gulf + Western's long pursuit of growth and diversification led to a large company, but not one prized by investors. General Mills, in the wake of losses in the toy and apparel businesses, refocused its efforts on the core food business by spinning off the peripheral activities. And RCA, prior to its purchase by General Electric, bought and then sold its finance business, CIT, within a four-year period.

The diversification, and subsequent restructuring, of some of these (Arco, Gulf + Western, General Mills) and other companies have been greeted with remarkable consistency by the investment community: first, a declining or flat stock price associated with diversifying acquisitions, and then a stock price surge with the efforts to narrow the focus of management. For example,

Gulf + Western's (G + W's) stock price has increased by about 180 percent since the change of management that elevated Martin Davis to the leadership in February 1983. (The S&P 500 has also improved, but by less than 50 percent over this period.) G + W's stock appreciated by only 13 percent over the entire three-year period prior to the change, while the S&P 500 advanced by about 30 percent. Davis' contribution has been a major divestiture program, the most recent being the sale of the consumer and industrial business to Wickes for about $1 billion. The result is a more streamlined, competitive group of businesses that gets more attention from management and is thus more attractive to investors.

Divestitures of profitable businesses can also benefit stockholders. Esmark, in 1981, broke up its energy subsidiary and sold the pieces to Mobil and other petroleum companies. At the same time it announced a commitment to the consumer products business, and a large stock repurchase to return capital to investors.

The reason for the divestiture was not that the energy subsidiary was performing poorly; in fact, it had contributed over 40 percent of Esmark's profits in 1979. Esmark's management was unwilling to undertake the capital commitment required to grow the business. Announcement of the planned sale, and the renewed focus on consumer products, resulted in a 68 percent stock price gain during June 1981, the month that the plan was made public.

Another restructuring, also in 1981, was the sale of the ethical pharmaceutical business by Richardson-Merrell. Again, management was unwilling to commit to the necessary capital expenditures, R&D in this case, required to achieve profitable growth in a competitive environment. The announcement of the sale—to Dow Chemical, a company willing to make these expenditures—was greeted favorably by investors. Richardson-Merrell's stock price jumped by over 20 percent in the two weeks surrounding announcement of the sale.

Several conclusions are obvious: If a company's management does not understand a business, they can add value by selling it to a management that does. Also, where a company cannot, or will not, adopt the appropriate strategy for a business, they can nevertheless access this value in a sale to another company that will. These observations may seem rather mundane, but oddly, many companies have ignored them. The evidence is the presence, indeed the flourishing, of corporate raiders.

Corporate raiders prey on managements deploying stockholder funds inefficiently, especially in declining businesses. Where existing management may be growing the company by investing in uneconomical activities (oil and gas exploration, for example), the corporate raider can create value by reducing investment and returning capital to stockholders. The raider calculates that the resulting stock price gain will more than compensate for the initial premium required to obtain control of the company.

It is a good bet that fear of a corporate raider accounts for many of the recent restructurings. Last April, Atlantic Richfield (Arco) announced massive changes in their operations and finances, including the following:

1. The sale of all (2,200) Arco gasoline stations and refining operations east of the Mississippi River.
2. Sale or closing of all mining and metals manufacturing operations.
3. A 50 percent reduction in expenditures for oil and gas exploration.
4. A commitment to repurchase about 30 percent of the outstanding stock, and a 33 percent dividend increase.

Arco's stock price increased by more than 20 percent during the week of the announcement. There are several reasons for this dramatic response, but none have anything to do with Arco becoming an easier company to understand. Rather, management indicated that instead of investing additional funds in oil exploration—an activity that the market seems to value less with each passing day—it will return cash to stockholders. Interestingly, recent research indicates that announcements of expenditures for exploration and development during the period 1975–81 have resulted in stock price declines. Announcement of all other types of capital expenditures has resulted in improved stock market values. (See "Corporate Capital Expenditure Decisions and the Market Value of the Firm," J. J. McConnell and C. J. Muscarella, *Journal of Financial Economics*, September 1985.) It seems that Boone Pickens' idea of creating royalty trusts is right after all. By creating a trust to hold income-producing properties, management guarantees that the cash flow will go directly to investors, and will not be used to subsidize uneconomical expenditures elsewhere in the company.

SPIN-OFFS

Another interesting restructuring device is the corporate spin-off. In its pure form the spin-off involves no cash; it is merely a distribution of stock in a subsidiary company. The end result is two separate and independent public corporations with the same stockholders. Academic research over the last several years indicates that spin-offs are viewed favorably by investors. The combined value of the two companies after the spin-off often exceeds the value of the single company before the distribution. Explaining this phenomenon has also led to some confusion among financial market observers.

For example, the primary explanation for Allied-Signal's huge spin-off of multiple businesses is that it allows the company to shed unprofitable operations. This is misleading. The management of Allied-Signal will no longer have to worry about the performance of these businesses, *but the stock-*

holders will. The spin-off does not result in a change of ownership; the same stockholders will benefit, or suffer, from the performance of the departing businesses. A spin-off should not be confused with a divestiture.

The existence of a "conglomerate discount" is also used to explain why spin-offs benefit stockholders. As before, however, there are better explanations. First, while the spin-off does not result in a change of ownership, it does change management. In fact, the greatest benefit to stockholders arises from a spin-off of unrelated activities, but not because it makes the company easier to understand. Instead, the spin-off often results in a senior management team more familiar with the company's operations and markets. The stock price gain therefore reflects the market's expectations for improved performance. There may, of course, be other reasons: the spin-off streamlines the decision-making process, allows incentive compensation awards to be linked directly to stock price improvements, and may result in better information being communicated to investors.

While all of these actions are desirable, it should be noted that the benefits can be obtained without resorting to a spin-off. What is required is a commitment to managing the business for the company's stockholders, careful attention to signals provided by the market, and the confidence that sophisticated investors are capable of ferreting out the fair value of the company's operations. If management is unwilling to make this commitment there are always the corporate raiders.

COMMENTARY:
A FRAMEWORK FOR SETTING REQUIRED
RATES OF RETURN BY LINE OF BUSINESS
by Bennett Stewart

To create value for shareholders, capital should be allocated only to those businesses where the return earned is likely to exceed the cost of obtaining capital. In this context the cost of capital is not a cash cost; rather it is an opportunity cost equal to the rate of return investors could otherwise expect to earn on investments of equivalent risk. Thus, a company like Apple Computer, which borrows no money and pays no dividends on common shares, has a positive cost of capital—and in fact quite a high one, given its level of risk—even though it has no explicit cash costs.

All companies have four important costs of capital: (1) a cost of capital for business risk, (2) a cost of borrowing, (3) a cost of equity, and (4) a weighted average cost of total (debt and equity) capital.

1. The *cost of capital for business risk* is the return investors require to compensate for the variability in operating profits. All other costs of capital are determined either directly or indirectly by the level of risk in the business. In practice, it may

be estimated by adding a premium for business risk to the rate prevailing on relatively risk-free, long-term government bonds.

2. The *cost of borrowing* is the required return for credit risk, or the risk in receiving contractual principal and interest payments on debt. It can be estimated by the current after-tax yield to maturity on the firm's long-term debt obligations.

3. The *cost of equity* is the return sought to compensate for the risk in the bottom-line profits available to shareholders. By paying fixed-interest payments out of uncertain operating profits, bottom-line profits are riskier, or more volatile, than operating profits. The cost of equity accordingly is equal to the cost of capital for business risk plus a financial risk premium to compensate investors for the additional earnings variability introduced by leverage. Like the cost of capital for business risk, it may be estimated by adding a premium for business *and* financial risk to the prevailing rate on government bonds.

4. The *weighted average cost of capital* is the blended cost of the firm's debt and equity capital. It is calculated by weighting the individual costs of debt and equity by the relative proportion each represents in the company's target financial structure. Conceptually, it is equal to the cost of capital for business risk less a discount to reflect the tax savings from deducting interest.

The weighted average cost of capital is the *most important* of the four capital costs because it represents (1) the hurdle rate for capital budgeting computations, (2) the standard for evaluating past rates of return on total capital, and (3) the target for future operating performance. But it is not appropriate for all corporate uses.

Consider the case of a diversified company with several different lines of business. The weighted average cost of capital for the consolidated company may be useful as a benchmark for generally reviewing performance and setting goals for overall performance. In most cases, however, individual hurdle rates should be assigned to each division or SBU to reflect differences in business risk and debt financing capacity. Requiring all operating units to cover a single cost of capital may unfairly penalize low-risk businesses and inadvertently subsidize high-risk ones.

OVERVIEW OF THE FRAMEWORK

In general, the most reliable source for assessing risk is share prices. The market communicates its estimate of risk through fluctuations in share values. Unfortunately, share prices are of little use in distinguishing differences in risk among product lines within a company. Consequently, a framework is needed for measuring business risk that directly evaluates the riskiness of individual operating activities.

Stern Stewart & Co. has developed a procedure for estimating how investors would perceive the risk of divisions and SBU's (as well as private companies) if they were publicly traded, stand-alone companies. Our research focused on the operating characteristics of approximately 3,000 publicly traded companies in the United States and Canada. After grouping the companies into fifty broad industry categories, a sophisticated statistical process was employed to identify the significant relationships between various financial ratios and beta, an index of investment risk. These ratios in turn were grouped into four "Risk Factors" which, when weighted according to their importance, can be used to explain the differences in risk among companies in the same overall industry. (An example of this method is presented at the end of this paper.)

The importance of this technique is its application to measuring hurdle rates for divisions and private companies. The first step in the procedure is to identify the unit's industry classification. A "Risk Index" is assigned that represents the average business risk for the designated industry group. (A sample of these business risk indices is exhibited on the following page.)

In the next stage of the procedure, the unique operating characteristics of the unit in question are compared to the industry average. To the extent the ratios differ from those of the average company in the industry, the unit will be assigned to a higher or lower risk category. This process yields a predicted "Business Risk Index" (BRI), which reflects all the adjustments resulting from the analysis of the four Risk Factors. The BRI represents what the "beta" on common shares would be if the unit were all equity financed and publicly traded.

THE RISK FACTORS

The calculation of the BRI focuses on a series of ratios grouped into four Risk Factors. The four Risk Factors found to be most important are:

1. Operating Risk
2. The Risk in Achieving Profitable Growth
3. Asset Management
4. Size and Diversity of Operations

Each of these is discussed in more detail in the following sections.

1. Operating Risk

The first set of ratios measures the risk in achieving a predictable level of operating profitability over time. It gauges investors' confidence (or lack thereof) in predicting future rates of return on capital already employed. When a unit's profitability is judged to be more unpredictable than that of other companies in the industry, its risk index, and thus its required return, are adjusted upward.

		Bus Risk +	Fin Risk =	Equity Risk
1	Mining & Metals	1.43	.21	1.64
56	**Miscel Insurance**	**1.15**	**.34**	**1.49**
27	Motor Vehicles	1.01	.20	1.21
9	**Construction**	**.99**	**.42**	**1.41**
32	Air Transport	.99	.77	1.76
36	**Media**	**.99**	**.29**	**1.28**
28	Aerospace & Defense	.95	.34	1.29
35	**Publishing**	**.95**	**.21**	**1.16**
23	Pollution Control	.95	.28	1.23
7	**Oil & Gas Services**	**.95**	**.37**	**1.32**
24	Electronics	.94	.28	1.22
29	**Railroad & Transit**	**.93**	**.31**	**1.24**
22	Producer Goods	.92	.25	1.17
45	**Leisure Time**	**.91**	**.36**	**1.27**
25	Office Equipment	.90	.43	1.33
16	**Forest Products**	**.89**	**.32**	**1.21**
3	Aluminum	.87	.14	1.01
42	**Durables**	**.86**	**.37**	**1.23**
11	Real Estate	.86	.33	1.19
30	**Trucking & Freight**	**.84**	**.35**	**1.19**
10	Construction Materials	.84	.32	1.16
50	**Miscellaneous**	**.83**	**.47**	**1.30**
46	Photographic	.83	.20	1.03
17	**Paper**	**.82**	**.27**	**1.09**
43	Lodging	.81	.62	1.43
4	**Precious Metals**	**.81**	**.28**	**1.09**
31	Water Transport	.80	.37	1.17
41	**Housewares**	**.79**	**.19**	**.98**
21	Tires & Rubber	.79	.25	1.04
54	**Miscellaneous Finance**	**.79**	**.50**	**1.29**
47	Distribution (General)	.79	.32	1.11
2	**Iron & Steel**	**.78**	**.27**	**1.05**
40	Textiles & Apparel	.78	.29	1.07
18	**Packaging**	**.78**	**.22**	**1.00**
37	Cosmetics	.77	.15	.92
20	**Agricultural Chemicals**	**.76**	**.24**	**1.00**
39	Health Care	.75	.34	1.09
5	**Coal & Uranium**	**.75**	**.26**	**1.01**
38	Drugs	.73	.19	.92
53	**Mortgage Finance**	**.73**	**.87**	**1.60**
	ALL INDUSTRY AVERAGE	**.72**	**.28**	**1.00**
8	Refining & Distribution	.70	.23	.93
49	**Services**	**.69**	**.48**	**1.17**
19	Chemicals	.69	.28	.97
6	**Oil & Gas**	**.69**	**.34**	**1.03**
48	Distribution (Food)	.66	.29	.95
12	**Agriculture/Food**	**.64**	**.23**	**.87**
44	Restaurants	.62	.55	1.17
34	**Gas Utilities**	**.60**	**.31**	**.91**
13	Beverages	.58	.22	.80
26	**Telephone & Telegraph**	**.57**	**.32**	**.89**
14	Liquor	.52	.14	.66
15	**Tobacco**	**.47**	**.07**	**.54**
33	Electric Utilities	.34	.30	.64

2. Risk in Achieving Profitable Growth

Our research demonstrates that unrealized investment opportunities create an additional risk for investors. As the perceived value of future investments change, this leads to dramatic movements in share prices and great risk for investors. For example, as IBM's success in personal computers became apparent, investors marked down the likely value from Digital Equipment Corporation's (DEC's) participation in the office of the future. The result: DEC's stock price fell by nearly $30. Similar dramatic stock price movements have been experienced by Apple Computer, Genentech, and Peoplexpress. The common attributes are rapid growth, great profit potential, and high P/E multiples.

It is precisely these attributes that our statistical research revealed as conveying high business risk. Accordingly, a single measure of risk is derived by weighting the unit's rate of return and growth rate. A business unit whose combined score is higher than that of its business peers will be deemed to have a higher price-earnings ratio and more risk in achieving continued profitable growth.

3. Asset Quality

The Risk Factor that measures the quality of a company's assets has four components: Working Capital Management, Plant Intensity, Plant Newness, and Useful Plant Life. Maintaining low and stable levels of working capital—inventory and receivables, less payables and accruals—relative to competitors demonstrates a superior budgeting and control capability. Managing working capital effectively also provides an additional source of cash during recessions and, in expansionary cycles, minimizes the need for external capital to grow. This is viewed positively by investors and results in a reduction in the company's BRI.

The extent to which a company is more plant-intensive than other companies in its business suggests that management has established a dominant position through a low-cost production capability. The fact that management is willing to commit a large amount of fixed capital is an indication of management confidence that results in a reduction in the Risk Index.

Also, the newer the plant, the less is the perceived risk in a company's assets. Older plants, because of their higher operating cost, generally are the first to be shut down in a recession, only to be reopened in expansionary times. As a result, companies operating older, less efficient plants will experience more volatile returns over a business cycle than companies with new plants. Thus, they are penalized with a higher risk index.

A related characteristic is useful plant life. Having to replace important assets frequently exposes the company to risk, and is a sign of rapid and often unpredictable technological change. In contrast, longer-lived assets

STERN STEWART & CO. FINANCIAL REPORT   INTL BUSINESS MACHINES CORP
BUSINESS RISK ANALYSIS

Industry Risk

Industry Number	Industry Segment	(1) Standard Risk Index	(2) Weight	(3) = (1)x(2) Contrib to Risk Index
25	Office Equipment	0.90	100.0	0.90
			100.0%	0.90

Adjustments For:

Number	Risk Factor	(1) Standard Value	(2) Weight	(3) = (1)x(2) Contrib to Risk Index
1	Operating Risk	−0.71	0.11	−0.08
2	Risk in Achieving possible growth	−0.12	0.12	−0.01
	Profitability	0.20		
	Growth	−0.20		
3	Asset Quality	0.54	−0.11	−0.06
	Work Cap Mgmt	0.52		
	Plant Intensity	0.30		
	Plant Newness	−0.09		
	Useful Plant Life	0.08		
4	Size and Diversity	0.23	−0.04	−0.01
	Size	0.19		
	Foreign Income	0.14		
Adjustment		−0.81	0.20	−0.16
Business Risk Index (BRI)				0.74

STERN STEWART & CO. FINANCIAL REPORT   DIGITAL EQUIPMENT
BUSINESS RISK ANALYSIS

Industry Risk

Industry Number	Industry Segment	(1) Standard Risk Index	(2) Weight	(3) = (1)x(2) Contrib to Risk Index
25	Office Equipment	0.90	100.0	0.90
			100.0%	0.90

Adjustments For:

Number	Risk Factor	(1) Standard Value	(2) Weight	(3) = (1)x(2) Contrib to Risk Index
1	Operating Risk	−0.29	0.11	−0.03
2	Risk in Achieving possible growth	0.54	0.12	0.07
	Profitability	−0.37		
	Growth	0.69		
3	Asset Quality	−0.53	−0.11	−0.06
	Work Cap Mgmt	−0.81		
	Plant Intensity	−0.23		
	Plant Newness	0.54		
	Useful Plant Life	0.07		
4	Size and Diversity	−0.38	−0.04	0.02
	Size	−0.03		
	Foreign Income	−0.56		
Adjustment		0.53	0.20	0.11
Business Risk Index (BRI)				1.01

are viewed by investors as providing operating stability and, hence, serve to reduce risk.

4. Size and Diversity

Absolute size of assets and the diversification of earnings sources tend to stabilize a company's performance. The size of the company often suggests the degree of market power it has in its industry, the length of its track record, all factors generally associated with lower business risk. Also, geographic diversification is viewed as mitigating overall business risk. The reason is that a company's investment in other countries reduces investors' exposure to business cycles in the United States.

IBM VERSUS DEC

To illustrate how our framework for measuring business risk takes all these factors into consideration, we have included sample printouts comparing IBM and DEC.

Not surprisingly, the exhibit reveals that even though both companies are in the office equipment business, IBM's risk as perceived by investors is far less than that of DEC, for several reasons.

- IBM's operating earnings are more stable.
- IBM is less profitable on average and grows less rapidly than DEC, and therefore will sell at a lower P/E. This means that investors in IBM have less of a gamble on uncertain future results.
- IBM's asset quality and management are superior.
- IBM is much larger and derives a greater portion of its operating income from foreign operations, which diversifies risk exposure.

Though the business risk measurement procedure illustrated above has been developed only recently, it is available in Stern Stewart's software system, "Corporate Financial Reports." This risk framework is now being used by a number of diversified companies, as well as companies in the food, oil, and forest products industries.

V

The Leveraging of Corporate America
A DISCUSSION OF CORPORATE CAPITAL STRUCTURE

INTRODUCTION

Is there such a thing as an "optimal" capital structure for the public corporation? What are the real benefits and costs of leverage? Does the relative
scarcity of triple A–rated companies suggest that corporate America is acquiring a greater appreciation of the value of debt financing? Is the triple
A company in fact an anachronism, one that promises to be eradicated once
and for all by ever larger corporate takeovers? Do the leveraged buy-out
and "junk bond" phenomena have any implications for the financing of
"blue-chip" corporations?

These questions have in the 1980s attained a prominence, and indeed
perhaps an urgency, that may be unprecedented in our corporate history.
For, along with the recent wave of corporate restructuring activities—mergers, divestitures, leveraged buy-outs, spin-offs, and stock repurchases—we
have seen a large number of companies undergoing dramatic changes in
capital structure. In the leveraged buy-out movement, for example, private
companies have been supporting debt-to-asset ratios upwards of 90 percent.
We have also seen large public companies, traditionally levered at 50 percent
debt-to-equity or lower, resorting to the "junk bond" market to make large
acquisitions and, in so doing, raising their debt-to-equity ratios well above
one. At the same time, many corporate restructurings have included major
stock repurchase programs which may reflect a more explicit, permanent
decision to leverage the capital structure. And, lest you think these are wholly
unrepresentative cases, Standard & Poor's Chief Economist, David Blitzer,
reports that over the period 1982–84, the total equity of all non-financial
American companies fell by $77 billion while total short- and long-term
borrowings increased by $492 billion.

Critics of the widespread restructuring activity view this apparent leveraging of corporate America as one of its most alarming by-products. A

number of other observers, however, have hailed these changes as reflecting a belated recognition by corporate treasurers that the tax advantages of debt financing can add significant value. Still another group views both of the above arguments with skepticism. They contend that although corporate restructuring may have increased the optimal amount of debt in *some* corporate capital structures—in large part because it increases the value of the corporation itself—the principal use of this new debt has been to provide the *means* for executing the restructuring transactions (for example, the use of junk bonds to finance an acquisition).

In the "Discussion of Corporate Capital Structure" which follows, two distinguished academics discuss the causes and import of these new developments with two corporate financial executives, an investment banker, and a representative of one of the major bond rating agencies. Joel Stern opens the discussion by suggesting that many public corporations may well have been significantly underleveraged prior to the recent changes—perhaps because of a managerial aversion to risk-taking. Increasing pressure from stockholder activists, Stern argues, may now be forcing managements to lever up their balance sheets. Provided there is a major tax advantage to borrowing, corporate decisions to maintain "reserve borrowing power" may simply be extending invitations to corporate raiders. (As a matter of general interest—and this is not meant to confuse anecdote with evidence—both of the companies represented in this discussion were relatively conservatively leveraged corporations which, after this discussion took place in May, have since become subsidiaries of their now highly leveraged acquirers.)

Stern's position, which as always contains at least an element of devil's advocacy, attracts plenty of opposition. For example, the University of Rochester's Clifford Smith voices strong doubt about the proposition that we are now witnessing a permanent increase in corporate America's use of debt financing. According to Smith, much of the leverage is merely a means to the end of changing corporate ownership; that is, it is not leverage per se that is allowing corporate managements to pay large premiums to acquire other companies (or to take their own private), but rather the value added by the transfer of ownership itself. As Smith also suggests, the leveraged buy-out and junk bond phenomena may be attributable in part to the fact that a number of growth industries appear to have "matured" in recent years. And, as Stewart Myers argued in a 1976 paper ("The Determinants of Corporate Borrowing"), and as Michael Jensen has argued in a series of papers (most notably, "Takeovers Are Reducing Waste in the Oil Industry") defending the restructuring of the oil industry, maturing companies that are rich in tangible assets and generating lots of excess cash are prime candidates for highly leveraged capital structures.

DHC

THE LEVERAGING OF CORPORATE AMERICA
A DISCUSSION OF CORPORATE CAPITAL
STRUCTURE
May 24, 1985

JOEL STERN, MODERATOR: On behalf of all of us involved with the *Midland Corporate Finance Journal*, I would like to welcome you to this discussion of corporate capital structure. I want to begin this morning by considering a number of general issues in capital structure planning:

1. Is there such a thing as an "optimal" capital structure? What are the real benefits (and costs) of leverage? Are American companies making full use of those benefits? Do the leveraged buy-out and junk bond financing phenomena have any implications for the financing of "blue-chip" corporations? What are the other major considerations in setting capital structure targets?

2. What are the primary factors affecting a company's bond rating? and of what use, incidentally, are bond ratings to a corporate treasurer in formulating a capital structure target? Does the relative scarcity of triple A–rated companies suggest that corporate America is acquiring a greater appreciation of the value of debt? Is the triple A company in fact an anachronism, one that promises to be eradicated once and for all by ever larger corporate takeovers?

3. Then we can move on to specific financing questions: Why should management prefer fixed-rate to floating-rate debt financing? What are the real as opposed to the alleged benefits of all the new kinds of financing instruments that have been introduced in the past few years, such as zero-coupon bonds, interest rate swaps, floating-rate preferreds, convertible exchangeable, commodity-linked, and otherwise-indexed bonds. More generally, we would like to explore the process of financial innovation: How permanent are the benefits it promises, and who stands to benefit the most from the process—corporate issuers, investors, or investment bankers and other financial intermediaries?

With this as overview, let me introduce the members of our panel, who bring to the table an interesting diversity of viewpoints and experience.

CHESTER GOUGIS is a Group Vice President of Duff and Phelps;

ANDREW KALOTAY is a Vice President of Salomon Brothers in its Bond Portfolio Analysis group;

CLIFFORD SMITH is Associate Professor of Finance at the University of Rochester and an Editor of the *Journal of Financial Economics*;

BENNETT STEWART is my colleague at Stern Stewart & Co.;

ROBERT TAGGART is Professor of Finance at Boston University and Editor of *Financial Management*;

BRIAN WALSH is Assistant Treasurer of General Foods; and

HARRY WINN is Treasurer of American Hospital Supply.

ACADEMIC PERSPECTIVES ON CAPITAL STRUCTURE ___

JOEL: As you all know, the purpose of the *Midland Corporate Finance Journal* is to bring to the attention of senior financial executives the most important research taking place at the premiere graduate schools of business. The centers of research at the moment that are doing some of the most outstanding work are places that we all know—places with names like the University of Chicago, Wharton, the MIT Sloan Shool, Stanford, and so forth. But one of the most undervalued of such institutions is the University of Rochester. We have with us a representative from Rochester today, Clifford Smith; and we're very happy, Cliff, that your organization spends so much time training people so well while, at the same time, failing to market that fact. We rarely like to publicize this fact, by the way, because this allows us to hire their graduates at well below fair value.

Anyway, Cliff is a representative of that breed of serious researchers that keeps our magazine going, and what I would like to do today is to begin the program, as we have often done in the past, by asking Cliff to give us the academic research community's version of the "big picture" on corporate capital structure.

I have here on my lap a copy of an article from the *Journal of Finance* published in July 1984 called "The Capital Structure Puzzle." The author of this piece, incidentally, is Stewart Myers of MIT's Sloan School, who is widely recognized by his colleagues as perhaps the most authoritative writer on matters of corporate capital structure. And the article begins as follows:

This paper's title is intended to remind you of Fischer Black's well-known note on "The Dividend Puzzle," which he closed by saying, "What should the corporation do about dividend policy? We don't know." I will start by asking, "How do firms choose their capital structures?" Again, the answer is "We don't know."

The capital structure puzzle is tougher than the dividend one. We know quite a bit about dividend policy.... We know stock prices respond to unanticipated dividend changes, so it is clear that dividends have information content.... We do not know whether high dividend yield increases the expected rates of returns demanded by investors... but financial economists are at least hammering away at this issue.

By contrast, we know very little about capital structure. We do not know how firms choose the debt, equity or hybrid securities they issue. We have only recently discovered that capital structure changes convey information to investors.... In general, we have inadequate understanding of corporate financial behavior, and of how that behavior affects security returns.

So, I guess, Cliff, the question I am asking is whether you think there is really such a thing as an optimal capital structure? Given the uncertainty expressed by Stew Myers, what do serious researchers today believe are the benefits and cost of leverage? You might even give us some historical perspective on how our thinking has evolved over the past twenty-five years or so.

CLIFF SMITH: I think it is important to admit from the start that entire books have been written on this topic; and it is going to be very difficult to summarize the range of analysis that has been brought to bear on this issue in such a brief discussion. But, given this limitation, it is useful to go back a little more than twenty-five years. Any serious academic analysis of the capital structure issue is going to go back to the Modigliani and Miller paper published in the *American Economic Review* in 1958. That paper established the following proposition: If you grant me three assumptions, I can logically demonstrate that the structure of the liability side of the firm's balance sheet is a matter of irrelevance.

JOEL: Irrelevance in terms of the impact it has on the value of the shares?

CLIFF: On the value of the wealth of all the claimholders of the corporation. The market value of the firm is unaffected by the structure of the liability side of the firm's balance sheet if (1) there are no taxes, (2) there are no transaction costs, and (3) we hold constant the firm's current and future real investment decisions. Given these three assumptions, the structure of the liability side of the firm's balance sheet won't affect the real cash flows that are ultimately being divided up among the claimholders of the corporation.

Of course, as a company takes on more and more debt, there is more risk imposed on the bondholders; and there is also more risk imposed on the equityholders. As a result, both of those claimholders' returns are going to have to be higher. However—and this is perhaps the least intuitive aspect of the Modigliani-Miller proposition—although additional leverage raises the expected return to both the bondholders and the stockholders, the expected weighted average return to the firm's claimholders is unaffected; that is, the firm's weighted average cost of capital remains unchanged.

The way that works boils down to this: Let's suppose a firm that is financed 100 percent with equity has a set of real activities that are going to require a rate of return of 15 percent in the marketplace. If that company then issues enough debt to retire, say, 5 percent of the equity, that debt would be essentially risk-free; and let's say that investors require a 10 percent rate of return on riskless debt. But if you issue substantial amounts of additional debt, the rate of return required by the bondholders is going to rise above 10 percent; and the required rate of return to the equityholders is going to rise above 15 percent. But the weighted average is still going to come out to 15 percent. So, in this sense, and given the three assumptions I mentioned earlier, there is no benefit to increased leverage. It is true that the firm's EPS will increase as long as it earns a rate of return that is higher than its after-tax cost of debt; but this gain will simply be offset by a corresponding increase in the return demanded by stockholders for bearing additional financial risk. As Stew Myers likes to make this point, "There is no magic in leverage."

BENNETT STEWART: Cliff, isn't the theory behind that the idea that investors in the marketplace can essentially undo the capital structure decision that management has made? So that, for example, if I buy both the bonds and the common shares in the company, I have in effect bought a security which matches the underlying operating cash flows of the business. And this in turn means that no matter how you carve up the cash flows themselves, the bonds and the common stock together would have to sell for what the underlying cash flows are worth.

CLIFF: Yes, that is an easy way to think about putting the firm back in its unlevered state. If you buy 1 percent of the equity and 1 percent of the debt, then the payoffs you're going to get (again, given that there are no taxes and no contracting costs, and that we are holding those real investment decisions fixed) are those you would have gotten if the firm had no debt.

JOEL: Aren't you assuming, though, that the market behaves in a very sophisticated manner?

CLIFF: Yes, I am assuming the same sort of sophisticated behavior that seems to show itself every time people suggest that the market can't really figure out what is happening with, say, changes in accounting techniques. You try and put together trading rules based on the proposition that investors are fooled by accounting gimmickry; and, by golly, it almost always seems that there are enough sophisticated people in the marketplace that stock prices are unaffected by accounting games. And stock prices will also discount the effects of leverage on earnings per share.

JOEL: So, then you are not going to try to make a case for a particular form of capital structure on the assumption that markets are dominated by unsophisticated or irrational behavior on the part of investors?

CLIFF: That's correct. I think your argument for a sophisticated market is somewhat more plausible, though, if you make it in a slightly different way. The stock market, like any other market, is going to have prices determined at the margin, not by the average investor. The fact that the average individual in the marketplace is probably neither well-informed nor financially sophisticated tells me nothing about how market prices are set— because those individuals, the average investors, are unlikely to have much of an impact on prices. The people that are much more likely to be determining the prices in this market, the "marginal" investors if you will, are backed by large amounts of capital. Those people are typically the best informed and often have a comparative advantage because of better access to trading opportunities. They may also be a member of a firm that owns a seat on one of the stock exchanges. So, competition among market professionals seems vigorous enough to generate a set of prices that reflect a very sophisticated understanding of financing methods and how they affect corporate values.

JOEL: Isn't it true though, Cliff, that the position Modigliani and Miller (M & M) formulated back in 1958 would not account for the significant differences in debt-to-equity ratios among industries, or even for significant differences within the same industry? Because if capital structure is really irrelevant, then there should be no preference for one capital structure over another. If corporate managements are catering to the sophisticated investors you're talking about—those investors who base their pricing decisions on concepts of value-maximization, if you want to call it that—then you would not expect differences in capital structure to be caused by anything other than an irrelevant managerial preference, or simply by random choice.

CLIFF: If you laid that argument out in front of a logician, I am afraid he would have some problems with it. If this irrelevance proposition were correct, then in fact *any* distribution of capital structures would be consistent with it. You could have large cross-sectional variations across industries and small cross-sectional variations within industries or vice versa. In fact, the proposition makes no predictions about what corporate capital structure ought to look like. Therefore, the only way you are going to demonstrate to a logician's satisfaction that capital structure matters is to come up with a theory that makes specific predictions about the cross-sectional or time-series behavior of capital structure, and then demonstrate that that theory is statistically consistent with the empirical evidence.

JOEL: Well, let's take it the other way then. Let us assume that there *is* a consistent pattern of debt-to-equity ratios in various industries. Would you consider that to be *inconsistent* with the proposition that capital structure was irrelevant?

CLIFF: Well, yes, an observed pattern would lead me to suspect that capital structure is not irrelevant, and that management's decisions about how much debt to employ might be driven systematically by certain industry-wide or economy-wide factors. But what is incumbent upon us as academics is to generate a set of theoretical propositions that would imply a certain distribution of capital structures—one which could then be tested empirically by examining the data on firms across industries and over different time periods.

JOEL: And you clearly don't have that as of Modigliani and Miller's 1958 paper. So what happens, then, to the original M & M proposition if you introduce corporate taxes into the picture?

CLIFF: Well, I personally think that the most important contribution of the M & M proposition to our understanding of corporate capital structure comes from taking that irrelevance proposition and standing it on its head. Remember, that proposition rests on three critical assumptions: no taxes, no transaction or contracting costs, and real investment policies are independent of financing policy. If you take that argument and just turn it on its head, then it says the following: If financing policy is important, then it can be important for only these three reasons. One, the firm's choice of financing policy affects its tax liabilities. Two, there are important differences in contracting costs that arise because of the firm's choice of financing policies. Three, there are important interdependencies between the firm's choice of financing policy and its investment policy.

The profession collectively turned most of its attention very early to the first two points: taxes and contracting (or bankruptcy) costs. Modigliani and Miller themselves first looked at the implications of the tax deductibility of interest payments. And because greater debt seems to imply an increasingly larger tax benefit, consideration of tax effects alone would seem to dictate the maximum possible use of debt by the firm; in the extreme, it would suggest that all firms would be 99.9 percent debt.

Yet we do not see companies choosing to employ extremely large amounts of debt. So, to come up with a factor that would offset this tax effect, people started thinking about things like the out-of-pocket contracting costs associated with severe financial distress, sometimes known as "bankruptcy costs." Jerry Warner, however, found that for a sample of railroads that went through the bankruptcy process, the out-of-pocket bankruptcy costs turned out to be a very small amount, at least relative to the value of the assets of the corporation when the financing decisions were made.

BENNETT: Did these estimates include the cost of negotiating with bankers and getting the accountants involved, and the loss of management time in reorganizing or liquidating the company?

CLIFF: That is an important point, and my feeling is that our studies here reflect an academic myopia. I can remember Merton Miller insisting on the importance of distinguishing between financing decisions and investment decisions. That principle became so ingrained that most people in the academic community were willing to look at only those costs that were consistent with a *fixed* investment policy. Those costs turned out to be things like incremental lawyers' fees associated with the fact that you wound up in bankruptcy.

But academics did not take account of the fact that the management of a company under financial duress makes different investment decisions and does different things with its time than it would under normal conditions. They did not consider that the investment activities that go on under the supervision of a bankruptcy court judge when a company is in reorganization are likely to be very different from what they otherwise would have been.

BENNETT: There is possibly even a change in the management itself.

CLIFF: Possibly, or even more likely, an entirely new management team.

But, anyway, I think that a lot of the work that has taken place in the last five to ten years suggests to most people in the academic financial community that taxes are not as important an explanation for capital structure as we once thought. A lot of the earlier confidence in this argument has been shaken by more attention to the tax implications of debt to the investors holding that debt.

JOEL: Let me see if I can summarize all this, then. The first step back in 1958 was that the overall returns to all claimholders are unaffected by whether a firm has no debt or has almost all debt. It makes no difference. Then we introduce corporate income taxes. In this case, interest expense becomes a tax-deductible item reducing taxable income. The effect of that implies that a debt-to-equity ratio of, say, a million to one would maximize the value for the shareholders because they would get the greatest tax benefit. Now, you are saying that the next step is the consideration of problems of financial distress, such as bankruptcy costs. With this added factor, you would then expect that the tax benefits of debt financing would be offset by financial distress costs at high debt ratios. Therefore, there would be some kind of optimal capital structure—one which would balance the tax advantage against the expected costs of financial distress. You are suggesting, however, that the work of Jerry Warner—who I believe was one of Merton Miller's students—concluded that the bankruptcy costs were really quite small.

CLIFF: Yes, the measurable, *out-of-pocket* bankruptcy costs were small.

JOEL: So, as a consequence, if you were hopeful of coming up with optimal capital structures that were consistent with actual experience, based on the balancing of the tax benefits and the financial distress costs, those hopes were gone because the financial distress costs appeared to be much too small to be the balancing factor.

CLIFF: Yes, the capital structures of companies like Kodak and DuPont, which have virtually no debt, would be very difficult to explain.

JOEL: So, you are suggesting, then, that even if bankruptcy costs are not an important consideration in the capital structure decision, the tax benefits of debt financing may not be nearly as substantial as we once believed, largely because of the offsetting effect of the taxes that some investors are forced to pay on interest income. And this combination of factors—potentially high costs of financial distress and the relative insignificance of the tax advantage—may explain some of these surprisingly "low" debt ratios that we see for some blue-chip companies.

CLIFF: That's right. In this continuing saga of financial economists coming to grips with increasingly complicated logical propositions, the next thing that Merton Miller looked at was the tax disadvantage to individuals from holding corporate bonds relative to equities. Debt financing, for example, tends to generate ordinary income for individuals, while most of the cash flows to investors from equity claims are passed through to the stockholders on a more tax-advantageous basis, in the form of capital gains or through other alternatives.

JOEL: So, therefore taxes might not matter at all, in which case there would be no tax benefit for debt financing?

CLIFF: Yes, that's right. But let me point out another severe problem for anybody who wants to build this whole house of cards on taxes: corporations issued debt on a regular basis long before there was an effective corporate or personal income tax in this country.

BENNETT: But if there is no tax benefit to debt financing, then aren't you back to the world of capital structure irrelevance?

CLIFF: No. There are other important factors. For example, because debtholders have a senior claim on the corporation's assets, they collect less information about the companies' operations than do equityholders. Thus, issuing both debt and equity could allow a more efficient sorting of investors according to their investment in information and their risk-bearing preferences. And then there are the real costs of financial distress we discussed earlier.

BENNETT: Do you have any evidence on what has happened to debt ratios over long periods of time?

CLIFF: I saw a study that was done a few years ago by Merton Miller which suggested that, over a very long period of time—more than a hundred years I think—there had been very little change in the aggregate amount of debt issued by U.S. companies. And that period of time encompassed several different tax regimes. But Bob is probably more qualified to talk about this than I am.

BOB TAGGART: As Cliff says, it's hard to identify a pronounced trend in debt ratios. There is some evidence that corporate debt ratios were quite high around the turn of the century and then actually declined somewhat through the early 1920s, right after the income tax system was instituted. Debt ratios then fell further in the wake of the Great Depression and into World War II. They have climbed somewhat in the post–World War II period. But, at any rate, as Cliff suggested, it is hard to match up long-term trends in capital structure with changes in the tax code. For corporations in the aggregate, a theory of optimal capital structure that is based only on tax savings from the deductibility of interest does not appear to explain the facts very well.

LEVERAGED BUY-OUTS

JOEL: Harry, as Treasurer of American Hospital Supply, what do you think about the enormous debt ratios we have been seeing in all the leveraged buy-outs? The explanations we have heard so far do not seem to account for why a firm that has a ratio of debt to total capital of, say, 30 percent as a public corporation suddenly has a ratio of debt to total capital of 90 percent when it goes through an LBO. Does the form of organization suddenly change, such that it changes management's risk-taking propensity or greatly enlarges the company's ability to support debt?

HARRY WINN: I don't think it is the form of organization. I think it is the change in the company's focus that is going to be the important difference. In a leveraged buy-out, management is willing to take on a lot of debt because it has set itself a fairly predictable course. It feels quite confident in its ability to project the cash flows generated by the business—the cash flow necessary to pay down that debt and still earn a (very high) rate of return for itself and for its investors.

The case of a public corporation is different. In that case, there is generally not that kind of assurance about the future. They can't project the future as well; and, consequently, they may want to play it a little safer.

JOEL: So you are telling me that because we suddenly have a change in the corporate "focus," the corporation can now leverage itself to these otherwise unheard-of levels, consistent perhaps with what we might see some individual investors doing with their own portfolios. There must be something in this special form of organization that enables the firm to take on what appears to be a very high debt-equity ratio—one that would be considered irresponsible perhaps in a public debt market.

HARRY: I think many times a shift occurs in a company's investment policies. Even if there isn't a change in management, the existing management team all of a sudden may come to the realization that many of their potential investments may not be worth doing, and some of their present operations may not even be worth continuing. And this realization causes them to narrow their focus on the one thing they do especially well. Management then may want to "bet the ranch" on their ability to execute, and this process leads to the leveraged buy-out.

JOEL: But why doesn't this process take place within the framework of a conventional organization, within the public corporation? Why does this concentration of "focus" require an LBO and the move to a private corporation?

CHET GOUGIS: Well, Joel, two things usually happen in an LBO. One is that you suddenly have managers becoming owners as well as managers. This makes the managers a lot more comfortable making very risky decisions, such as taking on a lot of debt or selling assets. It reduces managers' concern that if they make a risky decision and it doesn't work out, even if they have correctly assessed the risk, they are going to be fired.

JOEL: I have a problem with that explanation. If it were in the interest of stockholders to create the most value by having a high debt ratio, and the only way we can do that is by making managers owners as well, then why wouldn't it be in the interest of stockholders to encourage the management to have large ownership positions in public corporations as well? This way the rest of us could also enhance the value of our portfolios. At present, the only way this value enhancement seems to happen is through the LBO when all the rest of the public shareholders like you and me have been kicked out. Management is left in. They create the value by availing themselves of these high debt-equity ratios, and we have got nothing.

BOB: I think you do see some trend toward larger proportionate ownership positions by management. This has been true, for example, among many of the companies that have engaged in stock repurchase programs.

CLIFF: Joel, I think your analysis of the stockholder consequences of LBOs is incomplete in at least one important way. The average return to the stockholders being bought out in these LBOs—the average buy-out premium over market—is about 56 percent. So the existing stockholders are not being "frozen out" of the process by any means.

Also, as others have been suggesting, the LBO is a different kind of transaction. It is something that is perhaps more akin to mergers and tender offers—other kinds of corporate control transactions that suggest that something about the ordinary day-to-day internal control system of the corporation has gone amiss. It is a very dramatic transaction, a fairly unusual transaction, one that is designed to get the corporation back on track. As a result, I don't think we are going to learn a lot about the capital structures of IBM or General Motors or most of the New York Stock Exchange listed firms by focusing at this early point in the conversation on leveraged buy-outs.

BOB: There is also reason to believe that a leveraged buy-out is not likely to be a successful transformation in all companies. One of the major functions of the corporate form is to separate risk-bearing from the management of assets. The benefit of that separation is that it allows talented, but partly risk-averse, managers to run a corporation. In the LBO, by contrast, a lot of the risk is placed on some managers. For those managers, a combination of high risk and high reward may be the ideal motivation; for others it may not.

CLIFF: I also think that the nine-to-one debt ratios we are seeing in these deals are more illusory than real, in the following sense. What is the first thing that happens after one of these LBO deals is consummated? My impression is that one of the primary objectives of the firm is to get that debt ratio substantially reduced as quickly as possible. That is one of the primary uses that any internally generated cash flows are devoted to. And in fact they may go even further and sell off certain assets of the corporation and use the proceeds to retire part of this debt. So it seems to me that financing this deal with a very high amount of debt is not really a long-term financing strategy for the corporation. Therefore, maybe we ought to be a little more careful about separating these perhaps very different motives for using debt financing.

JOEL: Yes, I see your point. But let me carry my line of thinking a little farther. The principal purpose of an LBO, to my mind, is to improve the rate of return on capital very substantially—and I mean the operating return here, the cash flows before financing charges. Why? Because the only incentive for the management that is now a large equity player to bring the debt down is because at a later date they intend to sell equity at a much higher value than the price that was paid to take it private in the first place. There is no reason for lenders to bring their position down if the firm is successful in creating new equity value.

So, initially, there may be some uncertainty in the lenders' minds as to whether management is going to be able to pull it off. And that first effort is made to see if they can really add significant value to the firm before they worry about the debt retirement. There is a debt retirement schedule, to be sure; but there is no incentive to accelerate that payment. The lenders want to be very certain that the equity value that is being created is in line with their early expectations.

CLIFF: I don't disagree with your point about the change in the operation of the assets. That's the motivation for this LBO. But I do disagree with your notion about the use of the debt. The debt that is acquired in these LBOs is acquired for a very specific purpose. There is always a very well-defined maturity schedule; it is something that the lender insists on. In fact, the maturity structure or required sinking fund payments reflect an agreement between the borrower and the lender that this debt is going to be brought down to much lower levels over a very short period of time.

JOEL: Yes, but the only real reason why lenders ever ask to be repaid is merely to see if the borrower can do it. Especially with so much at risk in one particular group of assets and one particular company, it is incumbent upon the lender to monitor carefully the progress that is being made in creating value here. As a result they ask for a particular rate of debt payment. I would venture to say, however, that if the company were very much more successful than the lenders had anticipated, the lender would go back to the borrower when the debt was to be repaid and he would say, "I was only kidding about the repayment. You can keep the money." Because the lenders only make money when the loans are out, not when they are recalled.

CHET: Do we have enough history, though, to suggest that it is common in LBOs to lever up the assets and then to keep on rolling over that debt and maintain those initially very high debt ratios?

ANDY KALOTAY: I think the intention, at the very outset, is to get the debt ratio down. For example, I was involved in proposing a structure for a debt issue of Chevron; they were in the process of borrowing several billion dollars to fund an acquisition. We put specific provisions to provide for Chevron's repayment of that debt—sinking fund provisions and covenants which would provide the lender with a reasonably secure position.

JOEL: Yes, but putting those constraints on themselves simply enables them to borrow the money in the first place. And the reason the loan covenant restrictions are placed on the firm is to monitor its *ability* to repay the debt—not to repay the debt per se—because the firm Chevron could issue new equity to retire the debt at any time.

CLIFF: Joel, I have a problem with the last part of your statement. When the firm has a significant amount of leverage on its balance sheet, issuing equity has the effect of reducing the risk faced by the existing bondholders. Unless you pre-arranged the deal so that the equity issue was anticipated by the bondholders when they originally priced their bonds, you are just playing Santa Claus to the bondholders.

JOEL: I didn't mean to imply that I would recommend that a firm have an equity issue to bail out the bondholders. The point that I wanted to raise is that when firms borrow money and they are asked to repay, we shouldn't take that request too seriously. Because the lenders would be quite pleased to keep the money out there at the given rate of interest which is supposed to compensate them for the risk they are taking. Junk bondholders, for example, don't really want to get their principal back. They like earning that rate of return and they would have to incur transaction costs to start the process again. They just want to see if the borrower can do it.

But the point I am making is this: What the management and their supporting investor group really want to do in LBOs is to see if the gamble that they took is likely to pay off. If it is likely to pay off, then they want to create the most value they possibly can by making the greatest possible use of the tax shelter provided by debt financing.

To return to my real question, Why can these special players in the LBO game support nine-to-one debt-equity ratios when public corporations seem to have nothing like that? Is it because Mr. and Mrs. Joe Average America can't sleep at night if American management levers up the balance sheet?

BRIAN WALSH: Public companies access traditional capital markets whereas the nature of the debt that goes into an LBO tends to be custom-made. Equity kickers are not unusual and all aspects are negotiable. Often the providers of the equity are also the providers of the debt. Certainly, the maturities are very different. So, the nature of the LBO debt is very different from traditional public or private markets.

JOEL: When I say nine-to-one, I have to admit that some of that is merely for its entertainment value. I happen to like the number nine. And you are right: it turns out that some of the debt is really part of the equity. So, the debt ratio may be only four-to-one.

BRIAN: But you know what else happens, Joel? I have looked at some of these deals, and most of them have requirements that the companies get that ratio down to one-to-one in five to seven years. So while the present value of that tax shield you get over those five to seven years may be substantial, the final intention, perhaps requirement, is to wind up with a more normal capital structure—say 50 percent debt.

What seems to me to happen in LBOs is, first, you have got a very different kind of debt; and, second, there are constraints put on the debt that really force you to make major changes, such as the sale of a business or tighter working capital management, reduced inventories, faster collections, and so forth. You basically have a situation where a public company is taken over by management backed by an investor group, and it is given a different type of structure for a discrete period of time. And all the players in the game clearly have to be ideal. The intention is typically that after a period—probably less than ten years—they will take the company public and reap their reward.

Now, the question is, what role does the financial structure play in this process of creating value, sometimes enormous value, for investors? My feeling is that the value created is much more a function of what they do with the company than of the change in financial structure. The financing, I'm convinced, is largely the tool that allows the investor groups to compete with public corporations in these takeover contests.

An LBO, after all, is a form of project financing. Take any project financing—an iron ore development, for example, or anything that has discrete, readily identifiable cash flows. You structure a debt security around those expected cash flows; you take those flows, package them, and then give it to an investor who is ideally suited to take the risks you're imposing. Investors in LBOs also get four or five points over the going rate of interest—a point we haven't mentioned. So, in effect, the company is paying a premium for its debt of something like 50 percent over market rates.

BENNETT: Yes, but junk bonds with their high rates of interest have a lot of tax benefits, too. First of all, the higher interest cost is tax-deductible. And, as you are pointing out, junk bonds are very much like income bonds—bonds which pay interest only when the company has enough earnings to pay the interest. What junk bonds achieve here is the transformation of equity into a tax-deductible form similar to the effect of income bonds which, like preferred stock, are riskier, and in many ways comparable to equity instruments. On a tax basis alone, it seems sensible to me to convert an equity cost into a form that is tax-deductible.

BRIAN: Okay, but I am not sure the average investor would be at all comfortable with your proposition. You are dealing with a situation where you have paid an enormous premium for the company; and then you are financing the purchase at nine-to-one with debt that is costing you an extra 400 or 500 basis points—although, yes, it is deductible. You have to get into a position where you are making money very quickly under those kind of conditions.

BENNETT: Whatever money was made, though, would be fully sheltered. Take the example of what Club Med did a couple of years ago. The interest rate paid to investors was tied to the occupancy rate at the hotel which was being financed by that investment. It was a profitability-linked form of financing, in essence a tax-deductible form of equity which minimized the financial risk of the company.

BRIAN: Yes, but that was a very esoteric type of financing. It appeals to a particular type of investor; and it is not the kind of instrument that is likely to be issued by large, public corporations with any regularity.

ANDY: Brian is making an extremely important point, one that I think is well worth emphasizing, and it is that the kind of debt in these deals is very different from conventional long-term corporate debentures. This is a point that is typically ignored in academic discussions of capital structure. In fact I have read a good deal of the research on capital structure, and that experience, combined with much that I've heard today, reinforces my suspicion that many academic generalizations about capital structure are not very informative or helpful. In order to understand corporate capital structure you have to begin by understanding that there are many, many kinds of financial instruments; and to lump them together under the titles of "debt" or "equity" obscures important differences among them.

The typical academic study looks only at the book value of debt. They don't look at the market value of debt. They don't attempt to determine the average life of a debt issue. They don't look at call provisions. How many studies do you see that look at pre-payment provisions on the debt? You keep talking about the big picture, but how many of the academics have looked at issues such as how the sinking fund provision and the call price affect the pricing of bonds? And, when you look at these new bond issues, you have to consider the very important differences in the provisions attached to them. Most obviously, the average life seems to be much shorter. Five to seven years is the average maturity for this new LBO and acquisition financing.

JOEL: Do you know why that is?

ANDY: Because the company intends to retire the debt. If the company does not put these repayment provisions in the debt contract, it cannot retire that debt—even though it may have the cash on hand. So what do you do with that cash if you do not have the flexibility of prepaying that debt?

JOEL: Why would you want to prepay the debt?

ANDY: Because they never intended to have all that debt in the first place.

THE LEVERAGING OF CORPORATE AMERICA _____

JOEL: We are seeing fewer and fewer triple A–rated corporations these days, and I suspect they are a vanishing breed. If there is a significant value to debt financing, then why should any corporation continue to maintain a triple A credit rating? A reference was made earlier to the IBMs and DuPonts and the Eastman Kodaks. And, Brian, I am sure it was only out of deference to you that we did not include General Foods in this category.

The reason why this was of some interest to me in terms of the LBO is that LBOs seem to take place with firms where the assets provide highly predictable, or less variable, cash flows. The same is true of a company like General Foods. And yet for a long time General Foods had almost no debt and maintained a triple A rating on its bonds. General Foods has gone the route from having practically no debt to having a debt-to-total capital ratio, at least in book value terms, of something like 30 to 35 percent. My first question for you, Brian, is what led you to make the change? The second: If you were going to make the change, how come you decided to go to only 30 percent and not to the nine-to-one ratios that LBO firms use? Do you have to have an LBO type of organization to get the debt-equity ratio up that high? Can you answer in 30 seconds or less?

BRIAN: Well, I guess that any 3,000 mile journey begins with the first step, as they say.

Our debt policy at General Foods has become more aggressive in recent years. The reason we were able to take this stance was in part because of the size and predictability of our cash flows. We recognized that in order to achieve growth in a maturing market, we would either have to buy it through acquisitions or change our internal investment policy to spend a great deal of money on growth opportunities. Then our question was, how should that type of growth be funded in the best interest of the shareholders? On the basis of our own investigation of the various opinions on capital structure policy (which were well summarized in Cliff's introduction), we found that there was a good deal of uncertainty in the current thinking on what is the most appropriate debt policy for a public corporation. There certainly is not universal acceptance that the risk implications and earnings impact of high leverage should be given less weight than the cost of capital and other concepts argued by academics.

JOEL: But if debt financing does create value for stockholders, then in view of the recent tendency for LBOs to be unfriendly transactions, especially when there is a lot of debt used to effect the transaction, one would think that a firm like General Foods, where the cash flows are highly predictable, might be a likely candidate for a takeover or an LBO. This might be one of management's concerns at General Foods.

BRIAN: I think the answer to that is an overlay of business pragmatism on top of some of the concepts that have been talked about here today. First of all, I don't think that there would necessarily have been any change in our capital structure at General Foods if there hadn't been a business need, a need to finance growth.

JOEL: Then you are suggesting that even if debt turned out to be cheaper than equity, you would not have moved to increase the ratio of debt to equity, say, by borrowing money merely for the purpose of buying back your shares?

BRIAN: Something has to attract your attention first. And I think the primary impetus that encouraged us to look at the conceptual benefits of debt financing was a need for funds to support growth.

JOEL: So you needed some form of external finance because the internally generated cash flows did not meet the capital requirements for business. And then you turned to the question, should General Foods issue debt or equity?

BRIAN: That is right. In other words we knew that we had to finance this growth. The question then was, what is the most appropriate way to finance this growth, given that our basic objective is to increase shareholder wealth? So we reviewed the work on capital structure that Cliff summarized and we basically came to the conclusion that the tax deductibility of interest makes debt a cheaper source of capital than equity—within limits. That is a proposition which we as a corporation have come to accept.

So, our financial policy is to use debt in conjunction with internally generated funds to a level that is consistent with retaining our current access to all capital markets at any time. This recognizes the desire to lower our cost of capital, but gives weight to the fact that some capital markets dry up from time to time and that we do need the ability to be flexible in finance. So we raised our leverage ratio to around 30 percent debt to capital. But we didn't go to 80 or 90 percent because, by doing so, we would have restricted our access to the major capital markets and thus limited our flexibility.

All of this, of course, translates into maintaining a bond rating the company feels comfortable with, and the acceptance of less than a triple A. In fact, we are now a double A.

JOEL: Why didn't you take it a step further? Wouldn't a single A still give you the flexibility and access to capital markets you wanted?

BRIAN: That requires consideration against a specific need, and the economics of that need versus the flexibility remaining. Of course, the cost in terms of the basis points between being a double A or a triple A is insignificant when measured against the overall cost of capital implications of leverage.

BENNETT: Yes, but remember the point that Cliff made right at the outset. The additional basis costs you have to pay for more debt are really a matter of irrelevance. They simply reflect the degree of additional risk that bondholders are being made to bear. The stockholders are also being asked to bear more risk; but because of the tax advantage of debt, the total return required by all securityholders (that is, the weighted average of all debt and equityholders) actually goes down as you issue more debt, at least up to a certain point.

BRIAN: Well, I understand what you are saying. But I have always believed that risk transfers from the bonds to the equityholders in "brackets," if you will. Academics treat financial risk as if it were clearly perceived by the market as a continuum, as a linear relationship, between the amount of debt financing and the amount of risk and required return demanded by stockholders. But I find this model difficult to accept. I have to think that it works on a kind of step function with large discontinuities.

CLIFF: You mean that there is a threshold level of debt which has to be exceeded before the debt actually is perceived as risky?

BRIAN: Yes, I certainly think there is an initial threshold, and then from there you work upward in steps, with large jumps between categories. I can't believe that the market is so sensitive that it responds by raising its required rate of return with each incremental addition of debt to the capital structure.

HARRY: I think that the market groups companies together in risk categories both according to capital structure and on an industry-by-industry basis. The equity market looks at a group of stocks with roughly the same kind of risk profile and looks for a similar rate of return from each. When setting required rates of return, the market certainly may look at companies in the same industry group and differentiate them on the basis of capital structure differences, but I suspect that those differences would have to be pretty significant to count very much in the pricing process.

JOEL: Brian, if it turned out that you foresaw capital requirements that were fairly large (and let's assume that you might have one or two major acquisition candidates), what would you do if you had satisfied yourself that having a higher debt ratio was beneficial to your shareholders within a certain range, and then the acquisition prospects suddenly fell through? Would you have recommended that General Foods borrow large sums of money and repurchase its own stock to accomplish this levering of capital structure?

BRIAN: In fact we are now doing just that. General Foods is in the process of a major program of stock repurchase. And one aim of that stock repurchase is to ensure that our capital structure is kept in the type of range that we have now become accustomed to.

Our motive for doing this is to maximize our company's growth potential. We as financial management have a responsibility to keep our cost of capital as low as we can—certainly vis-à-vis that of our competitors, which we look at very carefully. It allows us to promote projects and investments that presumably we wouldn't undertake unless they promised to give us a return in excess of the cost of capital. In fact we are wedded to the principle that all of our investments have to offer a rate of return that exceeds our cost of capital. The lower we can keep our cost of capital by using debt financing, within the constraints I have already described, the more projects we can undertake and the more we can grow the company.

JOEL: OK, so you have decided to have a double A rating on your bonds. What if someone else were to come along and say, "No I think a triple B would be just fine, and I am therefore going to raise the debt-to-capital ratio to 60 percent. The way I am going to do it is through an unfriendly tender offer. I am going to borrow large sums against your overcapitalized assets." What would have to happen in your opinion to change management's view about moving to a higher debt ratio? Do you think that General Foods, having once accustomed itself to a 30 percent debt ratio, may begin to think about moving toward leverage as high as 50 or 60 percent?

BRIAN: It seems to me that corporate America is moving toward higher leverage, and the old norms, for example, being set by rating agencies are changing. In particular, those companies, such as General Foods, with strong cash flows and prominent market positions seem capable of raising leverage without significantly impairing credit standing. Certainly this thought process would be applied when major funds are needed in the future.

THE CASE OF AMERICAN HOSPITAL SUPPLY _____

JOEL: Harry, what about the capital structure of American Hospital Supply? Is your case similar to that of General Foods, or are you still using very little debt?

HARRY: As you are probably aware, we are in the process of merging with Hospital Corporation of America (HCA). We had a debt-equity ratio prior to the merger of only about 12 percent. So that was on the low end of the range.

JOEL: What is HCA's debt ratio?

HARRY: HCA is fairly highly levered, around 58 percent debt to equity.

JOEL: So why did a company like HCA, with such apparently different risk preferences, want to merge with an organization as apparently risk averse as your own?

HARRY: Well, I'm not sure I would call our strategy "risk averse." I would say that we were simply saving our debt capacity for special circumstances, for special opportunities. The truth is that, during the seventies, we were really comfortable with a low debt profile. As we moved into the eighties, we recognized that we needed to make a change in our business. Our traditional supply business was characterized by an important market share position and subject to changes in market demand. Given the cost pressures in health care, we knew that if we stayed in our corner of the health-care business, we would be in a slow hold pattern. Making a change to other businesses through incremental stages, however, did not seem an appropriate strategy.

So we made the decision to align ourselves with a company that is closer to the provider base of health care. That is the rationale for our merger plan with HCA.

JOEL: Were you involved in the process of valuing the two companies to be merged?

HARRY: Yes, I was.

JOEL: The reason I am asking the question is this: If the tax-deductibility of interest expense creates value when capitalized, and you came to this deal bringing a 12 percent debt ratio to their 58 percent, then did they at

[Editor's note: Since the date of this meeting, Baxter Travenol Laboratories has made a successful offer of $51 cash for each American share which also provided for the cancellation of the HCA transaction. Baxter's offer clearly anticipated the use of American's debt capacity.]

any time bring up the idea that they could afford to pay a higher price for you due to the underutilization of this debt capacity?

HARRY: Yes, that was certainly one of the expected benefits of merging, but that was not the sole reason for the merger.

JOEL: No, I am not saying that it was the most important motive. But, to get back to this point, did you use a valuation procedure that incorporated and even *quantified* the tax benefits of debt financing in determining the prices to be paid?

HARRY: Yes, we did. But, as I said, this was not the primary motive for the merger.

But let me talk a little more about why we at American Hospital have chosen to keep a fairly low debt profile, and why the leveraged buy-outs may not be an appropriate comparison. Looking at capital structure from the perspective of a public company is a very different thing from the perspective of an LBO management, who are taking calculated risks with their own equity. One of the things that keeps a management from going to a nine-to-one debt ratio is its own uncertainties about the future. Some of our assets at American Hospital have a higher risk profile than others. For example, 30 percent of our assets are in California where the possibility of an earthquake is a real issue. We have to have a strategy for catastrophe and that has got to be part of the capital planning process. Because of these uncertainties, we know we want a large equity component in our capital structure. We know why we have that large equity component, and we strongly believe that our capital structure is in the best interest of our shareholders.

Cliff earlier mentioned the financial distress level as being the bottom range of acceptable capital structure. But I would look at it a little differently. To my mind, financial distress comes well before the creditors begin to close in. You have a financial problem, I think, at that point when the financing activity of the company interrupts and disturbs the primary focus of management: namely, the operating side of the business. As a manager of a public company, I am not going to feel comfortable with the notion that my debt level scrapes the bottom criterion of "financial distress." Management does not want to get in the situation where attention to financing matters interrupts its primary operating focus and interferes with its operating plan.

EVALUATING CREDIT: THE BOND RATING PROCESS _____

JOEL: Brian, when you are estimating your debt ratio at General Foods, do you talk about debt ratio in terms of book values or in terms of market values?

BRIAN: We talk in terms of book values.

BENNETT: Well, Brian, you may calculate your overall leverage ratio in terms of the book values of assets and equity. But you are also taking market values into account, at least implicitly, when you pay attention to interest coverage ratios and return on capital measures—measures which are in some sense proxies for the market value of the company. So that indirectly the quality of the cash flows and the market value of the current level of this activity are more important determinants of your debt capacity—more important than, say, book debt-to-equity ratios.

CHET: This is certainly true from the standpoint of what we at Duff and Phelps look at in rating corporate bonds. We look closely, for example, at interest coverage ratios, at the cash-flow variability of the company over time, and at other measures which reflect a company's ability to repay its debt. And these measures have become all the more important to us because book leverage ratios are becoming less and less meaningful as a result of the proliferation of different types of debt instruments and accounting methods. So, for purposes of credit evaluation, we are increasingly relying on more market-based measures of leverage.

BENNETT: Marriott Hotels produces in their annual report statements of both accounting book value and leverage ratios and estimates of the market value of their equity and market leverage ratios. In fact they periodically have their properties appraised on the basis of the cash flow they generate. And, of course, for a company like Marriott, the debt-to-equity ratio expressed in terms of market values is considerably less than in terms of book values.

Marriott has also spun off into limited partnerships some of their hotel properties whose market value is not recognized on their books. My question is, are they doing this because they feel that they will not otherwise get credit for the debt capacity of those assets? I think such things may be a way of providing more information to the market.

CHET: This may be a matter of perspective, but I think that you should still look at the book value of debt to equity when making credit evaluations. That is certainly something that we continue to pay attention to. On the other hand, you can find two companies that have the same rating; and while one company may have a fairly high, say, a 58 percent debt-to-capital ratio, the other may have significantly lower leverage. The explanation for this apparent puzzle is that if you look at these two companies from a cash-flow standpoint, it may tell you a very different story about the financial risk of that particular company than simple book value measures of leverage.

HARRY: Which ratio do they look at most carefully when the rating is on the borderline?

BRIAN: I would think interest coverage is probably the most important one.

JOEL: More important than the stability of operating cash flows?

BENNETT: Well, more important than book ratios. But you're really both saying pretty much the same thing.

CHET: Interest coverage is an important ratio in our analysis. And, as Bennett is suggesting, it is really, in a sense, a reflection of market values, of the cash-generating capacity of the firm's assets. In practice, what we actually do in rating a company's bonds is to go through the exercise of projecting out the cash flows to the company over the next five to seven years, and then look at coverage ratios and the internal funds-to-debt ratio in each of those years.

BENNETT: I have a question, then. If the stock market is properly capitalizing the future expected cash flows of a company in its stock price, as the efficient market hypothesis would predict, why wouldn't you simply calculate the market debt-to-firm value ratio? This ratio would give you a reasonable proxy for the debt-servicing capability or creditworthiness of the company. This way, the only time a forecast would be necessary is when the forecast differs from what investors in the marketplace are saying. Why would you want to base your debt capacity considerations on a different forecast than the forecast implicit in stock prices?

CHET: Because as a rating agency we have access to inside information. When a company makes rating presentations to us, they share with us product plans and forecasts that are often strictly confidential. Some people would say that there is no *new* information contained in bond ratings at all. But if the rating agencies provide any value, it may in large part come from acting as an information processor. We are the agent for the investors who gets to hear this inside information and who provides them in effect with the assurance that they are going to get a security that has credit quality.

Also, management is very often concerned that they are going to have to issue debt securities at a higher interest rate than is justified because it has positive inside information about the company that it cannot communicate to investors. Based on such information, a company may not be nearly as risky as it looks to an outsider. Such information, which can be relayed to a rating agency in a private presentation, may allow the company to issue its bonds at a substantially lower cost.

BENNETT: Why wouldn't it pay the management to have that same discussion with equity investors? This way the stock price would reflect that same information. Why not make a presentation to Value Line? Then you could communicate inside information to equity investors by having your Value Line rating upgraded.

CLIFF: Bennett, I think a firm would open itself up to some kinds of regulatory liability if it started making forecasts to stockholders. Companies have a fiduciary relationship with investment bankers and with bond rating agencies that doesn't expose them to the same kinds of liabilities. So, if market prices are reflecting a very different view of the future than what is reflected in management's forecast, management can use a bond rating agency to provide investors with a sort of guarantee that there is not some important undisclosed negative information.

Another important consideration is that management may be very hesitant to make public statements about some very important piece of inside information because the release of that information might damage the company's competitive position vis-à-vis suppliers or competitors. If you think back on that Texas Gulf Sulphur problem with insider trading, the reason they didn't release the information about their discovery of high-quality deposits was that they were in the process of acquiring mineral rights on surrounding properties. They got permission from the SEC not to have a public release of the information because to have done so would not only have signalled to the stockholders of the corporation that maybe the stock deserved a higher price, it would have also provided a signal to the people they were bargaining with over the price of their most important input. So, in this case (and I suspect there are many cases like this), it was quite important at that time to keep that information private.

BENNETT: So you are saying they could go to a rating agency to disclose that kind of information, and thus get kind of an indirect credit from investors for doing so?

CLIFF: They could go to a rating agency and say, "We have had a major mineral find. We have got a contract with you that says you can't trade on that information."

JOEL: Yes, but if Duff and Phelps had this inside information that caused it to raise the company's bond rating, then surely the equity market would interpret that rating change as conveying significant positive information. That should function as an unbiased signal to the market that the shares are undervalued because of significant undisclosed information.

CLIFF: I agree with that, but at the same time it wouldn't be the kind of information signal that could be unraveled by the mineral rights owners in that particular area of Canada. So, while it might have a positive effect on investors' perceptions, it wouldn't affect the negotiations with suppliers.

JOEL: But certainly that would signal them that something is going on over there. It would be far better, it seems to me, to stay away from Duff and Phelps for a time period.

CLIFF: It may be. All I am saying is that there are two basic reasons why going through an intermediary with some of this information is different from a general public announcement.

CHET: It is certainly not true that companies share all of their inside information with us. Management obviously makes a judgment about whether it wants that private information to be reflected in its bond rating.

JOEL: Management may be providing this important information to rating agencies as a substitute way (instead of public announcements) of signalling their prospects to the market. But if they could convincingly demonstrate to the market that they had valuable assets that were not being recognized by the market, successful communication could lower the cost of their debt, or increase their debt capacity, by affecting lenders' perceptions.

But once it is generally recognized that significant inside information is being disclosed in rating agency presentations, then anyone who wants this information badly enough is going to start camping out on the agencies' doorsteps. If I knew my competitor were making a presentation to a rating agency, and I was convinced that those presentations and subsequent rating changes were a great source of information, then I would wind up watching the way my competitor walks out of a Duff and Phelps meeting. If he was doing a mumbo rhythm, I would say to myself, "Buy that stock." That would be my signal. So I am not convinced that management can use presentations to rating agencies to provide substitute signals to keep certain parts of the market uninformed and other parts of the market well-informed.

CHET: There is no doubt that advance knowledge of a bond rating change could be valuable information to an investor, just like advance knowledge of a merger or tender offer. Somehow, though, despite the efforts of clever investors who may camp outside of the offices of rating agencies, merger attorneys, financial printers, and others with "inside information," the market can still be surprised.

THE JUNK BOND MARKET AND CORPORATE DEBT CAPACITY

BENNETT: Let me ask you a question, Chet. There are only about 700 companies in the United States that have a bond rating. Why aren't there more companies that have chosen to have their bonds rated? What are management's considerations in deciding whether or not to have its bonds rated?

CHET: Well, as in most financial decisions, you weigh the benefits against the costs. A debt rating generally costs between $10,000 and $25,000. Companies are willing to spend this money because the information conveyed by the rating agency to the market will, all things equal, lower their financing cost relative to what it would be without the rating.

JOEL: The point that I would like to address here is this: Many people have said to us that the reason they don't have their bonds rated is because their ratings would be very low. They have never used the public debt market and they don't feel they ever could. But this brings me to the subject of the junk bond market. How do you account for what appears to be the almost unbelievable growth in the so-called "high-yield" bond market, that market for debt securities that are rated less than investment grade?

CHET: The junk bond market is a substitute for other types of debt financing—for bank financing, for example, or private placements. The development of the junk bond market really began with private individuals and selective institutions. It was really very much akin to a private placement market where the investors themselves did the kind of credit analysis that a rating agency like Duff and Phelps would do. In other words, the investors would become very involved with the borrower, probably getting much more information than would have been available in a public market setting.

JOEL: Does this mean that the private placement market is a substitute mechanism for a rating agency like Duff and Phelps? Does this represent a form of competition for the rating agencies?

CHET: Yes, in one sense, but not in another. Private financings have always really been analyzed by the lenders themselves. When GE Credit or Hancock or Prudential makes a large investment in an LBO, they have always done, and will continue to do, an analysis that may be a lot more thorough than what we are allowed to do because they have access to better and more complete information. So that method of financing has always been out there. It is not really a competitor, though. What we really provide is information for the larger market—for the pension funds that are making a number of investments in a large range of these things and that don't have a staff like a GE Credit that will thoroughly analyze every deal. So, when the junk bond market first started, the wider institutional involvement was not there. But what you have seen in the last year is a progressive broadening of that market.

HARRY: It has become "securitized," if you will; it's now available and packaged for you and me.

CHET: We did a rating recently for Peoplexpress. And while I wouldn't call their paper junk bonds, clearly that is a high-yield security that they want a broad market for. And I think we are going to see more and more of these high-yield issues to fund normal corporate uses as you have more and more of the smaller banks in the midwest and pension funds wanting to invest in higher-yield bonds.

JOEL: What implications does the junk bond market have for the blue-chip companies of America? Chet, you are an evaluator of credit. Why is there this incredible discontinuity in the levels of corporate debt financing? You have companies going up to, say, 50 to 60 percent on the one hand; and then you have private companies up at 90 percent; and there appears to be nothing in between. Then, suddenly something called junk bonds comes in and a lot of companies start levering up through the public debt markets. Are you telling me that it was only prohibitively high interest rates that was keeping public companies from using more leverage?

CHET: There are a few people who are using that kind of leverage, and their names are Boone Pickens and Carl Icahn.

BRIAN: That's right, Joel. It depends on what they are going to do with your billion dollars. Pickens and Icahn are using the billion dollars to buy control of the company. For management to take another billion dollars for normal capital expenditures is a very different story.

JOEL: They can use the money to buy back their shares.

CLIFF: These junk bonds are a relatively new phenomenon. I agree with Chet that higher-yield debt instruments have been available for years through private placements. And that the formation of junk bond markets is simply a way of getting these securities out to a broader market. So that I think the development of the junk bond market is more of a change in form than in substance. Before there were simply no close substitutes available in the marketplace.

I also agree with your point that these things have gotten a lot of attention lately because of a set of very specific uses for which these bonds have typically been issued. I don't think that the existence of junk bond issues suggests that the average public company is underleveraged, or that adding a large amount of additional debt would significantly increase the value of the average corporation.

DEBT RATIOS AND COMPETITIVE POSITION _____

JOEL: Let me try this proposition out on you. The similarity of debt ratios within industries has a tendency to support the view that those industries are highly competitive. Assuming additional use of debt adds value, then if one firm in an industry moves to a significantly higher debt ratio and thereby lowers its overall cost of capital, then it will be able to lower the prices on its products and gain market share. This pressure in turn would force its competitors also to move to a higher debt ratio in order to maintain market share. In other words, they have to lower the price of their products, and the only way they can do it may be by raising their debt ratios.

CHET: But there is an alternative explanation of why companies in competitive industries have similar debt ratios. In competitive markets, returns tend to be lower and the source of internal funds tends to be lower. Therefore, a company in competitive markets has to go out to the capital markets more than companies in protected industries. And if you look at the Stew Myers paper, which describes an inherent bias on the part of management to use debt rather than new equity, then that bias may explain how those companies in competitive industries end up with large amounts of debt.

JOEL: The reason why that doesn't really make much sense to me is that people would not normally do things in a big way that have no effect on the value of the firm. If there is such a bias which adds no value, then I would argue that some value-maximizer is going to be waiting for the opportunity to come swooping down on underleveraged companies. Furthermore, if there is a tendency to move toward a particular debt ratio based on what the price cutter is going to do, then I would ask this question: If we are moving toward a sufficient number of LBOs that have very high debt-equity ratios, my argument would be that some double A companies will eventually be forced to move to higher debt ratios whether they want to or not. They may even have to issue junk bonds to remain competitive on the prices of their products.

Consider the case of Dr Pepper, which has gone the LBO route. If my hypothesis is correct, Dr Pepper should be cutting prices like crazy, thereby forcing Coke and Pepsi to cut their prices. In order to compete, Coke and Pepsi may have to raise their debt ratios every bit as much as Dr Pepper's.

BRIAN: I don't think so, Joel. They are going to have to service all that debt at Dr Pepper. It is Dr Pepper that will end up bringing its debt ratio down.

CLIFF: Joel, you are getting dangerously close to the assertion that a lot of debt is good and even more debt is better. I think there are also some substantial costs associated with having a lot of debt, and that these costs vary across firms and across industries.

JOEL: I agree, Cliff. But what I am suggesting to you is that in industries where the assets provide highly stable cash flows, we may have a lot more LBO candidates than we thought—companies which may be able to support a lot more debt if owned by an aggressive shareholder-value maximizer like Carl Icahn.

The question I would ask of you, Cliff, is why are some firms like General Foods increasing their debt ratios *now*? Brian, you said your firm is committed to the proposition that debt financing is cheaper than equity, at least when used within prudent limits. So your debt ratio went from 12 percent to 30 percent debt to capital. My question, again, is: How come you stopped at 30?

BRIAN: Well, Joel, I think that a certain amount of debt adds value, but too much debt can have a negative impact on your share price performance. Now, the LBO is at the extreme edge of this investment risk-reward spectrum. And investors in LBOs have so far been buying businesses supported by assets whose liquidation value is probably equivalent to the price they have been paying.

You see, Joel, I am trying to differentiate between situations where these nine-to-one debt ratios are being used and situations where they are not being used. The corporate raiders have been going after the type of companies that offer safe bets. They may like strong cash flow, but they are generally buying companies that are rich in undervalued assets. So that if push comes to shove, they can break the company apart and pay off the debt.

HARRY: I agree with Brian. The corporate raiders and LBO investors are only going after the lay-ups. They are not interested in the jump shots, in the riskier companies.

JOEL: I would say they are going for even three-point shots, as long as they are highly confident they can make them. In other words they are going for cash flow that is highly stable across time.

HARRY: Look at it this way. General Foods is already levered to 30 percent debt to capital. You might be able to take them to 45 percent and still have the same degree of confidence in your ability to service that debt and maintain your access to capital markets. Joel, you and I are both talking about predictability.

JOEL: Well, let me talk about the case of one LBO that I am somewhat familiar with. When Dr Pepper was going through the LBO process, I asked the chief financial officer, "What is going on here?" He said, "Well, the answer is of course that debt is cheaper than equity. And because of our very stable cash flow, they think they can do the deal at a nine-to-one ratio." So I said to myself, "If what he is saying is correct, then what does that imply for our friends at General Foods?" If a higher debt ratio does create a lot of value, then will General Foods soon be forced to make some changes that it is not anticipating?

BRIAN: Joel, I think the fallacy of your argument is twofold. One, the big deals have been done such that the financing risk that comes to the equity holder from the nine-to-one debt ratios is potentially covered by the protection afforded by the assets.

CHET: I said a little bit earlier that very few of these deals are really expected to stay at nine-to-one. In the great majority, the strategy is to bring that debt down very quickly. And sometimes the debt is reduced through the sale of assets. These assets are not "undervalued," but I would often call them "underutilized" assets—assets that may have a much higher value in a different context. It is the undeveloped land sitting on the company's balance sheet, for example, or it may be the operation earning substandard returns (and which is never expected to earn an adequate rate of return) that continues to have its requests for more capital granted by headquarters—these are the kind of things that attract corporate raiders' attention.

JOEL: Can I ask you a question, Chet? Why didn't these managements that bought their public companies and took them private create that value for shareholders by disposing of the assets *before* they had the LBO?

CHET: That is a question I really do not have a good answer for. Just as I don't have a good answer for why you have all these companies with incredibly large cash balances that are earning only money-market rates of return. There must be more productive uses for that corporate capital.

THE VARIATION OF DEBT RATIOS ACROSS INDUSTRIES __

CLIFF: There are two strategies that we can follow in looking into this capital structure puzzle. Let me just lay them out and suggest that there might be some advantages to moving on to a slightly different track. One thing that we can do—and this is what we've done for the most part today—

is to focus on firms that have had dramatic changes at a point in time in their capital structure. We can try to explain why a particular firm that had a low debt ratio has chosen to go to high debt ratio, or vice versa.

The other possibility is to look at capital structure "cross-sectionally" if you will, to see if there are some discernible, predictable patterns of capital structure in various industries. We may be able to say something about how the chemical industry's average capital structure differs from that of the steel industry, or something about the capital structure of regulated utilities versus unregulated firms. Then we can try to explain these average tendencies. Finally, we can look at individual firms within that industry that deviate from the average and try to explain that deviation.

At this state of our knowledge in finance, I feel a lot more comfortable about approaching capital structure along this second line. If someone said to me, "Here is a company that just substantially increased the debt in its capital structure. I want you to explain, first, why they did it; second, why did they do it when they did it, not six months earlier, not six months later," I would just have to throw my hands up in the air.

Now, Joel, you raised the point that if we try to look across firms and determine which kinds of firms tend to have a lot of debt, one of the most likely determinants of capital structure is the stability of operating cash flow. I would argue that more fundamental than the stability of cash flow is the kind of asset that they are lending against. For example, firms that have a set of *tangible* assets—"bricks and mortar," if you will—are likely to be able to support a lot of debt. There is little uncertainty about how those assets will be used by management. They are general assets that can be transferred from one owner to another with little loss in value. Those kinds of assets represent relatively good collateral for loans.

At the other extreme of this continuum are firms—even well-established companies with long records of stable earnings, firms perhaps like Kodak or IBM—whose primary assets are intangible, assets that take the form of things like trademarks, advertising, patents, research and development activities, and perhaps a well-developed organization. To bring a project that right now is in an R&D phase and to turn it into a set of realized cash flows is going to require a whole sequence of managerial decisions over a number of years. The value of those kinds of projects tends to be much more sensitive to how they are financed, much more vulnerable to the wrong kinds of management incentives that can be created by heavy debt financing. These assets are not very well suited as collateral for loans.

I would like to suggest that one of the things that differentiate the DuPonts, the IBMs, and the Kodaks, on the one hand, from the steel companies or the regulated utilities (although there are some other things going on there as well), is that the nature of the underlying assets is different in a very fundamental way.

BENNETT: As an example of that point, I've noticed that tank car companies, which have very fungible and collaterized type of assets, generally choose to borrow money rather than issue equity. In fact, it seems to me that as a general rule, those companies that can support a lot of debt—those companies that lenders are willing to lend to—generally tend to have fairly large debt ratios. And this seems to be an argument against the capital structure irrelevance proposition we began with. The fact that companies with tangible assets tend to use a lot of debt suggests that there must be substantial benefits to debt financing.

CLIFF: I tend to agree with that. But what we are saying here is that there appears to be a cost associated with more debt, and that that cost varies in a systematic way across firms with different activities and asset types. Therefore, it doesn't seem to me that you want to say, "Well, the fact that regulated utilities seem to have used a lot of debt and over a long period of time means that Kodak must be making a mistake."

The one observation that I think is most appropriate to this capital structure question wasn't made by a financial economist, but by an architect, Louis Henri Sullivan. He said, "Form ever follows function." If you want to understand the form of the financing—that is, the structure of the liability side of the firm's balance sheet—then it is crucial to go back and take a look at the underlying real investment policies that these firms are following. That, I think, is where the majority of the explanation of capital structure is going to lie.

BOB: I think that ties in well with the case of General Foods. General Foods, as Joel has observed a number of times, has a debt ratio that is well below nine-to-one. It is true that General Foods may historically have quite stable cash flows, but part of the reason that they are so stable is that they have a set of market franchises which they need to feed through research and development and advertising on new products. So it may be very different from Bennett's tank car company; there may be a large amount of managerial discretion with respect to future investments.

BENNETT: But shouldn't their bond rating reflect the fact that their assets don't seem to support much debt? So if General Foods has a double A bond rating, presumably the rating agency is telling the company they could borrow far more than they do.

CLIFF: Nobody is saying that General Foods couldn't borrow more. The question is, If they borrowed more, would the value of General Foods be higher or lower than it is now? All I am saying is that I am quite sympathetic to the notion that a company's capital structure may affect its value. The fact that corporations hire very talented people in finance-related activities seems to me a well-reasoned investment in personnel.

JOEL: I have a question for you, then. Why, over the same period of time, do we see such high variance between firms in the same industry at the same time? Pepsico has a fairly high debt ratio, Coca-Cola almost no debt. And why was General Foods financing themselves at a debt ratio of, say, 12 percent when other food processors like Ralston Purina or Pillsbury or General Mills were using considerably more debt?

ANDY: Once again, I don't think you are going to understand private capital structures unless you get down to specifics. If you want to find out why Pepsi and Coke have different capital structures, I think the way to do it is to talk to the specific personnel in the department who can probably explain it to you.

PENSION FUND LIABILITIES AND OFF-BALANCE SHEET FINANCING

BENNETT: We haven't approached the subject of off-balance sheet financing as yet, and the effect that such financing has on a company's debt capacity. One of the biggest is the pension fund liability, which has the most senior claim in bankruptcy courts according to ERISA. When we take such liabilities into account, many companies have far more leverage in a real economic sense than the accounting books would suggest. As a matter of fact there have been studies showing that swings in AT&T's pension portfolio from year to year could conceivably double or wipe out that company's profits. So it would seem that a large part of a company's debt capacity may actually be used in funding off-balance sheet liabilities. So, my question is, to what extent are off-balance sheet items like pension fund liabilities affecting the capital structure decision of companies?

HARRY: The FASB has been at work on this pension problem and should issue a ruling by the end of this year which would force companies to adjust their accounting numbers to reflect the economics of these liabilities. But, in general, I think that very imperfect, very limited information is getting out to the marketplace about off-balance sheet financing. For example, I have a captive finance company that gives us off-balance sheet financing. And we did it specifically for that purpose: to preserve our debt capacity and financing flexibility. Even though it was disclosed, we felt that it was giving us extra flexibility because it was being ignored by the market. We felt we could use $50 to $100 million with no effect on our ratings.

CLIFF: There are other off-balance sheet claims against the corporation, things like product warranties that represent fixed claims against the corporation's future cash flows, that also would affect how much debt it wants to maintain.

BRIAN: Chrysler issued those five-year warranties, and that made a lot of sense.

CLIFF: It makes a lot of sense if you have the federal government coming in to underwrite a certain set of your fixed claims. But it's a little different in the case of companies in the consumer industry—say, the tampon and Tylenol problems—cases where the Fed is not providing the insurance. Most finance discussions ignore these real liabilities.

HARRY: Yes, and some of the insurance markets are falling apart. I know of a company in our industry where the liability policy is now one-fourth of the coverage of last year's, and it cost ten times what it was before. Now the existence of these kinds of exposures is certainly going to place some limits on the use of debt.

BRIAN: Yes, potential liabilities have to be factored into your choice of capital structure, even though these liabilities are not reflected on your balance sheet.

FLOATING-RATE DEBT AND INTEREST RATE SWAPS _____

BENNETT: Well, let's move on to consider some of the new financing instruments that managements have been using to meet their overall capital structure objectives. There are a great variety of issues to consider, and not much time remaining, so let's just focus on some fairly specific questions: Why, for example, would management prefer to issue fixed-rate rather than floating-rate debt? I am talking about *long-term* floating-rate debt, not just short-term bank debt. Most treasurers I have talked to have a strong preference for fixed-rate debt. They typically say, "Well, at least with fixed-rate debt we know what our debt is going to cost us." Would it make any sense for companies in uncertain times to issue floating-rate debt instead of the conventional long-term fixed-rate issue?

HARRY: The tease for the treasurer is the shape of the yield curve. When you are facing a positively shaped or "normal" yield curve, then the corporate treasurer has a strong temptation to stay with short-term debt.

BENNETT: I am not talking about short-term rates now. I am talking about long-term money where the rate of interest floats.

HARRY: I understand. But those long-term issues typically are tied to short-term rates like LIBOR. You are talking about long-term money that carries a lower rate on principal and doesn't have to be paid back for a fairly long period of time. As a treasurer you have got to make judgments about the yield curve, about how it looks today and how that is going to change.

However, the fact that today you have interest rate swaps available substantially reduces the risk of judging incorrectly. You don't have to worry about call provisions anymore. If in fact you were wrong on your judgment, or you see the basis for your judgment changing, then you can go out and do a swap and change your floating rate into fixed, or fixed rate into floaters.

BENNETT: But in that case you are still losing money. By swapping you're simply cutting your losses.

HARRY: I agree that the only person who doesn't lose something is the one who only borrows at bottoms in the interest rate market. I'm talking about the ability to manage debt costs and optimize.

In the past, American Hospital never wanted more than a third of its debt costs to float. With these new tools we now feel comfortable allowing more than half of our debt to float, at least at present debt levels.

BRIAN: With these new financial instruments, you can really separate the kind of pricing and the structure of the debt from the funding decision. At any point you can switch it.

BENNETT: Are you saying that the reason you are doing that is that you think you can predict interest rates better than the prediction built into the yield curve?

BRIAN: No, but what it does is to protect you from your own prediction of future interest rates. In the old days, you would say, "I think long-term rates are going down, so I am going to fund short term until I reach that time when I think I should lock in those lower long rates." So, then you would lock in at a fixed rate; and in retrospect, on the basis of what rates did later, you either made a good decision or a bad decision. These days, however, you can swap at any point from floating to fixed, from fixed to floating, and from one currency to another currency.

ANDY: But these new instruments still don't prevent you from betting on rates, and thus making the wrong decisions.

BRIAN: Yes, but you do have some added flexibility because the market generally comprises investors with differing views on future rates.

ANDY: Well, yes, you have the liquidity to get out of the instrument, but it still costs you; the mistake has still imposed a cost on the company.

BENNETT: What these new instruments allow you to do is to make more and more bets, and thus more precise bets. My question, though, is whether or not you can consistently win by making these bets? Is this a game worth playing?

HARRY: Well, I have saved a good deal on financing costs through swaps—in some cases, over 200 basis points through the use of currency swaps. Swaps allow firms with the ability to efficiently access specific markets to combine with other firms with similar abilities, but in different markets. The mechanism results in an arbitrage that isn't being made by those usually functioning as market intermediaries.

ANDY: There are also tremendous financing opportunities that now exist in the floating-rate, tax-exempt market. Here companies and municipalities are issuing floating-rate, tax-exempt bonds which exploit the fact that the yield curve on municipal bonds is, and has always been, positive. We are talking about spreads between long and short rates that are much more than 200 basis points; in fact, they typically range between 500 or 600 basis points. The yield curve has always been positive, never negative, and there are very good reasons for this. So by having these long-term, floating-rate instruments that are tied to short-term rates, the issuing companies are getting enormous savings on their interest costs.

ASSET/LIABILITY MANAGEMENT

CLIFF: One of the things that this discussion highlights is that it is a lot more difficult now to read a firm's balance sheet and understand its capital structure because of all the things that don't necessarily show up there. It is difficult to look at many corporate balance sheets and tell exactly what is going on without a very careful reading of the footnotes.

I would argue, for example, that this question about the effective maturity of the debt has something ultimately to do with the effective duration or interest sensitivity of the projects that the firm invests in. Those firms whose projects have cash flows that are quite sensitive to interest rates—think about a commercial bank, for example—are going to use short-term or floating-rate liabilities to fund their assets. If you see a savings bank or a savings and loan association, you are going to see longer-term liabilities that correspond to their longer-term assets. And I don't think that is accidental. By matching those effective maturities of the asset and liability sides of the balance sheet, companies are engaging in certain kinds of hedging.

If you want to think about interest rate risk, though, you have got to think about the *whole* structure of the asset side of the balance sheet and then about the *whole* structure of the liability side of the balance sheet. For example, the firm may have entered into a swap that's only disclosed in the footnotes, if at all. As a consequence, determining the effective interest rate sensitivity or effective maturity of the liability side of the balance sheet is a lot more complicated now with new tools for financial engineering.

HARRY: In the last year Sears made a major adjustment of their liability side because they felt the asset side of their business was really sensitive to interest rate changes. I thought this was an appropriate application of this concept.

CHET: I think you also have to look at these new financing tools from the investor's as well as the issuer's standpoint. A lot of these new instruments were created to satisfy a demand on the part of buyers who also have a certain liability structure of their own; insurance companies and pension funds are classic examples. They wanted to get assets that matched their liabilities. Zero coupons, for example, arose in part to meet this need of pension funds to immunize their portfolio of liabilities.

CLIFF: One of the things that instruments like swaps do is to unbundle a set of financial characteristics that previously came only in packages. Now you can take one collection of financial characteristics and, say, separate the sensitivity to interest rates from the maturity characteristics. You can unbundle that package and sell the life insurance company what it wants, and sell the other characteristics of the cash flow claims to a commercial bank. By splitting the old security apart and giving the components to the people who value them the most, the issuer gets a higher price for its debt or, alternatively, ends up paying a lower yield.

ANDY: One particular service that I am involved in at Salomon Brothers is to look at our corporate clients' entire liability portfolios. We compute the duration of their entire portfolios of outstanding bonds on an after-tax basis. What we have tried to bring to the attention of industrial companies is the need to look at the interest rate exposure of their revenue or asset sides; and then to try to design a matching liability structure.

THE PROCESS OF FINANCIAL INNOVATION _____

BENNETT: Let me move away from asset/liability management for a second. You are saying that there are now benefits to corporations from issuing unbundled securities and selling them to different markets to get the benefit of lower-cost financing. My question is, wouldn't it make more sense for financial intermediaries to do the repackaging?

BOB: Corporations started issuing zero-coupon bonds partly because of the tax advantages, but also partly because of a special investor demand. Investors didn't want to bear reinvestment risks; so then financial intermediaries stepped in and began stripping conventional securities to meet essentially the same demand. So there is a lot of competition to do exactly this repackaging.

BENNETT: But the value of these innovations is soon competed away in the marketplace.

BOB: Yes, that's right. We started off this discussion talking about the Modigliani and Miller proposition. I see that proposition as essentially a statement about capital market competition. It doesn't say that all financing decisions are necessarily unimportant. Rather it says that if corporations can gain any advantage through purely financial transactions, such transactions will attract a lot of competitors. It says in effect that whatever the corporation can do to repackage its securities, people out in the capital market—whether individual investors or financial institutions—can do just as well under competitive circumstances.

BENNETT: I don't see why the corporation would benefit at all from this process. I would think that the intermediaries capture all the benefit of these financial innovations.

BOB: The intermediaries generally do capture most of the benefits, unless there is some unique advantage the corporation has relative to the intermediaries.

CHET: Sure, but the corporation may benefit simply by having lower transactions costs. For example, a corporation with very long-term projects would be likely to issue a zero-coupon bond, which means that it has no required outlays until maturity. This arrangement keeps them from having to go back into the capital market each year to finance the interest and principal payments that might be due on this.

ANDY: In the case of zero-coupon bonds, we have been talking about stripping treasury bonds of their interest payments to create a zero-coupon government bond. Well, the federal government has responded by issuing zero-coupon bonds itself.

CLIFF: To understand the role of these financial intermediaries, consider what happened when we first observed some of these exotic interest rate and currency swaps. We saw firms with very aggressive financial officers doing things that on the face of it looked like very unusual transactions—things that had little to do with the complexion of the firms' assets. For example, a company may have issued Deutsche mark–denominated debt when they didn't have an obvious mark exposure. What they were really doing was swapping themselves back out of the exposure, and winding up with cheaper dollar financing.

HARRY: I came close to doing a transaction where we would have borrowed at a fixed rate in yen, swapped it to fixed-rate dollars, and then swapped it to floating-rate dollars. The point of the whole deal would have been to reduce my commercial paper costs by 40 basis points.

BENNETT: If you can make money doing that, why wouldn't it pay for a pension fund to raise money in Germany and turn around and advance you the dollars?

CLIFF: Well, yes, the point that Bennett is making is right; I think that this market has matured. The opportunities for picking up 40 basis points by doing something that on the face of it seems bizarre are the kind of opportunities that are competed away very quickly. What you are eventually left with is that only those companies that have some real business reason for engaging in a swap (say, for example, because underlying circumstances have changed such that where it once made sense to issue debt in marks, their business has changed and they now want to be in dollars) are prime candidates for a currency swap.

You won't for long have the opportunity to lower your cost of borrowing by taking a long detour to get from A to B. The shortest route for corporations in financing is usually the right one because these intermediaries come in, create much deeper markets, and arbitrage the difference of getting from A to B by going through C.

HARRY: That's right. I never got my 40 basis points. I never did the deal. The best I could have gotten was 30, so I said "no." It was just too complicated. For that amount of work the savings were too small.

CLIFF: But if you had been there six months earlier, you would have done it. The rate of financial innovation in that marketplace is so rapid that the window of opportunity—that brief period when companies are doing something that is new, innovative, and therefore there are some rents to be made—is getting smaller and smaller.

BENNETT: Speaking of financial innovation, what do you think of the Dutch auction that Jack Bennett at Exxon did a little while ago? Exxon went directly to the capital markets to issue their securities. There were no underwriters involved in the process. The securities were offered directly to the ultimate investors, the intermediaries were cut out of the process entirely, and Exxon saved a lot of money.

CLIFF: That's true, Bennett, but who bid for the securities? I suspect that the underwriters outbid the investors.

BENNETT: That may be true, but the cost to Exxon was much, much less than the cost of going with a more traditional underwriting.

CLIFF: I suspect that that kind of opportunity to bypass the underwriters is not going to be available for most companies. Underwriters provide a certifying function for investors, and it is only the Exxons, the largest public corporations, that are going to be able to do without the services of an underwriter. The savings from bypassing your investment banker, as in the case of self registration, are probably only available to a limited number of companies.

ZERO-COUPON BONDS

BENNETT: Let me ask another question, a more general question. How can a financing instrument simultaneously be both an attractive financing vehicle for the corporation and an attractive investment for investors? Because it seems that whatever yield is paid to investors represents a cost to the company.

ANDY: I think the answer to your question will expose the fallacy of the thinking underlying so many economic theories. How much do you know about Japanese tax laws? Do you know why the Japanese are buying zero coupons?

BENNETT: Because the capital gains rate is zero to Japanese investors.

ANDY: Yes, but the answer is a little more complicated than that. European institutions are also buying them, but for some other reasons. Japanese institutions are buying them for still other reasons. You have after-tax investors in the United States that are buying for their own reason. But what you want to do from the corporate perspective is to create that set of liabilities that minimizes the cost of the overall financing process.

BENNETT: My answer to your question would be that there were some major tax benefits to zero coupons. The corporation could deduct the amortized discount from its corporate income. Japanese investors pay no taxes on capital gains, and zeros effectively convert ordinary income into capital gains for them. So, if you consolidate the U.S. and Japanese government together, then zeros were the most effective vehicle for evading the taxation of the two governments combined.

ANDY: In March of 1979 there was an article in the *Journal of Finance* in which Myles Livingston "proved" that zero-coupon bonds would never be issued. At the same time he was devising this proof, we at Salomon Brothers were at the beginning of a very successful effort to design and market these securities. So what was missing in Livingston's proof? He assumed that taxes were symmetrical. At the same time interest rates started rising, investors were crying out for zero-coupon bonds. What finally made zeros so successful was the tax treatment combined with the very high level of interest rates in 1980 and 1981. There was an incredible flood of zeros because by that time the tax advantages were overwhelming. So, even though investors and issuers were very much aware of these tax effects, the academic community was slow to see it.

DOES CAPITAL STRUCTURE MATTER?: SUMMING UP ____

BRIAN: One thing you have to understand is that corporate managements respond differently to their common mission of improving stockholder wealth. I think that most people believe, and very logically so, that the principal means of improving shareholder value is by improving operating performance. As long as management shows growth and improving returns, it is essentially doing its job by stockholders. So, there will always be some skepticism about the notion that management can significantly influence shareholder wealth solely by looking in a more sophisticated way at its capital structure and lowering its cost of capital.

JOEL: You are right, Brian. I would also argue that the overwhelming majority of a company's value is created at the operating level. What we are trying to determine is that, holding operating performance constant, what incremental value can be added from the use of debt financing? My feeling is that small changes in the debt ratio have little effect. But, if you go from a zero debt ratio to something like 50 percent debt to capital, the creation of value might be on the order of an increment of 20 percent. So, while operating performance is certainly the most important determinant of stock prices, the effect of capital structure changes can also be consequential for some companies. I am convinced that some companies are not making the fullest use of the tax advantage of debt that they could.

BRIAN: I think there is a problem with this, Joel. If you go back to Cliff's introduction, there is enough uncertainty that you really have to work at accepting the proposition you just made. First of all, you need a receptive management, one that is comfortable with the proposition that debt adds value—because the natural inclination is to play it safe.

JOEL: Well, there may be some urgency about the resolution of this matter. I'm not sure we can always permit management the luxury of five to ten years to mull it over. Because there are value-maximizers out who understand that the tax benefits of debt financing can be significant.

CHET: To return to your earlier comparison, Joel, I think it is possible that the capital structures of Coke and Pepsi are not really as different as you are suggesting. Coke is triple A and Pepsi is a low double A. And though their book debt to capital ratios may look a lot different, the interest coverage ratios and other proxies for *market* leverage ratios may be quite similar. If you look at a true, market-based measure of debt leverage, then the difference between the capital structures of Coke and Pepsi may not be that different. What this may mean is that, in some cases, you may be able to go from 20 percent debt to 40 percent debt in book terms and still only get a single-letter downgrading.

JOEL: That is an intriguing possibility. If the cost of adding that kind of leverage is only a single-letter downgrade on the rating, then there may be a lot of value that can be added without sacrificing much in the way of financing flexibility.

BRIAN: Cliff, is there any evidence that says that the specific nature of the debt structure has any influence on shareholder wealth apart from savings in basis points here and there? To my mind the primary focus of shareholders is on the target capital structure, not on the specific financing instruments that go to make up that structure. Has any work been done to differentiate the effects of issuing different kinds of debt securities on shareholder wealth—or, more recently, on the implications of swaps and other hedging techniques?

CLIFF: That work is really at a formative stage at this point.

BRIAN: Would you say, then, that any kind of debt by definition is better than equity?

CLIFF: No. I don't think anybody but Joel in his role as devil's advocate would strongly adhere to that sort of position.

BRIAN: So what type of debt by definition is good?

CLIFF: Well, as Andy has pointed out, debt is a much more heterogeneous commodity than academic discussions tend to acknowledge. Jerry Warner and I spent a long, long time writing a paper that would call more academic attention to the details of standard bond contracts—to the differences in covenants restricting corporate dividend policy, restricting additional debt, and establishing sinking funds and call provisions. I had hopes that our work would at least make academics aware of complexities that investment bankers have been familiar with for a long time.

ANDY: Yes, this is an obvious point. There is essentially only one kind of equity issue. But in the case of debt there are many, many variations.

CLIFF: Yes, debt issues can differ not only by coupon and maturity date, but also by provisions in the covenants, by seniority, by convertibility, by callability.

BRIAN: I know the terms of debt issues differ, but my interest is in whether that differentiation affects shareholder wealth in any systematic way. For example, if a company has 40 percent debt in its capital structure, and that debt is all carrying floating rates, does that have a different effect on a company's stock price than if its debt were all carrying fixed rates?

CLIFF: If you told me that there are two electric utilities and one has financed itself with twenty-year floating-rate instruments and the other has financed itself with twenty-year fixed-rate instruments, then I would expect shareholders in those two companies to be affected very differently. And a lot of that has to do with the characteristics of the assets of those corporations and the cash flows that are going to be generated.

ANDY: I have been doing some work on that issue. I have looked at the debt structure of dozens of major electric utilities. What you generally find is that the average maturity of most of their debt issues is between twelve and seventeen years. If you look at telephone companies, but not Bell system companies, the average life varies between twenty-three and twenty-four years to about twenty-six or twenty-seven years. Now there are some cases— gas transmission companies for example—where the debt maturities are much shorter, say, three years to about seven years.

CLIFF: The reason you see this is that in the case of a gas pipeline, as soon as the recoverable reserves of the field at one end of that line give out, the whole pipeline is worthless. So those gas transmission debt issues will include special sinking-fund provisions in order to extinguish that debt— presumably before the assets that serve as the collateral become worthless.

BRIAN: What I am really wondering myself, though, is whether the shareholder wealth concepts that we use really are keeping track of these very sophisticated moves that are going on in the capital markets? Because if they are not, then we could be making a big mistake.

HARRY: I think there is still a lot of uncertainty about how the marketplace views a lot of debt on corporate balance sheets; this is still a major point of contention.

BENNETT: In response to Brian's question, though, about whether the financial instruments the company chooses affect stock prices, the answer to that question is obviously yes. If a company that can raise tax-exempt instead of taxable financing fails to do so, then it quite clearly penalizes its stockholders. Clearly, there are ways to affect stockholder value through financing—by reducing corporate or investor taxes, by reducing transactions costs, and by preserving company incentives to undertake the right investments. These variables are all affected by the company's choice of capital structure and financing instruments.

BRIAN: Yes, Bennett, I can see these differences translating into lower costs *over time*. I guess the question I am really asking is whether the intrinsic economic impacts of a new financing are reflected immediately in stock prices in any systematic way.

CLIFF: Let me try and restate your question in a slightly different way. It seems to me that you are saying that every time you try to structure a debt issue, you have to make a pragmatic business decision. And, in some sense, I think that what you would really like is more theory, not less, to base your decision on. What you would like is more direction from carefully crafted academic studies that would give you more confidence in what kinds of issues you should focus on in trying to decide whether you should issue, say, fixed-rate or floating-rate debt; whether the debt should be callable or not; whether the call provisions should be prohibited in the first five years and only come in after that, or should it be ten, or should they be callable immediately.

What you are really asking for, I think, are useful guidelines for a set of very important managerial decisions. And my strong feeling is that if the academic finance community is going to be successful in the long run, we are going to have to address all those much more specific financing issues. We are going to have to provide convincing theories supported with strong evidence. We are going to have to show which things matter in which dimensions, and demonstrate the magnitudes of the trade-offs in making these decisions.

BRIAN: You have already given a very straightforward example of the floating-rate versus fixed-rate decision. Let's say my judgment is that I can save over the life of the instrument twenty-five basis points per year for five years. Now, that might be, on the face of it, a good economic decision. But what if the stock market looks at that floating-rate debt and says, "I really don't like that because it converts into a major risk from interest rate changes." So, even though I may have obtained some expected interest savings, the market may lower my stock price because of my increased interest rate exposure. It is this kind of subtlety that I am looking to the research for.

CHET: The use of floating versus fixed-rate debt certainly affects the level of financial risks perceived by the market. We can't forget, after all, that there is a real cost for a firm getting into financial distress. And these costs are not just the cost of the lawyers representing you in bankruptcy court. The real costs are all the constraints on your decision making that financial distress brings about.

So a big cost of issuing the wrong kind of debt is that if it raises your financial risk to the point where the market thinks you're now a much riskier firm, then the market is going to raise your required return and lower your stock price. For example, if the electric utility issues floating-rate debt, they may save a few basis points; but they may also face a significant danger that if interest rates rise, the regulatory commissions may refuse to allow them to pass those higher interest costs through to consumers.

BOB: We are now seeing the beginnings of a literature with the kind of studies that I think you would like to see. For example, we are beginning to look at the stock market's reaction to all kinds of securities issues. And the main thing we are finding is that it is awfully difficult to interpret the results. For example, it is invariably found that when companies issue new equity, the market's reaction is negative. And this is not as a result of the equity issue per se. The reaction occurs upon the announcement of the new issue, well before the new stock is actually out.

Now, that finding doesn't necessarily mean that the equity issue was a bad idea. It may mean that management's decision to issue equity at that time conveyed information to the market about the real value of the company (it may, for example, suggest that management feels the company is slightly overvalued relative to its prospects)—information that would likely have come out sooner or later anyway. It is important to distinguish, therefore, between the effect of a financing decision on shareholder wealth and the information the decision might reveal about other aspects of the company's operations.

BENNETT: Well, you know, Bob, this makes me think of Merton Miller's old comment about the effect of dividend policy on stock prices. He said that trying to determine the effects of the dividend on stock prices was like trying to hear the piccolo player in the orchestra. Some of the things you are talking about are so subtle, and are taking place when so many other things are happening, that they are virtually impossible to detect with any precision.

CLIFF: That may be true, Bennett. But, at the same time, I am strongly convinced that financing decisions do affect the value of companies. As I said much earlier today, the way to approach financing decisions is to stand the old M & M proposition on its head. If financing policy matters (and I have little doubt that it does), then it matters only because of those factors I mentioned above: taxes, contracting costs, and potential incentive problems if the firm gets in financial trouble. So companies making financing decisions will have to consider matters such as: Are there provisions in the tax code that would make it better to issue fixed versus floating rate debt? Are there important contracting costs associated with one versus the other? And, finally, is one type of financing more likely to interfere with management's investment policy? A good financial officer will focus his attention on these three issues.

BENNETT: There is no question that financing decisions matter. It's just that they may matter a lot less than most chief financial officers and many investment bankers would contend. But with that I would like to thank everyone for taking part.

COMMENTARY:
SOME GUIDELINES FOR SETTING
CAPITAL STRUCTURE TARGETS
by Bennett Stewart

OVERVIEW

A company's financing policies should be designed to support management's operating goals. So long as management attempts to undertake all projects that promise adequate rates of return, financing policy should be subordinated to investment decisions. Unfortunately, all too often management permits financial goals to dominate good business judgment; the result is that value-adding investment opportunities are lost due to inadequate funding. In our view, shareholders are served best when the financing plan provides management with the flexibility necessary to meet its business objectives.

The development of an appropriate financing plan involves a three-step procedure. Management first should prepare a business plan *without* considering a limitation on capital availability. In this way the financing plan can truly accommodate the cash needs of the business plan. Moreover, management can count on capital being available if the proposed investments cover the cost of capital.

When all scenarios of the corporate business plan are completed, the next step is to tailor a financial plan that will, first of all, fill the needs of the business plan. Secondly, it will incorporate all management's financial goals. These goals include a debt financing policy which achieves a prudent balance between funding growth with low-cost debt and allowing adequate financing flexibility. The policy may be expressed in terms both of a financial posture as measured by a bond rating and of a target ratio of debt-to-capital employed.

The final step is to identify the most attractive sources of preferred and common equity capital to finance any cash deficit remaining after debt financing. If operating cash requirements exhaust debt financing capacity under the target debt-to-capital ratio, serious consideration should be given to reducing the dividend or eliminating it altogether. If the additional retained earnings are insufficient to maintain management's target debt-to-capital ratio, then a comparison should be made of the relative costs of raising external equity through preferreds, new common, or rights issues.

In this framework for devising financial policy, there is *no* trade-off between paying dividends and undertaking new investments, or between paying dividends and raising additional debt. Rather, the trade-off is between paying dividends and raising external equity financing. In other words, the optimal dividend policy is one that is truly residual to investment and external financing policies.

In the remainder of this article, I discuss issues involved in setting financial goals and provide the reasoning required to formulate a consistent policy on dividends, new common, and preferred equity issues. Because a company's financial goals are closely interrelated, each must be set with the others in mind.

TARGET CAPITAL STRUCTURE

In establishing an appropriate debt financing policy, two opposing factors should be taken into consideration. First, there are distinct advantages to the use of debt financing because shareholders receive a tax deduction for interest charges incurred. As leverage is increased, management is able to lower the weighted average cost of (debt and equity) capital by blending greater proportions of lower cost debt with smaller proportions of more expensive equity, thereby reducing the hurdle rate for new investments and potentially increasing the share price.

On the other hand, higher leverage introduces additional fixed charges which increase financial risk and impair financing flexibility. Firms with high financial risk may be forced to issue new equity under difficult money market conditions when equity is very expensive. They also may be required to spend additional time and effort to comply with more stringent loan covenants and restrictions.

In resolving the pros and cons of debt financing, management should try to maximize the benefits of debt financing while maintaining financial risk at a "manageable" level, one which assures management of adequate financing flexibility. In our view, financial risk is manageable when the firm is reasonably well protected against economic downturns, changes in industry conditions, and company problems which might depress earnings.

BOND RATINGS

It is useful to classify financial risk in terms of bond ratings since these provide a framework for analyzing the risks important to all creditors. Furthermore, relating the financial posture adopted to a particular bond rating facilitates a determination of the availability and cost of funds in both the private and public debt markets.

When selecting a particular bond rating and financial posture to pursue, management is really choosing a desired level of financing flexibility. We define financing flexibility to be the degree to which a company's financing options are kept open for raising funds while keeping the equityholders of the company within an acceptable risk level in any economic climate. A company with too low a level of financing flexibility could be forced to raise common equity at an inopportune time to meet a need for funds.

Financial planners must decide what bond rating is right for their company. There is really no one correct bond rating for any particular company. The choice will depend on the levels of financing flexibility and financial risk the company feels comfortable with. We only say that a company should not seek a financial risk level that would endanger management's financing flexibility and give rise to an undue risk of insolvency. In our opinion, companies with ratings of less than Baa/BBB (triple B) on their long-term senior debt run this risk.

While countless factors affect companies' debt capacity, we have found five which together are most important in explaining bond ratings. Stern Stewart has developed a bond rating simulation framework which focuses on these five factors. Such a framework can aid the long-range financial planning process by showing the projected effect of a company's operating performance and alternative financing strategies on its credit standing.

Briefly, the technique, which is based on a statistical concept known as "discriminant analysis," involves identifying the key quantifiable characteristics that play a major role in determining the financial strength of a company. Each of these characteristics is assigned a "weight" based on its relative importance, and then a weighted "score" of financial strength is calculated. The score is then put on the Bond Rating Score Range to determine the estimated rating (AAA, AA, etc.).

A description of the factors and an interpretation of the significance of each in determining financial strength is presented below.

1. *Size*: Company size, as measured by total assets, is the single most important factor. It acts as a proxy for the company's ease of access to capital markets, a proven track record, continuity and depth of management, control over markets, and diversification of activities by product line and geography. In general, the larger the company, the higher the bond score.

2. *Risk-Adjusted Return*: The risk-adjusted rate of return measures both the level and stability of the economic earnings of a company. The level of earnings is important because it provides a good indication of the profitability of a company. And, for any given leverage implied, the higher a company's return on total capital, the more likely it will be able to pay interest expense out of earnings. The stability of earnings is also important to creditors because they do not participate in the capital gain rewards accorded equity investors. Consequently, creditors wish to avoid the earnings fluctuations caused by economic cycles.

   The risk-adjusted return, which is computed by subtracting one standard deviation from the five-year average rate of return on total capital, provides an indication of the minimum rate of return a company may be expected to earn approximately 83 percent of the time. To calculate the return on total capital each year, we divide NOPAT by total capital employed. Higher risk-adjusted returns strengthen a company's bond score.

3. *Long-term Debt-to-Capital Ratio*: The three-year average of a company's long-term debt-to-capital ratio is a measure of the financial risk of a company. This measure averaged over a three-year period is a better measure of permanent leverage policy than the debt-to-capital ratio in any one year; hence, it is a better measure of the expected future financial risk of a company. The higher the long-term debt-to-capital ratio, the weaker the bond score will tend to be.

4. *Pension-Adjusted Liabilities-to-Net Worth Ratio*: Pension-adjusted liabilities to net worth is calculated as total liabilities plus the lesser of 50 percent of unfunded pension liabilities or 30 percent of net worth, divided by net worth. This is a good measure of asset protection in the event of bankruptcy, since pension-adjusted liabilities include the off-balance sheet liability of unfunded pension liabilities. This liability is senior to almost all other liabilities and can be substantial. Federal bankruptcy law states that a company can be forced to pay up

to one-third of its net worth to cover unfunded pension liabilities. It therefore seems reasonable that the higher this ratio is, the lower the bond score will be.

5. *Investments and Advances to Unconsolidated Subsidiaries-to-Capital Ratio*: Calculated as a percentage of total capital, this measure indicates the proportion of capital of a company that is already supporting debt. The equity in unconsolidated subsidiaries supports debt on its own books and can not be relied upon to support parent debt as well. Higher ratios of investments and advances to unconsolidated subsidiaries-to-capital will pull down the bond score, all else constant.

CALCULATING A BOND RATING SCORE

To calculate a bond rating score, one would multiply the values of each of the five factors above for a particular company by their respective weights. An example of a 1980 bond rating for a company follows:

	Value	× Weight	= Score
Natural Log of Total Assets	4.71	0.6660	3.14
Five-Year Mean less Standard Deviation of NOPAT/Average Total Capital	15.65%	0.1146	1.79
Three-Year Average of Long-Term Debt/ Total Capital	35.00%	−0.0298	−1.04
Pension Adjusted Liabilities-to-Net Worth	0.60X	0.4658	−0.28
Investments and Advances to Unconsolidated Subsidiaries/Total Capital	5.00%	−0.0247	−0.12
BOND RATING SCORE			3.46

Bond Rating Score Ranges

BBB	BBB/A	A	AA	AAA
3.2	4.0	4.2	5.1	6.0	7.4

In this example, the bond rating score is 3.46, corresponding to a bond rating of BBB for the company's long-term, unsecured, senior debt. Every year SSP&M studies the 300 + industrial and service companies with rated debt and updates the "weights" which, when multiplied by the five factor values, determine the estimated bond rating.

By using the above five factors to calculate bond scores we were able to assign over 80 percent of companies in a holdout sample to their approximate bond rating category. Of those misclassified, the bond score generally was on the borderline of the actual rating, and never was the error larger than one rating grade. In addition, research has shown that bond rating changes lag actual market risk changes: bond rating agencies change bond ratings only after the underlying financial health of the rated company has changed. We believe our ratings are as good as or better than (and in some cases are more up to date) the rating agencies' ratings. Thus, the 20 percent "misclassification" may not be a misclassification at all.

All things considered, the results of our bond rating classifications compare very favorably with our experience using a more traditional rating approach involving a comprehensive study of financial ratios, competitors, and management. While qualitative factors are no doubt important in assigning bond quality and should be considered as a means of supplementing a quantitative method, the accuracy of the bond scoring model demonstrates that the essence of a company's financial condition can be captured by focusing on a few independent characteristics of real economic significance.

BOND RATING USES

In addition to providing an accurate reading of a company's overall credit quality, the bond scoring framework can help to assess the contribution to corporate debt capacity made by individual divisions. Further, the extent of the financial benefit due to diversification and to the consolidation of divisions under a corporate umbrella can be estimated separately.

In the same way, management can evaluate the financial synergy, if any, expected to arise from an acquisition. (A larger post-merger company may be able to increase its target debt-to-capital ratio while maintaining its same bond score.)

However, perhaps the most significant application of the bond scoring method is to help management formulate long-range financing objectives. Such objectives should be commensurate with prospective operating performance and investment spending plans. To do this several operating forecasts, corresponding to a range of possible economic scenarios, should be prepared. Then the bond rating warranted under alternative dividend policies can be estimated using the scoring methodology. Once this is done, management can evaluate the complex trade-offs among dividend payout, financing flexibility, and the use of low-cost debt funds in devising an optimal financing strategy.

With the aid of this technique, the impact of dividend policy and prospective operating results on the company's credit standing can be estimated by examining the trends of projected bond quality. Once agreement is reached on an acceptable level of financial risk, management can select the optimal combination of debt funding and dividend policy.

While certainly not a complete substitute for judgment and experience, our bond scoring method is both simple to employ and highly accurate in assessing financial risk. Moreover, the subtle trade-offs of operating performance and financial policy with credit worthiness that are too complex for the human mind to discern are implicitly accounted for in the scoring framework by focusing on a few independent factors of genuine economic consequence. As a result the facilitation of strategic financial policy formulation is perhaps the most significant contribution of the bond scoring technique.

VI

Giving Executives the Right Incentives
A DISCUSSION OF MANAGEMENT COMPENSATION

INTRODUCTION

A recent *New York Times* article (August 19, 1984) dubbed ours "The Age of 'Me-First' Management." There is little that is tentative about its opening statement:

It doesn't take a revolutionary to figure out that something is amiss in American business today; that a 'me-first, grab-what-you-can' extravagance increasingly appears to be cropping up among the nation's top executives. It shows itself in the disproportionate salaries and bonuses paid to so many corporate chiefs....

Offering a smattering of anecdotes and selective opinions (which, of course, is standard journalistic fare), the article goes on to buttress its basic contention that we are now experiencing an unprecedented "failure of corporate stewardship; a breakdown in management's accountability to shareholders." The tone of the article, like that of so much press commentary on this issue, is that of moral certitude and denunciation—as if to say, "We have offered *prima facie* evidence of corporate management's culpability, the case is closed, bring in the federal regulators."

From the academy, meanwhile, we are hearing something very different, both in manner and matter. It seems doubly peculiar to us, moreover, that the message from our finance scholars was completely ignored by the article above. For, in another article published by the *Times* some three months *earlier* than the piece cited above, the University of Rochester's Michael Jensen and Kevin Murphy report a set of findings that surely merited (at the very least) mention by a journalist who presumes to announce an "age" of unprincipled management. Jensen and Murphy state that "the best scientific evidence currently available" (reflecting "the consensus of more than 60 leading academicians at a recent University of Rochester conference" on management compensation) suggests that "executive salaries are determined by the market, and that changes in compensation are strongly related to company performance."

What distinguishes such "scientific evidence" from the findings of most journalistic reportage? As a popular saying among economists has it, the unspoken assumption underlying most financial journalism is that " '*data*' is the plural form of '*anecdote*.' " What the emerging science of financial economics offers, in place of a few, handpicked "war stories," are the results of subjecting masses of empirical data to rigorous statistical analysis. What we get from this process are the broad *averages*—the representative case, not the one which thrusts itself on our attention (or, more likely, is thrust upon our attention by the media). The unaided eye notes only the most visible aspects of the terrain; broad underlying shifts can be detected only by more sensitive instruments which allow us to range through time. (And a certain amount of historical perspective is useful, we think, in distinguishing "ages" one from another.)

The available scientific evidence on management compensation points to conclusions like the following: executive decisions are strongly influenced—no surprise here—by provisions in their compensation plans; the market responds positively, on average, to the adoption by companies of compensation plans; it reacts negatively to deaths of CEOs (except in those cases where the CEOs were also the founders of the company), suggesting that most CEOs are worth significantly more to their companies than they are paid; and companies with dispersed stock ownership are much more likely to undertake conglomerate mergers than those with relatively concentrated ownership.

On the issue of executive pay and its correspondence with corporate performance, the research shows a small positive correlation between annual stockholder returns and changes in the level of executive salaries and bonuses. Financial economists argue, however, that there are good reasons why we should not expect this correlation to be overly strong, even under the best of all possible compensation schemes. One of these reasons centers on another research finding: namely, that annual changes in the amounts of executives' salaries and bonuses are dwarfed by changes in the value of their stock (and stock option) holdings in their own companies (which turn out to be substantial). This fact alone would suggest that the interests of management and stockholders, at least on average, cannot diverge too sharply.

In the "Discussion of Management Compensation" below, Michael Jensen insists that a far more plausible case can be made for the argument that American corporate executives are now being "systematically and seriously underpaid." In making this case, Jensen points to certain fairly recent phenomena: the shunning of industrial companies by newly graduated MBAs from the best business schools; the large and ever-growing disparity between the pay scales of large public corporations and those of private organizations, such as investment banking, law, and consulting firms; and, perhaps most important, the proliferation of leveraged buy-outs, which Jensen attributes in large part to the inadequacy of current executive rewards—which in turn is attributed to political pressures exerted on the large, visible public corporation. ("We are allowing the Ralph Naders of the world," complains Jensen, "to set the agenda in this business of executive compensation.")

To argue that the market for executive labor is reasonably efficient, however, given the political constraints within which it must operate, is not to suggest that the status quo cannot be improved upon. And the "Discussion" generates a number of proposals for changing current incentive plans. These proposals are concerned for the most part with designing measures of corporate performance, and thus compensation criteria, which most closely align the interests of management and stockholders.

For example, Lou Brindisi, director of Booz Allen's compensation consulting practice, reports a growing disparity between executive pay and corporate performance caused, in large part, by a focus on EPS growth as the primary gauge of performance. Throughout the seventies, Brindisi maintains, many companies reported steady increases in EPS, while their stock prices remained flat or even fell. According to the results of a 1983 Booz Allen study, inflation-adjusted ROE does a much better job of explaining stock market performance, and it accordingly provides a more reliable measure of corporate performance.

Even more radical departures from current corporate practice are proposed by Mark Ubelhart, Hewitt Associates' national practice leader in "Corporate Finance/Compensation." Ubelhart proposes four alternatives to conventional, accounting-based measures of performance like EPS growth and ROE. They are (1) forecasts of discounted cash flow for evaluating divisional performance; (2) cash flow–based returns on investment; (3) relative shareholder returns; and (4) market-indexed stock options.

In "Performance Measurement and Incentive Compensation," the article which follows the discussion, Bennett Stewart offers an extended critique of accounting-based performance measures. In their stead he proposes a measure of cash-flow rates of return on total corporate investment—one which converts conventional accounting income data into estimates of operating cash flow. What further distinguishes Stewart's proposal from traditional, accounting-based criteria is his suggestion that, for highly cyclical industries, performance standards be adjusted *after the fact* for general economic and industry-wide conditions, thereby shielding management (especially operating management) from uncontrollable risks.

DHC

GIVING EXECUTIVES THE RIGHT INCENTIVES: A DISCUSSION OF MANAGEMENT COMPENSATION
December 4, 1984

JOEL STERN, MODERATOR: On behalf of all of us associated with the *Midland Corporate Finance Journal,* I would like to welcome everyone to this roundtable discussion of corporate executive compensation. As you are all well aware, the level of executive pay and its correspondence to corporate performance have become very controversial subjects. They have brought forth highly charged statements from legislators, academics, journalists, and corporate critics of all species. What has been noticeably lacking in this dispute, however, is careful economic analysis of the issues at hand. I would like to use this discussion to shed the light of economic reason— or, if this sounds too overbearing, at least to bring some responsible economic analysis to bear—on this question which has elicited such emotional responses from so many "experts" representing such a variety of disciplines.

To provide some structure for the discussion, I will begin by sketching out some of the major issues we want to confront here today:

1. Is the level of compensation received by American top management excessive, as some critics claim? Furthermore, is it true that year-to-year executive rewards bear little relation to annual stockholder returns? Is it true that firm size, not profitability, is the major determinant of compensation? and if so, is this a serious problem?

2. How are management compensation contracts typically designed, why are they designed this way, and what problems arise from such agreements? How prevalent are EPS and EPS growth as measures of performance, and what explains their popularity? What problems have you seen arise from the use of such measures? What is the ideal measure of performance for evaluating managers?

3. What are the barriers to adopting innovative compensation schemes in the public corporation? To what extent are companies going private in order to improve management incentives? What sort of compensation programs are adopted by private companies, and could they be used in public companies?

4. *Business Week* recently featured an article arguing that money managers were ruining corporate America by forcing management to focus on the short run to the detriment of longer-term corporate interests? Is this really a problem? And if so, how can management contracts be structured to overcome this problem?

5. Stock options as a form of compensation have been on the decline since the change in tax treatment and the poor market performance of the seventies. One objection to options is that their value reflects so many economy-wide uncontrollable factors. What about using some form of market- or even industry-indexed stock prices or options?

6. Furthermore, what about the use of flexible budgets in which performance standards are adjusted for general economic or industry conditions? This would allow operating management, at least, to be insulated to some extent from events beyond their control. What are the pros and cons of adopting relative performance goals?

7. How is corporate acquisition behavior affected by existing management compensation programs? Do the managers of acquiring firms typically increase their own compensation as a result of acquisitions? What about the managers of acquired firms? Are golden parachutes worth their cost to stockholders? Would

executive stock options be a better way of aligning management-stockholder interests in acquisitions?

8. Academics argue that it is not only compensation contracts that force executives to pursue stockholder interests, but also the threat of takeover and the existence of a well-functioning executive labor market. In your experience, does the market for executive talent effectively discipline managers who exploit their own stockholders? and how effective is such a discipline in curbing management's tendency to pursue its own interests at the expense of its stockholders?

9. Are corporate compensation committees, as sometimes alleged, largely under the thumb of top management, or do they exercise a major monitoring function on behalf of stockholders? The American Law Institute has proposed some amendments to the Business Judgment Rule which would change the composition of corporate boards of directors, restrict the autonomy of corporate managements, and regulate executive compensation. What is the likelihood of such legislation being passed? and what will be the effect of such legislation on the American corporation?

We have with us this morning a distinguished group of financial economists, investment bankers, and compensation consultants who are well prepared to provide perspective on these questions. They are:

LOUIS BRINDISI, who is Senior Vice President of Booz Allen & Hamilton, Inc., and a member of the Firm's Board of Directors. Lou is the managing officer of Booz Allen's Executive Compensation Strategy Practice;

CARL FERENBACH is a Managing Director of Thomas H. Lee Co., a firm specializing in the arrangement of leveraged buy-outs. Carl was formerly head of Merrill Lynch's M & A Department;

MICHAEL JENSEN is LaClare Professor of Finance and Business Administration, as well as Director of the Managerial Economics Research Center, at the University of Rochester's Graduate School of Management. Mike is currently Visiting Professor of Business Administration at the Harvard Business School;

ALAN JOHNSON is a principal consultant at Sibson & Co., a compensation consulting firm in Princeton, New Jersey. Alan was formerly part of Hewitt Associates' compensation consulting practice;

DAVID KRAUS recently formed his own consulting firm, David Kraus & Co., which, in conjunction with Arthur Andersen, advises corporate clients on executive compensation. Dave was formerly director of McKinsey's compensation consulting practice in Chicago;

DAVID LARCKER is Professor of Accounting at Northwestern University's J. L. Kellogg Graduate School of Management. Dave conducts research primarily on questions related to executive compensation;

MARK UBELHART is Hewitt Associates' national practice leader in the field of Corporate Finance/Compensation. Mark was formerly Vice President and Administrator of Harris Trust and Savings Bank's Corporate Financial Consulting Division; and

BILL WHITE is Hay Management Consultants' national practice director for executive compensation.

JOEL STERN: Before I begin this discussion, I would like to point out that although I am supposed to be the moderator of this discussion, things tend to get out of my hands very quickly (especially when Michael Jensen is present, who, for all his free market advocacy, is really a monopolist at heart). But having made this disclaimer, I'd like to begin by asking David Larcker to review some of the highlights of the research he has done in the area of management compensation. Dave, you no doubt have seen Lou Brindisi's editorial in the *Wall Street Journal* criticizing current compensation plans. How does your research bear on the controversy? What do your findings suggest about the way corporations compensate their executives?

DAVID LARCKER: Well, Joel, as you know, academic research tends to lag somewhat behind popular thinking. Executive compensation has certainly become a popular topic of discussion in the financial press. While questions about the level of executive pay and its consistency with stockholder interests have engaged legislators' and the general public's interest for years, it is only recently that we have begun to analyze—in a rigorous, statistical way—the economics of management compensation.

The existing body of academic literature—now fairly slight but growing rapidly—can be broken down into three general areas. The first group of studies concerns itself with the question: *Do compensation contracts really "matter"?* That is, do managers compensated in different ways tend to make different decisions? There is empirical evidence to suggest that the form of the compensation contract can influence the risk-taking, decision-making horizon, and expenditure decisions of management. Moreover, we have evidence that the adoption of "long-term" contracts is associated with an increase in shareholder wealth.

The second group of studies focuses on the question: *What are the determinants of the level or size of executive rewards?* More specifically, we are asking whether, or to what extent, the level of executive pay corresponds to shareholder returns. The evidence indicates that there is a modest positive correlation between changes in executive compensation and changes in shareholder wealth.

The third group of studies concerns the issue: *Does the labor market play a role in motivating executives?* Or, alternatively, how does the labor market go about assessing the value of an executive? What evidence we have here—and it is still pretty slight—suggests that the labor market does consider the effects of managers' past decisions on shareholders when setting his opportunity wage. And this finding is consistent, of course, with the idea that the labor market helps to provide some control over management's behavior.

To summarize, then, the academic literature on compensation is relatively new and the results are somewhat preliminary. But the research does provide some useful insights into parts of the controversy about executive compensation. Especially interesting, I think, is the finding that changes in compensation contracts—particularly the adoption of new long-term contracts such as performance plans, perhaps restricted stock—are associated with a significantly positive security market reaction.

One problem with interpreting this finding, however, is that there is always an interplay between changes in corporate strategy and changes in the structure of executive compensation contracts.

JOEL: Could you elaborate on that point a little?

DAVE LARCKER: It is hard to attribute the increase in shareholder value *solely* to the adoption of the new compensation plan. We are not sure whether the market is responding to an expected change in management incentives and performance from putting in the new plan, or whether the adoption of a new plan generally occurs at the same time as a general revamping of corporate strategy. A third possibility is that management puts in a new plan to benefit itself when it expects the firm to do well in the near future. And the market may interpret the institution of the new plan as conveying positive insider information about the firm's prospects.

ALAN JOHNSON: You mean, then, that the adoption of the plan may work like a stock split? That is, the split itself may have no economic effect at all, but it functions as a signal to the market about what the company may actually be thinking about doing?

DAVE LARCKER: Well, I think that when companies announce changes in their compensation plan, the market interprets this announcement as both an internal and external signalling device. Management is conveying to capital markets information both about improvements it hopes to make in managerial performance, and about its view of the firm's future.

LOU BRINDISI: I doubt very much that the market is responding *just* to the compensation plan. In my experience, companies often restructure their compensation programs as part of a major reorganization, including sometimes a change in the company's basic strategic thrust. Three years ago, for example, Sears adopted a new compensation plan as part of a major reorganization and strategic change. These kinds of changes often provide a positive signal to the investment community. If you tie in a management compensation program together with a major change in the company's portfolio of businesses, and perhaps a new set of executives, then the market is going to respond to what it perceives to be a very different company.

DAVE LARCKER: You are right, there is a strong interplay between the two. I guess the real issue is this: if there is a corporate strategy change, I think most management consultants would agree that we ought to design new incentive contracts for the senior executives in a manner consistent with the goals of the new strategy.

DAVE KRAUS: However, since the ultimate objective of strategic planning and strategic management is shareholder-value creation (i.e., higher stock price), it would seem to follow that stock options are an ideal long-term strategic incentive for executives.

DAVE LARCKER: I think stock options are a good idea, but with some qualifications (and I think the discussion will get around to these later). But let me go back to Lou's point about changes in management incentives taking place in the context of changes in business strategy. We don't really have much hard data on this; in fact, we are just starting to accumulate this sort of data. But as Lou just pointed out, when you see major corporate strategy changes, you also commonly see compensation contracts being changed in a manner which is (presumably) consistent with completion of those strategies. And this in turn may lead to the increase in shareholder value which our studies detect.

BILL WHITE: If the shareholders really don't have all the available information about what these proposed changes are—either in strategy or in the linkage between strategy and the new compensation plan—I think it would be very difficult for the market to interpret the significance of such changes.

LOU: I don't agree with that. I think that the market is pretty efficient. The market is dominated by the most sophisticated players, by the very large institutions that make the major investment decisions. Individuals are becoming a smaller and smaller part of the market. And I think if management makes a strong effort to communicate its story to the dominant investors in the market, the market will *anticipate* the new value to be created by strategic and compensation changes.

MIKE JENSEN: Lou, I have a question for you. I have spent quite a bit of time over the past few years thinking about organizational problems and organization theory. And my investigations have convinced me that the way we do performance measurement—that is, which measures we use and how we tie management rewards and punishments to those measures—must be integrally tied to the rest of the organization's structure, its plans and its basic strategy. However, my forays into this field of organization theory leave me with the strong impression that changing incentive compensation, especially at the middle and higher levels of the organization, is political dynamite. Senior management may sometimes change the whole strategic thrust of the company, but they can't bring themselves to change the compensation scheme in conjunction with it. Or, in other cases, they may change the compensation plan, the way they measure and evaluate performance and then administer the rewards, and then fail to implement the rest of the organizational changes that are necessary to complement the comp plan and the strategy change. It is like trying to bake a brownie while only putting in half the ingredients.

Do you management compensation consultants find this to be a common experience? And if so, do you try to coordinate these different corporate areas and functions?

LOU: We do. As you know, Booz Allen has had a strategic management practice for a long time, one that goes back well beyond the recent growth of all the strategy boutiques. About four years ago, we became convinced that there were three interrelated functional areas in a corporate organization: business strategy, organizational structure, and the financial reward system. So within Booz Allen, we brought a troika of practices under one umbrella. This allows changes in business strategy to be coordinated with changes in the structure of the organization, which in turn leads to changes in the reward system.

MIKE JENSEN: And you actually have people from all of these different areas talking to each other?

LOU: We use common resources. Our people who work on strategy studies for the client also work on the organization piece and then on the compensation piece. So we use the same people to do all three of those things within the firm. What we would like to do, obviously, is to start with the strategy, then go to the organization, and go to the reward system. And when we are successful in dealing with one of these three problems, we often find ourselves working with the client to deal with the others. Of course, they're absolutely interrelated; you can't do one without doing the others.

THE PERFORMANCE SCORECARD

JOEL: Lou, let me ask you a question. You say that the market is well-informed. That no doubt leads you to develop a set of criteria by which management should be judged—criteria that are consistent with the way the stock market evaluates corporate performance. What financial measures of operating performance do you typically recommend as the basis for managerial rewards?

LOU: It all depends upon the company, the industry it is in, and the stage of the company's development. But let me start by saying that all companies should be evaluated along two dimensions: (1) their real rate of return on stockholders' equity and (2) their rate of equity growth. All of our market analysis at Booz Allen, whether by industry or by individual company, has shown that the market rewards companies that earn higher rates of return on equity than investors can earn on comparably risky securities. Companies with consistently sustainable high real returns on equity tend to sell at high multiples and large premiums over their book values.

But applying these principles to a specific company is easier said than done—again, mainly because different companies are in various stages of development. Take a company like Combustion Engineering, which has several different lines of business. They are engaging in a major strategic effort to redirect those businesses so that they can begin to achieve acceptable rates of return on investment. Eventually they are all going to have to get to a point where their returns on equity exceed their cost of equity. But until they get within reach of this point, the major focus of their incentives will have to be on strategic goals, rather than on purely financial ones. This means repositioning the businesses, perhaps downsizing the businesses, until such time as they can achieve an acceptable rate of return on equity.

JOEL: Dave, what is your response to that?

DAVE LARCKER: This notion that corporate price-to-book ratios are highly statistically correlated with the comparison of return on equity (ROE) to the cost of equity capital (COE) has become the basis for much general management consulting; and it is now being extended into executive compensation consulting. But it is not at all clear to me that the correlation between these two ratios justifies the use of the ROE/COE ratio as the scorecard for compensation purposes. The ROE measure is obviously an accounting-based measure, one which suffers from all the problems, the arbitrary allocations and distortions, to which accounting numbers are prone. So you are comparing this highly flawed, *accounting-based* measure of return on investment with the COE, which is a *market-determined* required rate of return. I just don't think the two numbers are comparable.

Also, I don't think that the notion of maximizing market to book is necessarily synonymous with increasing shareholder value. The increase in shareholder value means, of course, share price appreciation plus dividends earned over some period of time. But an increase of market to book doesn't necessarily translate into higher returns to stockholders. For example, we could decrease the denominator of that ratio—that is, the book value of the firm—and the market to book will rise without having any positive effect on stock price. It may be that the return on equity compared to the cost on capital is a good measure. But I don't think it is a good measure simply because it is correlated with market to book.

MIKE JENSEN: Can I interject here? It seems to me that those who talk about return on equity are clearly going in the right direction. But implementing a compensation scheme based *solely* on rates of return, or on differences between the return on equity and some estimate of the cost of capital, is clearly wrong.

LOU: Why is that?

MIKE JENSEN: A simple analysis will indicate why. Suppose you had a range of projects returning from 100 percent to 2 percent. And the appropriate cost of capital was 10 percent. In this case, you wouldn't want to maximize the *difference* between the return on equity and the cost to capital. You want to maximize the net present value by taking all the projects that promise to return at least 10 percent.

JOEL: So what you are suggesting is that the value of the firm should rise for all projects taken which are expected to earn more than their cost of capital?

LOU: What is the cost of capital? Every business has a different cost of capital. So a 10 percent return in one business may be acceptable while a 20 percent return in another may be substandard.

MIKE JENSEN: Sure, Lou, I agree with you: the cost of capital depends on the individual project. It is not necessarily a single number, but let's assume it is just for simplicity. This is a very simple point. If you array all projects on the basis of the rate of return, and then evaluate managers only according to their realized average return on investment, you are going to be paying them to *reduce* the size of the business. You are encouraging them to take on that one project with the highest promised rate of return, and to turn down all the rest of the projects which may have a positive NPV. In this sense, maximizing ROI, as Dave was saying, is not necessarily consistent with increasing shareholder value. What you want your manager to do is to accept all projects which promise to earn their cost of capital.

JOEL: You are saying that the value of the firm is maximized when the rates of return just equal the cost of capital.

MIKE JENSEN: Yes, when the expected return on the *last* project taken equals the *marginal* cost of capital.

JOEL: So, the rule is: Take all projects down to the cost of capital. If you try to maximize the *spread* between the average returns on capital and the cost of capital, you may have to forgo projects which would otherwise increase shareholder value.

DAVE KRAUS: I totally agree with Joel's last comment. Maximizing the *percentage spread* would always lead to decisions to eliminate the least profitable businesses and products (including those with returns in excess of the cost of capital) and thereby shrink the size of the business. The objective should be to maximize the *total dollar-spread*.

LOU: Well, I agree with you all in principle. But over the last several years, the message from the stock market seems to have been that smaller is better if you can get a higher return on equity—in the short term at least. I have seen many, many companies that have been rewarded by the market for paring their operations. Gulf + Western, for example, has been doing this for the last six months, and its stock price has gone up appreciably.

MIKE JENSEN: Yes, but the point is, that kind of performance measurement function is not only going to motivate managers to drop out of losing businesses, it is also going to motivate them to drop out of profitable businesses and thereby eventually reduce shareholder value. The logic of that is inescapable.

ALAN: Yes, it is better to have 18 percent of a lot rather than 20 percent of a little.

MIKE JENSEN: Absolutely. That is the whole point. Of course, if you hold the level of investment or the number of projects constant, then it is true that you want to motivate people to maximize the return on that level of investment. But that is not the issue. So often what happens when we specify these performance measurement systems and link them to a reward system for managers, we end up motivating them to do things that destroy value.

STOCK OPTIONS

JOEL: If you wanted to ensure a perfect harmony of interest between management and stockholders, why would it not pay simply to abandon all forms of incentive compensation other than stock options?

MIKE JENSEN: Well, I think the answer to that is relatively simple. If you want to pay managers in a way that is perfectly correlated in a one-to-one fashion with the return to stockholders, you can do that. You can give them phantom stock, or stock appreciation rights, or something like that. But doing that throws out the baby with the bathwater. It throws out one of the major advantages the corporation has over all other forms of organization.

The major advantage of the corporation as a form of organization is that it allows the spreading of risks. It allows for the separation of risk-bearing, which is largely the function of investors, from the day-to-day running of the company, which of course is the function of management. If you load all of that risk back on management, you are going to get another set of undesirable consequences. So by insulating management from at least *some* of the uncertainty that is due not to their decisions, but rather to changes in the level of interest rates or international trade considerations, you create value for shareholders. You create value by allowing the risk-bearing to be accomplished at lower cost.

So the problem we are stuck with here is one of achieving the proper balance between linking management's interests with stockholder interests by making them bear a lot of market risk, and, at the same time, insulating them from some of that risk. As Dave Larcker points out in his article ["Executive Compensation, Corporate Performance, and Stockholder Wealth: A Review of the Evidence," *Midland Corporate Finance Journal*, vol. 2, no. 2 (1984)], the appropriate amount of market risk that management should bear must carefully weigh two opposite effects. To the extent we are able to separate the results of managerial actions from the effects of exogenous factors—factors management cannot control—we are clearly much better off. We can reduce the amount of risk we ask them to bear. But, at the same time, we want to tie their interest to that of the shareholders. That is clearly desirable. But, of course, we are never going to do either of these things perfectly. It is a trade-off.

JOEL: What would you recommend in order to accomplish that goal as close to perfection as possible? If stock options are not the final answer, then what is a better mix for tying management's interest to shareholder's while, at the same time, not placing certain excessive risks on management?

MIKE JENSEN: Well, there is no single, simple answer to that. As Lou said earlier, it is going to depend on the company—where the company is in its history, and what the general business conditions are. But I like the concept proposed in the Stern Stewart article [see Bennett Stewart's Commentary at the end of this chapter]—the concept of "economic value added." That measurement doesn't have the problem, which Dave and I were talking about earlier, of motivating people to reduce the size and the value of the firm. I think that it has got generally the right dimensions.

But clearly that's not everything. You have to relate to divisional managers, you have got to relate the concept to the kinds of things that they can control. And that is not going to be easy.

JOEL: As an aside, Mike, would you be in favor of having large corporate organizations spin off their individual operating units, so that the equity of each of these operations trades on the market? This way, options or stock appreciation rights could be offered to those managers whom you are trying to motivate without the benefit of a market test—managers whose performance would otherwise be buried within the large conglomerate form.

MIKE JENSEN: The existence of those capital markets, and the fact that they solve this valuation problem for us, is enormously advantageous. And my impression is that at least a number of companies are taking parts of their organization public for exactly this reason: to provide a much better handle on performance measurement and thus provide stronger incentives for divisional operating management.

LOU: An extension of this question, which is really a fascinating one, is this: Can the public corporation provide the same kind of incentives that private corporations can? When you see all these LBOs, all these companies going private, you know there are lots of different motives, such as tax reasons, debt reasons, and so forth. But greater flexibility in incentive compensation is clearly one of the major motives for going private that every LBO expert talks about.

Now, if I were an investor who was going to put up a lot of bucks to take a company private, and I was designing the compensation package for a small group of managers, I would offer them a certain level of straight salary—one which would afford them a certain life-style. And to that salary I would add a piece of the equity, and that would be it. It is like going back to the compensation model of the 1960s, when we had basically only salaries and stock options. Annual bonuses were very small then, and there were no such things as long-term performance plans.

JOEL: Why do you think the characteristics have changed?

LOU: At the beginning of the seventies, inflation began to rise, and this raised interest rates and the corporate cost of capital. Corporate rates of return on investment failed to match this increase in cost of capital, and the stock market came down. It was this substandard stock market performance that led companies to adopt larger annual bonuses and to institute the new long-term performance plans.

And, incidentally, it wasn't that the stock market wasn't working properly. The companies themselves weren't working. For a ten- to twelve-year period, their returns failed to rise with their higher cost of capital, causing their stock prices to stagnate.

DAVE KRAUS: Stock options are usually an appropriate incentive for top management of a public company, but not always. Consider a company that consistently earns a 50 percent return on equity and pays out all earnings as dividends (because of the requirements of owners or limited management resources). Management is doing a great job here, but the stock price is not likely to change. Options would not be an appropriate incentive here because they fail to reflect total return to shareholders (stock price increase plus dividends).

BILL WHITE: There are other drawbacks to using stock options that I would like to point out. One is the aggregate nature of the stock market's evaluation of the performance of any given company, and the time space of that. At any point in time, there may be a lot of "noise" in the stock market's evaluation of that company. For long periods of time the stock market might be prospective, looking out toward the effect of oil prices, or of any variety of macroeconomic variables that might influence the company's fortunes somewhere well down the road. So that an individual executive may find himself unable to influence those aggregate types of investor decisions—because they have to do with economic characteristics and industry characteristics as well as management's performance.

For this reason, the use of surrogate financial measures gives a manager the advantage of focus. The real test of management is an ability to react adaptively to the challenges that are presented through time. Like the case of the rat pushing the lever to get a pellet of food, pushing the lever—or, in this case, meeting a set of financial goals—becomes a valuable surrogate in very ambiguous times, in those times when the stock market results have so much noise (even though, as Lou suggests, market prices may in fact be accurately portraying some fundamental problems with corporate performance).

JOEL: I have a question for you, then. Since management is supposed to function as the steward of stockholder savings, why do you think managements should not have to share the bad times with their shareholders? Do you think that managements should have been receiving large bonuses during that period of time when their stock prices were flat or even falling? Stock options didn't work because the stock market was doing poorly. Do you think it was right for the board of directors to select an alternative means of compensation so that management did not have to suffer the consequences that the shareholders were suffering?

BILL: I think there is a disengagement which goes back to the agency theory which emphasizes the conflicts between the management perspective and the shareholder perspective. I think there are times when management will take a short period of time to revive itself. If you are in a losing situation, then to move to a more positive (or a less negative) situation can merit the bonus even though collectively the firm isn't doing that well.

On the other side of the coin, I do believe...

JOEL: But that is not what you were saying before. You were saying that there were forces that were exogenous to the firm. Let's assume a changing government policy of some sort had affected the shares of all companies. Now, let's assume the share prices then declined for that reason and the shareholders were doing worse. You are saying, "Let's assume that management was doing the best it can under those circumstances and yet the company is not doing well..."

BILL: Well, what I was saying was that because of the "here-and-now" assessment of the market, management doesn't appear to be doing as well for the time being—because the organization's strategies are not yet apparent to the market. That is essentially what I am saying. But, on the other hand, I do believe that management should have some market-based incentives— some stake in the firm that will identify their interest with the shareholders' over time.

So, the strategy is typically forward-looking, and management is executing the first leg of that; but the effects of that strategy may not be reflected in financial results or in the stock price for some time.

JOEL: Are you suggesting that the market does not have the information to evaluate the new strategy and, therefore, the share price is not reflecting the values that are yet to be created?

BILL: It is not a perfect equation; often the market does not have adequate information on the new strategy. It does over time; but at any specific point in time, the market may not be properly reflecting the future value of that strategy.

For example, there are insider trading rules which recognize that some individuals have "more perfect" information than the market at large. Possibly management believes that a decision or new strategy will be more effective if information about it is kept within the most senior levels of the firm. I suppose the key is that the market is quite effective in "collecting" and "assessing" information available to it, but it does not have "perfect" information.

MARK UBELHART: In order to eliminate part of the randomness of stock price movements, there are a couple of choices. I have proposed the use of *market-indexed* stock options. Alternatively, as Bennett Stewart argued in his article [see Commentary at the end of this chapter], you can index corporate operating rates of return against the market-wide or industry average rates of returns. The advantage of this kind of indexation is that, at least to some degree, you can focus on those things controllable by management.

You may not want to do that exclusively. It might be that the compensation committee says what you are saying, Joel. They may say, "We want our managers to suffer with the stockholders. That is our posture, that is our compensation philosophy." But for a compensation committee that wants to insulate the managers to some degree from those exogenous variables, then indexation offers at least a partial solution.

JOEL: Where does Hewitt Associates come down on that one?

MARK: We don't come down entirely on one side or the other. We don't believe that there is any single compensation scheme that is right for all companies. The plan has to be designed to fit the objectives of the company.

My article, which I just mentioned, offers three different proposals for evaluating managerial performance. One is based on cash-flow rates of return, a second on total shareholder returns, and a third on the present value concept which gets away from the problems of ROE we were talking about. All three of these are more suitable economic measures, I think, than ROE and all three would fit with some companies.

In other cases, though, we might recommend straight salary. The company may not want their executives to face any risk. And I think in some cases that might be right.

ALAN: One point Michael Jensen made that we shouldn't overlook is that the corporation is a much more efficient bearer of risk than an individual executive. The closer we tie an executive to this corporation, which is affected by exogenous variables, the more money that executive would expect to make. Somehow we have assumed that if we link all compensation to the performance of the company, the total level of compensation will stay the same. We will just divide it in different pieces. But I think the total will depend on how you divide the pieces, on how much risk you make the executive bear.

MIKE JENSEN: Lou earlier made the comment that management should be made to bear a lot of market risk, a lot of uncertainty. Now, I agree in the sense that I would want to be a shareholder in an organization where the managers' welfare was tied, in some way, to what happens to the stock. But that doesn't mean that I'd want *all* of their compensation tied that way (and I don't think Lou said that). My reason is this: if the executive requires a premium for bearing that risk that is much larger than the capital market charges us to bear that risk, then we are better off unloading some of that risk on a capital market. That is an important reason why these companies go public to start with—why they are no longer owned by an entrepreneur or by a very small group of stockholders.

JOEL: That doesn't address the question I raised before, though. And that is, why not have the individual operating units publicly traded, and have direct equity incentives for the operating managers?

ALAN: Well, what I am saying is this: if you tie all of the compensation of a division manager of Exxon to Exxon's stock price, he is going to want to make more money because he is taking on an awful lot more risk.

JOEL: What is so wrong with that?

ALAN: There is nothing wrong with that. But remember the charges of the "madness" of American executives' compensation that are being leveled in the public forum. If the politicians think $4 million is mad now, then what are they going to say about $14 million.

THE COMPONENTS OF EXECUTIVE PAY

JOEL: Can we ask Michael Jensen if $14 million in annual compensation for a corporate executive is madness?

MIKE JENSEN: No, I don't think it is mad at all. In fact, let me say that a responsible case can be made for the argument that top-level executives of American corporations are in fact systematically and seriously *underpaid*. And that is now reflecting itself in the quality of people moving into the managerial ranks, and it is going to become more clear as time goes on. This case, although it would require a lot of data to substantiate it, could be made at least as strongly as the counterargument has been made in the popular medium. But I do have some suggestive casual evidence that indicates that the top executives of our corporations are not being paid their real economic worth.

But let's consider first the charge, carried by articles in *Fortune* and elsewhere, that there is no correspondence between executive pay and corporate performance. Discussion of this issue has taken place in a much too narrowly defined field. I have some numbers in front of me, produced by my Rochester colleague Kevin Murphy, who conducted a study of the compensation of top-level managers in seventy-two manufacturing firms over the period 1964 to 1981. (The numbers I will give you are in 1983 dollars.) He has gathered compensation data on 4,500 executive years in his sample. Of these 4,500 years, 943 were for CEOs. He has broken out the average salary plus bonus—that is, the total pay—and then attempted to measure how changes in pay related to changes in stock prices. He also looked at what happens to the average value of executives' stock holdings in their firm (which include only direct holdings, not stock in trust or family).

Here are some of his findings: In years when a firm's stock returns were less than minus 30 percent (and there were 101 such cases), the average salary plus bonus for those executive CEOs was $479,000. The average loss that they took on their stock holdings was $1,563,000. At the other end of the spectrum, when the stock returns were greater than a positive 30 percent, the average salary was, again, about $475,000. But the average increase in the value of the executive stock holdings (which do not include changes in the value of their options) was $2,500,000. On average in his sample—

looking across all the executives, not just CEOs—the average executive's holding in the company exceeded $4 million in market value (again, in 1983 dollars).

It wouldn't make sense for a board compensation committee to set the compensation package for a CEO, or for other key executives in the organization, without taking into account the executive's portfolio holdings in the company. If I, as a director, know that the executive has got $4 million on the line in this organization—and maybe it is a highly risky organization—I know that this executive's feet are tied to the fire to a non-trivial extent. Maybe it is not enough, maybe it is too much. I don't know. But I would be foolish, as a designer of the compensation package, to ignore that when I am talking to him about what his salary should be. Because what I decide about his salary is undoubtedly going to influence his decisions with respect to those stock holdings.

And what I'd like to find out from you guys is whether or not these factors are taken into account in devising a total compensation package. And if so, how? I don't see them discussed.

DAVE KRAUS: I do not believe that an executive's personal stock holdings should be taken into account in the decision to determine the level of total annual compensation. Personal stock holdings reflect private investment decisions and should be independent of compensation. To do otherwise would motivate executives to avoid long-term investments in their own companies.

DAVE LARCKER: Mike is talking about the *mix* of compensation here, not the total level. What he is saying is that discussions in the financial press, like the Carol Loomis article in *Fortune*, ignore all the shares that are held by the executive. It is clear that, at least on average, the interests of management and shareholders' interest are firmly tied. Mike is saying that if an executive already has a lot of stock in the company, it doesn't make sense to pay the guy a very small salary and then give him mostly stock options. Because you are giving him more claims that are going to be hard for him to diversify. And he is going to become very, very averse toward risk.

LOU: What about the first time he cashes in and goes into alternative investments?

DAVE LARCKER: Yes, but we see that they are holding $4 million, on average, of their own company's stock.

LOU: What would you do if they held $4 million of real estate instead? It is an alternative investment. Would you offer them only cash and options in that case? And, furthermore, are you going to change my pay every time I change my portfolio?

ALAN: I think the key point, though, when you think about the elements of compensation is this. You wouldn't say to yourself: "This guy is holding $4 million of the stock already." Think of the typical stock option range—

let's say 100 percent of salary, which might represent about $500,000 a year in stock options. Now that has a lot of value to it. The problem is, most companies aren't going to raise his salary by $250,000 or $300,000 *instead* of granting him this amount of stock options. The reason: the higher salary figure would show up in the proxy. So companies are limited there. Nor are they going to offer an additional $200,000 or $300,000 in cash bonus to replace those stock options. Nor will they grant him a supplemental retirement plan.

So there are many companies where an executive owns enormous amounts of stock. And among them there are also many companies that continue to pay a large proportion of executive compensation in the form of stock options, even while knowing that the executives already have a large piece of their own net worth in company stock to begin with.

MARK: I think there are also some companies that choose different incentive plans in lieu of that. These plans take into account not only the executive's portfolio of assets, but also his *attitude* toward the risks that he faces. Our own compensation practice, for example, attempts to focus in on that attitude. When we talk to executives we interview them to find out what their risk-bearing orientation is, and then design the comp plan to accommodate those risk preferences.

In fact, I can give you an example of a company which was a candidate for takeover where an executive wanted salary continuation and benefit continuation. The comp committee and the board of directors wanted to grant him huge options so that if the company was sold, he would come out well ahead of what he was asking for in salary and benefits. But he was a risk-averse guy, he didn't want that.

LOU: The company was a candidate for takeover? Then why pay him a nickel after it had been bought?

MARK: The board wanted to give him a lot of reward through options if that occurred. He didn't want that. So you can either choose a different manager with a greater risk orientation, or you can meet his risk orientation somewhere in between.

DAVE LARCKER: You can't lose sight of why these incentive contracts exist in the first place. We are trying to pay this manager in such a way that provides him with incentives to take actions that make the shareholders better off. As Mike pointed out earlier, there is not one best sort of scheme, or one best performance scorecard, because you have to take into account not only the kind of company and the risk associated with the company and the environment that it works in, but you also have to consider the manager's preference regarding risk (this person's wealth and the mix of his other assets). And even though it is a personal decision regarding what portfolio this person holds, you can't ignore those other types of issues when you go to design both the level and the mix of the executives' compensation.

DAVE KRAUS: We must remember, though, that the primary purpose of executive compensation is to motivate people prospectively, not to reward them fairly on a retrospective basis. Therefore, we should be willing to trade off some theoretical purity and complexity in order to achieve simplicity. People cannot be motivated by programs that they don't understand.

For example, in theory, a sales compensation plan should probably take into account considerations like uneven territory potential, product mix sold, margins achieved, sales training contributions, and so forth. But the plan would be so complex that salesmen wouldn't understand it. So instead we pay the salesman a percentage of his sales. This approach may have theoretical weaknesses, but it is directionally correct and the salesman knows what he has to do to earn more money.

The same considerations apply to executive pay. Thus, I don't see much wrong with performance measures like return on equity, or even growth in earnings per share. Generally, they aim in the right direction.

MIKE JENSEN: No, not EPS. I think Joel has done a sufficient job of showing the problems you can run into using EPS and EPS growth as your performance measure.

LOU: I agree with you, Mike. I think that the end of EPS measures as the basis for compensation is coming.

But I just really don't agree with you on your consideration of individual preferences. If I were a shareholder who owned a large stake in a company, I would want the company to be run by a CEO who was willing to take prudent risks. I am not going to pay a guy who is not going to take risks. I don't think individual preferences have anything to do with that. I couldn't care less about individual preferences. What I care about is this: Do I have a chief executive who is going to be able to make some bold portfolio moves into some growth opportunities?

DAVE LARCKER: But wait a minute. If the guy has a very high dislike of variability ...

LOU: Then he shouldn't be CEO. But let me get back to the case of a private company. Let's say you own the private company. Now, are you going to pay a CEO to be risk-averse? Of course not.

DAVE LARCKER: No. But, at the same time, let me just suggest that all CEOs are risk-averse in some sense. Now if that is the case, then what I would like to do is to design a contract (and Mike and others at Rochester have certainly talked about this at some length) which is going to offset the manager's risk aversion in some way—whether it be through an option-based contract or some other means. I am simply saying that the best mix of an executive's compensation (assuming the size of it is fixed)—which includes so much in salary, so much in options, and so much in performance plans and other types of accounting-based options—should, and generally does, depend upon variables like how risky is the firm and what this guy's propensity toward risk is.

LOU: I only agree with half of that statement: the risk of the firm matters, but not the individual's attitude toward risk-bearing.

ALAN: Executives will have to be more aggressive if they want to manage in the 1980s and 1990s. I think you have to say that the times are tougher now, more competitive. And though everybody is risk-averse to some extent, if an executive is not willing to stick his neck out somewhat to take some calculated risks, the board may have to get rid of him.

DAVE LARCKER: One way to overcome that problem is to redesign the comp plan to include a lot of stock options. This may give the manager a much stronger incentive to take on riskier projects (although only those, of course, where the expected returns justify the risks taken).

ALAN: Yes, but you don't always say to the executive, "Do you feel good about this comp plan?" Because he is going to say, "No, I don't. I don't like it," and he will come up with eighteen good reasons why it should all be salary and benefits and early retirement.

CARL: That is not actually the way it works. You do have to ask him what he wants. He is running the company, and you are dependent on him. Put yourself in the shoes of the chairman of the compensation committee who has got the responsibility of compensating this guy. It is hard to replace a CEO. It is a big job. It may take a year. It may disrupt your entire business. It is an extraordinarily difficult thing to do. The preferences of the managers have to come into the equation when you're designing the compensation package. You just can't design a program that you think is neat and say, "He is going to run it."

GOING PRIVATE

JOEL: Can I ask Carl to tell us if he can, without revealing privileged information, what kinds of things he does with the compensation plan when he takes a company private? First of all, do you make major changes? and how far down the organization do these changes go?

CARL: It depends on the company and its current compensation plan. How management feels about the comp plan is important because you need to have a management group that is going forward in concert with the investor group. But the *first* thing you worry about is, how much stock they are going to get and how they are going to pay for it. The standard we apply there is that we want management to continue to function normally. We don't want people up at night worried about the fact that they have taken on a lot of personal debt to own their interest in the company. At the same time, you want management to feel that it's their company—they own it even if they only hold 15 percent of the stock.

MIKE JENSEN: Does that mean you will work out ways to help them finance their stock interest at a lower rate?

CARL: We will get them their stock, and they can assume from day one going forward that unless something bad happens they are going to own it. And the cost to them is not going to be material.

MIKE JENSEN: So, going back to the earlier stuff we were talking about, this is a way of reducing the manager's risk. How much stock ownership do you offer management? and how far down the organization do you go in terms of stock ownership?

CARL: Size of the company is an important variable. If you are buying a big company, then you are talking about more people and more dollars in absolute terms. But, as a rule of thumb, we offer management about 15 percent. The balance will be owned by us, or by money under our control, and probably by whoever supplies the mezzanine debt, whether it is an institution or a seller. Typically, we will own 50 to 60 percent.

In developing this scheme, you need to do a couple of things for management. Besides setting up a compensation plan for your core management group, you need to allow room for people to grow. Since you have got to assume you are going to be private for five years or more and probably independent for that period of time, you must allow for growth in a dynamic organization. It is going to change and you hope that people are going to grow up within the organization, and you need to be able to bring them into the ownership circle.

So we look at management's cash comp plans in terms of where they have been, what they can influence, what you want them to influence going forward, and what they will own or can expect to own. Developing such plans is an iterative process that has got to be done cooperatively if you are going to get the right set of objectives.

One objective you know is going to become very important is debt repayment. It becomes very important in a manager's life for some period of time. And then you have to set other operating objectives. Those are things that you need to understand in developing a comp plan.

In general, we go out of our way not to disrupt the existing plan. If they have got reasonable salary and bonus comp plans built into the organization, we probably won't change them materially for a year or two. *We assume instead that ownership will be the great motivator.*

MIKE JENSEN: Is this true of lower levels of the company, too?

CARL: Right. All the way down.

JOEL: Are there any new bonus plans you put in aside from the provision of new equity?

CARL: We have put in bonus plans to enable people in effect to buy their stock when they didn't have the cash to pay for it, and we've put in two-tiered plans where one is a short-term plan based on the current year's performance designed to enable a manager to pay the interest on his personal stock loan. But he has got to achieve certain levels of operating income. In this plan, we look at the directly "influenceable" operating results as those that go down to EBIT. We ourselves have a fair amount of control over the financing policy, so we leave the measurable, bonus amount above the EBIT line. Then you can run a short-term compensation plan which is a single-year type of thing.

JOEL: And what about the longer term?

CARL: The longer-term plan can also be based on EBIT. Or you can measure free cash flow, which is the other key operating measure.

MARK: There was a company where Carl and I worked together in arranging and designing an LBO. The short-term incentive plan was changed from relying on an income-based accounting measure to a cash-flow measure. A long-term plan was based on the company's debt-equity ratio. This combination provided management with an incentive to generate cash flow in the near term and also in the long term to reposition the company's capital structure at a lower level of leverage.

COMPENSATING DIVISIONAL MANAGEMENT IN CONGLOMERATES

CARL: Joel, let me return to your suggestion that conglomerates spin off part of their operating units. In theory I think it would be a good idea to give operating management stock options whose value appreciated with the success of their own individual operating units.

But the fact is, if I were the operating manager being offered your deal, I wouldn't accept it. I wouldn't take your deal because I wouldn't want to be the CEO of a division that was 20 percent publicly owned and 80 percent owned by a parent corporation. This security would be illiquid. And, remember, I would have to report to my biggest stockholder. I wouldn't be able to make decisions independently. And if my public shareholder's expectations were bigger than the expectations of my biggest stockholder, then I would be caught in the middle. And that would be a bad deal.

I would do it the other way around. I would rather issue a note and have my former parent own 20 to 30 percent of the company. If I do great, they'll make out. But they won't be in control. Management or the investor group will control. This way the guy who is going to run the company won't be in the middle between a controlling megacorporation and a small group of shareholders. Because he or she has no choice but to report to the biggest shareholder.

MARK: And the minority group will price the security accordingly.

JOEL: The problem I see is that a number of companies are permitting operating units (which represent relatively small fractions of the total value of the company) to go the LBO route and then become very successful as private companies. What that has meant is that all of that value created by going private has been lost to the existing shareholder base. Why not find a way to retain that operating unit by improving the compensation, and thereby retain that extra value for the shareholders?

CARL: Generalizing about compensation is very hard. It is one thing for General Motors, it is another thing for IBM, still another thing for Apple Computer; and these cases are all different from that of a private company like Signode Industries.

JOEL: Let's say you are advising a company that is a large conglomerate. Assume they have a group of outstanding scientists who are turning out fantastic products, but that there is no way that the relative value they're creating is going to find its way into their pockets. Let's say they are part of a little operating unit and that they are rewarded with stock options in the parent.

I realize, Carl, that you have a special interest in the LBO area, but let's assume that you were advising the board and the board said to you, "We want to avoid an LBO." What is the best alternative to an LBO or to the partial public offering I have suggested? I am thinking in particular about companies like IBM, which seems periodically to lose groups of people who go off, start their own companies, and make out very well for themselves. Is it possible that there is something wrong with the way in which IBM is compensating its people? Are they somehow encouraging entrepreneurial people to leave the company? Are you saying perhaps that the people who leave do so because they want a higher risk-reward profile than IBM is willing to provide them?

CARL: Yes, I think that is right.

JOEL: But I think there must be tremendous value being lost through that decision, through that kind of approach to compensation? My question is: How can IBM fashion a compensation scheme for their people so as to retain them and add all of that value to IBM?

CARL: Well, I guess another way of framing that question is this: If you have norms within your organization, as an IBM does, with its well-established corporate culture, how far from your norms can you deviate to accommodate small groups of entrepreneurs? I for one think it is pretty hard to go very far outside of your norms without disrupting the main body of your company.

JOEL: What about firms that don't have such an established corporate culture? I am thinking of firms out in Silicon Valley that have reached a certain size. They are nowhere near a giant company. But they also have individual division and product areas that are suddenly creating new values.

ALAN: Let's talk about Apple Computer's Macintosh, for example. Apple is reputed to have had special bonuses for people who worked on Macintosh. We could argue that the several thousand dollars they gave people wasn't enough. Management didn't offer those kinds of payments to anybody else; they violated all the cultural norms.

Theoretically, of course, you could say we should pay them for the value of what they created. But there was no contract before the fact. It was an after-the-fact arrangement. People are thinking, "He got too much," "I should have gotten more," "Why didn't the people who developed the Apple II get it?," and so forth. So I think the best thing for Apple to have done, in the case of the Macintosh computer, was probably to have done nothing.

JOEL: But then they might have lost those people who developed that product, and who will now be stimulated to find other new products.

ALAN: Well, the checks are being cashed. There is no reason those people won't leave *now*. Once the check is cashed, there is no reason those people won't leave and use that capital to start a new, possibly a competing, company.

JOEL: But what if Apple Computer were to spin off an operating unit called Macintosh, Inc. that was trading in the market? And say the key people were given options in that particular security? Then I think those entrepreneurs could be induced to stay with Apple for a long time.

MIKE JENSEN: Well, I think the most important question here is: Who did Apple lose as a result of these special payments? Who did they lose in the organization? Did anybody actually quit?

ALAN: You don't see the unrest in any of the six people who have gotten checks; they haven't left. But what about the other 4,000 people in the firm. You are never going to be able to measure the cost to the company in terms of dissension, reduced morale. So, if IBM gives a special deal for its PC division, for example, so that this PC division makes these people wealthy, you will never see the guy who is irritated inside the business and leaves IBM.

JOEL: The reason I brought up the issue about IBM is that, in this case, it is clear that hundreds of millions, perhaps billions, of dollars in value have been created by people who left IBM to do something else. And I wanted to find out why such value couldn't have been created *within* that organization, within that corporate structure, called IBM. Someone has got to be sitting on the board of IBM saying, "How much value do we have to lose before we change the compensation procedure?"

DAVE KRAUS: It isn't necessarily true that value has been lost as a result of the compensation plan. Many, if not most, of the best managed companies (e.g., IBM, Procter & Gamble) have compensation and other human resource management programs that produce more talent than they productively employ. Thus, they tend to become net providers of talent to their respective industries. In fact, it can be argued that being a net provider of talent to the industry is the ultimate measure of the success of corporate human resource programs.

JOEL: How much value is lost in Procter & Gamble because they lose this talent elsewhere? That is all I am asking.

DAVE KRAUS: Judging by the success of that organization, probably a lot less than in other companies with different programs for managing people.

JOEL: That is the question. IBM's stock price went up X percent over a period of time. But what if it could have gone up by X percent plus billions more if we had retained the people. And I want to know, from all our compensation specialists here, how you could design a plan that will keep an IBM from losing its most talented people.

DAVE KRAUS: I don't believe any corporate compensation program could (or should) keep people bent on being entrepreneurs. As an aside, these may or may not be the most "talented" people. Recognizing this, good companies hire and train sufficient numbers of executives and salespeople to meet their needs after normal turnover.

JOEL: Yes, but the reason they are hiring more salesmen than they need is because they can't keep the people because they haven't got the right compensation.

ALAN: The point comes down to this: Even though IBM may be a net exporter of good people, if you try to cut a special deal for everyone, you may destroy the organization that IBM now is. In so doing, you may lose a lot more than you gain.

JOEL: I am not trying to do it for *everyone.* I am just trying to do it for those people whose distinctive contributions have clearly added value—identifiable, quantifiable value—to the company. We are not talking about many people relative to the population of IBM.

ALAN: Yes, but how many people would hear about it at IBM?

MIKE JENSEN: May I interrupt here? There is a miscommunication, I think, between the two of you, and I would like to try to clear it up. I agree with the point that Alan is trying to make, and we are systematically ignoring it. In large organizations, even in smaller organizations, one has to be very careful about cutting special deals with people and about how you sell these deals after they have been made. Walking in, especially after the fact, and sprinkling a few dollars here and there can create all kinds of tensions within an organization. So that how you implement plans and how they are sold as part of the general compensation packages is enormously important. And Alan, I believe, is saying, "All right, let's tackle the whole problem of how we integrate the compensation package with the cultural environment; and let's try to do it in a way that doesn't cause us to lose a lot of people either because of envy or feeling of maltreatment."

But if you find people who are really good, as Joel keeps saying, and you don't pay them enough, and if they see they can do a lot better on the outside, they are going to leave. And IBM has certainly sluffed off a whole range of these.

THE LEVEL OF EXECUTIVE PAY ————————————————

MIKE JENSEN: But let me put the case in the following way. I think it is ludicrous that an organization like Kodak, in my hometown of Rochester, New York, pays its CEO *only* three quarters of a million dollars. It is absolutely ludicrous. And this is not unrepresentative of large corporations.

LOU: What should they pay them?

MIKE JENSEN: Well, before we talk about the appropriate level of total pay, let's divide executive pay into three components. This will help, I think, to structure our discussion a little.

First of all, let's think of an executive's compensation as the *expected value* of his total compensation package on average and over time. Setting the expected value of that package at the right level is enormously important, because if you set it too low, you are not going to get as high-quality people as you would otherwise get. They are going to go elsewhere. But if you overpay, of course, you are giving away stockholder funds.

The second, and probably less important, aspect of the compensation package is the composition of the package—the fringe benefits, opportunities for tax deferrals, and so forth. And this is very important. But I think corporations on the whole do a pretty good job in taking care of this aspect of compensation, though we probably can always do better.

The third component of the compensation package is what I call its "functional form." And that incorporates a lot of things. But, in plain English, we want to know how pay is related to performance. To think about it in a very simple fashion, picture a graph depicting the relationship between corporate performance (however measured) on one axis and executive pay on the other axis. I am oversimplifying the issues, but what we want to know is whether the functional form, the relationship depicted on the graph, is a straight line, whether it is gently sloped, or whether it is very steeply sloped. Now, it is more complicated than that because for one thing there is a time dimension which cannot be captured on this graph. For example, there is every reason to pay people less now and more later, and this will not show up in our two-dimensional picture.

But, to return to my original point about the total compensation package, I believe that the political constraints and the difficulties associated with both the political sector and communicating with shareholders have resulted in a situation in which the top-level managers of American corporations are underpaid. The expected values of their payoffs are too small.

LOU: Why do you believe that?

MIKE JENSEN: Well, mainly from comparing those numbers with what I see in alternative occupations, in alternative uses of those corporate executives' time. For example, consider the total compensation of partners in small, privately held organizations, or investment banks, or law firms. In fact, the whole phenomenon of going private, of the leveraged buy-out, is being driven in part by the inadequacy of compensation schemes in the public corporation. It is very difficult for top-level corporate managers to become really wealthy. It just doesn't happen. They don't have the dollars. And I believe it is because we are being too stingy in paying them. In particular, we are not making it possible for them to earn $10, $20, or $30 million for exceptionally good performance for their stockholders.

What this means is that public corporations are losing the entrepreneurs. The entrepreneurs are being filtered out of the system long before they ever get to the top level of the hierarchy. And in the long run, this is clearly going to have an effect on how well the American public corporation is run.

Let me give you some evidence from the Harvard Business School (where I am currently on leave from Rochester). Harvard is one of the major suppliers of executive talent in the United States, and the more recent experience of Harvard alumni is indicative of a widespread phenomenon.

First of all, the placement statistics indicate that it is becoming more and more difficult to get Harvard MBAs to take jobs in large organizations, and especially in manufacturing and smokestack industries. They tend to go to small organizations—entrepreneurial organizations, investment banking, or consulting firms. Harvard MBAs get starting salary offers which are very large—so large that it would take them five to ten years to reach that level in smokestack America. And they would have to put up with a lot of baloney along the way.

Second, Howard Stevenson, a colleague of mine at Harvard, has been analyzing results of Harvard alumni surveys for a number of years. These surveys keep track of people who have been out of school for from five to twenty-five years. Howard's analysis indicates that although annual incomes are roughly constant across large and small organizations, the net worth of respondents declines substantially as the size of the organization in which they work increases. This latter phenomenon—the inverse relationship between personal net worth and the size of the organization—is especially strong among those respondents classifying themselves as "self-employed." The difference in total wealth becomes very large as you move along this continuum from larger to smaller companies. There are very few really wealthy people among those who work in (including even those who get to the top of) large organizations.

Furthermore, the surveys also ask a set of questions involving job satisfaction: basically, how happy are the individuals in their jobs? And, again, it is the people with the small organizations who say they are happiest and the people in the large organizations who are unhappiest.

Think about the guy who is running Kodak or General Motors today. As one of the compensation people told me, that is a twenty-four–hour–a–day job, seven days a week. You give up your family. You are in the public eye all the time. And compare that with what goes on in the investment banking world. That is not an easy life either, but the pay is much, much better. You can get very wealthy in that business. It is not unknown for the underwriting partners in certain major firms to have average incomes of $5 or $6 million a year.

Now compare that to what goes on in corporate America. It is ludicrous. The corporation is being hamstrung. And I think that the results of this are going to be very clear. The leveraged buy-out movement is perfectly consistent with this phenomenon of underpaid corporate executives. Look at these very low top-level salaries—with no or very few opportunities to make millions of dollars when you do very well, even when you may be creating billions of dollars in shareholder wealth. And when you cascade that down in the organization to the divisional level—four, five, or more levels down in the hierarchy—then you get payoffs that are even more ridiculous. Academics can make more money than that and take a lot less risk. There is something wrong with this system.

LOU: I agree 100 percent with you. And I want to make two additional comments. One gets back to the issue that Joel brought up. We have corporations that have embedded value in their portfolio, whether in the form of growth opportunities (the kind IBM capitalized on) or undervalued assets (as in the case of a division of, say, a W. R. Grace). Then, all of a sudden, we see a bunch of guys leaving to set up a new firm to compete with IBM. Perhaps through a leveraged buy-out. Now, Joel's question from the shareholder value perspective was absolutely on target: Why aren't we as a corporation getting that added value? The reason is as simple as this: large corporations don't do untraditional things in rewarding divisional or SBU management.

Now a spin-off is an absolutely appropriate way of rewarding divisional management. If there is embedded value in a strategic business unit and they are not taking advantage of it, then spin the damned thing off. Give the management 10 or 20 percent of the stock. Have a public market, and let these executives rewrite the economics of the business, which they couldn't do within the constraints of the organization. So we have got to be thinking of untraditional things. That is number one.

My second comment is this: Many chief executives don't have a good understanding of the shareholder value potential of their companies. Joel, you referred earlier to the *Wall Street Journal* article I wrote in response to Peter Drucker. Well, as I said there in print, how much can Sears afford to pay its new CEO for creating some $6.4 billion in stockholder value through some bold strategic moves?

MIKE JENSEN: A lot.

LOU: What are you going to pay Bill Stiritz as chairman of Ralston Purina for creating $2 billion in stockholder value in two years? He did this by being a risk-taker, and by restructuring the portfolio of the company. You can't pay these executives enough.

MARK: One solution we have proposed to the problem of rewarding *divisional* management is to value the business unit using discounted cash flow. And I do know of some corporations—although they are few and far between—that have adopted this approach. There is no reason, Joel, why companies couldn't keep their entrepreneurial managers and retain that value. They could place a value on the division or SBU today, and then tell the managers, "You will get X percent of the increase in that value over the next three-year period." Three years later they would then use the same discounted cash-flow technique to establish the value of that division.

I think this is a better solution to the problem of compensating divisional management than, say, having a minority interest trade on the stock market—simply because it *is* only a *minority* interest. Using our approach we can value the division as if it were a controlling interest. And I think there are also some corporations that are using the principles of DCF valuation to create phantom stock for their units and create value-based incentives which rival those held out by LBOs. As yet, however, there aren't very many of these plans because of their complexity. You have to get people to agree either on independent evaluations or on the valuation model, and that is difficult.

ALAN: I think it is more than just the complexity. I think that people get squeamish about the amount of dollars involved. IBM got very squeamish when the chairman realized a multi-million dollar gain in stock options. And, remember, a few million dollars relative to a $75 billion market value is infinitesimal. And if you don't want to give the chairman $10 million plus, you certainly don't want to give somebody four levels down $2 million. I think that is the overriding concern: people get extremely squeamish about these levels of pay.

BILL: Let me talk about the relationship between size and risk, which may pull into perspective some of these points. I don't think it is any coincidence that when you look at portfolio management for investment advisors in pension funds, you discover that after they go over about $5 million in funds managed, the results tend to get worse. You take a look at many businesses and what really happens (and I think this is a general psychological tendency) is that as you get more assets under your control, your desire to insure yourself against risk goes up. I think that explains to some extent the mediocre results of large funds, at least on average, versus the very good results of the small. In the case of smaller companies, you have got less to lose and therefore the risk in some of those situations is a lot more palatable. And I think the entrepreneurial spirit has been more strongly associated with those smaller units that are more directly under managerial control.

ACCOUNTING MEASURES OF PERFORMANCE _____

JOEL: I want to turn the subject around to something that is much more infantile than what we have been dealing with, but I still have a distant interest in it. Can anyone tell me what his experience has been with regard to the use of accounting measures in incentive compensation plans? Are accounting measures something you recommend to your clients? And what about the short-run/long-run issue raised, for example, by a recent issue of *Business Week*. I keep hearing that managements are being paid on the basis of short-run accounting results, which is detrimental to the shareholders' interest and which, if we can believe *Business Week*, may be ruining the economy.

MARK: There is no question that accounting measures are the most widely used in incentive arrangements. But we are slowly getting away from these, and moving toward cash-flow measures of performance. Companies have long been using discounted cash-flow analysis (DCF) to evaluate investment decisions. And about ten to twelve years ago, they also started using DCF widely to price acquisitions. They are also using cash-flow analysis in strategic planning.

The final step in this process, it seems to me, and the one that we now seem ready to make, is the use of these same cash measures to monitor corporate investments, to measure corporate profitability and to evaluate executives' performance. In the area of performance evaluation and management compensation, cash flow is now starting to take the place of accounting earnings, of EPS, as the critical variable. This is especially important for corporations that are capital-intensive and those that are experiencing productivity problems. And it is imperative, of course, for LBOs or private companies, where cash is king.

But the majority of public companies are still measuring their performance with accounting measures. The executives of these companies go to security analyst meetings, and if somebody says, "What is your earnings per share next quarter?," they fail to recognize that what the security analyst is really asking for is earnings *surprises*—something that may provide information about the long-run prospects for the company. The executives think security analysts are concerned only about accounting effects. As a result, they come back from those meetings with their notions confirmed that accounting drives stock prices, and that the company must therefore continue to evaluate itself with its standard accounting methods.

JOEL: That reminds me of a story. I am a director of a company where, when I joined the board, I discovered that incentive compensation was tied to the bottom line. And I said to the chairman, "What do you think of the idea of switching to after-tax cash flow measures so that at least when we come to this question of inventory, we make the right decision to convert to LIFO? This way we will reduce our tax bill, and have more cash in the bank." And he said, "We can't switch to the LIFO inventory accounting because the bonus formula is based on earnings and earnings would be lower if we switched over to LIFO inventory." This also affected their return on equity.

My question, then, is: What do you tell your corporate clients in these situations?

MARK: My apologies to Dave Larcker as an accounting professor, but we tell them that the accounting doesn't matter.

JOEL: It sure matters to boards of directors. Can you imagine, we have just been told that a major bank in Chicago has decided to sell its building to boost its net worth? Now, if the market value of the building is known, why are they using the accounting-based information to make that decision? They will have to pay taxes on the gain.

ALAN: The bank has to boost its net worth to keep its charter. If they don't meet their capital adequacy requirements, that accounting will have some very real effects on the bank's future operating profitability. They must satisfy the regulators.

MARK: There was another interesting case, one involving stock appreciation rights. The CEO's stock appreciation rights totally wiped out the net income of the company—because the stock went through the ceiling. The expenses to the income statement turned the company from a profitable one into a loser, at least on an accounting basis, for the year.

Now, the economics of stock appreciation rights are identical to the economics of stock options. So if the company is willing to offer stock options, it should be equally willing to offer stock appreciation rights instead. The accounting treatment differs, but this is another one of those cases where the accounting doesn't matter. What I am saying is that the market for securities generally—though maybe this doesn't apply to regulators or certain subsets of the market—but the market as a whole reflects real economics and not accounting cosmetics.

CARL: Isn't it true that the stock appreciation rights granted executives are not expensed for tax purposes?

MARK: Only when it is cashed in do you get the tax impact.

CARL: But if I exercise my right, don't you pay me cash? Whereas, if I exercise my option, don't I pay you cash and then I can go out and sell the shares?

MARK: Yes, but even though the accounting treatment is very different, the underlying economics to the company are the same whether you issue stock options or appreciation rights. In the case of appreciation rights, a corporation could then go out and issue enough securities to pay you the cash. The company would then be in the identical cash or economic position that it would have been had it given stock options instead.

DAVE LARCKER: Mark is saying that the quarter-to-quarter gain or loss applied to the bottom line depends essentially on how the stock price moves relative to the striking price.

JOEL: From your own experience and research, Dave, are most companies using the accounting model of the firm to structure their incentive compensation plans?

DAVE LARCKER: I think Mark is absolutely right. The primary corporate scorecard, if you will, is earnings or growth in earning per share. There has been a widespread adoption of performance plans from the mid-seventies forward, and virtually all of those plans are based on either EPS growth or return on equity. And, of course, we all know that accounting measures have a lot of potential incentive problems. Joel, you've been talking about these problems for years. Al Rappaport has been talking about them.

But, at the same time, I also think that accounting numbers are providing us with some valuable information about executive performance. And for this reason I think it makes sense to base at least part of the management compensation scheme on accounting-based numbers. One of the benefits of using accounting numbers is that it allows you to move away from basing compensation entirely on share price changes. In other words, you get some risk-sharing kinds of benefits.

The problem, of course, is that you can play a lot of tricks with these scorecards. But the fact that they continue to be used so much suggests to me that their use is not completely detrimental to the corporation. Otherwise I would think that we would be seeing some steps taken by shareholders to force changes in these performance and compensation scorecards.

DAVE KRAUS: When are we going to acknowledge that assessing executive performance is a judgmental and not an arithmetic process? A senior executive's term of office is usually two, or maybe five to ten years. But his decisions and actions impact company performance for ten to thirty years. Current accounting measures or current cash flows don't begin to measure this long-term performance. In fact, they place undue and unhealthy emphasis on short-term performance. For example, I am fairly certain that most successful food or cosmetics companies could totally eliminate all their advertising and thereby increase earnings and cash flow for the period between now and senior management retirement dates, but at the expense of long-term shareholder value-creation.

JOEL: Well, executives would be unlikely to take that course of action because the market would respond to that kind of thing negatively. And after the share price deteriorated, management would probably be tossed out by the board of directors.

DAVE KRAUS: Thus, and this is my point, we should not necessarily conclude from a high current cash-flow rate of return that management is doing a terrific job.

LOU: The effects of that kind of strategy would show up very quickly in a rapidly declining market share.

DAVE KRAUS: I agree, Lou, it would be a disaster, but I disagree that it would show up very quickly. Cash-flow rates of return might look very attractive for the duration of the executive's term in office.

DAVE LARCKER: I guess that issue really is this: You have got, if you will, two views of the firm. One is the standard accounting view of the firm;

the goal there is to maximize reported earnings or EPS. The other is the economic model, in which the goal is to maximize free cash flow. Now the question is, does one of these models dominate the other in terms of providing the correct incentives?

I am not aware of any hard evidence that really comes to bear on that point. A lot of the discussion—certainly in the popular press and even in some of the academic literature—concerns those types of issues: Can managers do things that are detrimental to the shareholders while earning large bonuses? The example of FIFO versus LIFO is a good example of the problems that can arise.

JOEL: Also important is the issue of acquisitions. If acquisitions are being evaluated on the basis of EPS effects, then that may explain why so many of the deals we have seen, especially in recent years, have penalized acquiring companies' stockholders. On the other hand, I have also had the experience where people say to me, "The acquisition made good business sense, but we didn't do the transaction because of the amortization of goodwill." I said, "Well, why is that?" And they said, "The bonus is tied to the growth in earnings."

So, my question is: What are the people in this room advising boards of directors to do to overcome these problems? I am kind of curious to know what you are telling them.

DAVE KRAUS: Much depends on the stage in the life cycle of the firm. In the early stages of development neither profits nor cash flow is a good performance measure; market share might then be the best indicator of executive performance. For example, IBM's leasing policies in the 1950s and 1960s didn't help current profitability or cash flow, but they helped to maintain and expand market share.

JOEL: Forgive me for my ignorance, but why would the decision to lease rather than sell have made a difference? It seems to me it is basically a pricing decision. If they were to cut the price of their equipment, they would have sold the equipment instead of leasing it. So why was the sell/lease decision important in terms of the market share there?

DAVE KRAUS: Two reasons. First, their cost of capital, particularly equity capital, was less than that of most of their customers. Second, leasing freed their customers from the risk of technological obsolescence.

LOU: Joel, I would like to respond to your initial question. When we advise companies, we begin by pointing out that accounting measures of performance, whether short term or long term, can be dysfunctional in enhancing strategeic management behavior. They are not designed to promote the creation of dominant positions in the marketplace, positions that will give you sustained high cash flow and shareholder value-creation. What we are advising companies to do is to put more strategic performance imperatives and measures in their short- and long-term bonus plans.

We had a client, a major company in the Midwest, which has been very,

very successful in restructuring its long-term incentives away from EPS goals, away from financial goals designed merely to boost EPS. And that is the right thing to do.

JOEL: Because you think that will enhance the value of the company?

LOU: That's right. That is the right thing to do.

JOEL: Why wouldn't the strategic results be reflected somewhere in financial numbers that would relate back to the share pricing?

LOU: It will.

ALAN: It is also important because you are trying to get focus on people's behavior. The whole process is valuable, not just the end result. You are saying to the management of Sears, or whomever, that there are certain ways that you can achieve success over the long run. Perhaps it is by adding stores, cutting inventory, improving the quality of labor relations, exploiting technological innovations, or whatever. And the strategic plan is not only going to serve as a link to shareholder value, but also as a communications tool. We are using the compensation plan not only to reward management for success, for creating stockholder value, but also to communicate how we want to achieve our strategy.

If you simply tie compensation to stock price through a program of stock options only, there is no communication value. Then you are simply saying, "Go out and win the war. But we're not going to tell you with our compensation program how that goal is to be achieved."

JOEL: If I am a director of a company, why should I care how the operating managers go about achieving their results in terms of benefiting the shareholders?

DAVE KRAUS: Because those operating managers are likely to be retired long before their achievements are fully recognized and finally assessed by outside investors.

ALAN: But consider the case for stock options. You probably would not get agreement from the top hundred people at IBM about the validity of using stock prices to measure IBM's performance. Some of them believe the stock market is rational, but many believe it is irrational. So if instead of offering management stock options, you say, "At IBM our goal is to develop three new products or to have a certain percentage of sales for new products," that statement communicates to everybody involved how we want our profits to be achieved.

LOU: I think we are focusing too much on IBM. IBM is organizationally unique.

CARL: Let me give you another example. Emerson Electric is a public company whose policies are well-known and which focuses on all the realities of this world: namely, that some analysts seem to care about whether or not the company's earnings per share go up from quarter to quarter, but they also care about how it is doing in its various markets, how effectively it manages its capital, and so on. It gets all of that feedback and uses it in its planning process. It has a fairly simple matrix for planning. But every manager of an operating unit in this company has to develop a plan, has to live with its plan, and has it monitored by what, in effect, is a board of directors (which is really the senior management of the company). This board spends a lot of time—generally meeting once a month—to monitor the performance of those operating managers. Their feet are held to the fire and they are compensated according to their ability to operate the plan.

And the company's earnings do in fact go up. When it looks like it is going to be a recession year—and this company has a number of cyclical businesses—they tighten up. They tighten up hard. That is part of the plan. Everybody plays to that. The earnings per share go up, relatively speaking, as a consequence. This company is in a lot of mundane businesses, but they have held their multiple. The stock price appreciation has been not spectacular, but it has been good. It has appreciated at the rate of growth of the company. And they have been able to use the stock as a means of compensation.

But it is just blocking and tackling. It is dealing with realities. And it is a reality that some portion of the market focuses on the bottom line. You just can't ignore it.

JOEL: The question is not whether it focuses on what appears to be the bottom line. It is possible that the bottom line correlates very well with cash-flow profitability, especially over long periods of time. The question is, Why would you want to get to the front part of the house by walking in the back door?

CARL: Why didn't you ask your director to change the inventory costing method so you are comparing apples and apples? Then nobody would care whether you were using FIFO inventory.

JOEL: You would pay more taxes.

CARL: No. I'm suggesting you use LIFO for taxes and FIFO only for the compensation analysis.

JOEL: Yes, that would be OK. But when I confront boards of directors with these questions, they generally say, "Everybody else ties compensation to EPS or the bottom line. In fact, we have had people come in from this company and that company and they told us the way to set up a bonus plan is to do it in accordance with things like earnings per share, earnings per share growth, return on equity, and so forth."

But this brings to the really critical question: Does the market know what it is doing? Why should we assume that the market prices are set based on the economic model of the firm when managements seem to be driven by the accounting model?

DAVE KRAUS: The stock market doesn't always know what it is doing. In the 1920s stock prices correlated with dividends. Someone figured out that dividends could only be raised if profits were higher and in the 1940s stock prices correlated with profits. Then someone figured out that issuing more shares diluted profits and in the 1950s stock prices correlated with EPS. Then someone figured out that past growth in EPS, if sustained, would increase future values (at the same multiple) and in the 1960s stock prices correlated with *growth* in EPS. Then someone figured out that EPS growth cannot be sustained without adequate profitability and in the 1970s stock prices correlated with ROE. The current school maintains that underlying cash flow is a better indicator of long-term profitability than an accounting figure like ROE, so here we are in the 1980s convincing ourselves that cash flow explains the stock market and shareholder value-creation. Let's all get together ten years from now to discuss how we went wrong.

LOU: All these things have changed. In the 1960s stock prices were driven by EPS growth.

JOEL: How do you know that?

LOU: Well, what I mean is that EPS growth in the sixties went hand in hand with high real returns on equity. There was a low rate of inflation then, corporate costs of capital were accordingly lower, and corporate returns on investment were higher than investors could earn on bonds or other alternative investments.

ALAN: I think part of the problem, though, is that you have got a lot of CEOs and senior managers who don't understand the investment community. We all know that investment banking firms and brokerage houses repeatedly turn out those widely real prognoses of companies they cover. They talk about book values and EPS and projected earnings and all of that.

But in the back room of the most sophisticated houses, no one really believes a word of what they are saying. So, there is a problem when you read the standard analysis that comes out of the *Wall Street Journal*'s investor column. You will read, for example, "We think Procter & Gamble is a good buy. We expect the multiple to be around eleven, here is our projected earnings figure, and so here is what the share price is going to be." Now, this is all very nice, very simple, but the people in the back room of the investment bank think that this kind of analysis is a joke.

The market has nothing to do with any of that. But the CEO hears that. He gets up in front of the analysts—analysts whom the people in the back room often don't think an awful lot of—and he keeps hearing the language of earnings, earnings per share, and standard P/E ratios. Meanwhile, the very sophisticated investment bank, where some of the best people make $6 million in a year, think all this talk about EPS is a big joke.

JOEL: What kind of response do you get, then, from the compensation committee or the board of directors when you confront them with a model that seems to be at variance with their conventional wisdom?

ALAN: There are two things to keep in mind here. One is that the compensation board has no incentive at all personally to adopt anything that is aggressive, that is the slightest bit risky. Because they can take no share of increasing the value of the company. But they may get sued. They may have their name in the press. So the point is, if you are a director of International Harvester, people see the enormous payouts Archie McCardell got in the year Harvester was hurting, and they don't look kindly on that.

So, as a board member, you want to be very conservative. You want to pay "competitively," which means you want to pay down the middle of the road. You have no personal incentives to take enormous personal risks.

JOEL: Then how do innovations ever take place in the area of incentive compensation?

ALAN: What happens is this: One large company that is very well thought of will lead the way. Take the case of Sears, Roebuck and Co. Sears, Roebuck adopted an innovative plan, one which proved to have great benefits for shareholders, and this has opened the door for other, less prestigious, firms. Now, for example, the comp committee at Zayre can say Sears is leading the way. Now we are no longer taking the risk. Sears has already done it. So the way is to follow the leader.

JOEL: Can you tell me how Sears, Roebuck came to the conclusion they had to make a change?

ALAN: Somebody at the company had an expensive consultant come in and tell them how to do it—or how to do what they wanted to do. Because somebody has to break away. (But, then again, I have a client that decided to break away because they either didn't know what everybody else did or didn't really care.)

CARL: But something else had to happen in that Sears' case. Okay, the consultant was called in. But something else probably would have had to happen on that Sears board. And that is that some group of people had to support it. Somebody had to get excited about the change.

LOU: Let me return to your first question, Joel: What happens when you go to the compensation committee to try to convince them to base the plan on economic value? As Bill Fruhan of Harvard says, getting companies to change their focus from EPS to economic value is a tough sale. It is a tough sale to get compensation committees to structure incentive plans around the concept of economic value. But we are getting it done through a program of management communication.

JOEL: In the case of Sears, Roebuck, the new plan was put in place after a period of hard times. Would I be wrong in saying that management was driven to make these changes by the sense that they had to do something to get their stock price up? Are companies in general more willing to consider innovations when they are under pressure, perhaps in fear of a takeover?

LOU: Those conditions certainly help in bringing about change.

JOEL: So you mean to tell me the entrenched corporate culture that resists innovation can be overwhelmed by an immediate need?

LOU: We had a major communications client here in town that was doing very well. We told their chief financial officer, "You are running the business on the basis of the wrong economic model. The incentive plan is focused on the wrong variables." He liked what we were proposing, but he got only a modest response from the senior management. The chief executive's bonus was based on earnings per share; and earnings per share was going up and the stock price along with it. So there wasn't much we could do to convince him that the company needed a different comp plan.

DAVE KRAUS: Well, "if it ain't broke, don't fix it."

LOU: Now, let me return to the Sears case for a minute. Sears did some very innovative things. But it was essentially a three-part process. First of all, they were embarking on a new business strategy—very bold, high risk. Second, we had to change the organizational structure to correspond to the changes in the company's portfolio of businesses. And third and last, we had to determine how best to motivate the managers in the key positions.

Our first job in this process, then, was to convince the board of directors that they had the potential to increase shareholder value by about $13 billion.

JOEL: Do you mean just by paying them bonuses based on the economic rather than the accounting model of the firm?

LOU: By reinforcing the new business strategy with an innovative way of compensating and motivating the key players. We convinced them to discard the accounting model of the firm for purposes of performance evaluation, and we devised an incentive plan that was very different from what Sears had been doing in the past and from industry practice in general.

JOEL: What did the people on the board of directors who were traditionalists then say to you? How did you overcome their resistance?

LOU: It was an education process. But there were a couple of directors who understood shareholder value-creation, who understood the market valuation process. They understood Sears' strategy, they understood the strategic challenges. And they said, "We are willing to take the risk of providing non-traditional kinds of compensation plans and we will hold out the offer of big bucks to the people who succeed."

JOEL: But supposing the company is in trouble?

LOU: That helps.

JOEL: The company was having difficulty.

LOU: Sears was at a low point at that particular time. The fact of the matter, though, is that their decision to make the changes was driven more by their sense of an opportunity for shareholder value-creation. They saw the possibility in a new strategy, in a new organization with a very strong chief executive officer. And the compensation committee was willing to take the risk of introducing an innovative, non-traditional comp plan to motivate the people to execute that new strategy.

THE LEVEL OF EXECUTIVE PAY REVISITED _____

ALAN: Well, as Michael Jensen said, when you think about the dollar amount of the potential benefits to Sears, Roebuck from those innovations, the risk they were taking seems miniscule. If Sears wanted $20 million to develop a new store, the board would have rubber-stamped that proposal in fifteen seconds. But if we proposed a comp plan providing $20 million for top executives for great performance, the hours we would have to spend worrying about that $20 million payoff are enormous because of the political arena that we are now working in.

MIKE JENSEN: I want to reemphasize this point because I don't see it talked about. We are allowing the Ralph Naders of the world to set the agenda in this compensation business. If you think about the magnitude of the potential losses to stockholders from underpaying the very top-level people in the organization—and not just the CEO—the total amounts of money in executive compensation packages are dwarfed by the magnitude of the shareholder value that is created by good management or destroyed by bad management. Those payments to senior executives are miniscule in comparison to what is at stake for stockholders; you can't even see them.

But, to repeat, the potential losses to stockholders, and to the economy in general, from underpaying our corporate executives, or paying them in the wrong direction, are enormous. Take somebody running an organization the size of Kodak or IBM or Sears. If one hiccup is wrong, 1,000 times the amount of money that could have been spent correcting the compensation problem is down the drain. If you bring people into that level of the organization who aren't of the very highest caliber, who aren't willing to take risks and to work the kind of long hours and to bear all the other pressures, then you are weakening the corporate form of organization.

One reason I know that this is happening right now is that Carl Ferenbach and other people like him are busy taking these bureaucratic nightmares private, honing them, and turning them into high-powered racing cars that are competing in this same market with public companies. And you have got this block of technicians coming out of engineering schools and MBA programs who are busy starting new enterprises and competing all the time with these tired bureaucracies. The notion that very large organizations can't go right down the tubes and out the door is clearly gone. It is happening and we are looking at it.

If we broaden the perspective, I think we are seeing this enormously productive machine—the public corporation—being hogtied by the political environment and by the cowardice of people who don't really understand what is at stake. The controversy is being generated by people who are, therefore, not only cowardly but intellectually unprepared to carry on the debate and the discussion at these levels. And I think it is time it stopped.

JOEL: Well, to approach this controversy from another standpoint, what about the often-heard claim that the compensation committee is controlled by the people who they're trying to compensate?

MIKE JENSEN: It is clear that they are not. If that were true, why would corporate executives set their salaries at such a piddly level compared to the earnings of the major partners in a Wall Street law firm, who regularly make over a million dollars a year? I have no doubt which job I would choose were I given the choice.

JOEL: So, then, the only way you expect significant changes in incentive compensation practices is through changes in the nature of the public debate and in the political process?

MIKE JENSEN: I don't actually think that the process of public debate is likely to have much of an effect. It may. I would like to see it tried. But what I really think is going to happen is that the Carl Ferenbachs of the world are going to win out, and a much larger fraction of economic activity is going to take place in private companies.

JOEL: What would have to take place to change the public's mind about the role of the corporation and the private sector generally?

MIKE JENSEN: I am not optimistic about the chances of this happening. It doesn't pay people who aren't directly involved to spend very much time thinking about and understanding the complexity of these problems. And they are enormously complex. So when the employee on the production line, the middle manager, or the politician in Washington or Albany looks at numbers of three quarters of a million dollars, he can't imagine that anybody is worth that much. This is true whenever people look at numbers that are much over the $150,000 to $200,000 range. What you have is an educational problem that is not likely to be resolved. The reason, simply, is that even if we find out what the right economic analysis is, you will never get people to spend the effort to understand it. Instead they will emote.

ALAN: How much do you think Iacocca was worth, Mike? People will look at a folk hero like Iacocca and say, "He is worth it." Or, to take another example, no one is criticizing Steve Jobs at Apple Computer.

MIKE JENSEN: Or Michael Jackson. But Iacocca didn't get those rewards, and Jackson and Jobs are "owners." People have a different attitude toward "owners" than managers.

DAVE KRAUS: I'm not sure I agree with all this. Maybe the rest of the world is right and the United States is wrong on how to pay executives. Many national economies of countries in Western Europe and Asia have outperformed ours in the last twenty years, yet executive pay is far lower there than in the United States. You could also argue that there are legislative, executive, regulatory, and judicial people in Washington who have a bigger economic impact than any large-company CEO. Maybe these people should be paid more than corporate executives.

LOU: There is a vast cultural difference between the United States and these other countries. We are not driven by cultural aspirations. To a far greater extent here than anywhere else in the world, it is money, net worth potential, that provides the most powerful incentive.

ALAN: That may be a partial explanation, but more important, I think, is the abundance of other opportunities here. I don't know if there are law firms in Tokyo where people make a million dollars or investment bankers who make $5 million. But if the pay scales in Japan are roughly the same for everybody in different professions, with no opportunities to make salaries like those provided by American private firms, then there is going to be far less pressure pushing up the salaries of corporate executives.

But here in the United States, as long as we are not going to regulate compensation at Goldman Sachs, we are going to have a problem if we regulate Exxon. As long as people can leave Exxon, and there is the potential for these people to go to Goldman Sachs, you're going to get a migration of the top talent to the Goldman Sachses of the world.

When I think about Peter Drucker's argument that the pay of American corporate executives should be limited to some multiple, say fifteen times, of the average wage-earner's pay, then I want to suggest that Drucker's speaker's fees be limited to some small multiple, say one and a half times, of what a speaker in Japan makes. Peter Drucker is not regulated, but he wants to regulate what other people make. And this is the fundamental problem we're facing now. We can't regulate everybody equally, so we are going to regulate only these very visible people whose salaries we periodically make known to the public. No one knows what Peter Drucker makes. But I suspect he makes at least four times what his counterpart in Tokyo makes.

JOEL: How do you account for Drucker's argument? Is this consistent with his positions on other business issues? Is he the kind of person who is an interventionist in general? How do you account for him coming out with a statement like that, given the information that you and he must both have about the relative compensation of American executives?

MIKE JENSEN: I just do not understand Peter Drucker's position. It makes absolutely no sense to me.

ALAN: It is a very popular one.

MIKE JENSEN: I don't understand why he takes this position, but it is clear to me what the results of this policy would be. I have no doubt whatsoever in forecasting what the results would be if his suggestions were adopted. We wouldn't have to bother to shoot ourselves in the foot. We would have just shot ourselves in the chest.

DAVE KRAUS: You may not agree with him, but I believe Drucker is saying that the large, private corporation is gradually losing its economic freedom and evolving toward a quasi-public organization. And as that evolution takes place, it should follow that pay differentials between the private and public sectors should begin to narrow.

MIKE JENSEN: As a purely positive matter, as a purely factual description of what has been happening to the public corporation, I agree with you. But whether or not that's good is a different question. In fact, it is clear to me that it is very bad. And it is bad for two reasons. One: it is going to reduce our wealth. It is going to reduce the standard of living in this country, and throughout the rest of the world as well. Two: it is going to reduce freedom. It is an infringement of our basic liberties, and that is exactly what is going on.

The end result of this development (and I was in print a number of years ago forecasting this) is that the corporation, as the publicly held but private organizational form of business we now know, is very likely to be destroyed. And I am just watching that happen. It was in 1976 that I published that forecast, and I still see things moving down that road. And the Peter Druckers of the world are not helping us avoid this disaster.

LOU: I have one last comment here. If the public corporation is an endangered species, in part because of the inability of public corporations to provide adequate pay for top management, a big part of the problem I think is that public companies can't get income to their people in a tax-efficient way. The income of corporate executives is taxed largely at ordinary income tax rates, 50 percent, while private companies can readily convert ordinary income into capital gains, which are taxed at 20 percent. We don't have the public forum for doing this, but the big business community needs a way of getting capital gains into the executive compensation package. ISO's today are peanuts. We have no way for a public corporation to get capital gains into the hands of its key executives. And this is one of the big reasons we are now seeing leveraged buy-outs. This is why you see major companies like City Investing going private. If there is one thing we can do politically to change compensation, we ought to get capital gains back into these compensation packages.

RELATIVE PERFORMANCE MEASURES

JOEL: Before we close, let me turn briefly to a matter we have touched on earlier. To what extent should incentive compensation plans attempt to insulate management from exogenous factors that are beyond its control? Let's say, for example, that you could filter out economy-wide and industry-wide effects on an individual manager's performance. Do you think that this would be a good idea? Furthermore, can it be done successfully?

For example, we worked with a firm in the oil service business to design a relative performance plan. Consider their situation. In 1981, when the oil price was about $38 a barrel, the demand for oil services was very high. As a result, the company achieved a pre-tax, pre-interest return on assets of almost 40 percent. And there were enormous bonuses paid during early 1982 for that 1981 performance. In 1982 the price of oil came down sharply and the economy was in deep recession. The combination of those two forces drove down the returns to approximately 19 percent.

So, in early 1983, we were asked by the president of the firm what we thought of their idea of paying no bonuses for 1982's performance. In fact I remember him saying, "Of course we shouldn't pay bonuses based on such poor performance." And I said, "Well, how do you know your *man-*

agement's performance was so poor?" He said, "Take a look at the numbers." I said, "Yes, but the numbers were affected by factors that your management has no control over, no way of responding to: namely, the oil price and the state of the economy." He said, "Yes, but we paid enormous bonuses in 1982 for 1981's performance, which was boosted by these same factors." So I said, "Maybe we will discover that the 1982 performance was actually *better* than the 1981 performance when you adjust for the effects of the economy on the industry as a whole. Maybe you should have paid bonuses in 1983 for 1982's performance, but not in 1982 for 1981's. But the more important issue there is this: motivation and morale in the organization may be hurt if people feel that their incentive compensation is determined primarily by factors that are clearly beyond their influence."

Another benefit of this kind of program, incidentally, is that you need not have caps on the amount of the bonus—because there is no possibility of a windfall being built into the profits. And this is important, I think, because when you feel the sky is the limit, you are much more likely to reach for the sky. You are not going to do that if there is a 15 or 20 percent cap on your bonus.

What does anybody here think about this proposal?

DAVE KRAUS: You can argue this from two points of view and reach different conclusions. One is to assume that a corporate executive is an administrator, agent, or hired manager whose job is to implement strategies and decisions as established by the board of directors. If you subscribe to that point of view you would want to insulate him from the impact of uncontrollables. The other point of view is that management will best serve shareholders if he is subject to the same risks, rewards, and outside influences as stockholders.

In response to your case of the oil service company, I would not alter the pay program. If the chief executive had concerns about the compensation program, he should have voiced them in 1981.

JOEL: Incidentally, I always suggest that the board of directors and the comp committee review the rules that have been set in place, don't you?

DAVE KRAUS: Yes. The compensation plan should be based, at least in part, on judgmental evaluations. In other words, judgment should be provided for in the plan and exercised within the context of the plan. This is different from exercising judgment by changing the plan each year.

JOEL: No, I'm talking about actually *quantifying* the terms of the plan. You can actually set a formula that would say, if real growth was the following and if industry conditions were the following, then your hurdle rate, your minimum acceptable rate of return on net assets, would be as follows. And if you beat that hurdle rate, then this is the kind of bonus that you would earn. I am saying that you can quantify these expectations.

There seem to me to be two types of bonuses that are paid in companies. One type is called the "act of God" approach. At the end of the year, the chairman or the operating head looks at you and says, "Good boy, here is the amount for you." The other approach is where, at the beginning of the year, a contract is essentially entered into between the operating people and their subordinates. The people who are subordinates know what they can earn through bonuses if they achieve certain pre-specified objectives. Now, I clearly prefer the second to the first for the simple reason that the second has a much more desirable effect on morale and motivation.

DAVE KRAUS: Many bonus plans are based on some mix of quantitative (formula-based) and qualitative (judgmental) bases for determining awards. There is a trade-off involved in establishing this mix. Quantitative (formula-based) plans provide the strongest incentives because executives know in advance what they need to do to earn a bonus; but this approach also carries the greatest potential for inequities. Qualitative (judgmental) plans are probably the fairest to executives, but this approach is deficient in incentive value. The central issue in designing bonus plans is how to sensibly combine these approaches.

JOEL: Do you have caps on the plans you put in place?

DAVE KRAUS: We try to avoid caps, but they are sometimes necessary in situations that are unusually uncontrollable or unpredictable. The strongest incentive for a salesman selling pencils, for example, would be to pay a penny for every pencil sold. He knows that if he sells 8 million pencils he'll earn $80,000.

BILL: Joel, I think there is a big risk in what you are proposing. You have got essentially two choices: to condition the risk or not to condition the risk. If you condition the risk, you can say, "These macroeconomic and industry factors are exogenous, they are beyond the control of the particular manager; and we want to separate out the management contribution to the process." I think that proposal is excellent for motivational and focus reasons.

But it also begs a second, bigger issue. Namely, if you are in the oil business or the S&L business, and if you are comparing yourself to a peer group so that you essentially condition out all those industry-wide risks, then management has no incentive to confront the larger question: Should we continue to be in the oil business or the S&L business? In order to guarantee that management's interests are united with stockholders', you have to make management bear some of these outside risks. Management should always be looking at its performance in an absolute as well as a relative sense: Not merely how am I doing relative to my industry group, but how is my industry doing relative to the market as a whole? Where are my greatest opportunities to create shareholder value?

For a short period of time, you might want to use relative performance measures to attempt to isolate management's contribution. That is fine for survival purposes. But carry it to the nth degree, and you could wind up like the S&L. The one who was bleeding least survived the longest, but all of them were finally going out of business. In the long run, you have got to be concerned about shareholder value-creation in an absolute, not a relative, sense.

DAVE KRAUS: Joel, I have one other comment about your plan for the oil service company. Although there was probably a short-term benefit derived from modifying the plan in 1982, repeated revisions, over the long term, tend to erode the integrity and incentive value of the plan. Over time executives will come to expect and anticipate plan revisions in any unusual or crisis situation.

LOU: But that is not what Joel is saying. He wants to remove from the evaluation process the distortions caused by cyclicality, economic factors, oil prices, drilling activities—all these variables which can't be controlled. And I agree with Joel that you can attempt to quantify the effects of these outside factors. I agree with him that, in highly cyclical industries, measuring relative performance by removing the effects of exogenous factors is the right way to go.

Now, it's true that a relative performance plan might not encourage management to get out of substandard businesses when they should. But one way to accommodate this issue of whether they should be in a given business or not is simply *not to cap the bonus.* So, for example, if the high rate of return in a cyclical business like paper products is 18 percent, don't cap the bonus at 18 percent. Have management face the offer of very big bucks if they can earn, say, 24 percent. This way management will have an incentive to redeploy assets into different kinds of businesses.

But relative performance measures, the indexing of actual results according to industry- and economy-wide returns, is clearly the next level of sophistication in management compensation.

MARK: You can index to the industry in the near term, and to a broader measure, such as the S&P 400, over the long drive.

LOU: Of course, over the long haul, it is a zero-sum game. If the program is structured properly, management rewards over the entire business cycle should reflect the company's average performance over the cycle—just as if you had allowed the bonus to fluctuate up and down with the cycle instead of cushioning management from the effects.

ALAN: What might make sense in your oilfield services industry may not make sense in another kind of company. Consider General Motors when it was not an active stock. When imports suddenly took off, management could have argued that they should be insulated from the effect of those imports on their profits. But some people could say, with justification, that those problems were coming for years; and that management, by failing to anticipate these problems, should be held responsible for dealing with such problems. I think it made sense for General Motors not to pay bonuses in 1980 or 1981 or 1982.

DAVE LARCKER: I think you have to be careful about how you use this notion of relative performance. The good side of relative performance is that you do insulate the manager from some of these risks that are out of his control. Perhaps it will allow them to hone in on a variable which more closely reflects the actions a manager has taken.

There is a downside, though, and it can be illustrated in an example like the following. Let's say that some manager is in industry A, and the return for industry A is 10 percent, and everybody knows it is 10 percent. And let's say he has relative performance stock options where the striking price varies according to market prices. Now this manager looks out there and he sees another industry, B, and although its expected return is 10 percent, he looks at it and says, "Well, it really looks like we can earn 15 percent in this industry. So maybe I should redeploy assets from industry A to industry B."

Now let's say he does just that, and indeed the return for industry B turns out to be 15 percent. Well, under a relative performance scheme, it turns out that he would really have no incentive to change industries because he was being evaluated relative to industry B's higher rate of return, not relative to the rate of return that he would have earned had he stayed in Industry A. So you have to be careful about the kind of incentives you provide management with relative performance measures.

MIKE JENSEN: But Lou's suggestion that the bonus not be capped is a solution to this problem you're talking about, Dave; and it is, I think, a really ingenious one. By not capping the bonus, you do motivate the executive to search for investments where the returns are higher, even though you are insulating him. And that is really a neat proposal.

The other way is to have a mixture. The same thing is true even with adjustments for interest rates. We really can't know what is and what is not under management's control because, by changing the nature of the business in various ways, management can adjust to uncertainties in all of those exogenous variables to one degree or another. And, as Dave and Bill and Lou said, you don't want to insulate them completely from all those uncertainties and risks. On the other hand, if you move lower down in the organization (and in some ways I think that the compensation packages that exist at lower levels in the organization are in the aggregate more important than what exists at the top), you might want to protect those managers who clearly are not in a position to respond to such risks.

CLOSING REMARKS

JOEL: In closing this meeting, I'd like to turn again to David Larcker. Dave, since you had the pleasure (at least I hope it was a pleasure) of opening this meeting, were there any loose ends that we did not get to that you feel you would like to address at the end?

DAVE LARCKER: Well, perhaps the most important thing the academic research has established is that executive compensation is not independent of shareholder value. And this, of course, contradicts much of the claims that we have been seeing recently in the financial press. The data we now have suggests that corporate executive compensation practice is not total "madness." (But this, of course, should not be interpreted as saying that there is not a lot of room for improvement in our current compensation plans.)

What we have not talked about very much today—and it is an issue which I think is absolutely critical in analyzing the compensation and incentive questions—is the functioning of the market for executive labor. This is another area where we really don't know very much. Does it play a role in management incentives? Does the manager's opportunity wage reflect the profitability of his decisions over time? My suspicion is that this market provides management with strong incentives to act in the interest of stockholders.

JOEL: Is it also possible that once you and others have completed that research, we will have a reason to have another meeting like this?

DAVE LARCKER: I hope that is the case.

JOEL: Thank you all very much for coming.

COMMENTARY:
PERFORMANCE MEASUREMENT AND
MANAGEMENT INCENTIVE COMPENSATION
by Bennett Stewart

Incentive compensation plans should be designed to build morale, retain good managers, and promote decisions that will benefit shareholders. Only seldom does this really happen. All too frequently investors get shortchanged by compensation plans that encourage management to achieve short-term, accounting-oriented goals having no direct bearing on companies' values. The framework we have developed is intended to reward management only when value is created for investors.

A wide body of research has demonstrated that the primary determinant of stock prices is the adequacy of the corporate return on total capital in relation to the cost of obtaining that capital. While other factors are important, and should be considered in any comprehensive evaluation of performance, management's compensation should be based in large part on the relationship between the corporate return and investors' demanded return. This helps to ensure that management wins the competition for capital, not just the competition for business. Growth adds to the value of shareholders' investment only when an adequate standard of profitability is met as well.

Stern Stewart & Co. has developed a combined measure of profitability and high-quality growth that we call "Economic Value Added," or "EVA."

As the basis for incentive compensation, it focuses management's attention on the critical problem of allocating and managing capital. In our society, where savings rates are low relative to those in countries like Japan and Germany, and where real interest rates may be kept high by the prospect of large government deficits, efficiency in utilizing scarce capital becomes all the more important. EVA-based compensation plans thus help to achieve both a favorable allocation of resources and high stock prices for investors.

Another problem with most incentive compensation plans is that management gets shortchanged when the value of sound operating decisions and long-run strategies is temporarily distorted by fluctuations in economic conditions. Simply stated, most plans today compensate the business cycle, not management. It is no wonder that management loses incentive, avoids taking risks necessary to remain competitive, and even seeks employment elsewhere. Our approach avoids this shortcoming by considering the stage of the business cycle and the performance of competitors in appraising performance.

Briefly, it involves a statistical procedure to analyze the effect of broad-based economic and industry conditions on the profitability of the company over, say, the last ten years. This produces a simple formula that can be used to separate the performance reported in any given year into components attributable to: (1) general economic conditions, (2) industry-specific factors, and (3) the distinctive contribution of management. By so isolating management's performance, such a compensation plan is not only fairer to management, it also benefits investors by encouraging managers to adopt a longer time horizon for creating value. The practicality of the approach is indicated by the fact that in recent years it was adopted by numerous companies in industries as diverse as airlines, soft drink bottling, and oil services.

Before discussing the major features of the plan, however, we look at the shortcomings of some of the most common management compensation standards now employed. The benefits of adopting an incentive plan based on the cash-flow measures incorporated in EVA should be clarified by this discussion.

THE PROBLEMS WITH COMMON MEASURES OF PERFORMANCE

The most widely used standards of performance are earnings, earnings-per-share, return on equity, and growth sales or profits. From the point of view of the shareholder, all of these measures are seriously flawed. Management can achieve any one of these goals without necessarily increasing the value of shareholders' investment.

counting Measures Mix Finance with Business

For example, bottom-line earnings and earnings-per-share (EPS) are both subject to criticism because they reflect the outcome of financing as well as operating decisions. Managers can increase earnings through financial leverage created with preferred stock or debt financing. Such increases do not necessarily benefit common shareholders.

Consider that any company can use debt to increase earnings as long as the after-tax rate of return on investment exceeds the after-tax cost of borrowing money. Today high-grade corporate bonds may cost as little as 6 percent after-taxes. Thus corporate investments, including acquisitions, that yield more than 6 percent will increase bottom-line earnings if financed with debt. This is hardly tantamount to meeting an acceptable standard of profitability.

The reason is simple. Investors will not ignore the additional financial risk they bear. Bottom-line earnings will vary more over a business cycle, and hence will be riskier, due to the contractual obligation to meet fixed interest payments each year. The lower P/E multiple that investors will assign due to greater risk will more than offset any increase in earnings, and the company's share price will fall. Only if profits from the investment cover the full cost of debt and equity financing will investors benefit.

The Problem with Return on Equity

Like earnings per share, a return on equity (ROE) standard can also be manipulated through leverage. It should be the intent of senior management to compensate officers for operating decisions that add value to the company and not for financial actions having no effect on shareholder values. Another problem, unique to the ROE standard, applies to companies with convertible securities outstanding. As the company's stock price moves above the exercise price of the convertible, there will be a point at which it will be in the interests of the common shareholders to call the convertible and force conversion. In fact, it is a source of controversy as to why so few convertibles are actually called when this point is reached. One reason may be that the conversion to common stock will increase the book value of the equity, thus reducing the calculated return on equity. Again, if ROE is the primary standard of performance, the interests of managers and shareholders may be at odds.

Accounting Fails to Represent Cash Flow

A still more serious flaw of accounting measures of performance is their failure to reflect cash flow. This can result in decisions which, while boosting EPS, harm shareholders. Just two examples are the LIFO/FIFO decision and the amortization of goodwill in acquisitions. As is well known, LIFO inventory accounting results in lower earnings (relative to FIFO) but lower taxes as well. Thus, rewarding management according to earnings, rather than a cash-flow standard, encourages management to pay higher taxes—this despite an impressive body of evidence showing that investors respond favorably to changes from FIFO to LIFO inventory accounting.

Many companies also regard amortization of goodwill as an important issue in undertaking acquisitions. In fact, some companies refuse to undertake acquisitions if pooling of interest accounting cannot be applied. But since amortization of goodwill represents neither a cash cost nor a tax shield, shareholders are neutral towards this expense.

There is compelling evidence that what matters most to investors is how much is paid for an acquisition relative to the (cash-flow) benefits realized, and not how the acquisition is subsequently recorded. Managers, however, may be biased against even strategically sensible acquisitions if their compensation is based on achieving an earnings target.

Accounting Misses Value

Accounting measures are especially misleading when earnings and value go in opposite directions. For example, under present accounting procedures, outlays for product development, market-building, and research are expensed in the year in which they are incurred. Accountants insist these outlays should be expensed because their future returns are uncertain. Businessmen, however, know that such outlays create value and therefore should be capitalized.

It is true that these expenditures are among the most risky that a company makes and that, in many instances, individual outlays do not pay off. In the aggregate, though, it is these outlays that provide the foundation for the future value of corporate America. Investors do not require every expenditure to pay off, but only that there be enough winners creating enough value to cover the cost of the losers.

To compute the return on their investment, investors relate the cash benefits realized in future years to their initial cash outlay. To be consistent in measuring performance, management should adopt the same "full cost" accounting procedure employed by investors. R&D and market-building expenditures should be capitalized, not expensed as accountants prescribe.

Using EPS as a corporate yardstick encourages management to shy away from the risks associated with new investment. It causes management's decision making to focus on the near-term costs of value-creating expenditures without considering the longer-term benefits they may bring. The time horizon for payback thus narrows considerably, putting American managers at a disadvantage to their more patient foreign competitors. To remedy this problem, incentive compensation plans should encourage managers to focus on the determinants of long-run value, not on short-run earnings.

Accounting Misleading in Acquisitions

An even more serious shortcoming of EPS arises when evaluating acquisitions consummated through an exchange of shares. EPS will *always* increase following a merger with a company bearing a lower P/E ratio; it will *always* decrease after a merger with a higher P/E ratio company. Is it therefore logical to conclude that the acquisition of companies with lower P/E ratios will always benefit investors, whereas the acquisition of higher P/E ratio companies will always be harmful? Stated differently, can an acquisition be judged "good" or "bad" without knowing whether there are any operating synergies to be realized or if the premium paid is excessive? Instinctively we know the answer is "no," but why is our intuition right?

The answer lies in the fact that P/E ratios change in the wake of acquisitions to reflect either an improvement or a deterioration in the overall *quality* of earnings. The dilution in EPS following the acquisition of a higher multiple company can be offset by an increase in the P/E multiple, so that the stock price need not be adversely affected. The multiple will rise because higher quality earnings are added to lower quality earnings. Add high octane gas to low octane gas, and the rating will increase. The same is true of earnings.

The opposite happens with the acquisition of a lower multiple company. It is true that EPS will increase, but it is possible that the dilution in the multiple will more than offset it, leading to a lower stock price. Investors care about *both* the quality and the quantity of earnings in setting stock prices. EPS represents only one-half of a two-part equation.

In conclusion, EPS is misleading as a basis for judging the merits of undertaking an acquisition with an exchange of shares. Companies that currently sell at high P/E ratios can make acquisitions that harm shareholders while at the same time increasing EPS. By diluting their P/E ratio, such companies mortgage their future in order to show higher per share earnings today. Equally questionable is the reluctance of the management of companies selling at modest P/E ratios to acquire attractive candidates just because of potential earnings dilution. This would happen less frequently if management incentive compensation plans focused on the real determinants of share value.

Growth Misleading

Operating managers frequently are preoccupied with increasing sales, both absolutely and relative to their competitors. Their motivation is to be the biggest and the best in order to win against their business competitors.

Unfortunately, managers with a single-minded determination to compete for business may wind up losing the competition for capital that drives stock prices. Without considering the additional resources required to achieve growth, management may fail to provide an adequate return on shareholders' investment. Thus, rewarding sales growth may give management incentives inconsistent with investors' objectives. Stock price may suffer as a result.

Growth in earnings also is a tempting objective. Many of the most successful companies in America today have long, uninterrupted records of rapid earnings growth. Their impressive performance has earned them stock price multiples that are the envy of businessmen everywhere. It seems only sensible to conclude that rapid growth in earnings should be the first priority of management. However, it is the *quality* of growth, not the quantity, that is of overriding concern to investors. Growth without adequate *profitability* will reduce stock price.

A brief illustration will make this point. Assume that all we know about two companies, "A" and "B," is that they are expected to grow at the same rate of, say, 10 percent a year. At this stage, it is a silly question to ask which company, "A" or "B," is more valuable. Obviously, we expect them both to sell at the same price.

With a single additional piece of information, we can conclude that "B" is more valuable than "A." Suppose we are told that "B" requires relatively little investment in new capital to sustain its growth, whereas "A" requires a substantial amount of new investment each year to keep its earnings growing. "B" sells at the higher price and P/E because it requires less capital to produce the same stream of earnings as "A." Stated differently, "B" sells at a higher price because it is able to earn a higher rate of return on capital than "A."

THE RETURN ON TOTAL CAPITAL

The best indicator of the investment quality of any company, then, is its rate of return on total capital. This answers the first question influential investors ask of management: "What am I getting out of the business relative to what has been put in over time?" The more successful a company is at earning high returns on capital, measured in relevant cash-flow terms, the greater will be the value of its shares.

In addition, by calculating the return on the *total* amount of debt and equity capital employed, this procedure eliminates biases introduced by changes in the financial structure of the company or by changes in interest rates. And by reversing non-cash charges to earnings, and by capitalizing all value-building expenditures, this measure of performance will be unaffected by goodwill amortization or by accounting expenses for R&D and marketing.

By comparing the return on capital with the cost of capital, management can determine whether it has been successful in adding value to shareholders' investment. The cost of capital can be interpreted as the *total* return that debt and equity investors collectively require for accepting the (operating and financial) risks inherent in the company's securities. Management should be responsible for earning at least this return because investors expect to do just as well by investing in a diversified portfolio of other companies' securities having similar risk.

ECONOMIC VALUE ADDED

Because the spread between the return on capital and the cost of capital is a major determinant of share prices, our recommended incentive compensation system uses this as the primary indicator of management's performance. Our compensation framework also encourages management to grow the company, but not by sacrificing required profitability. This is done by calculating a measure called "Economic Value Added," a procedure that involves multiplying the spread between the return on capital and the cost of capital by the amount of capital management has invested in the business.

Economic Value Added is equal to the difference between the level of earnings management achieves and the level of earnings investors require as compensation for bearing risk. More formally, it is calculated as follows:

$$EVA = (Return \ on \ Capital - Cost \ of \ Capital) \times Average \ Total \ Capital$$

If the return on total capital is less than the cost of capital, EVA will be negative, providing an indication that the capital could have been more productively deployed elsewhere. If the return is greater than the cost of capital, EVA will be positive. This means that management has been able to create value for investors by satisfying customers' needs more efficiently and creatively than their competitors.

There is a direct link between EVA and share price. Investors will bid share prices to a premium or discount to the value of capital employed that is equal to the present value of anticipated future EVA. Companies like Hewlett-Packard, Johnson & Johnson, and Procter & Gamble sell at premium prices because their managements have demonstrated an ability to invest funds to earn attractive rewards for investors. On the other hand, steel companies justifiably sell at discounts to the replacement value of assets employed because management is incapable of earning a sufficient return. EVA and share prices thus go hand in hand to motivate the proper allocation and management of capital.

To be more specific, management is provided with three important incentives when the goal is to increase EVA. These are: (1) to improve the efficiency of existing capital employed, (2) to commit new capital to projects where the rate of return exceeds the cost of capital, and (3) to liquidate and redeploy capital from underperforming operations. These important incentives are missing, in large part, from all of the more commonly employed techniques for evaluating management performance.

It may appear that strategic objectives such as the attainment of a high market share, or the development of high quality products, are not recognized in EVA. In fact, these achievements will be rewarded through EVA provided their returns outweigh their costs. In our framework, goals relating to the competition for business are not ends in and of themselves, but are subordinate to the generation of value—that is, the competition for capital. Consequently, management is provided with an incentive to formulate strategic plans that will be highly regarded by the investment community.

Turnaround Situations

In the application of these principles there are special cases that will require additional adjustments. As an example, consider a "turnaround situation"—one which is characterized by low profitability, not just at the present time, but for several years prior. In this case, a straightforward calculation of EVA will always result in a judgment of inadequate performance, and a low or perhaps non-existent bonus for several years. Under such conditions, the question becomes how to motivate a talented manager to take on the challenge of bringing an underperforming division up to an adequate standard of profitability.

The best method of compensation in "turnaround" situations is to reward managers on the basis of the *change* in EVA over a pre-determined period of time. Thus, if the current year's EVA is negative, but is less negative than the prior year's, this constitutes an improvement in performance that should be rewarded. In this way, new management is not penalized for inheriting the problems created by past decisions, and is compensated for achieving progress towards reaching the benchmark standard (the cost of capital). In addition, the manager can be required to break even in EVA within, say, five years.

Compensation based on the change in EVA is also appropriate for an overperforming division. In this case, the present manager should not be rewarded for benefits derived from prior decisions, but only for *additional* value created for investors in future years. Last, for the more normal situation, where a division or company is earning a return just about equal to its cost of capital, the unadjusted measure of EVA would be the appropriate measure for setting incentive compensation awards.

THE EFFECT OF FACTORS BEYOND MANAGEMENT'S CONTROL _____

In reviewing the adequacy of EVA it may also be important to give consideration to prevailing conditions, both in the economy and in the company's industry. To the extent that these conditions are beyond management's control, management should not be penalized (or rewarded) for returns due specifically to such external factors. Instead, management should be required to perform better in good years, so as to offset the inevitable shortfall incurred during poor years. Only in this way will incentive compensation reward good performance, not good luck.

A major shortcoming of almost all incentive plans we have reviewed is that they require the attainment of some fixed standard. On an annual basis the standard generally is established in a budget prepared before the year has begun. In today's volatile economic climate there is no guarantee that the economic conditions contemplated in the budget will materialize. Variance from budget then measures the accuracy of management's budget forecast rather than the quality of management per se. If the economy sours midway into a year, management is apt to lose all motivation once they realize their bonus is unattainable for reasons beyond their control. Most managers will simply write the entire year off, while the truly outstanding ones may be inclined to seek employment elsewhere.

Even when the bonus is tied to the attainment of strategic objectives stretching out over several years, there is no assurance that the time span will begin and end with comparable business conditions. For example, a five-year incentive plan that expired in 1982 would have begun in the expansionary year of 1977 and ended in a recession year. Any improvement in the company's strategic condition over that period would have been buried in the business cycle. (In fact the vice chairman of a major electrical equipment manufacturer told us that this turn of events was creating a severe morale problem among senior operating managers who received no long-range incentive bonus in the previous year, even though they had unquestionably contributed to the company's success over the past five years.) With the great uncertainty over where interest rates, inflation, and economic growth are heading, it becomes even more crucial to design long-range incentive plans that are flexible enough to accommodate unforeseeable changes in business conditions.

Index

JOEL M. STERN is Managing Partner of Stern Stewart & Company, a New York-based corporate finance advisory firm. A frequent guest panelist on the national television program *Wall Street Week*, he is the author of *Analytical Methods in Financial Planning* as well as *Measuring Corporate Finance* and currently serves as Adjunct Professor of Finance at Columbia University's Graduate School of Business.

DONALD H. CHEW, JR., is a Founding Partner of, and Director of Publications for Stern Stewart & Company. He is the editor in chief of the distinguished *Midland Corporate Finance Journal*.